Polygraph 17

The Philosophy of Alain Badiou

CONTENTS

Introduction 1
Matthew Wilkens

Depending on Inconsistency: Badiou's Answer to the "Guiding Question of All Contemporary Philosophy" 11
Peter Hallward

And Being and Event and … : Philosophy and Its Nominations 27
Oliver Feltham

The Cantorian Revolution: Alain Badiou on the Philosophy of Set Theory 41
B. Madison Mount

Topography and Structure 93
Jason Barker

Nothing but a Truth: Alain Badiou's "Philosophy of Politics" and the Left Heideggerians 105
Oliver Marchart

"I Love (u)": Badiou on Love, Logic, and Truth 127
Lindsey Hair

How Much Truth Can Art Bear? On Badiou's "Inaesthetics" 143
Élie During

Something Else Is Possible: Thinking Badiou on Philosophy and Art 157
Nico Baumbach

Badiou and Beckett: Actual Infinity, Event, Remainder   175
Andrew Gibson

Badiou, Derrida, and *The Matrix*: Cultural Criticism between Objectless Subjects and Subjectless Objects   205
Stefan Herbrechter

Badiou without Žižek   221
Bruno Bosteels

One or Several Events? The Knot between Event and Subject in the Work of Alain Badiou and Gilles Deleuze   245
Bruno Besana

Badiou: The Grace of the Universal   267
Eric Alliez

The Badiou-Event   275
Carsten Strathausen

"Fault lines": Simon Critchley in Discussion on Alain Badiou   295
Edited by Jon Baldwin and Nick Haeffner

Contributors   309

Introduction

Matthew Wilkens

Thanks in no small part to the previous work of many of the contributors to this volume, and to their new interventions collected here, the time when any English-language publication devoted to Alain Badiou's thought was required to open with a lengthy synopsis of the same is now behind us. Peter Hallward's *Alain Badiou: A Subject to Truth* and Jason Barker's *Alain Badiou: A Critical Introduction* have provided book-length studies of, and critical engagements with, Badiou's body of work as a whole, and the editors' introductions to each of Badiou's texts in translation offer specific accounts of their individual subject matter. Rather than attempt to add to this corpus, the following introduction aims to supply an overview of the essays collected in this issue of *Polygraph*, to explain their groupings and interrelations, and to suggest starting points for readers interested in further exploring certain topics in Badiou's oeuvre.

The first two contributions, by Peter Hallward and Oliver Feltham, respectively, together do much of the work that might otherwise have been expected here, since both address in broad terms the structuring dichotomy of Badiou's thought, that of being and event. Hallward's piece, "Depending on Inconsistency," begins by laying out Badiou's claim for the ontological priority of the multiple over the one, a priority that Badiou identifies as characteristic of "all contemporary philosophy worthy of the name." As Hallward demonstrates, however, Badiou's philosophical contemporaries and rivals—among them Deleuze, Lyotard, Derrida, and Žižek—respond to this realization in at least two ways that differ importantly from Badiou's own. First, they continue to search for (and usually claim to have found) exceptional experiences of jouissance or of an encounter with the Other, hence of a direct encounter, however fleeting or ineffable, with a reality not conditioned by the situation from which it is glimpsed. Second, they equate this encounter with the event, a move that simultaneously divides the event from the situation in which it occurs and reinstates it as the unified term on which experience is based. Badiou's project is to avoid both of these consequences, i.e., to understand the event as a disappearing "connotation" of a situation's inconsistency, but not as a revelation or experience of it. Hallward goes on to draw out from this point a number of Badiou's positions concerning truth and subjectivity, each of which helps to make clear the nature of the relationship between the original terms of the dichotomy. "An event offers an opportunity," he concludes, "for us to acknowledge an implication of what we are"—opportunity, but not necessity; this is Hallward's (and Badiou's) point, that being ("what we are") cannot be made equivalent to the event as its manifestation, nor can the event be said to follow necessarily from the knot of conditions under which it takes place.

While Hallward's essay considers what might be called the macro-scale implications of Badiou's theorization of being and event, situating his work with respect to that of other contemporary thinkers and distinguishing his conclusions from theirs, Oliver Feltham's "And Being and Event and …" concentrates more specifically on the technical details of Badiou's mathematical ontology. Feltham's objective, however, is less to provide a comprehensive account of this ontology than it is to understand what it means for philosophy to be "conditioned … by generic truth procedures" located outside philosophy proper. He begins by identifying three "metaontological theses" in Badiou's work: the thesis of schematism, the thesis of the real, and the praxiological thesis. The first of these makes the claim that the representation of any situation must always exceed its presentation; in the case of infinite situations (as are all actually existing historical situations), by an infinite degree. The thesis of the real holds that acceptance of the thesis of schematism entails a conception of both the subject and the event as "inscribed" within ontology, but connected to it only in the mode of "impossibility." The subject—that non-individual entity responsible for recognizing and acting in fidelity to an event—forces the awareness of an inconsistent multiplicity, a multiplicity that cannot exist within the given situation, but that is (or will be) no longer inconsistent in the new situation to which the subject's fidelity gives rise. Feltham then proceeds to unpack Badiou's understanding of the subject in this context, and to elaborate on the praxiological thesis, which accounts for the emergence (in practice) of a new state of the situation as a result of the subject's contingent embrace of an event. In contrast to the thesis of the real, which is devoted to a disjunction between being and event, the praxiological thesis concerns the possibility of a synthesis (however tenuous) between them. Feltham concludes that the task of philosophy is the recognition and naming of these "disjunctive syntheses as they emerge in singular truth procedures," and ends his contribution by sketching the consequences of this conception.

[Readers interested in Badiou's theory of the subject may wish to see the essays by Stefan Herbrechter, Bruno Besana, and Carsten Strathausen later in the issue.]

A number of the contributions to this volume take up Badiou's use of set theory and its connection to ontology as a step toward examining other aspects of his thought. B. Madison Mount's essay on the "Cantorian revolution," however, is the lone direct and sustained engagement with his philosophy of mathematics, and is perhaps the best such treatment yet to have appeared in English or in French. Mount begins by situating Badiou's ontology within and against the historical development of theories of the infinite through Cantor and Gödel, with particular attention to issues surrounding the Continuum Hypothesis. He then goes on, in the second section, to analyze the ways in which Badiou seeks to develop a line of thought "transverse" to what he calls the grammatical or constructivist, generic, and prodigal orientations of contemporary philosophy of mathematics. Specifically, Mount reads at length meditations 28–30 of *L'être et l'événement* in order both to show the ways in which Badiou derives a closed or noneventual understanding of constructivist thought from Leibniz's metaphysics and to suggest the alternate conceptions that might be drawn from—or in alignment with—the same source. Mount's essay will thus be of particular relevance to those interested in Badiou's generally dismissive treatment of constructivism past and present, as well as to those seeking a more complete understanding of his position vis-à-vis other mathematical philosophies (and philosophies of mathematics). Finally, it provides a useful complement to and extension of Hallward's appendix to his *Badiou* on the technical details of Badiou's mathematical thought; see especially sections 1.2 and 2.2, which treat the Continuum Hypothesis and the large cardinal axioms in meaningful and comprehensive detail.

The next seven essays are devoted to specific problems in the other generic procedures—politics, love, and art, in that order—identified by Badiou. Jason Barker's "Topography and Structure" is the first of two papers concerning the implications of a Badiouian politics (or metapolitics, since Badiou is careful to separate philosophical reflections on the truth procedures from the work of the procedures themselves), which he distinguishs from that of Althusser and others in the domain of "revolutionary ontology." His argument turns mainly on the problems of determinism and structure—terms that, while natural to conventional Marxism, Barker argues are not foreign to Badiou himself. He concludes that where Althusser's politics is characterized by overdetermination, Badiou's remains necessarily "underdetermined," open to the unpredictable irruption of an event, a thesis that he illustrates with respect to the Israeli-Palestinian conflict and its relationship to an existing politico-economic order.

Oliver Marchart's essay on Badiou and what he calls the "left Heideggerians"—a group that includes Nancy, Lacoue-Labarthe, Lefort, Rancière, and others—argues that the perceived gap between their anti- or post-foundationalism and Badiou's professed Platonism is much smaller than is generally believed. After reviewing the useful distinction between politics [*la politique*] and the political [*le politique*], as well as Badiou's critique of the latter as inextricably tied to "capitalo-parliamentarism," Marchart goes on to analyze Badiou's "politics of the real," emphasizing its separation of politics from social bonds and from any foundation in communitarianism. As a truth procedure, any specific politics in this sense is necessarily linked to a political event, one that is collective rather than individual, open (or infinite) rather than closed, and directed against the finitizing power of the state. This evental source of political truth is the central moment of Marchart's argument; he finds in the unconditioned unpredictability of the event—its exteriority to being—and in the link between essentialism and evil as procedures that reject the event, a suitably non-foundational origin for any existing politics, which in turn allows him to link Badiou's political thought to the same left Heideggerians Badiou sometimes dismisses as sophists. Marchart closes, however, with a series of questions concerning the ability of Badiou's conception to account for the pragmatic difficulties encountered by any situated, actually existing, and necessarily compromised politics.

[Readers interested in a different and specifically Deleuzian critique of Badiou's politics may wish to consult Eric Alliez's essay later in this volume.]

The amorous truth procedure is the subject of Lindsey Hair's essay, which seeks both to explain Badiou's debt to Lacan and to locate the formulations that result from it with respect to alternative conceptions of sexuation and sexual difference. In the case of Lacan, Hair emphasizes the "non-relation" of sexual difference, linking it to Badiou's insistence that the two "positions" of experience are both exhaustive ("there is no third position") and "absolutely disjunct." Nevertheless, the positions are related by way of the void they each include, a situation clearly analogous, if not directly equivalent, to the functions of both lack and the *objet a* in Lacan. Hair then goes on to treat in some detail the difficult problem, again in both Badiou and Lacan, of heteronormativity in the sexuation of the two disjoint positions. Although she stops short of offering definitive conclusions concerning the ultimate adaptability of Badiou's model to situations of love outside the hetero-monogamous paradigm, she does suggest that once we have accepted love as a truth procedure of the Two in Badiou's sense, it is difficult to avoid the force of his conception.

Art, the last of Badiou's truth procedures, is the object in one way or another of the next four essays. Élie During's "How Much Truth Can Art Bear?" is an evaluation of Badiou's response to the Platonic question posed in its title. It is no surprise, of course, that Badiou finds art capable of producing truth; During's purpose is not to reiterate this claim, but to trace both the assumptions and the consequences of inaesthetics, the specifically philosophical engagement with art's truth. During's first conclusion is that inaesthetics is necessarily local, concerned with individual artistic products and situations rather than with art "in general" outside its historical specificity. With this in mind, he turns to Mallarmé, one of Badiou's favorite examples, observing that his work is of interest to Badiou precisely because it produces a void or lack in being, rather than merely announcing the presence thereof. Mallarmé's poetry thus provides, according to During, a properly artistic event, one that it is the job of philosophy (in the form of inaesthetics) to recognize and to maintain. During then goes on to address a number of complications and potential objections to this view, most significantly those concerning a potential hierarchy of the arts, the status of the individual work of art, and the critique of Badiou's position developed by Jacques Rancière. Finally, he closes with an analysis of art's educational or didactic potential under Badiou's conception, concluding that inaesthetics is ultimately a kind of slogan for an understanding of art that does not allow it to be excluded from political efficacy.

Like During, Nico Baumbach offers an analysis of Badiou's inaesthetics as such, though with an emphasis on, and detailed reading of, Badiou's own most recent inaesthetic production, the "Fifteen Theses on Contemporary Art." This is to say that instead of examining specific works of contemporary art in an attempt to intervene in the artistic procedure itself, Baumbach and Badiou alike seek to formulate a set of principles according to which art functions as a truth procedure within our own situation. The seeming tension in this case with During's conclusion that, for Badiou, inaesthetics is not concerned with "art in general" is less pronounced than it may appear; as During and Baumbach both emphasize, a contemporary inaesthetics is contemporary in the most literal sense, it is of its time and drawn from the conditions of its specific situation. Thus the diagnoses and prescriptions for art offered by Badiou in the "Fifteen Theses" are specific to artistic production as it now exists, even when they do not name individual works. With this analysis in mind, Baumbach works first to establish the nature of the relationship between philosophy and art, a task with important implications not only for inaesthetics, but for any reading of Badiou's philosophical system in relation to the generic procedures. He concludes that art both "wounds" philosophy and puts it into question, since it forces philosophy to respond to truths that philosophy does not itself produce. Baumbach's reading of the "Fifteen Theses" then seeks to elucidate the philosophy produced in fidelity to the dicta of contemporary art, among them a rejection of "the will to formal innovation" and an absolute resistance to both imperialism and identitarianism. The essay concludes with a number of open questions about the inaesthetics, some of which—most notably those concerning the rejection of classical aesthetics and the specific figures of Badiou's modernity— are both shared with During and taken up in part by the next two articles.

Following these two relatively abstract studies of Badiou's inaesthetics are more applied essays by Andrew Gibson and Stefan Herbrechter. Gibson's piece reads Beckett as producing a body of work that is "much closer to mathematics than it is to most literature," characterized as it is by a "will to abstraction, … withdrawal from the world of which it nevertheless retains a residual trace, … concern with extraordinary paradoxes …, and formalization of material that is threatened with drastic inconsistency." To the extent that both Badiou's ontology and his theory of the event represent attempts to deal in generic terms with this same set of problems and concerns, Gibson argues that the two writers can be illuminatingly read together as "vestigial or melancholic modernists" characterized by their engagement with what he names the "pathos of intermittency." In order to demonstrate the plausibility of the connection, Gibson devotes a large portion of his essay to a lucid elaboration of Badiou's mathematical ontology and its relationship to the event (which, makes this a useful companion piece to B. Madison Mount's more technically demanding contribution to this volume). He then goes on to explain Badiou and Beckett's divergent emphases on the "remainder," the material of everyday life and of historical experience untouched by the grace of the event. Gibson's claim is that Beckett's work provides a sustained examination of the results of the event's rarity, i.e., that Beckett's work complements Badiou's by drawing out the existential consequences of his metaphysics. Gibson thus closes his essay with insightful short readings of several of Beckett's texts, including *The Lost Ones*, *Lessness*, and *Waiting for Godot*; readers interested in more extended engagements with Beckett's work in this context may wish to consult Gibson's engaging afterword to *On Beckett*, the collected English translation of Badiou's writings on Beckett.

In "Badiou, Derrida, and *The Matrix*," Stefan Herbrechter presents a detailed reading of just one work of art, the Wachowski brothers' film named in his title. He argues that *The Matrix* can be can be understood "'as if' it fulfilled the criteria of Badiou's notion for an event," an event Herbrechter identifies with the end of humanism and the moment at which posthumanism is born. Thus, on his reading, Neo is a figure for—and the film is symptomatic of—the kind of posthuman (or perhaps nonhuman) subjectivity that is both a central feature of Badiou's theory and the site of a potential contemporary truth procedure. Herbrechter argues that Neo's Christ-like "resurrection" as an element of the matrix functions effectively as an allegory of the posthuman event, and that the related aspects or consequences of this event—its subject, the truth procedure to which it gives rise, the void or real it reveals—map out the domain of our posthuman situation. He goes on to compare this model to related theories advanced by Derrida and Žižek, concluding that they are largely compatible, in fact that they require one another; Badiou to supplement the others' elision of truth, and they to supply his lack of a meaningful concept of the other.

Following this series of interventions focused on the individual truth procedures is a group of essays devoted to evaluating the overall standing of Badiou's project and his relationship to other philosophers, and which return time and again to the problem of subjectivity. The first of these is Bruno Bosteels' careful disentanglement of Badiou's thought from Slavoj Žižek's widely-received interpretation of it. Bosteels argues that Žižek attempts to present himself as the secret or repressed truth of Badiou, a move that operates through the now-traditional framework of Lacan's "Kant with Sade." He identifies and responds to three principal critiques raised by Žižek: that Badiou is a closet Kantian (or, alternatively and paradoxically, Deleuzian); that he fails to follow out the consequences of his own politics of subtraction; and that he does not take into adequate account the lessons of Lacanian psychoanalysis, specifically those concerning the death drive. Bosteels then offers a critical comparison of Žižek's "act" and Badiou's "event," concluding that the former is split in Žižek's work between Lacanian and Badiouian usages without the possibility of a successful resolution. This analysis leads Bosteels, finally, to two sets of speculations, one on the status of truth after psychoanalysis, and the other on the effectivity of Žižek's frequent readings of the form "Y with X," which he argues depend crucially on the logical or ontological (if not always the strictly temporal) priority of the second term.

The next intervention is Bruno Besana's "One or Several Events?" a detailed and illuminating interpretation of Badiou's theory of the event, its link to a new subjectivity, and the points of disagreement on both matters with Deleuze. Concerning the event, he observes that what separates Badiou from Deleuze is the presence in the latter of an insistence on the ultimate univocity of being. In Deleuze, he argues, this leads to the conclusion that every apparently individual event—or one might better write "occurrence"—is in fact a manifestation of the single event of being (a formulation that necessarily equates being and event). Badiou, on the other hand, is perfectly willing to sacrifice the univocity of being in favor of a meaningful distinction between individual events and between the orders "being" and "event." This disagreement extends to their respective conceptions of the subject, which Deleuze understands as entirely immanent to its situation in every case, whereas Badiou forsakes such immanence, arguing that it reduces subjects to what Besana calls "the simulacra of identities, … the multiple phantasms of the same One." Instead, a Badiouian understanding of the subject holds it to be the "presentification"—the making present, in both the spatial and the temporal senses of the word—of an event, a formulation that makes plain the impossibility in any meaningful sense of a strictly immanent event. This is related, of course, to Badiou's denunciation of constructivism as a "closed" ontology (concerning which, see B. Madison Mount's essay in this volume), and it is a similar charge that lies at the bottom of his quarrel with Deleuze, one that may or may not be a matter of taste, as he claimed in his *Deleuze*.

Continuing this debate is Eric Alliez's contribution, itself the culmination of an exchange of essays with Badiou, which is included here as a Deleuzian counterpoint to Besana and Badiou's arguments. (This seems especially relevant now that Badiou's "One, Multiple, Multiplicities," to which it responds, is available in English translation; see *Theoretical Writings*, 67–80.) Although he claims for them a shared "radical antecedence of politics" to ontology, Alliez denies categorically many of the points central to Badiou's reading of Deleuze, most importantly the characterization of Deleuze's thought as a "Platonism of the multiple." Alliez argues that Badiou's attempt to "reestablish the truth of Deleuzism, if necessary *against* Deleuze himself" results in a fundamental misprision of Deleuze's insights, one that can be maintained only by ignoring Deleuze's collaborations with Guattari. This produces in Badiou, according to Alliez, a "Lacanized" psychoanalytic vision of multiplicity as "the event of nothing destined for all" that is wholly incompatible with any theorization of multiplicity as multitude.

In "The Badiou-Event," Carsten Strathausen offers a more sympathetic, but ultimately critical, reading of Badiou's project. His central question concerns the object named in his title, an "event" in philosophy named for Badiou and grounded in his thought. But there can be no such thing as a philosophical event, he observes, asking why many of Badiou's adherents and exponents nevertheless "entertain [this] nonsensical proposition." His answer is that the idea of a Badiou-event suggests the possibility that not only Badiou, but philosophy itself can and do "*matter* in the most radical sense of the term" as interventions in their situation. Strathausen remains skeptical, however, of Badiou's ability to unite theory and practice (or philosophy and politics), which he argues remain separated by Badiou's "decisionism," a problem that in turn concerns the nature of subjectivity. In order to define the contours of Badiou's theory of the subject, Strathausen compares it to those of Laclau, Althusser, Butler, and Derrida, concluding that it most closely resembles Derrida's, but with the important difference that Derrida is able to account for the genesis of the decision by locating it outside the subject, which then becomes the passive recipient of the Other's demand. There follows a related discussion of "situation," which Strathausen contrasts to Luhmann's systems theory and which he claims must result in the supposition of a transcendental "thought" outside any situation and capable of evaluating its constituent elements. All of this leads Strathausen to conclude that what is needed in contemporary politics is, instead of Badiou's theorization of rupture and militancy, a rigorous commitment to participation in liberal-democratic institutions and procedures, i.e., to a wholly immanent process of political change. Badiou is valuable in this case, then, as a reminder that these institutions cannot be taken for granted, that they must be chosen and supported, defended even, against their opponents on the left as well as those on the right.

The final contribution to the issue is the transcript of a discussion between Simon Critchley and members of the audience to whom he presented a paper titled "Ethics as Subjectivation." Since the debate is introduced with care and concision by Jon Baldwin and Nick Haeffner, I will observe here only that it is pursued with vigor and intelligence by its participants, and provides a fitting conclusion to the issue, taking up as it does a wide range of topics and questions raised in the preceding essays.

It is my hope that this issue of *Polygraph* will help to shape the growing debate in anglophone criticism over the interpretation and direction of Badiou's thought. As is plain from the above synopses and even more evident in the essays themselves, there has yet to be achieved a broad consensus on many of the issues central to Badiou's project, a state of affairs that makes this a particularly interesting moment at which to participate in the conversation about it. The interventions collected here advance this conversation both in the common ground they are able to find on a number of topics and in the contradictions they maintain on others. To this we can say only "keep going!" and look forward to the results. ∎

....

A Note on Notation

Badiou's mathematical notation is at times idiosyncratic. To the extent possible, we have retained in the present volume each individual author's usage, most of which remain fairly close to Badiou's own. An exception is B. Madison Mount's essay, in which standard notation has been adopted in some cases by the author so as to compare more easily Badiou's work with that of other philosophers of mathematics.

Table of Abbreviations

The following is not a comprehensive bibliography of Badiou's texts (for which, see Hallward's *Badiou*, among other sources). It is intended only to simplify citations in this issue; as such, it includes most of Badiou's book-length works, but none of his articles and none of the secondary work on his thought. References to the texts listed below are supplied parenthetically in the body of each essay, rather than in the notes (as is the case for all other references).

Note that English translations use the abbreviation of their French counterparts, followed by a lower-case *e*. In particular, *Ee* (Peter Hallward's English translation of *L'éthique*) should not be confused with *EE* (the French original of *L'être et l'événement*).

AM   *Abrégé de métapolitique* (Paris: Éditions du Seuil, 1998)
B   *Beckett: L'increvable désir* (Paris: Hachette, 1995)
C   *Conditions* (Paris: Éditions du Seuil, 1992)
CD   *Casser en deux l'histoire du monde* (Paris: Éditions du Perroquet, 1992)
CM   *Le concept de modèle: Introduction à une épistémologie matérialiste des mathématiques* (Paris: Éditions Maspero, 1969)

CT	*Court traité d'ontologie transitoire* (Paris: Éditions du Seuil, 1998)
D	*Gilles Deleuze: La clameur de l'être* (Paris: Hachette, 1997)
De	*Deleuze: The Clamor of Being*, trans. Louise Burchill (Minneapolis: University of Minnesota Press, 1999)
DO	*D'un désastre obscur: Droit, état, politique* (La Tour de l'Aigues: Éditions de l'Aube, 1991)
DP	*Monde contemporain et désire de philosophie* (Reims: Noria, 1992)
E	*L'éthique: Essai sur la conscience du mal* (Paris: Éditions Hatier, 1993); reissued, with new pagination, by Nous (Caen, 2003)
Ee	*Ethics: An Essay on the Understanding of Evil*, trans. Peter Hallward (London: Verso, 2001)
EE	*L'être et l'événement* (Paris, Éditions du Seuil, 1988)
I	*De l'idéologie* (Paris: Éditions Maspero, 1976)
IT	*Infinite Thought: Truth and the Return to Philosophy*, ed. Justin Clemens and Oliver Feltham (London: Continuum, 2003)
LM	*Logiques des mondes* (forthcoming)
MP	*Manifeste pour la philosophie* (Paris: Éditions du Seuil, 1989)
MPe	*Manifesto for Philosophy*, trans. Norman Madarasz (Albany: State University of New York Press, 1999)
NN	*Le nombre et les nombres* (Paris: Éditions du Seuil, 1990)
PM	*Petit manuel d'inesthétique* (Paris: Éditions du Seuil, 1998)
PMe	*Handbook of Inaesthetics*, trans. Alberto Toscano (Stanford: Stanford University Press, 2005)
PP	*Peut-on penser la politique?* (Paris, Éditions du Seuil, 1985)
RT	*Rhapsodie pour le théâtre* (Paris: Imprimerie Nationale, 1990)
S	*Le siècle* (Paris: Éditions du Seuil, forthcoming)
SB	*Samuel Beckett: L'écriture du générique et l'amour* (Paris: Le Perroquet, 1989)
SP	*Saint Paul et la fondation de l'universalisme* (Paris: Presses Universitaires de France, 1997)
SPe	*Saint Paul: The Foundation of Universalism*, trans. Ray Brassier (Stanford: Stanford University Press, 2003)
TC	*Théorie de la contradiction* (Paris: Éditions Maspero, 1975)
TS	*Théorie du sujet* (Paris: Éditions du Seuil, 1982)
TW	*Theoretical Writings*, ed. and trans. Ray Brassier and Alberto Toscano (London: Continuum, 2004)

THE CAMEL.

Depending on Inconsistency: Badiou's Answer to the "Guiding Question of All Contemporary Philosophy"

Peter Hallward

> *Sur les inconsistances*
> *S'appuyer.*

Our question concerns the relation between what *is* and what *happens*, between being and event. It involves, in turn: a presumption, a rivalry, an implication, a parenthesis, a comparison, a formulation, a solution, an example, an interruption, and a consequence.[1]

The **presumption** concerns the ontological primacy of the one or the multiple. Is the unit (*a* thing, a body, an entity, an identity, ...) the fundamental category of being? A philosophy that says yes to this question will agree with Leibniz, that what is not a being, or *one* being, is not a proper being at all. Such a philosophy will adopt among its central concerns the distinction, identification, and definition of individual entities or beings. It will be careful to supervise the appropriate means of representing such individuals, of discerning their characteristic features and guarding against their misrepresentation. It will seek to delimit, for each class of individuals, legitimate from illegitimate methods of description or analysis. Such, we might say, is the spontaneous philosophy of most contemporary work in cultural and literary studies—work marked by the effort to map complex identities or itineraries, to cultivate more sensitive forms of recognition and representation, more nuanced appreciations of context and perspective, and so on.

What about the alternative? What if multiplicity rather than unity is primary? Plato foresees the obvious consequence in his *Parmenides*: if the one is not, then any given instance of being must figure as "lacking oneness," as "limitless multiplicity."[2] Disqualification of the one will require, as a matter of course, that the multiple itself be thought as "without-one" [*sans-un*], as without constituent units or elements. Such multiplicity will have to be thought in terms of a "process of limitless self-differentiation." It will figure as "intrinsic self-dissemination" (TW 42). After Plato, this is what Lucretius anticipates with his vision of a boundless, inexhaustible scattering of space, "without limit in every direction."[3] Badiou accepts this radical disorientation of being as the exclusive ontological dimension of his philosophy.

If then the one can be said to be at all, it will only be as the derivative *result* of an operation performed upon this multiplicity. Rather than primary or constituent, every one should rather be thought in terms of a more fundamental making-one, a "one-ing" or one-ifying. Every unit is just the unifying of a multiplicity that is itself non-unified.

All contemporary philosophy worthy of the name, Badiou maintains, concurs in this decision to presume the "radical originality of the multiple."[4]

The **rivalry** that arises at this point is with Heidegger. Badiou recognizes the importance of Heidegger's attempt to depose the one (i.e., the entity, or individual beings) in favor of an exposure to being withdrawn from its identification as being-this or being-that, from its reduction to *quidditas*. He shares Heidegger's desire to break with metaphysics insofar as metaphysics can be defined as "the commandeering of being by the one," the subordination of being to the "normative function [of] … the one as unifying unity."[5] The reign of metaphysics involves the oblivion of being insofar as this preoccupation with the discerning of individual beings conceals and then erases "the initial or inaugural movement of the disclosure of being." So far so good. But Heidegger then goes on to link the metaphysical rule of the one to "darkening of the world," a darkening he further associates with "the flight of the gods, the destruction of the Earth, the vulgarization of man, the preponderance of the mediocre."[6] Heidegger's solution, of course, is to call for a return of the Gods, for the re-sacralization of the Earth, for the poetic illumination of language and man. Heidegger's solution, in other words, involves the renewal of means whereby we might cultivate the fragile *experience* of being as other-than-one. Badiou rejects this solution *in toto*.

The question then is whether the link between being and the one can be broken in a non-Heideggerian way, and the answer will depend on whether it is possible to conceive of being in such a way as to subtract it entirely from the domain of experience. Badiou insists that any alternative, i.e., any effort to think being in terms of a kind of experience or intuition—for instance, Deleuze's effort to think being as creative energy or vitality—will inevitably return being to the dominion of the one. A properly subtractive ontology, therefore, must proceed in line with the assumption that being conceived as multiple rather than one (i.e., being withdrawn from any reference to the one, from any notion of either a constituent unit or immanent limit) will by the same token remain inaccessible to all inspection, observation, or definition. Pure multiplicity must have no immanent limit or predicate other than multiplicity as such, since "such a constraint would confirm the power of the one as the foundation for the multiple itself" (TW 41). Because it exceeds any possible "envelope," because there is nothing that can gather it together as *a* being (let alone as *an* object) or as an instance of any distinguishable predicate or concept, pure multiplicity can never figure as the object of experience. Multiplicity figures as indiscernible pure and simple. (More, it must figure as *infinitely* multiple and thus in a sense as infinitely indiscernible—"since there is no immanent limit anchored in the one that could determine multiplicity as such, there is no originary principle of finitude" and infinity is simply "another name for multiplicity as such" [TW 45]).

Which means: insofar as we can speak of it at all, insofar as it can be the "object" of discourse, the being of multiplicity can figure only as the object of a pure implication. Inaccessible to any procedure that might discern or identify it, multiple being *is* only insofar as its being is *implied*.

This is the critical step taken by Badiou's ontology: it articulates the fundamental being of being in terms of a purely **implicative** structure. Although anticipated up to a point by Plato and Lucretius (among others), Badiou claims that the only rigorous version of such a structure is the one developed by axiomatic set theory in the wake of Georg Cantor's pioneering achievements in transfinite mathematics. Only strictly axiomatic thought makes it possible to think multiplicity without ever conceiving of it as a sort of object or referent that might then be defined, represented, experienced, intuited, and so on. "The most crucial requirement for a subtractive ontology is that its explicit presentation take the form of the axiom," because only axiomatic thought can posit purely undefined terms and then prescribe the set of procedures or connections that might manipulate them in an internally consistent way; such manipulation exhausts all that can be said of or about these terms. The implication of an axiom can *never* become the object of a possible experience (however problematic or unsettling the nature of such experience). Only axiomatic thought, in other words, can fully subtract the entire dimension of experience or interpretation and thus "tear itself from everything that still ties it to the commonplace, to generality, which is the root of its own metaphysical temptation" (TW 44–45).

What the axioms of set theory prescribe are precisely the steps whereby, at the most abstract level of thought, any given unit or one is determined as the result of an operation which proceeds "upon" a multiplicity that is itself without-one and withdrawn from all presentation or exposure. When I count out any indifferent collection of things as so many units or "ones," I perform an operation that "one-ifies" or treats-as-one each resultant unit. Badiou's most basic ontological premise is that every conceivable "situation" can be considered as a collection or rather collect*ing* in this sense.

Before going any further it might be worth, **parenthetically**, briefly recalling the basic features of the ontology that Badiou develops on this rudimentary basis. The key idea, we know, is that in any given collection or set, every element that counts as one unit for that set is the *result* of its being collected as one or its being put-into-one. The process that collects or counts as one the elements that belong to a numerical situation (say the situation made up of ordinary whole numbers), of course, is nothing other than the process of counting as such: this is the process determined by the basic axioms of set theory. In other situations (i.e., in situations that contain something other than merely ontological, or mathematical, elements), the process that makes-one or "structures" whatever belongs to the situation is as variable as these elements themselves. The elements that belong to the set of students, or employees, or citizens, for example, are structured by the processes and criteria that define these groups and distinguish them from non-students, from the unemployed, from unauthorized immigrants, etc. Ontology *per se* has nothing to say about the nature of such empirical processes. But it's clear that each of the units thus collected or presented in such a set counts in the same way, precisely as one among ones. Presentation itself is always perfectly egalitarian. Insofar as it belongs to or is a member of the set, each element counts as one and no more than one.

Egalitarian presentation, however, is in every set supplemented by the re-presentation of each element, organized in such a way as to guarantee a dominant, hierarchical *order* to the structure of the set. This meta-structure is what Badiou calls the "state" of a situation. In our set of students, for instance, each counts as one in terms of his or her presentation in a classroom, but the configuration of the education system will also ensure that each student can be ranked in terms of aptitude or achievement. Some employees, likewise, will be more valuable or more productive (or more deferential) than others. In any human or historical situation, the meta-structure will be organized in such a way as to secure the stability and dominance of its ruling group, or class. An obvious example would be the set of property-owners: as far as the prevailing order of the situation is concerned, though each proprietor will be presented as one equal member of the situation, in terms of how much they own some proprietors will literally "count" more than others. Members who own the smallest discernible amount of property will count least of all.

Now in any situation made up of individual entities of this sort, what is primary is of course the definition of the unit or entity involved; insofar as we are concerned with being-this or being-that (being a student, being an employee, ...) the one prevails over the multiple. Heidegger understood this perfectly well. The great effort of Badiou's ontology is thus to ensure that when we consider only being-*as-being*, i.e., being abstracted from the definition of any entity, being withdrawn from every ontic form of this or that, then what is primary is not any sort of discernible unit but rather pure, oneless multiplicity. The task peculiar to ontology involves not the presentation of students or citizens but the presentation of presentation itself. In other words, when we count out instances of counting itself, when we count not "a student" but an abstract "one" as such, then we must either say that such ones might be the primary units of being or else that they simply figure as the result of an operation performed on some other, more fundamental multiple being. The axiomatization of set theory in the first decades of the twentieth century confirmed that only the second option can provide a coherent foundation for the basic operations of mathematics, and it's this confirmation that conditions Badiou's decision that the only truly contemporary (i.e., post-Cantorian) ontology must be an ontology of the multiple rather than the one.

We can return now to the *implied* status of this multiplicity. Just as a situation made up of students presents nothing other than students, so too a situation that counts out numbers or units will present nothing other than units. Badiou accepts this part of Leibniz's principle: although the one is not primary, all that is ever presented in any situation are units that count as one for that situation. All that can be presented (and thus experienced, observed, described, …) in any situation are the elements that it discerns or counts as one. Since "nothing is presented that is not counted [as one] …, so from the inside of a situation, it is impossible to apprehend an inconsistency inaccessible to the count" (EE 65). If every such one is a result of an operation, however, it follows that the material upon which this operation operates must itself be not-one. By defining any one as the *result* of a counting-for-one we imply that "something" that is itself not one was thereby counted, or oneified. And since we accept that only these results (or ones) can be presented in the situation, we must also accept that nothing of this "something" can ever be presented (or experienced, observed, …).[7] All we can say is that our most basic ontological operation, the operation whereby we present any abstract unit or one, implies that what is thus made-one, or presented, is itself not-one and without-one, without immanent limit or boundary, and thus infinitely multiple.

Perhaps the most distinctive and unusual feature of Badiou's ontology, **compared** with those of his contemporaries, is the rigor with which he maintains this strictly implicative condition. Consider a few of the usual suspects, starting with Deleuze. Insofar as he orients his philosophy in line with the "imperceptible," with counter-actualization, with the dissipation of molar or recognizable forms of identity, Deleuze is in many ways no less subtractive a thinker than Badiou. It remains the case, however, that for Deleuze what survives this subtraction is a creativity or intensity that can not only be prescribed but also *lived*, sensed, or experienced, even if it is an experience that explodes the conventional subject of experience. Much of Deleuze's work is concerned with the composition and proliferation of intensive multiplicities, i.e., the dissolution of rigid forms of identity within a multiplicity that is itself directly available (as non-unified, as non-extensional) for intuition or experience. A large part of philosophy's task here is thus to assist in the navigation *through* multiplicity as such. The same applies, roughly speaking, to the work of Michel Serres. Lyotard is perhaps a little more complicated but belongs to the same general orientation of thought. For the early Lyotard, pure multiplicity, though it evades the conventional limits of discourse, can nevertheless be *figured*; the later Lyotard will insist that though a differend cannot be represented or resolved, we can nevertheless *bear witness* to this failure of resolution. As for Derrida, surely the most "implicative" of Badiou's philosophical contemporaries: despite his critique of presence and the phenomenology associated with it, he nevertheless dwells on the urgency of paradoxical or "impossible" forms of experience—the experience of a demand that can never be met, of a responsibility that can never be endured, a necessarily "secret" pathos that resists rational articulation. Ditto Levinas. And Žižek? He has always stressed that the Real is not some positive plenitude hidden behind the obstructive screen of the Symbolic but rather a sort of kink internal to the Symbolic itself. Nevertheless, much of Žižek's work orbits around the traumatic *experience* of precisely this kink, the experience of subjects confronted by the collapse of their Symbolic mandate, by the radical destitution of their authorized identity.

Though irreducible to an experience in any ordinary phenomenological sense of the word, the central categories deployed by all these thinkers are shot through with the vehemently experiential quality of *jouissance* or its equivalent. In each case, the approach is based on a sort of obscure experience, one that conveys some sort of demand at the same time that it renders this demand essentially problematic if not "impossible." The paradigmatic version of this scenario is what Derrida calls, after Levinas, our infinite responsibility to "every other as altogether Other."[8] The effort, in short, is still to orient (critical, ethical, political, creative, …) behavior directly in line with some intense encounter with our most essential reality, regardless of how complex or inaccessible this reality might ordinarily seem.

For Badiou, by contrast, there can be no experience of inconsistent multiplicity, and thus no question of either pathos or jouissance. Inconsistency is not only subtracted from the categories of presence or identity, it is also withdrawn from the domain of an "absent" alterity. It is as indifferent to the domain marked by a transcendent "trace" of the Other as it is to the immanent intensity of a Life that lives beyond the limits of the organism. The "experience" of inconsistency is precisely *not* an experience, but merely an implication occasioned by a momentary suspension in the rules that usually make experience intelligible.

We are now in a position, finally, to **formulate** our question. We know that Badiou takes it for granted that all genuinely contemporary philosophers agree that pure being as being (as opposed to being-this or -that) must be thought as multiple rather than one. Readers already familiar with his work will also know that for Badiou (unlike Spinoza, Heidegger, Deleuze, …), philosophy itself is not reducible to ontology: thought is capable of thinking more than what *is*, and a truth is a matter of what *happens* before it is a matter of what is.[9] But now: if the thought of being affirms the primacy of the multiple over the one, might the effort to think what happens involve reintroduction of the one?

"The guiding question of all contemporary philosophy" is precisely this: how are we to "avoid reintroducing the power of the One at that point wherein the law of the multiple begins to falter," i.e., at the point marked by the irruption of an *event* (TW 101)?

Whatever their ontological achievements, Badiou suggest that most (if not all) contemporary philosophers have failed to meet this additional challenge. In Deleuze, for example, an account of innovation or invention, of what happens insofar as it *happens*, seems to require a distinction along Bergsonian lines between the "extensive and numerical multiplicities" of mere static being and the "intensive or qualitative multiplicities" of dynamic creation or life. As Deleuze conceives it, "an event is always the gap between two heterogeneous multiplicities," a "fold between extensive segmentation and the intensive continuum" (TW 99). According to Badiou, it's in this gap that Deleuze reintroduces the power of the one, i.e., of the event as the singular occasion of *an* individuation or differentiation: the "unity" of such an event is precisely not derivative but primary. Its oneness is not the result of an operation but an instance of a fully primary or constitutive force. And Badiou offers some other examples: our guiding question is anticipated in Heidegger's shift from *Sein* to *Ereignis*, or—switching registers—in Lacan, where it is entirely invested in the thinking of the analytical act as the eclipse of truth between a supposed and a transmissible knowledge, between interpretation and the matheme. Lacan will find himself obliged to say that though the One is not, the act nevertheless installs the One. But it is also a decisive problem for Nietzsche: if it is a question of breaking the history of the world in two, what, in the affirmative absolute of life, is the thinkable principle that would command such a break? And it's also the central problem for Wittgenstein: how does the act open up our access to the "mystical element"—i.e., to the ethical and the aesthetic—if meaning is always captive to a proposition, or always the prisoner of grammar? (TW 101)

When they come to think the event, in other words, all of these philosophers fail to conceive of its unity as a result: banished from the domain of being, the one nevertheless returns here in the guise of a exceptional "act" or decisive "experience."

How does Badiou himself try to avoid this outcome? The problem, as he acknowledges, is very delicate. On the one hand, if we allow an *ontological* disjunction between being and event we appear condemned to follow Deleuze or Wittgenstein, and thus to reintroduce the one via the event, in its externality to mere being. On the other hand, if we absorb the event entirely within being then we seem to trap ourselves within a sort of "closed ontology" in which a break with the order of being is blocked in advance. Against Spinoza or Hegel, Badiou maintains that truth is a matter of what happens insofar as this breaks with what is. But against Deleuze, Badiou maintains that "multiplicity is axiomatically homogeneous," such that an event must figure "both as a rupture of the law of segmented multiplicities *and* as homogeneous to this law" (TW 99).

Badiou's **solution** to this double imperative is precisely to align the event with *inconsistent* multiplicity. The key to his notion of an event (and indeed to his project as a whole) is that when one occurs it is not presented as a consistent or discernible element of the situation but rather takes place as an exceptional indication of the inconsistency which, by this implication, figures as the very being of every such element. If an event occurs in a situation it occurs as something that the situation cannot count or discern. Rather than an imposing act or occurrence, an "event is always a perfect weakness because the being of an event is to disappear; the being of an event is disappearing."[10] More, as far as we can know or observe any situation, including the abstract ontological situation, it is never possible to *know* anything of an event. *An event can never qualify as an experience of any sort.*[11]

Badiou's careful reading of Françoise Proust's partially comparable conception of the event makes this point especially clear. Since an event fails to conform to the logic that determines what can appear, what can be recognized in a situation, so then "the visibility of an event is indiscernible from an invisibility." The event appears only as "always-already-disappeared" and "precisely because its whole being is its disappearing, what is at stake in the event itself has nothing to do with an experience." But this disappearing—and this is where Badiou begins to distance himself from the pathos of Proust's own emphasis on the passive *reception* of an evental affect—is also the occasion of a "radical power of affirmation" insofar as it "bequeaths the imperative to weave a truth" from its trace.[12]

Admittedly, Badiou's frequent reference to an event as an "exposure" or "revelation" of inconsistency invites some confusion here, as does my use, in the preceding paragraph, of the word "indication." If you ask *what* is thereby exposed or revealed, however, the answer is just what you would expect: nothing at all. All that can ever be shown of inconsistency is that which figures as empty or void in a situation, i.e., that which by the criteria of the situation counts as nothing rather than as one. The void presents nothing other than "inconsistency according to a situation" (EE 69), and an event is whatever manages to indicate or "reveal" this void.[13] On at least one occasion Badiou says that an event "connotes" the void (EE 204), which is perhaps the least ambiguous way of putting it. In any case, if an event is to be defined as an experience, this "experience" will figure only, very literally, as the experience of nothing. Such is the difference between Badiou's notion of an event and that of Deleuze (for whom it is a positive act of creation, or differentiation) or Lyotard (for whom an event, though it cannot be represented in the normal sense of the word, can nevertheless be experienced as a "sliding" or "fall," as a moment of "vertigo").[14]

However: though it is not an experience, an event is clearly not itself nothing. It can "reveal" only nothing, only the void of the situation, but this revealing as such is precisely not nothing but a *happening* (more precisely, an event both exposes the void of the situation and "interposes itself between the void and itself" [EE 203]). The event itself (the revealing, or exposing) occurs as an as-yet indiscernible or unidentifiable "addition" to the situation. Its indiscernible quality deprives this occurring of any phenomenological or experiential intensity, but its occurring can still be affirmed as real or *true*.

An event then is not mere non-being, it happens (and by happening, it "mobilizes the elements of its site"), but it cannot be described as an experience. So rather than describe it as an exposure or revelation it might be better, instead, to say that an event is the *occasion of an implication*. An event is simply an opportunity for some members of a situation, if they so decide, to affirm that which they can never experience or observe, namely the inconsistency that they and all other members of the situation indifferently and indiscernibly are. If these members take up this implication in a consequential way (and thus become "subjects" in its wake), it will entail fundamental transformation of the way a situation discerns its elements: such a transformation, of course, is what Badiou calls a truth.

This is why, initiated in the wake of such an event, "a truth does not draw its support from consistency, but from inconsistency. It is not a matter of formulating correct judgments, but of producing the murmur of the indiscernible" (PM 57). And this is why Badiou associates political justice, for example, with egalitarian *indiscernment*:

> We have too often wished that justice would act as the foundation for the consistency of the social bond, when it can only name the most extreme

moments of inconsistency; for the effect of the egalitarian axiom is to undo bonds, to dissociualize thought, and to affirm the rights of the infinite and the immortal against finitude, against being-for-death. Within the subjective dimension of the declaration of equality, nothing else is of interest save the universality of this declaration, and the active consequences to which it gives rise. Justice is the philosophical name of the inconsistency, for the State or society, of any egalitarian political orientation.[15]

Grounded only on an the implied status of that "unnamable being which is the very being of that-which-is …, art, science, and politics change the world, not by what they discern in it, but through what they indiscern [*par ce qu'ils y indiscernent*]."[16]

Any such indiscerning, however, always takes place within a precise situation of thought, i.e., in confrontation with particular mechanisms of discernment. To say that a truth is based on inconsistency always means, more precisely, that it is based on inconsistency *according to* a particular situation, or on the void of that situation. Badiou's most fundamental ontological assumption, remember, is that everything *is* according to a situation, including the implication of that inconsistency which cannot itself ever be presented in any situation. Inconsistency is the implication that before the count the one is not, but the count itself clearly precedes this implication; there is nothing prior to the count. So the implication itself, we might say, will always be specific to a situation. (And this difference might be enough to "distinguish," if we wanted to, the inconsistent being of human beings from the inconsistent being of other kinds of being. There is nothing "in" inconsistency per se, on the other hand, that might serve as the positive basis for such distinction. The absolute indistinction that inconsistency *is* can itself only be evoked in the ontological situation, precisely, which is the situation purged of all reference to being-this or -that, i.e., of being-human, being-material, etc.).

This is an argument, we might note in passing, for the necessarily exceptional nature of consequential change. We know that a situation both presents a certain set of elements and then represents them in such a way that some privileged elements "count" more than others. Badiou's point is that the only process that might allow all elements to count the same (i.e., that might allow equality to serve as the rule of representation) must be a process grounded not on the discernible qualities of any particular element in the situation, however worthy or admirable that element might be, but rather on affirmation of that indiscernible reality implied as the very being of *every* element of the situation. Since such a process cannot begin with an engagement with this or that element of the situation, it must begin instead with the mere occasion for such affirmation, i.e., with an event. Transformation of the prevailing order of the capitalist situation, for instance, will not proceed simply on the basis of a process that strengthens or empowers the discernible element known as the working class: it can only occur as the invention of new ways of indiscerning people in general, as the development of newly consequential ways of subtracting people from the various distinctions that serve to differentiate them in line with the interests of the status quo. (It remains the case, however, that in the capitalist situation such indiscernment will *begin* in the vicinity of the working class, insofar as that class gathers together the minimal or "fundamental" unit of what counts in that situation, namely property or capital: it's for this reason that the working class is what Badiou calls the "evental site" of this situation, and thus concentrates its "historicity," the location of its possible transformation [EE 199]).

A truth interrupts or dissolves the force of all established distinctions, so as to allow the elements of a situation to be represented simply as the indifferent, un-distinguishable members of a *generic* set.

But how then can an event "connote" inconsistency? Since a situation presents only inconsistent elements, since ontology only ever encounters or "experiences" consistent multiplicities (i.e., since mathematics only ever deals with discernible numbers), what does it mean to say that something could ever "indicate" inconsistency as such? Since a situation only presents whatever it can discern as an element, whatever it can count as one, what allows us to affirm, even by mere implication, the oneless multiplicity of that which is counted or discerned? There is just one possible answer: only **interruption** of the process that treats or counts as one the elements of a situation can offer an occasion to affirm that which is thereby counted or oneified. The basic, literally elementary operation that allows a unit to be distinguished as a unit, as *one* unit, must be thrown into momentary crisis.

Take the example of our propertied situation. The basic operation here is the conversion of any indifferent or inconsistent "stuff" (a piece of land, an object, a resource, a product, …) into units of property. This operation is bound up, of course, with a whole series of complex historical processes (appropriation, commodification, development of the legal system, etc.), but as far as analysis of the resultant set is concerned it can be treated as a literally elementary procedure. The most basic unit of this situation will be the simplest or smallest instance of "property-ification"—in the case of landed property, we might say that a "plot of land" is what serves as this most basic unit, such that the rest of the situation is made up of any number of plots or combinations of plots. Each such combination will endure as a stable part of the situation as a whole insofar as the elementary integrity of what it includes (i.e., individual plots) remains undisputed. This situation might be thrown into crisis, then, not through the revalorization of this or that particular plot but if the very notion of "treating land as something divisible into commercial plots" is itself threatened—if the effort to divide up elements of land stumbles against a valorization of land that resists such discernment, for instance, its valorization as sacred, or ancestral, or communal.

More precisely, what happens in such a moment involves a crisis in the *foundation* of a situation. In the terms Badiou borrows from set theory, this involves suspension of the "axiom of foundation." This axiom simply stipulates that whatever belongs to a situation belongs as one unit or as a combination of such units (two units, three units, four …), where the fundamental unit is precisely whatever qualifies as "one" rather than as none or as something mysteriously "less than one." A situation made up of words and combinations of words has, as its foundational unit or element, precisely the word—and not the letter, or phoneme, or gesture …. The situation of landed property includes plots of land that are or can be incorporated into ever larger divisions of land; each combination, conversely, is "founded" on the unity of the smallest discernible plot. A plot thus figures as the "elementary particle" of this whole system, beneath which there are not still smaller units or sub-particles (portions of earth, patches of ground, ...) but rather, so far as *this* propertied situation is concerned, nothing at all. The orderly sequence of successive sequences is what guarantees the stability of a situation, founded on the integrity of its simplest unit. So long as the axiom of foundation holds good, in other words, it ensures that each discernible element of the situation is made up of other elements of the situation, and that this applies right down to the most basic such element. One consequence of this arrangement is that no element can then be made up simply of itself, i.e., that no element can belong to itself.[17] The most basic element will just be the one to which *no* other discernible element belongs (the plot to which no smaller plot belongs).

What happens with an event, then, involves the suspension of such well-founded inclusion. Something happens which cannot be discerned in terms of any combination of the distinguishable units of a situation. Lacking any foundation in the situation, an event appears as a pure supplement, a moment of pure chance that tears an aspect of the situation—say an exceptional "piece" of land that cannot be bounded or "plotted" in the usual sense—away from the prevailing order of inclusion. "What happens—and, inasmuch as it happens, goes beyond its multiple-being—is precisely this: a fragment of multiplicity is wrested from all inclusion. In a flash, this fragment ... affirms its unfoundedness, its pure advent, which is intransitive to the place in which 'it' comes." And since it has come from no discernible place in the situation, since there is nothing in or about it that allows us to connect it to an identifiable cause or foundation, this "fragment thereby also affirms its belonging to itself, since this coming can originate from nowhere else."[18] To be sure, Badiou's theory of the evental site ensures that this coming will itself have a location in the situation, it stipulates that a crisis of foundation is possible only with respect to the most elementary unit of the situation (that unit to which no other units belong), but the coming or happening per se is emphatically *not* a consequence or corollary of this site (EE 215). To finish with the example of a landed situation: in some versions of this situation we could say that the place (the evental site) where the normal division and commodification of land might be challenged will be marked by the inclusion of aboriginal "pieces" of land (pieces which are technically included in a situation without individually belonging to it). But in order for this challenge to become effective something else must happen—an appropriation must be blocked, a sale interrupted, a claim made or refused, a stand taken and upheld, etc.[19]

Take one last example, one provided by the British situation. This situation presents or discerns individual Britons on the basis of elementary criteria of birth or citizenship (and so enumerates them all, indifferently, on the basis of identity cards or tax records, etc.), and it further represents or classifies them according to the criteria that order the situation in line with the interests of its ruling or dominant group (such that these individuals all count for more or less in terms of wealth, political influence, cultural impact, etc.). The basic operation here is the one that treats an inconsistent human "someone" as *a* Briton; the most "elementary" unit of the situation is not a person but a *British* person. An occurrence will only qualify as an event for this situation if it throws into question the discernible qualities of "British" as opposed to non-British, and thereby allows members of the British situation to consider, in a consequential way, what it means to be a person of *any* or *no* nationality. For instance: however unrealistic it might seem at present, it's at least possible to imagine a process which might allow us to consider asylum seekers precisely not as "asylum seekers," not as supplicants begging for inclusion within the well-founded British situation, but simply as people *indistinguishable* in political terms from those already included in that situation.

To return now to the thread of our discussion: since it "surges up as such beyond every count," since it is unfounded and thus indiscernible according to the elementary procedures whereby a situation identifies its elements, so then "it cannot be said that the event is One" (TW 101). An event as such *is*, like everything else in Badiou's system, a multiplicity or set (more precisely, a set to which belong both the elements of its site, and itself). As with any set, the "one-ness" of an event considered in this sense is not primary but derivative, it is the result of a process that makes-one. However, in the exceptional case of an event, the process that makes-one is *also* this one itself. An event is precisely an element that belongs to itself, hence an element that founds itself. (This is precisely why "ontology rejects it" [EE 205]). We must say then that an event is both one *and* not-one. Badiou opts to call it an "ultra-One," where "the essence of the ultra-one is the Two" (EE 228). An event is precisely *two* rather than one.

Appropriately, an event is "two" in two senses. On the one hand, since it takes place as something that the situation cannot recognize or discern, the occurrence of an event is guaranteed only by the intervention of those who affirm this occurrence—an event is thus the occasion for the two of a radical decision, the separation of *for* from *against*, the opening of a gap with no middle ground (EE 229). And on the other hand, an event takes place within that element of the situation (its evental site) whose own elements remain indistinguishable for that situation: an event occurs within a space that appears undifferentiated or anonymous. But insofar as its occurrence is declared and maintained by the subjects who constitute themselves in its wake, it duly occurs as *an* event, as something identified by a proper name. An event thus figures as "an interval more than a term, it establishes itself, through the retroactive intervention [of its subjects], between the anonymous void that borders its site and the in-addition of a name [*l'en-plus d'un nom*]" (EE 228).

Neither reducible to mere being nor wholly other than being, an event thus appears as an instance of "trans-being." Insofar as it happens, an event *happens* as one; insofar as it is, an event *is* not-one. Badiou's entire project endures in the tension between this happening and this is, between this one and not-one. Between the two there is nothing but inconsistency, and inconsistency is the object of unverifiable implication alone. It's on the sole basis of this most insubstantial of foundations that Badiou erects his whole conception of truth.

To put it in conventional Kantian terms: we *are* inconsistency (i.e., pure indetermination or unbounded freedom) but we can never experience what we are, we can never have some "supersensible" glimpse of our noumenal reality. We will never have some radical encounter, via our finitude or mortality, with our ownmost being. Instead, an event offers an opportunity for us to acknowledge an implication of what we are, and a truth is then the rational, inventive working out, step by step, of the consequences of this implication. A truth will allow for a new, as yet indiscernible representation of inconsistency with the terms available within the situation.

A truth is an infinite affirmation whose only ground is provided by the ephemeral occasion for a pure implication. A truth is a prescription occasioned by an implication.

This accounts for one of the most characteristic qualities of Badiou's work (and indeed of Badiou himself)—its combination of an almost imperturbable enthusiasm or serenity with an unapologetically militant conception of change. What is perhaps most distinctive about Badiou's philosophy is its effort to conceive of subjectivation in terms that are constitutively indifferent to the world as such: every subjectivation takes place in the world but proceeds independently of any mediation from the world. Subjectivation involves the evacuation of worldly distinctions. Though it invites pertinent comparisons with Saint Paul or Pascal, this indifference is obviously a consequence of Badiou's axiomatic or mathematical orientation. Mathematical thought, at least the classical version of it affirmed by Badiou, is from start to finish independent of both experience and world, and the paradigm of Badiou's notion of a subject has always been the subject not of religious fervor but of a mathematical proposition—a subject without identity or depth, a subject entirely absorbed in or carried by the articulation of a particular chain of reasoning, without any trace of existential "pathos" or "remainder."[20]

It is this independence that allows Badiou to conceive of subject and truth in purely **consequential** terms. Since there can be no experience (and thus no remembrance or commemoration) of an event, a truth persists in the exclusive dimension of the present, the consequential present. Dependent on nothing other than an implied inconsistency, Badiou's notion of truth has always been carried by an elementary confidence in itself, rather than any sort of belief in something else.

Subtracted from the logic of foundation or cause, a truth is a sequence sustained entirely by its effects. ■

....

1 Pending the translation of Badiou's *Being and Event*, I have instead based most of what follows on two decisive texts in the very useful new collection of Badiou's *Theoretical Writings*: "The Question of Being Today" (39–48) and "The Event as Trans-Being" (97–102). The epigraph is from Paul Celan, quoted in Badiou, "L'age des poètes," in *La politique des poètes: Pourquoi des poètes en temps de détresse*, ed. Jacques Rancière (Paris: Albin Michel, 1992), 31; also quoted in MP 53; IT 78; PM 58; AM 118. [For a list of Badiou's principal texts and their corresponding abbreviations, see the introduction to this issue.—Ed.] I'm grateful to Alberto Toscano for his penetrating comments on a first version of this essay.
2 Plato, *Parmenides*, 144B, quoted in TW 42.
3 Lucretius, quoted in TW 41. Badiou quotes Lucretius again in his essay on "The Event as

24 *Depending on Inconsistency*

Trans-Being": "From all sides there opens up an infinite space / when the atoms, innumerable and limitless, / turn in every direction in an eternal movement" (TW 102).

4   Alain Badiou, "Untitled Response," in *Témoigner du différend* by Francis Guibal and Jacob Rogozinski (Paris: Osiris, 1989), 109; cf. D 12. Badiou refers here from Lacan, Deleuze, Lyotard, and Derrida. This and all translations are my own unless otherwise indicated.

5   Martin Heidegger, "Sketches for a History of Being as Metaphysics," in *The End of Philosophy*, trans. Joan Stambaugh (New York: Harper & Row, 1973), 55, quoted in TW 39.

6   Martin Heidegger, *Introduction to Metaphysics*, trans. Ralph Mannheim (New Haven: Yale University Press, 1980), 38, quoted in TW 40.

7   Though it cannot be presented or perceived as such, pure or inconsistent "multiplicity is the inevitable predicate of what is structured, since structuration, i.e., the counting-for-one, is an effect. ... Inconsistency, as pure multiplicity, is simply the presumption that, prior to or above the count, the one is not" (EE 32, 65).

8   Cf. Jacques Derrida, *The Gift of Death*, trans. David Wills (Chicago: University of Chicago Press, 1995), 78; Derrida, *Politics of Friendship*, trans. George Collins (London: Verso, 1997), 68. Françoise Proust's call to "resist the irresistible" is another variant on this schema.

9   See in particular EE 391.

10 "The event is nothing—just a sort of illumination—but the consequences in the situation of the event" are entirely variable ("Ontology and Politics," IT 187).

11 "If the word 'experience' means anything," in Badiou's system, "it designates presentation as such" (EE 429). And an event indicates only "the inadmissible empty point in which nothing is presented" (PP 115; cf. EE 227).

12 Badiou, "Sur le livre de Françoise Proust, *Le Ton de l'histoire*," *Les temps modernes* 565/566 (1993): 240–42. It's essential to maintain, Badiou continues, that while an event involves "*déliaison*, the undoing of every related or bound figure of objectivity," it does not thereby confront us with the "raw," unbound stuff or essence of being, the "other side of being, as if the unappearing was the 'heart' of the appearing." No, an event is a supplemental implication, nothing more (or less) than an "incalculable excess," and it says nothing about any allegedly sublime "depth" in being (240). Andrew Gibson demonstrated the pertinence of a comparison between Badiou and Proust in a talk given at London Metropolitan University, 15 December 2003.

13 See EE 204; PM 88; AM 134.

14 Jean-François Lyotard, *Discours, figure* (Paris: Klincksieck, 1971), 135.

15 And he continues, quoting Celan again: "in matters of justice, where it is upon inconsistency that we must lean or rest, it is true, as true as a truth can be, that it all depends on you" (IT 77–78).

16 EE 377. "Since the truth of the situation is its inconsistency, a truth of this being will present itself as indifferent [*quelconque*] multiplicity, as an anonymous part [or subset] of the situation, consistency reduced to presentation as such, without predicate .... A truth is this minimal consistency (a part, an immanence without concept) which indicates in the situation the inconsistency that makes its being" (MP 90). Or again: "Since the groundless ground of what is presented is inconsistency, a truth will be that which, from within the presented and as a *part* of the presented, brings forth [*fait advenir au jour*] the inconsistency upon which, ultimately, the consistency of presentation depends" (MP 88).

17 Sticking with our example, we might say that the real estate market depends precisely on the impossibility of any one owner buying *all* land, every piece of land, as a single plot: the set made up of all plots of land cannot be itself a plot in the commercial sense of the term.

18 Badiou gives as his examples here: "a certain modulation in a symphony by Haydn, a particular command in the Paris Commune, a specific anxiety preceding a declaration of love, a unique intuition by Gauss or Galois" (TW 101).
19 For a useful analysis of an example along these lines, see Oliver Feltham's analysis of the landmark claim initiated by Eddie Mabo in Australia. Feltham, *As Fire Burns: Of Ontology, Praxis and Functional Work* (PhD thesis: Deakin University, 2000), 132ff.
20 There is perhaps no contemporary thinker more opposed to Badiou's orientation, on this precise point, than Giorgio Agamben, who seeks to articulate or bear witness to "that which remains" after the cancellation of all presentable distinctions.

AIR BIRDS.

THE EAGLE.

And Being and Event and ... : Philosophy and Its Nominations

Oliver Feltham

L'être et l'événement departs from two foundational statements:

- First, "ontology is mathematics because mathematics alone is able to speak of being as pure infinite multiplicities";
- Second, "transformational events may take place amongst these multiplicities—and so the new can occur in being."

The central task of *L'être et l'événement* is to articulate these two statements by identifying the connection between the mathematical inscription of being and particular events, particular emergences of the new. If one attempts to reconstruct this articulation, one finds that it is accomplished by means of a renewal of the concept of the subject and a grafting of the Lacanian concept of the real onto set theory; that is, the subject is placed as an operation between being and event, a transformational operation which takes place in the real.

It is tempting to extend Derrida's early prognosis of an infinite afterlife for Hegel by arguing that Badiou's articulation of subject, being and event also risks subsumption under the historical category of "inversions of Hegel" insofar as for Hegel the subject names the transformation which completes being as Absolute.[1] Badiou's philosophy, however, subtracts itself from any such subsumption: first, by means of its concept of transformation; and second, due to its having subtracted ontology out to set theory. Transformation, in Badiou's philosophy, goes under the name of "generic truth procedure"; contrary to Hegel, there is more than one such truth procedure, there is, in fact, an untotalizable multiplicity of them. Moreover, each truth procedure is *incomplete*. As for Badiou's nomination of set theory as ontology, it allows him to demonstrate the impossibility for ontology to schematize both the initial point of transformation—an event—and any supposed totality of being. Once set theory takes on the tasks of ontology there is no science of the Absolute.

This paper forms the first section of an extended reconstruction of Badiou's articulation of being and event. Its goal is a minimal determination of what actually occurs when philosophical practice is conditioned, in Badiou's terms, by generic truth procedures occurring in the domains of "art," "love," "politics," and "science."

I How to Pass through the Impasse of Being

The first characteristic of the articulation of being and event in Badiou's work is that there is a *disjunction* between the two terms. This disjunction is explicit in his system, yet it does not consist of a complete absence of distinction between the two terms. Rather it is the modality—impossibility and contingency—of those connections that do exist that generates the disjunction. There are two such connections; one intrinsic to the science of being qua being and the other extrinsic. Moreover, it is these two connections between being and event which allow Badiou to tie his theory of the subject—developed in the last section of *L'être et l'événement*—with one of the major results of his set theory ontology, its formal inscription of the "impasse of being."

The connections between being and event are established by three metaontological—philosophical—theses which all refer back to the same ontological statement: $|p(\omega_a)| \geq |\delta|$.[2] This statement affirms that if one considers the cardinality of the set of all subsets of an infinite set, then that cardinality is larger than any other infinite cardinal one may choose, provided that it is larger than the cardinality of the initial set. What does this mean? A subset is a partial collection of elements which belong to an initial set. Such a collection is said to be *included* in the initial set, whereas an individual element simply *belongs* to its set. Take for example the set α whose elements are β, γ, and δ: $\alpha = \{\beta, \gamma, \delta\}$. One subset of α is made up of the elements β and δ and it is included in α; this is written $\{\beta, \delta\} \subset \alpha$. All of a set's subsets may be collected together in turn to form a new set termed the power set. The latter is written $p(\alpha)$ where α is the initial set. Each subset of α is thus an element which belongs to the power set $p(\alpha)$. This belonging is written, for example, $\{\beta, \delta\} \in p(\alpha)$. The power set has a certain cardinality: the quantity of its elements. In set theory we know that this cardinality is larger than that of the initial set, that it exceeds the latter. With a finite set it is relatively easy to calculate this excess; that is, the difference between the cardinality of the power set and that of the initial set: it is given by the formula "two to the power of n," where n is the number of elements in the initial set. Take our set of three elements, $\{\beta, \gamma, \delta\}$. You will find that there are two to the power of three subsets in total—eight subsets—including the "maximal" subset $\{\beta, \gamma, \delta\}$ and the empty set $\varnothing$, which is a subset of all sets due to its special properties. Thus $p(\alpha) = \{\{\beta\}, \{\gamma\}, \{\delta\}, \{\beta, \gamma\}, \{\gamma, \delta\}, \{\beta, \delta\}, \{\beta, \gamma, \delta\}, \varnothing\}$. However, in the case of infinite sets, there is no formula available for the calculation of the quantitative difference between its power set and itself. With infinite sets, it is simply not known by how much a power set exceeds its initial set. In other words, the measure of the quantitative excess of the power set is, strictly speaking, undecidable.

On the basis of this ontological—mathematical—statement, Badiou constructs three metaontological theses. What is a metaontological statement? For Badiou, a metaontological thesis is a philosophical statement conditioned by ontological theorems, operations, or axioms. Such a thesis would concern the nature of presentation or representation, or the relation between the subject, the event, or truth, etc. For example, Badiou says that the distinction between a set and its power set schematizes the distinction between presentation and representation. "Presentation" is understood by Badiou in its most general sense, being a synonym for "situation" in his terminology and referring to any grouping of phenomena whatsoever, regardless of its nature, position, or modality. "Representation" is similarly taken in a general sense and designates all those mechanisms which are supposed to repeat contents without transforming them. According to Badiou, the relationship between presentation and representation is exactly that between a set and its power set. Consequently, at the level of philosophical statements conditioned by mathematics, Badiou can say that representation consists structurally of regroupings of elements of presentation, and that the number of such possible regroupings is always superior to the number of elements in the initial presentation. Note that this goes against the grain of our normal prejudice about presentation and representation, which is that visual or linguistic representations of a landscape or a person never manage to capture the complexity or "essence" of the latter. Following set theory ontology one can state that any complexity occurs purely at the level of representation.

For the moment let us identify the three metaontological theses and clarify their terminology:

- First, there is the *thesis of schematism,* which says: *the statement "$|p(\omega_a)| \geq |\delta|$" schematizes the "impasse of being" which occurs in any situation whatsoever.*

    In metaontological terms, this impasse is the immeasurable split between representation and presentation in a situation. Note that all situations are schematized by infinite sets for Badiou.

- Second, the *thesis of the real* says that *the forcing of the statement "$|p(\omega_a)| \geq |\delta|$" reveals both the trace of the event and of the subject in the discourse of ontology.*

    As we shall see later, forcing is a particular technique which provides us with conditional information about an indiscernible set. There are solely traces of the event and the subject in ontology because they are both excluded from its discourse due to their structure.

- Third, the *praxiological thesis* declares: there is no ontological response available to this split between presentation and representation, but there are practical responses furnished by generic procedures of fidelity.

    In other words, this split in being is solely measured within concrete procedures of transformation which can take place following the occurrence of an event in the domains of art, science, politics, and love.

The clarification of the three theses depends upon a reconstruction of the argument which supports them. As the first step of such a reconstruction let us examine forcing.

Forcing is a method for the construction of hypotheses in a formal language about the nature of a new set, using only the resources of an initial set. These hypotheses concern an extension of the initial set which will be composed of itself plus a new set, its generic subset. A *generic* subset is one that is indiscernible for the formal language that describes the rest of the initial set. "Indiscernible" means that this subset can neither be named nor known at the level of its contents by using the mathematical language that defines the initial set. The extension constructed by the addition of this subset to the initial set is termed the "generic extension." Normally, this generic extension would remain an indistinct myth, a vague virtual entity, a kind of mathematical phantom. However, thanks to the mathematician Paul Cohen's innovation in the 1960s, there is an operation which allows us to approximate the nature of this subset without discerning it; the operation of forcing. Using only the resources of the initial set and its formal language, forcing allows us to say, in reference to its generic extension, that a hypothesis concerning the latter's nature will be true if a particular element, with a certain relation to the hypothesis, turns out to belong to the generic extension. This hypothesis cannot concern the predication of a property that, once shown to belong to one particular element of the generic subset, would be assumed to belong to the entirety of the generic extension. For the generic subset to remain generic, it cannot be "discerned" in its totality, and so it cannot be said to possess any property in its entirety. The totality of the generic subset remains unknown; all that we know, at the moment of forcing the hypothesis, is that one particular element belongs to it.

The mathematical statement at the base of the three theses—"$|p(\omega_a)| \geq |\delta|$"—is actually the result of a particular forcing in ontology. It is not a theorem of set theory. In fact, it contradicts another well-known hypothesis in set theory on the cardinality of the power set. Formulated by Cantor himself, Badiou terms the latter the constructivist hypothesis; $p(\omega_a) = \omega_{S(a)}$. It affirms that the cardinality of the power set is that which comes just after or succeeds the cardinality of the initial set in the series of infinities. The result of this hypothesis—compared to our statement—is a drastic reduction in the excess of the power set over the initial set: it is a conservative estimate of the power set's cardinality.

The statement "$|p(\omega_a)| \geq |\delta|$"—which is the result of a particular forcing—says that in a generic extension the cardinality of the power set of an infinite set surpasses any given cardinality. This forcing thus demonstrates that the constructivist hypothesis is a radical limitation, a savage reduction of the power set's excess. This forcing shows us that it is compatible with set theory—that is, no contradictions result—to choose any cardinality as measure of that excess.[3] The quantity of elements of the power set thus exceeds that of the initial set not by any precise figure but by *any infinite cardinal figure whatsoever*, as long as it is superior. This is what Badiou terms the unmeasured, a quantitative gap or abyss which is impossible to measure. The constructivist hypothesis is thus revealed to be a contingent decision in set theory and not a theorem.[4]

The Thesis of Schematism

Badiou understands the statement "$|p(\omega_\alpha)| \geq |\delta|$" as a point of the *real* within the discursive field of mathematics (EE 469). That is, it is real insofar as it inscribes an obstacle, a gap, a point of impossibility which is unique to mathematical discourse and occurs in the very fabric of that discourse. It is impossible to definitively decide the quantitative excess of a power set over its set: this inscribes a point of undecidability with regard to quantity in mathematics, the very discourse which fixes quantity. At this stage of his argument Badiou employs the Lacanian concept of the *real* without any explanation. This concept, moreover, is quite problematic and subject to much variation in Lacan's own work. In any case what can be understood about Badiou's usage of the concept is that the point of the real acts like what we can term a *negative index*: it is negative because it is not a positivity like the smoke which is an index of fire, but rather an impossibility; it is an index because it indicates a necessary link between this point and an exteriority or an alterity with regard to discourse. It is not a matter of a substantial exteriority or alterity, but nevertheless this point constrains and shapes the development of mathematical discourse. In contrast, "reality" could be defined as what is *supposed* as being substantial, external, and possible in relation to discourse. In other words, a discourse can admit supposed relations with such a substantial exteriority by means of its mechanisms of reference. A negative index, on the other hand, allows no such supposition, nor any mechanism of reference.

Badiou declares that insofar as this point of the real is particular to the discourse on being qua being, it can only be a matter of Being in this mathematical statement (EE 311). What lies behind this claim? In the philosophical discipline of ontology, the problem of the relationship between the discrete and the continuum has a very long history, dating at least from Zeno's paradoxes. In set theory this relationship is thought in terms of the relation between the first infinite set—which numbers the discrete—and its *power set*—which numbers the geometrical continuum. This is precisely the relationship which our mathematical statement declares is impossible to measure. The consequence, once one allows that ontology is mathematics, is that this problem of the relationship between the discrete and the continuum is strictly speaking inexhaustible. For Badiou, the unavoidability of this point of impossibility in mathematics, and the unavoidability of what it schematizes—the discrete-continuum relationship—in the philosophical thought of being, necessitate that this unmeasure be a structure of Being: which he terms the "impasse of being."

The thesis of schematism declares that once one admits that every situation is infinite—that every situation is schematized by an infinite set—and that the state of this situation, or the representation of its presentation, is schematized by the *power set* of this initial set, then the statement "$|p(\omega_\alpha)| \geq |\delta|$" schematizes the impasse of being particular to each situation, that is, the gap between presentation and representation in each situation.

The Thesis of the Real

We are now in a position to explain the thesis of the real. It says that *the forcing of the statement "$|p(\omega_\alpha)| \geq |\delta|$" reveals the trace of both the event and the subject in* *ontology*. In short, forcing is the general schema, in ontology, of what Badiou terms the "law of the subject," examined below (EE 469). The particular forcing which produces this point of the real forms the *trace* of the ontological substructure of the subject because it is the point at which the event, which is excluded from the discourse of ontology, returns. This return implies the subject because for Badiou the event is both the origin of the subject and part of its composition. Consequently, this point of the real—" $|p(\omega_a)| \geq |\delta|$ "—the trace of both the event and the subject in the discourse of ontology, generates the first connection between being and event, a connection which is not so much *intrinsic to* ontology but rather *inscribed within* it. In other words, this real is an internal point of exteriority; it is a connection between something external or extrinsic to ontology—the event—and an ontological statement. The modality of this connection is impossibility.[5]

This all needs a little untangling. The argument which supports the thesis of the real is extremely knotty. It forms the stakes of the entire final section of *L'être et l'événement* and it passes through the schematism of the subject. Here I shall merely reproduce the order of the argument.

First of all, the subject is rare for Badiou; it is the contingent product of an unpredictable encounter between a person and an event in a situation. Sometimes, as a result of that encounter, the person recognizes that there is a truth at work in the event which concerns the established order of things in the situation. Badiou terms such recognition "subjectivization." "Subject" is Badiou's name for the actions which follow such a recognition and consist of the implementation of the consequences of the event's belonging to the situation. "Generic procedure of fidelity" is the name for the infinite set of these actions in their unprecedented unfolding. A subject is thus a finite "fragment" of a procedure of truth, of a procedure which globally transforms a situation. Badiou's subject is a subject of praxis: it transforms the world.

The schematism of the subject is a singular case in set-theory ontology because for Badiou, the subject, amongst all beings, is the only one which can be divided into matter and operation. The matter of a subject is the random collection of elements of a situation generated by the enquiries. Each enquiry examines the consequences of the occurrence of the event for each element of the situation as it is encountered. The collection of elements is random because the trajectory of these enquiries—which form part of the truth procedure—is indeterminate: if there were a principle, an order, or a destination determining the trajectory, the procedure would not be generic or new. The operation of the subject is the encounter itself with these elements of the situation plus the "forcing" of statements on the basis of such encounters about the probable global consequences of the completion of the generic procedure.

As both matter and operation, the subject is in an exceptional position in this ontology, an ontology that I would characterize as "flat." A flat ontology does not recognize two different genres of being, one named "matter," the other "operation"; a flat ontology recognizes one genre of being alone. In the case of Badiou's set-theory ontology, it is "multiplicity." Any operation, whether it takes place in a situation named "time" or not, can be schematized in ontology as a structured multiple. The complex differentiation that is often ascribed as the characteristic of time in philosophy is of no special import, being particular to certain temporal situations rather than a characteristic of all beings.[6] In any case, any temporal "dimension," however complex, can be written in set theory ontology as a structured multiplicity, just like any other situation.

Why is it then that the subject is exceptionally privileged in Badiou's flat ontology by being divided into matter and operation? Because it alone, amongst all beings, can transform the ontological structure of a situation by contributing to its supplementation by an indiscernible multiple. In contrast to Hegel, the negativity of the subject is contingent, rare, and fragmented for Badiou.

The Schematism of the Subject

Badiou identifies three constraints for the ontological or set-theoretical schematism of the subject. First, ontology possesses its own version—forcing—of what Badiou terms the fundamental law of the subject; that is, its operation of deciding upon the undecidable on the basis of the indiscernible (EE 439–40). Second, ontology cannot think the concept of the subject, that is, its operation (449). Third, what ontology can do, however, is think the type of being, the ontological substructure that corresponds to this law of the subject (449, 457).

How is ontology able to generate a version of the fundamental law of the subject?

First of all, a subject, according to Badiou, is the one who, as a fragment of a generic procedure of truth, has to deal with two instances of undecidability on the basis of an indiscernible (469). First of all, the subject engages with the undecidability of the orientation of this procedure, since there is no reference within the knowledges of the situation which will support a decision as to which terms of the situation should be the next to be examined (432). For example, there is nothing in the Australian colonialist situation which indicates to indigenous militants in which direction to proceed in order to follow the true orientation of an indigenous politics, whether it be land rights, public health, education, affirmative action, or cultural heritage, etc. The second encounter with undecidability concerns the hypotheses a subject makes as to the nature and the consequences of the truth procedure. The status of such hypotheses is undecidable because the procedure is unfinished and there are no criteria within established knowledges that would underpin an evaluation of these hypotheses (445). For example, even if a group might attempt to do so for tactical reasons, strictly speaking it is not possible to proclaim the general nature of indigenous politics per se from the restricted perspective of one set of actions: this is what lies behind one of the major weaknesses of a truth procedure.

The schema of these two undecidabilities in set theory is the following: by means of forcing, one can isolate statements expressed in the formal language of ontology which are undecidable in ontology: that is, a forcing is possible which shows that these statements are compatible with set theory, and another forcing is possible which shows the inverse; the contrary statements are also compatible with set theory. How then can the mathematician decide which are the correct statements? The procedure of forcing reveals points of undecidability.

Let's return to metaontology, to the action of a subject faithful to an event. Subjects in truth procedures do not remain immobilized before this absence of criteria for their action; they decide on these points of undecidability (445). First of all they do so by examining a term in particular—for example, what is "public health" in terms of indigenous sovereignty? Second, they decide upon hypotheses concerning the global nature of the procedure insofar as they say "if such and such an element turns out, upon investigation, to be connected to the event (thus belonging to the generic multiple of the truth of the situation), then the hypothesis relative to this term will be veridical in the new situation." At the level of our examples, this means that if particular experiments in public health practices turn out to be successful—or universally transmissible—then the ideas which have been employed could form the basis of a general declaration on indigenous public health.

In set theory, the ontological schema for these decisions on undecidability is forcing; that is, the operation which shows that an undecidable statement could be forced or decided by constructing a generic set. The generic set must be such that this statement will be veridical in the "generic extension" of the initial set; in other words, in the new set formed by the supplementation or extension of the initial set by a new element which was previously its indiscernible subset.

If ontology provides a version of what a subject does in a truth procedure, why can't it formalize the concept of a subject? Badiou's response appears to be problematic: ontology can think the multiple-being of the results of a subject's activity; that is, the generic set, but it cannot think the *acting* itself of such activity; which Badiou terms the "enquiring of the enquiry" or the "real of the procedure" (433, 438). This response seems problematic for a flat ontology as we saw above since the latter does not recognize a privileged global position for the situation of temporality, nor does it accord an inaccessibility for thought to the temporal situations it does recognize. Ontology can think particular operations which unfold over time, however particular they may be. Why then can't it think the operations of the subject?

Three reasons may be considered for this obstacle to thought: first, ontology cannot think the means of the operation; second, it cannot think the real of the encounters; third, it cannot think the relationship between particular operations and their horizon.

The means of the subject's operation are the name of the event, and the operator of connection; the latter allows the subject to decide if a term of the situation is connected or not to the name of the event (433). Ontology does not recognize the name of the event because its multiple-structure—a multiple which belongs to itself—is strictly prohibited, under pain of paradox, within set theory. The real of the encounters is quite simply chance: there is nothing which could tell the subject, whose multiple-stuff is formed from its enquiries, where the next enquiry will lead. For Badiou, ontology can think the results of these chance-driven enquiries but not chance itself at a local level.[7] Finally, the subject is the one who, on the basis of a particular stage of the incomplete procedure, anticipates its completion, its belonging to the transformed situation. Ontology thinks this anticipation in action—the creation of names for the new, the formulation of hypotheses concerning the nature of the new situation—by means of its concept of forcing, but at the level of the multiple, it cannot figure the gap between an indeterminate fragment of a generic multiple and the complete infinite generic multiple.

Despite these obstacles to ontological thought, Badiou affirms that ontology can think the type of being or ontological substructure which corresponds to this operation. He speaks of a *trace* of the being of the subject within ontology; a trace rather than schema because it is not a matter of a type of set but rather of a type of *connection* (468). In Badiou's argument, the trace of the subject in set-theory ontology is the operation of forcing itself. The operation shows that one can demonstrate, by means of a particular forcing of a generic procedure, that an undecidable statement in ontology is decided within a generic extension. This operation thus establishes a connection between the indiscernible—the generic subset—and the decision upon an undecidable. This is why it is supposed to provide the ontological substructure of the subject. The subject itself, as actions unfolding the consequences of an event, is nothing other than the *practice* of this connection between the indiscernible and the undecidable.

Immediately afterwards, in the argument of meditation 36, Badiou adds a sort of confirmation, a twisted confirmation of this relationship of trace between ontology and the subject. He says that the demonstration of the undecidability of the quantitative excess of the power set over its initial infinite set is one particular result of forcing, that is, of the ontological trace of the law of the subject, *because* it is precisely at this point of the real—$|p(\omega_a)| \geq |\delta|$—that the event returns. The event is both the *real origin* of the subject in the concrete truth procedures, and that whose lack contributes to ontology's difficulties in thinking the subject. Badiou then grafts Lacan's initial conception of the real—the real is what returns to its place—onto a later conception—the real is what cannot be presented in the symbolic order—by saying that the real of the event, being foreclosed from the presentation of ontology, is what returns to its place, this place being a place of impossibility, or a place of non-placement within the very discourse of ontology (468–69).

Badiou then adds a second confirmation of his thesis that forcing is the trace of the subject in ontology by saying that this relation is quite appropriate given that the point of the real marked in the statement "$|p(\omega_a)| \geq |\delta|$," otherwise known as the "impasse of being" is actually the "pass of the subject." This means that every subject of a truth procedure has to deal with the immeasurable gap between the state of a situation—schematized by a power set—and the situation itself at the level of its presentation—schematized by the initial infinite set.

Badiou maintains that the impasse of being is the origin of all thought and so of each of what he calls the four main orientations of thought—grammarian, transcendental, generic, and praxical. At the end of meditation 36 he declares that this thesis is clarified by the fact that the randomness or chance of truth procedures—which are procedures of thought, after all—is reproduced in set theory ontology itself when it formalizes this "impasse of being"; that is, when it inscribes an undecidability of quantity within its own discourse of quantification (469). It is this "reproduction of the randomness of truth procedures in ontology itself" which indicates why Badiou speaks of the "trace" of the being of the subject. It is here that this point of the real in the discourse of ontology— $|p(\omega_a)| \geq |\delta|$ —acts as a type of *negative index* of the real of each infinite situation, a real which is solely exposed via the activity of a subject following an event and an intervention.

Such is the argument underpinning the thesis of the real—the *forcing of the statement* " $|p(\omega_a)| \geq |\delta|$ " reveals the trace of both the event and the subject in ontology—the thesis which established the first impossible connection between being and event, a connection inscribed within the very discourse of ontology.

Strictly speaking, this connection takes place between being as impasse of being, and the event as a point of the real foreclosed from ontology. The connection passes via the subject, and via the ontological operation of forcing as trace of the subject. Moreover, this passage is fundamental to the argument of *Being and Event*: it is designed to complete its ambition.

The final confirmations of the argument for the thesis of the real make use of the proposition "the impasse of being is the pass of the subject." It is this proposition that lies at the base of the praxiological thesis; it is responsible for the second connection between being and event.

The Praxiological Thesis

The praxiological thesis declares that since the "impasse of being" is undecidable within ontology, it is solely decidable within particular generic procedures. Badiou terms the place of such decisions "the pass of the subject," which of course could be reformulated as "passes of subjects" (314–15, 469). How can this thesis be interpreted? One must situate oneself within the very procedure of a truth. In metaontological terms, the impasse of being is the immeasurable gap between presentation and representation, or between a situation and its state. In a truth procedure this immeasure of the state is exposed in three moments:

- First moment: the reaction of the state to the emergence of a new procedure is that of trying to control and contain it; by means of diversion, marginalization, or simple repression. Such control requires first that the new procedure be categorized. Due to the novelty of, say, the artistic or political procedure, the attempt at categorization at a practical level is doomed to defeat; for example, indigenous politics in Australia has shown again and again that, despite certain expectations, it is not a type of green politics. The consequence of such failure is a multiplication of attempts at categorization, which reveals the structural fact that the state could indefinitely continue such attempts at categorization without ever capturing what is actually at stake in the generic procedure.

- The second moment: from the perspective of subjects who make up part of the truth procedure—indigenous activists in Australia for example—there is the recognition that these attempts at representation will never manage to classify the new practice. In metaontological terms this is the recognition that the state will never cross the barrier between itself and what happens at the raw level of the event and its new presentations; it is incapable in principle of categorizing the indiscernible multiple. This is what could be termed the necessary moment of hysteria, again following the definition Lacan gives of the discourse of the hysteric: "there is no signifier of the Other which names me as subject."[8] Of course this is not a matter of individual psychopathology—such is not the Lacanian conception of a discourse—but rather of a moment which is structurally necessary in the construction of the new.

- Third moment: the subjects of the procedure affirm that the only representations which succeed in naming and transmitting a truth procedure will be the autochthonous representations which emerge from the procedure itself: this is what Badiou terms the formation of a "counter-state." See, for example, the rejection on the part of indigenous militants, of the term "reconciliation" as a name for the process of peace-making between the indigenous peoples and the colonizers; for many militants "reconciliation" boils down to collective therapy by and for the whites. The autochthonous terms which have emerged in the indigenous creation of a new political knowledge, are rather "sovereignty," "justice," and "treaty."[9]

These three moments constitute what Badiou terms the "fixing" of the state by the subjects of a generic procedure; the exposure of its immeasure in relation to presentation.

The praxiological thesis establishes the second connection between being and event, the non-ontological connection, which, strictly speaking, is a plurality of connections extrinsic to ontology. These connections are inscribed in the development of concrete generic procedures, on the condition that there are decisions in these procedures with regard to the immeasure of the state. The modality of these connections is that of a pure *contingency*, due to the chance of an event, an intervention and a series of enquiries.

That the first connection between being and event takes place in the modality of impossibility, yet is intrinsic to the discourse of ontology, shows that there is a clear *disjunction* between being and event. That the second connection takes place according to the modality of extrinsic contingency shows that there are clearly *syntheses* of this disjunction. According to Badiou's conception of philosophy, without these syntheses there would be no such thing as philosophy insofar as it circulates between particular truth procedures—its "conditions"—including ontology.

II What Can Philosophy Do with Disjunctive Syntheses?

Philosophy is thus a practice of nomination, a particular type of nomination which names the *disjunctive syntheses* as they emerge in singular truth procedures.[10] Each of these disjunctions interrupts an established order of things, each of these syntheses allows such an interruption to endure, to take on consistency, and to contribute to a new unlimited, egalitarian, and open ordering of things.

What difference does this notion of philosophy as the nomination of disjunctive syntheses make? How does it contribute to an interpretation of Badiou's conception of philosophy as the incommensurable space opened up between diverse truth procedures in the four fields of love, art, politics, and science? At this intermediate stage, three clear consequences appear.

First, that its nominations concern *disjunctions* indicates that philosophy's circulation amongst truth procedures does not and cannot aim at the unfolding of a unity that would totalize or make sense out of their diverse singularities. Philosophy does not aim to end with, or to make an end out of, these contemporary truths.[11] In other words, it does not set out to divine some common possibility between these truths. For Badiou, contemporary subjects of truths do not coalesce via the privileged means of philosophy into a single demiurgic über-subject beyond the world. Every time philosophy succeeds in naming the work of a subject of truth, it has to break apart and reorganize its own chains of concepts.

Second, that philosophy's nominations concern *syntheses* underlines that philosophy does, however, open up a *common* abyssal space for the thought of these truth procedures.[12] Each synthesis of being and event in a truth procedure contributes to the opening up of a new structure of being, of a new consistency. Philosophy therefore is not merely concerned with events as interruptions, but with the endurance and extrapolation of such interruptions into new organizations of historical situations. If philosophy were solely concerned with interruptions, it would risk, in the absence of any practical differentiation, unifying all events into one single form of rupture. Such is the risk run by Derrida's messianic conception of the event. It is the *practical* differentiations of different types of synthesis which allows philosophy to circulate between its conditions rather than becoming stuck to any one of them—see Austin's conception of philosophy as mere antechamber or laundry to science.[13] It is thus the failure to circulate between its different conditions that leads philosophy to risk or even claim its own auto or *hetero*-expulsion into one of its conditions.[14]

Third, each of philosophy's nominations turns a proper name into a common name. "Being" and "event" are two of philosophy's common names; in Badiou's work they result from his philosophical re-nomination of two proper names which emerge respectively in set theory and modern poetry, namely "∅" and "the unique Number which cannot be another." It is the commonality of names such as "being" and "event" which opens up an intra-philosophical communication between the nominations of different truth procedures.

This opening of communication is how philosophy contributes, in its own mode, to the transmissibility of truth procedures; it registers and retransmits what Badiou terms a generic truth procedure's universal address. Moreover, philosophy redirects such addresses towards *other* contemporary truth procedures. It thereby contributes to the linking-up of truths in another manner than those tragic, comic, and tragicomic imbrications which constitute the lives of certain individuals wherein truth procedures are instrumentalized by each other; politics is abandoned for the sake of love, art is dedicated to the service of politics, and so on. Philosophy thus runs an interference service which bypasses any instrumental articulation of truths in favor of the disjunctive voiding of final significations and ends, and the synthetic holding *open* of a commons for thought. For Badiou, philosophy is a clearing house for truth. ▪

....

1 "Misconstrued, treated lightly, Hegelianism only extends its historical domination, finally unfolding its immense enveloping resources without obstacle." Jacques Derrida, "From Restricted to General Economy: A Hegelianism Without Reserve," *Writing and Difference*, trans. Alan Bass (Chicago: University of Chicago Press, 1978), 251. It is interesting to note that forty years after Derrida's claim, it is not Hegel but rather a certain Wittgenstein and a particular Heidegger which dominate the field of "continental philosophy" in the anglophone academy. Hegel, *Phenomenology of Spirit*, trans. A. V. Miller, (Oxford: Oxford University Press, 1977), §18, and §20.

2 [For a note on mathematical notation, see the introduction to this issue.—Ed.]

3 Badiou presents a résumé of the demonstration of the forcing of the statement "$|p(\omega_a)| \geq |\delta|$" in section 4 of meditation 36 of *L'être et l'événement* (EE 328). [For a list of Badiou's principal texts and their corresponding abbreviations, see the introduction to this issue.—Ed.]

What roughly happens in this demonstration is that a particular generic set is constructed in such a way that each element of δ can be shown to correspond to a subset of ω_0, the first infinite set, the denumerable set of whole numbers. As such, the power set of ω_0 is shown to contain at least as many elements as δ has elements. In this manner the errancy of state excess is demonstrated and the statement "$|p(\omega_a)| \geq |\delta|$" is shown to be veridical in a particular generic extension (459–62).

This result then has retroactive consequences for the status of this statement within ontology. It is possible to show that if set theory—ST—is consistent, no statement λ which is veridical in a generic extension of ST can affect the consistency of ST; that is, ST + the statement is also consistent (457). Since such a statement is always compatible with ST (ontology), then it can have one of two statuses: either it is a theorem of ontology or it is an undecidable statement within ontology (458). Since the statement "$|p(\omega_a)| \geq |\delta|$" is not actually a theorem of ontology—other statements concerning the excess of the power set such as the constructivist hypothesis are also compatible with set theory, as Gödel demonstrated (328)—it is thus undecidable in ontology.

A particular operation of forcing within the construction of a particular generic set thus reveals—according to Badiou's philosophical gloss—a point of the real within the ontological discourse of set theory.

4 Badiou notes that it is actually Easton's theorem published in 1970 which shows that not just Cantor's hypothesis but *all* hypotheses as to the cardinality of the power set of an infinite set "are in fact pure decisions" (328).

5 One could argue that there is another impossible and intra-ontological connection between being and event: that of the matheme which schematizes the event; $e_x = \{x \:/\: x \in X, e_x\}$ (where X is the evental site whose elements—the x's—are not presented in the situation, and e_x is the event itself). The connection takes place in the form of belonging: the elements of the evental site belong to the event. However, in contrast to "$|p(\omega_a)| \geq |\delta|$," the matheme of the event is not an ontological schema, but rather a metaontological schema inasmuch as it is inadmissible in set theory ontology. It is inadmissible because it is impossible for a set to belong to itself; e_x in the occurrence. It is for this reason that this metaontological matheme schematizes the event as point of impossibility for ontology,

as the real of "what-is-not-being-qua-being." In fact, it is the axiom of foundation which guarantees that this point of impossibility remains excluded from the discursive field of set theory. This exclusion is operated due to the impossible contradictions which occur in a formal language when sets which belong to themselves are allowed. This impossibility was formalized for the first time as Russell's paradox with regard to Frege's formalization of logic and it can be summed up in the question "does the set of all sets which do not belong to themselves belong to itself or not?"

6   See for example, at the basis of his theory of Ideas, Plato's usage of Heraclitus on the sensible world as perpetually unstable for knowledge due to the changes concomitant with time.
7   For a critical interrogation of this point, I refer the reader to Ray Brassier's article "Nihil Unbound: Remarks on Subtractive Ontology and Thinking Capitalism," in *Think Again: Alain Badiou and the Future of Philosophy*, ed. Peter Hallward, 50–58 (London: Continuum, 2004).
8   Jacques Lacan, *Séminaire XVII: L'envers de la psychanalyse* (Paris: Seuil, 1992), 37.
9   See Stuart Macintyre, *A Concise History of Australia* (Cambridge: Cambridge University Press, 1999), 276.
10 Badiou himself borrows the term "disjunctive synthesis" from Deleuze in the context of his analysis of the idea of a "war on terror." See IT 158.
11 There is a proximity between my position here and some of Jean-Luc Nancy's arguments concerning philosophy in *Le sens de la philosophie* (Paris: Galilée, 1993). However, I hold Nancy's ontological commitments, against his own problematizing rapprochement in his essay on Badiou, "Philosophy without Conditions," to be quite simply incommensurable with those of Badiou. Nancy's essay can be found in English translation in *Think Again: Alain Badiou and the Future of Philosophy*, ed. Peter Hallward, 39–49 (London: Continuum, 2004).
12 See Justin Clemens for a rigorous insistence on the necessity of thinking the "quadrature" of the conditions when engaging with Badiou's philosophy; "Letters as the Condition of Conditions for Alain Badiou," *Communication and Cognition* 36, no. 1/2 (2003): 73–102.
13 For Austin, philosophy's task is to deal with all the residual problems which are currently insoluble and reformulate them in a manner which allows their scientific treatment, at which point they will become the subject-matter of a new science and depart the realm of philosophy. See J. L. Austin, "Discussion" after "Performatif-constatif," in *La philosophie analytique* (Paris: Éditions de Minuit, 1962), 292–93.
14 On what I take to be a proposed hetero-expulsion of philosophy into one of its conditions, namely mathematics, see Ray Brassier's article "L'anti-phénomène," in *Alain Badiou: De l'ontologie à la politique*, ed. Bruno Besana and Oliver Feltham (Paris: L'Harmattan, forthcoming), and my reply.

The Cantorian Revolution: Alain Badiou on the Philosophy of Set Theory

B. Madison Mount

In the foreword to the second edition of the *Critique of Pure Reason,* Kant famously claimed that the critical philosophy set out in his work was separated from the dogmatic metaphysics of Leibniz and Wolff by nothing less than a "revolution"—a complete perspectival transformation analogous to that unleashed upon the astronomical sciences by Copernicus' *De revolutionibus.* Kant's so-called "Copernican revolution," like the original heliocentric thesis, required years to become part of the common currency of philosophical practice, bearing with it *topoi* of "revolutionary" reversal and epistemic reorientation whose diffusion, not to say banalization, would ultimately reach from nineteenth-century historicism through Kuhn and Bachelard all the way to the infomercial landscape of modernity's crepusculum. For the post-Maoist Alain Badiou, however, the term "revolution" is to be used with more circumspection: underneath the myriad forms of the "theme of the Subject" that define modernity (MP 24),[1] there is one and only one radical transformation in first philosophy that truly separates the contemporary moment from the age of the great early modern system-builders—the Cantorian revolution.

The *prima philosophia* in question is to be understood, in accordance with the classical tradition, as ontology, but this term has a very specific sense for Badiou: the entire "meta-ontological" discourse of his most important work, *L'être et l'événement,* is explicitly governed by "the thesis of identity between mathematics and ontology," the affirmation "that mathematics, in its entire historical becoming, pronounces that which is sayable of being-*qua*-being" (EE 14–15). Ontology manifests the "situation" in which the pure multiple, the ground of all presentation, can be given. However, to the degree that Badiou reverses the classic adage of the medievals, *ens et unum convertuntur*, proclaiming that the One *is* not, that even the Lacanian affirmation "there is the One" [*il y a l'Un*] is inadequate, but rather "there is no one, there is only counting-for-one" [*il n'y a pas d'un, il n'y a que le compte-pour-un*] (31–32), ontology can operate solely in "a situation whose presenting multiple [*le multiple présentatif*] is that of presentation itself" (36). The "mathematical theory of the pure multiple" can only manifest the terms under which a multiple can be counted-for-one, without itself offering "a definition of the multiple" (49, 37). In so doing, it attests to the *excess* of the multiplicity of multiples over that which can be (consistently) counted-for-one. This multiplicity of multiples, in its fullest expanse, is the set-theoretical universe (the proper class of all sets, designated V). The kerygma of set theory is nothing other than the narrative of the modes of manifestation of V, a hymn to the excess inscribed within pure number chanted unceasingly by the denizens of what David Hilbert called "Cantor's paradise."[2]

In this article I attempt to offer an analysis of some elements of Badiou's interpretation of the "Cantorian revolution" and its relation to open questions in modern set theory. Specifically, I seek to connect Badiou's perspective on the ZFC axioms (the Zermelo-Fraenkel framework with the Axiom of Choice, the standard starting-point for modern set theory, which Badiou claims "concentrate the greatest effort of thought ever accomplished, thus far, by humanity" [536]) and their possible extensions with the insights offered by contemporary Anglo-American philosophy of mathematics. I claim that Badiou's analysis of the implications of the Axiom of Constructibility (a proposed extension to ZFC designated, for reasons that will be explained below, $V = L$, where L is the "constructible universe") in meditations 26–30 of *L'être et l'événement* offers a unique and persuasive explanation for one of the most interesting facts of contemporary mathematical practice: that $V = L$, despite its demonstrable consistency with ZFC and its extraordinary explanatory power, is almost universally considered by mathematicians to be false and to provide an inadequate picture of the set-theoretical universe. The fullest attempt to account for this fact in the analytic tradition is offered by Penelope Maddy in an extensive project culminating in her 1997 *Naturalism in Mathematics*, in which she attempts to defend $V \neq L$ on intramathematical grounds, driven by metatheoretical maxims that she names "MAXIMIZE" and "UNIFY."[3]

I contend that Badiou's notion of a "desire ... to think ontological thought" [*de penser la pensée ontologique*] (336), lying latent in the mathematician, can, if properly interpreted, permit us to integrate Maddy's maxims and her arguments for $V \neq L$ within a "decisionist" perspective on the philosophical vocation of mathematics. This perspective, which I take to be Badiou's, is far removed both from conventional metamathematical platonism and from Maddy's properly "ontic" focus on the autotelism of a mathematical practice built upwards from naturalized epistemology.[4] Moreover, as an examination of Badiou's reading of Leibniz in meditation 30 demonstrates, the notion of a primary ontological "decision" predicated on desires (understood in Lacanian, rather than empirical, sociological, or psychologistic terms) provides a matrix for a "strong" reading of the history of philosophy of mathematics—a reading in which the entire trajectory of a variegated tradition is taken to be intratheoretically legible, bearing a historicity that can be elevated to the level of a true philosophical concept. This "epochal" reading of the historicity of the mathematician's decision, located at the collision point of mathematical exigency with metaontology and with a praxis that always opens up toward the political, underpins Badiou's invocation of a "revolution" and explains the relation between his theory of mathematics and his larger philosophical project.[5]

This article presents these themes in three relatively independent parts; each part combines discussions of the mathematical implications of Badiou's interpretation of set theory with analysis of the more general philosophical stakes involved in the notion of the "Cantorian revolution." In general, I have assumed only a basic background familiarity with the ZFC axioms and the heuristic "image" of the set-theoretical universe on the part of the reader; rigorous definitions and other technical material are set with a wider left margin, and can be skipped by those already familiar with modern axiomatic set theory.[6] Sections 1.1 through 1.3 provide a schematic reading of the development of set-theoretical practice through the lens of Badiou's notion of the infinite, explaining how the search for a solution to the question of the continuum hypothesis led to Gödel's work on constructible sets; sections 2.1 through 2.5 read Badiou's meditations on constructibility and on the proposed large cardinal axioms (which entail $V \neq L$) against the arguments advanced by Gödel and Maddy; and sections 3.1 through 3.4 consider meditation 30, along with Leibniz's own writings on infinity and the nature of history, in an attempt to evaluate the connections between Badiou's general theory of the historicity of mathematics and his work as a whole and to offer a critique of his vision of the "constructible orientation."

1 The Making of the Revolution: From the Ἄπείρον to ZFC

1.1

Every revolution calls into being a temporal structure that orders itself retroactively around an instant of scission, which, once perceived, alone permits the revolution to be named as such; this compression, however, should not be allowed to occult the durative aspect of revolutionary time: the herald of the instant always appears before it can be named, and subsists beyond its crystallization into a single term. If this is true of political revolutions—and an entire historiographical tradition attests to this fact—it is no less true of *ontological* revolutions. Thus the name "Cantor" is to be read as a retrospective arrangement, a synecdoche for the sequence of works stretching from Bernard Bolzano's *Paradoxien des Unendlichen* of 1847, through the triumvirate of Richard Dedekind, Gottlob Frege, and Cantor himself, to the consolidation of the ZFC system in the 1930s and, ultimately, to the equiconsistency proofs of Gödel and Cohen and the discovery of forcing, which brought a close to the "classical" epoch of set-theoretical mathematics, at last rendering patent the internal coherence of the entire movement.

Badiou's reconstructive vision of the Cantorian revolution does not follow its historical order linearly, but reorganizes its development around the central concept of the infinite—a pure mathematical object freed from every ontotheological notion of divine transcendence: "The thesis of the infinity of being is necessarily post-Christian or, if one wishes, post-Galilean. It is historically linked to the ontological advent of a mathematics of the infinite ..." (EE 162). The paramountcy of this notion of the purely mathematical infinite is manifest in the very passage where Badiou invokes the phrase "Cantorian revolution":

> To be sure, the foundation of a "quantity of being" cannot be for us the one that Kant proposes for the quantity of objects of intuition, since Kant finds this foundation in the transcendental pregnancy of time and space, whereas we try to think mathematically the presentation-multiple [*la présentation-multiple*] *beneath* time (which is founded by intervention) and space (which is a singular construction, relative to certain types of presentation). ... But perhaps the major obstacle is still not there. The obstacle—it separates us from Kant, with all the depth of the Cantorian revolution—resides in the fact that ... the form-multiple [*la forme-multiple*] of presentation is generally infinite. (293–94)

Although Kant attempted to offer a justification not only for Galilean science but for the calculus of infinitesimals, his concept of the infinite remained fundamentally classical; as it was for Aristotle, his *infinitum* was still essentially the ἀπείρον, the "indeterminate" potentiality of a series to be expanded by addition or of a magnitude to be divided ever further into submagnitudes. In the First Antinomy, Kant argues that the completed infinite collection never exists as a single entity for the understanding, and the claim that it does can only lead to contradiction: "the true (transcendental) concept of infinity is this: that the successive synthesis of unity in the traversal [*Durchmessung*] of a quantum can never be completed." In a footnote, Kant adds that this infinite quantum "contains thus a collection [*Menge*] (of a given unit) that is greater than any number, which is the mathematical concept of the infinite."[7] The human intellect, confined to intuitions given in spatiotemporal form, is limited to synthesis over the given: *infinitum in actu* may properly appear, if at all, only as a limiting idea, not as a concept useful for the understanding.

The initial moment in the course of the Cantorian revolution is the reversal of this image of the infinite, in a mode that makes Kant's question seem badly posed from the start: it is not *the* infinite that is given to us to think, even limitatively, but rather an ordering of transfinite collections, and these collections, along with the cardinal and ordinal arithmetic that describes their properties, are no less amenable to rigorous conceptualization for being independent of spatiotemporal intuition.[8] This change in perspective begins with a transformation of the classical presumptions about the paradoxicality of infinite collections. The new approach, first sketched out by Bolzano and reinvigorated in Cantor's early correspondence with Dedekind, finds its clearest formulation in the famous §64 of Dedekind's 1888 monograph *Was sind und was sollen die Zahlen?* Dedekind's definition is remarkable in its simplicity: "A system S is said to be *infinite* when it is similar to a proper part of itself; ... in the contrary case, S is said to be a finite system."[9] The few previous attempts in the history of philosophy to give ontological *droit de cité* to an actual infinite had run aground on the apparent paradoxes involved in extending the operations performed by the understanding on finite quantities to infinite ones; particularly troubling was the "reflexivity" of infinite sets, known to the ancients but given new prominence by Galileo.[10] For Dedekind, this fact—seemingly repugnant to common sense—is precisely the defining trait of the infinite; the relationship of one-to-one correspondence ("similarity" or "equipollence") becomes the foundation of the crucial set-theoretical notion of *cardinality* [*Mächtigkeit*]—the concept of which Cantor would be the herald.

Badiou notes the crucial importance of this maneuver: "The most striking point of Dedekind's definition is that it determines the infinite *positively*, and subordinates the finite negatively. This is its particularly modern note, as almost always in Dedekind. ... This intrepid total secularization of the infinite is a gesture whose merits we (the maladroit partisans of "finitude," in which our religious dependence is still legible) have still not exhausted" (NN 51). The "recognition of the infinity of being" as "the infinity of situations" (EE 164) is not amenable to purely *intramathematical* justification; a demonstrably coherent arithmetic without the Axiom of Infinity (the assertion that an infinite collection exists) is possible, and can in fact—if suitably elaborated—offer succedanea for large parts of the "working mathematician's" practice.[11] Nor can a compelling *extramathematical* justification be sought from physics or from the philosophy of mind; Kant's antinomies ruled out the former, and the failure of Dedekind's attempt to deduce the existence of an infinite collection from a combinatorial conception of possible thoughts—which, as Bertrand Russell showed, rests on an illegitimate invocation of the notion of "an object" in general—would spell the demise of the latter.[12] Thus the turn to the infinite becomes, in Badiou's terms, a primary ontological decision: "just like the empty set, or zero, *the infinite does not allow itself to be deduced*; it is necessary to *decide* upon its existence axiomatically, which amounts to admitting that one holds that existence to be not a construction of thought, but a fact of Being" (NN 60–61).

1.2

Against the background of the notion of cardinality, the decision to posit the existence of infinite collections leads immediately to two questions. First, are all infinite sets capable of being compared in terms of size? In other words, is there a total ordering of the transfinite cardinal numbers? All of Cantor's most powerful results depend on the presumed existence of this ordering, which he termed the series of alephs: $\aleph_0, \aleph_1, \ldots, \aleph_\alpha, \ldots$, for all ordinal α—finite and transfinite.[13] Second, if this comparison is always possible, what can be known about the way any two given sets, and the sets that can be produced from them through elementary operations, relate in size? In other words, what are the laws of cardinal arithmetic? These two questions form the basis for the controversies that most directly influenced the development of set theory during the first third of the twentieth century: the debate over the Axiom of Choice (AC) and the attempt to demonstrate the continuum hypothesis. In 1904, Zermelo showed that the assumption that every transfinite cardinal is an aleph is equivalent to the assumption that a choice function exists on every set—a function f that picks out one and only one element from every nonempty set x that is itself a member of the set in question. The initial suspicion with which this axiom was greeted by mathematicians, and its subsequent acceptance—largely on grounds of mathematical indispensability—is well-known; I will not attempt to repeat the story here, except as it is relevant to the debate over the Axiom of Constructibility.[14]

Even with the acceptance of Choice, however, many of the most basic questions about the cardinal hierarchy remained unsettled. The most famous of these questions, the continuum hypothesis (CH), was first posed by Cantor in 1878. In modern terms (and assuming AC) his conjecture can be expressed as follows. The set of all natural numbers, $\mathbb{N}$, has cardinality $\aleph_0$: the smallest transfinite cardinal. (When speaking about the smallest transfinite *ordinal*, we will, in keeping with tradition, write ω or ω_0 rather than $\aleph_0$.) The set of all real numbers, $\mathbb{R}$, can be shown to be similar to the power set—the set of all subsets—of $\mathbb{N}$, $\wp(\mathbb{N})$. $\mathbb{R}$ thus has cardinality equal to that of $\wp(\mathbb{N})$. Cantor's most important early result in cardinal arithmetic shows that the power set of any set a has cardinality greater than that of a; in fact, under the definition of cardinal exponentiation, $|\wp(a)| = 2^{|a|}$. Thus $|\mathbb{R}| = 2^{\aleph_0}$. But elementary cardinal arithmetic does not answer how $|\mathbb{R}|$ and $|\mathbb{N}|$ relate in terms of the aleph hierarchy. Cantor hypothesized that there was no transfinite cardinal between $\aleph_0$ and $2^{\aleph_0}$—in other words, that $2^{\aleph_0} = \aleph_1$. Along with many other mathematicians, he would spend years trying, without success, to find a proof of this contention; it was at the top of Hilbert's famous list of unsolved problems presented to the International Congress of Mathematicians in Paris in 1900.[15]

By the 1930s, after decades of failed attempts at a proof, the possibility of a direct demonstration of CH by conventional means had begun to seem unlikely. However, the development of the Zermelo-Fraenkel standard axiomatization of set theory caused mathematicians to hope that the assertion (and the Axiom of Choice) could at least be proved to be consistent with ZF. (A direct proof of AC was generally assumed to be impossible, because Abraham Fraenkel had demonstrated its independence from an axiom system similar but not identical to ZF in 1926.)[16] Since the consistency of ZF cannot itself be proved in ZF (a consequence of Kurt Gödel's well-known incompleteness results of 1930–31), the best that could be hoped for in either case was a relative consistency proof: a demonstration that if ZF + the assumption in question is inconsistent, then ZF itself is inconsistent. For both AC and CH, the anticipated result came from Gödel in 1938–40, in a series of papers that made model-theoretic considerations an indispensable part of set theory and introduced the notion of the "constructible universe," the proper class of all "constructible" sets, designated L.[17]

Before giving a structural definition of L, it is necessary to explain precisely what Gödel sought to demonstrate. L constitutes a *model* of ZF: an interpretation in which the ZF axioms are satisfied.[18] Gödel demonstrated that both choice and CH (in fact, a stronger version of CH called the *generalized continuum hypothesis* or *GCH*, which states that for all α, $\aleph_{\alpha+1} = 2^{\aleph_\alpha}$) are satisfied in L, thus (by way of the Completeness Theorem) demonstrating relative consistency: neither ¬CH nor ¬AC can be proved in ZF if ZF is consistent. In 1963, Paul Cohen would provide the counterpart to Gödel's proof, demonstrating that CH cannot be proved in ZF if ZF is consistent, by producing a model in which ¬CH holds. Thus CH is rigorously *undecidable* within the framework of the axioms of ZF; if it is to be given a definite answer, this must occur by addition of a new axiom or axioms, not by any result that can be reached from the starting point of standard set theory.

To understand the form those axioms might take, it is necessary to discuss Gödel's model L in more detail. We can present L heuristically in a straightforward fashion by means of the recursive definition of a hierarchy of constructible sets. For every set a, consider all the sets that can be formed from a by a finite number of simple operations; call these the *definable subsets* of a and call their union Df(a). Let $L_0 = \emptyset$, $L_{\alpha+1} = $ Df($L(\alpha)$), and for a limit ordinal α (an ordinal that, like ω, is not the successor of any ordinal), $L_\alpha = $ the union of the sets L_β for all $\beta < \alpha$. L, the constructible universe, is just the union of all the sets in this hierarchy: $L = \bigcup_{\alpha \in On} L_\alpha$ where On is the class of all ordinals. The only difficulty lies in giving a rigorous formulation of what is meant by "a finite number of simple operations"; in technical terms, a set $s \in $ Df(a) if and only if there is a first-order formula φ in the language of set theory with a finite number of parameters $a_1, a_2, a_3 \ldots \in a$ such that $s = \{ x \in a \mid \varphi(x, a_1, a_2, a_3, \ldots)\}$.[19] L is thus, at every point, a precise analogue for the "intended" model of set theory, the cumulative hierarchy V which is built up by transfinite recursion from $\emptyset$. V_0 is taken to be $\emptyset$; its successors are given by $V_{\alpha+1} = \wp(L(\alpha))$ and, for limit α, $V_\alpha = \bigcup_{\beta < \alpha} V_\beta$; likewise, V itself is defined as $\bigcup_{\alpha \in On} V_\alpha$.[20] L differs from V only in that it includes, at each stage, not *all* the subsets of the previous stage, but only the *definable* subsets. However, precisely because L is a model of ZF, and every statement provable in ZF is by definition satisfied in L, it is not possible to prove in ZF that there are *any* sets that are not capable of being constructed from definable sets: in other words, it is not possible to demonstrate, operating solely within ZF, that $V \neq L$. Yet it is also not possible to prove within ZF that $V = L$, a result that follows directly from Cohen's proof of the existence of a model of ZF + ¬CH. (Since CH holds in L, if it could be proved in ZF that $V = L$, then there would be no model of ZF where ¬CH obtains. But there is a model of ZF in which ¬CH; therefore, $V = L$ cannot be a theorem of ZF.) For this reason, $V = L$ is a "safe"—and potentially appealing—candidate for an additional axiom to be added to ZFC (or ZF, since Choice is a theorem in the constructible universe). When so added, rather than merely hypothesized relative to the model-theoretic apparatus of an equiconsistency proof, $V = L$ (termed, under these circumstances, the Axiom of Constructibility) makes a strong ontological claim: non-constructible sets do not exist, so the model built by Gödel is nothing other than the "intended" model of set theory—the universe itself.

1.3

Gödel's and Cohen's intramathematical results demonstrating the limitations of ZF lead directly to an epistemological impasse. If ZF, whose axioms were intended to offer a foundation for all of mathematics on the basis of a rigorous thematization of the minimum "intuitive" characteristics of the notion of set, is powerless to prove either CH or ¬CH, does it make sense to say that CH has a truth-value at all? This question has been central to modern philosophy of mathematics; so central, in fact, that the members of the traditional *combinatoire* of attitudes toward mathematical practice—formalism, intuitionism, and platonism—are often sketched out in terms of their responses to the continuum problem. This taxonomy is the successor to the older logicist/intuitionist/formalist tripartition, which had already become sufficiently established by 1931 to serve as the basis for a series of set-piece manifestos by Rudolf Carnap, Arend Heyting, and John von Neumann on "the foundations of mathematics" published in *Erkenntnis,* the journal of the Vienna Circle founded by Carnap and Hans Reichenbach.[21] After Gödel's incompleteness theorems showed the limits of the classical (Fregean) logicist project, whose greatest monument was (and still remains) Russell and Whitehead's *Principia Mathematica,* the various versions of logicism current in the 1930s fell out of favor, perhaps unjustly; their place in the ideological *combinatoire* was taken by Gödel's own brand of set-theoretical realism, generally seen—although Badiou contests this judgment strongly—as the leading example of the general school termed "platonism."

The mathematical formalist, for whom there is no objective fact of the matter about a mathematical proposition beyond its deducibility in a logical system, claims that Gödel's and Cohen's results offer all the answers that are needed to the question of the continuum hypothesis: it makes no more sense to ask whether CH or ¬CH is "true," once its undecidability has been shown, than to ask whether Euclid's fifth postulate or its negation is "true." ZF + CH and ZF + ¬CH are both (to the best of our knowledge) consistent models of ZF and thus both different, but equally valid, "set theories," just as Euclidian, Lobachevskian, and Riemannian geometries are all equally valid mathematical systems. (All but the most extreme formalists concede that one axiom system might be more useful or interesting than another to study, but they argue that this fact is, in principle, of no epistemic relevance.)[22] The intuitionist believes that the question of the truth-value of CH is meaningless, but for an entirely different reason: he refuses to admit any mathematical object that cannot be "constructed" intuitively. "Construction," here, means something entirely different from the *formal* constructibility of L; it is a process that is absolutely non-formalizable, definable not in terms of any axiom system but only on the basis of the primary mental faculty of intuition. At least for the most famous early intuitionist, L. E. J. Brouwer, the concept of intuition in question is based on Kant's *Anschauung,* but freed from any dependence on a specific spatial model: to be intuitively constructible, Brouwer claims, is to be constructible to the mind in time from "the fundamental phenomenon of mathematical thinking, the intuition of the bare two-oneness."[23] The *only* objects that can be built out of this fundamental phenomenon, it is alleged, are $\mathbb{N}, \omega$, and the continuum. The intuitionist continuum, however, is not a set—$\mathbb{R}$ or $\wp(\mathbb{N})$ or anything equivalent thereto—but a pure limitative notion, "the 'between,' which is not exhaustible by the interposition of new units and which therefore can never be thought of as a mere collection of units."[24] For this reason the intuitionist does not accept the transfinite hierarchy or Cantor's proof, without which the problem of

CH cannot even be posed: "this power aleph-null is the only infinite power of which the intuitionists recognize the existence."[25] Thus, Brouwer claims, CH, "as stated [by conventional set theory] is without meaning; and as soon as it has been so interpreted as to get a meaning, it can easily be answered."[26]

In opposition to both of these positions, platonism fearlessly proclaims both the existence of a fact of the matter about CH and the accessibility of that fact, in principle, to "mathematical intuition": a nonconstructive, nonspatiotemporal faculty far removed from the cautionary strictures of either Kant or Brouwer. Gödel offered a paean to this faculty in an article entitled "What is Cantor's Continuum Problem?" written in 1947 and substantially revised in 1963, just before Cohen's proof. The later version expresses the central idea thus:

> [O]n the basis of the point of view here adopted, a proof of the undecidability of Cantor's conjecture from the accepted axioms of set theory … would by no means solve the problem. For if the meanings of the primitive terms of set theory as explained [in an appendix and footnote that allude to the intuitive "collective" notion of "set"] … are accepted as sound, it follows that the set-theoretical concepts and theorems describe some well-determined reality, in which Cantor's conjecture must be either true or false. Hence its undecidability from the axioms being assumed today can only mean that these axioms do not contain a complete description of that reality.[27]

For Gödel, it is mathematical intuition, "something like a perception … of the objects of set theory," that accounts for the fact that "the axioms force themselves upon us as being true." The "mere psychological fact of the existence of an intuition which is sufficiently clear to produce the axioms of set theory and an open series of extensions of them" means that either CH or ¬CH *must* be true; the task of the mathematician, aided by his primary intuition, is thus to find out *which* axioms "force themselves upon us as being true" and thereby enable an answer to the question.[28]

Gödel's results of 1938–40 on the constructible universe offer an immediate contender for one such axiom: $V = L$. $V = L$ settles CH; it settles GCH; in fact, its decisive force is so great that Azriel Levy claimed in 1979 that "one of the most profound open problems in set theory is to find a natural statement of set theory which does not refer, directly or indirectly, to very large ordinals … and which is neither proved nor refuted by the axiom of constructibility."[29] But does it force itself on us as being true? If not, are there considerations which could cause us ultimately to come to believe it true or false? Would these considerations be of a piece with Gödel's "mathematical intuition"? Or must this conception of the relation between intuition and truth—the philosophical calling card of the thinker whom Badiou names "the greatest, along with Cohen, of the continuators of Cantor" (CT 104)—itself be reinterpreted or replaced, if not by one of its classical (formalist or intuitionist) competitors, then by something wholly different?

Gödel himself, it seems, considered $V = L$ as a viable axiom candidate only very briefly. In the 1938 version of the paper that proved the relative consistency of ZF and ZF + CH, he wrote that it "seems to give a natural completion of the axioms of set theory, insofar as it determines the vague notion of an arbitrarily infinite set in a definite way"; however, as Penelope Maddy notes, it is difficult to view this as an unqualified endorsement.[30] By 1947, however, Gödel had come to adhere strongly to the contention that $V \neq L$. Following Maddy's analysis, we can isolate two reasons for this opinion. The first is developed at some length in Gödel's paper: $V = L$ implies CH and Gödel had decided that certain technical consequences of CH relating to point sets were highly implausible.[31] This extrinsic justification, however, only points the way toward the task left for mathematical intuition; Gödel opines that the "role of the continuum problem" may be "to lead to the *discovery* of new axioms which will make it possible to disprove" CH.[32] The second reason, based on "intuitive" considerations that would motivate such a discovery, is only dimly hinted at in 1947; even in 1963, Gödel is willing to offer no more than a single-sentence explanation of the heuristic principle that might lead one to identify a supplementary axiom, if proposed, as compelling in a way that $V = L$ is not: "from an axiom in some sense opposite to this one [$V = L$], the negation of Cantor's conjecture could perhaps be derived. I am thinking of an axiom which (similar to Hilbert's completeness axiom in geometry) would state some maximum property of the system of all sets, whereas axiom A [Gödel's name for $V = L$] states a minimum property."[33]

$V = L$ "states a minimum property" because it is ontologically restrictive: it constricts the extension of the term "subset of x" to "definable subset of x." For Gödel, this restriction appears to conflict with the impulse behind the primitive notion of "set," which takes for granted that *any collection* in the hierarchy can be joined into a set, regardless of its definability (unless it is simply so large, like V or On, that taking it to be a set would lead to a contradiction).[34] Precisely because "set" is a primitive notion, however, this combinatorial generality cannot be made explicit in the formal language of ZF; it is expressible only with difficulty even in natural language, as Gödel notes:

> The operation "set of x's" (where the variable x ranges over some given kind of objects) cannot be defined satisfactorily (at least not in the present state of knowledge), but can only be paraphrased by other notions involving again the concept of set, such as: "multitude of x's," "combination of any number of x's," "part of the totality of x's," where a "multitude" (combination, part) is conceived of as something which exists in itself no matter whether we can define it in a finite number of words (so that random sets are not excluded).[35]

The restrictivity of $V = L$, Gödel argues, is thus not merely an epiphenomenal feature of the formalization used in producing a constructible model in ZFC; $V = L$ manifests itself as fundamentally *limitative* relative to the irreducible content—however inadequately expressible it may be—of "set," and for this reason mathematical intuition compels us to find it implausible. Yet it is this final step, the keystone of Gödel's argument, that poses the most difficult problem for platonist philosophy of mathematics. Even granting that $V = L$ is limitative, why should this fact render it implausible? Why should the difference in intension between the pre-theoretical notion of the subset property and the subset property as it is used in the constructible hierarchy be counted as evidence for an *extensional* difference—the actual existence of non-constructible sets? This question can only be answered by asking about the *configuration of thought* that Gödel presupposes: why does the mathematical platonist seek after a "maximal property" rather than a "minimal one," and why does he believe—by virtue of a choice that is not itself capable of intratheoretical justification—that this desire is not merely a psychological fact, but the expression of an *epistemic orientation*? Why should the desire inscribed in the mathematician's thought track mathematical truth? It is this final conundrum, which ties the internal problematics of set theory to the infinitary exigency of truth—in the mode of "truths subtracted from knowledge" (EE 375), irreducible to any propositional encyclopedia—that underlies Badiou's consideration of the Axiom of Constructibility in *L'être et l'événement*.[36]

2   Platonism, Naturalism, and Desire: Badiou and the "Orientations of Thought," *V = L*, and Large Cardinal Axioms

2.1

The tripartite taxonomy of formalism, intuitionism, and platonism stenographs the institutional *rapport de forces* of a key battleground of modern analytic philosophy, and, in so doing, provides a map through which the philosopher can retroactively capture the subjectivating force of his decision; it is, for better and for worse, the dominant matrix of ideologization of the Cantorian revolution. For Badiou, however, this model is radically inadequate: not only does it falsify the metaontological status of the problem, but, by misreading "platonism" as though it were determined by a simple "criterion of exteriority (or transcendence) of mathematical structures (or objects)" (CT 95), it occults the crucial connection between mathematics and thought. Mathematical thought is νόησις in the plenary sense, rather than mere representation, and this point, more than any other, separates Plato from mainstream mathematical "platonism":

> The fundamental concern of Plato is to declare the immanent identity, the co-appurtenance, of the object known and the knowing mind, their essential ontological commensurability. If there is one point where Plato is the son of Parmenides, who affirms "The same is at once thinking and being" [*Le même, lui, est à la fois penser et être*], it is this one. Inasmuch as mathematics touches upon [*touche à*] being, it is intrinsically a thought. And reciprocally, if mathematics is a thought, it touches upon being itself. The theme of a knowing subject who would have to "aim at" [*viser*] an exterior object—a theme whose origin is empiricist, even when the object in question is ideal—is entirely inappropriate to Plato's philosophical usage of the existence of mathematics. (CT 96)

Badiou's own position, as will become clear, is not quite that of the Parmenidean τὸ γὰρ αὐτὸ νοεῖν ἔστιν τε καὶ εἶναι (in which, in any case, the ipseity of τὸ αὐτό is not quite identity, as Heidegger famously pointed out).[37] Yet the "touch upon being" of mathematics is unquestionably part of his own set of philosophical commitments; and it is from this insight that he is able to reread Gödel against mainstream "platonist" interpretations of the type I outlined in part 1. Most importantly, Badiou interprets Gödel's notion of "mathematical intuition" in light of the "ontological commensurability" he theorizes, finding in the set-theorist's assertion that "the question of the objective existence of the objects of mathematical intuition (which, incidentally, is an exact replica of the question of the objective existence of the outer world) is not decisive for the problem"[38] a vindication of the Platonic notion of being immediately and immanently accessible to thought over and against the "platonic" fixation on existence and externality. This, according to Badiou, is the true lesson of the *Meno*: "The Idea is always already there. If it were not capable of being 'activated' in thought, it would remain unthinkable" (CT 96).[39] For Plato, as for Gödel, the thinking that is (within) mathematics orients itself to the immanent truth of its Idea: yet this truth is anything but the correspondence of an intentional act with its transcendent *representatum*. Notwithstanding Gödel's somewhat misleading use of the phrase "criterion of truth," the logician's essential insight, on Badiou's reading, is that mathematical truth is not simply an *adequatio intellectus et rei,* for the "object" of mathematics fundamentally does not give itself objectally, that is to say, as an exteriority: it does not have the heterogeneity to noesis of the post-Scholastic *res* or *objectum*.[40] Instead, "'truth' is never anything but the name of that through which, in a single process, being and thought mate [*s'apparient*]" (CT 101). The truth of mathematics is its touch upon being, yet this touch, far from being the manipulative grasping of an *ob-jectum* or *Gegen-stand*, is a noetic caress.

It is this prioritization of the immanent character of every mathematical truth that obliges Badiou to superimpose a different triptych on the traditional schema of formalism/intuitionism/platonism. The crucial taxonomy is no longer that of the ideologies of philosophers of mathematics, but that of the *orientations of thought produced within—but transgressing the limits of—ontology (mathematics) itself*. All of these orientations can be assessed, Badiou argues in meditation 27 of *L'être et l'événement,* in terms of the ways in which they respond to CH and to "the abyss that separates numerical discreteness from the geometrical continuum" (EE 311).[41] The paths of approach to the abyss are three in number: first, the "grammatical or programmatic" tendency (312), later associated with the term "constructivism,"[42] which takes its departure from a "linguistic" notion of the combinatorics of being and from the Leibnizian doctrine of the identity of indiscernables; second, the "generic" approach, which rejects the primacy of the linguistic and seeks instead to fix a "matheme of the indiscernible" itself (313); and, third, the logic of "prodigality" that seeks to "differentiate a gigantic infinity which prescribes a hierarchic disposition in which nothing more can wander" (313–14). Each of these orientations has an accompanying concretization, which bridges the space between "mathematical ontology," the kernel that "does not constitute by itself any orientation in thought, but … must be compatible with all, discerning and proposing the being-multiple that they require" (314), and the metaontological mapping propelled by the "excess" of the multiple over its presentation (312). Alongside these three paths, however, Badiou names a *transversal* orientation of mathematical thought, which is to be identified with his own focus on the primacy of the decision:

> But a fourth path, discernable since Marx, taken from a different slant by Freud, is transversal to the three others. It holds, in effect, that the *truth* of the ontological impasse allows itself neither to be grasped nor thought in immanence to ontology itself or to speculative metaontology. It assigns the de-measure of the state [*la dé-mesure de l'état*] to the historical limitation of being so that, unknowingly, philosophy reflects it only to repeat it. The hypothesis of this path consists in saying that one can only *render justice* to injustice from the slant of the event and the intervention. There is no need to be alarmed over a de-linking [*dé-liaison*] of being, because it is in the undecidable occurrence of a supernumerary non-being that every truth procedure orients itself, including that of a truth whose wager would be this de-linking. (314–15)

The transversal orientation does not claim that the truths to which the plurality of competing intratheoretical claims attest are *simply* reducible either to "ontology itself" (that is to say, a result within the space of ZFC and its possible extensions) or to the "speculative metaontology" produced by philosophy of mathematics, which is necessarily blind to the historicity of the primitive rapport in being, the mode of being's being-counted (and counting out or dis-counting the "illegal" non-being which alone, in its "de-linking," makes the consistency of being as a totality possible). Rather, the transversal orientation seeks to reckon with the plural *truths* of the mathematical aporia as processes of truth-production in the conjuncture of ontology and metaontology. It rehistoricizes the decisions of the other three orientations and, in so doing, brings the discursive system engendered by the Cantorian revolution into conversation with the post-Galilean but pre-revolutionary moment of modern philosophy, whose conceptual innovations are captured and restructured by the *dispositif* of "philosophy of mathematics": "The three orientations also have, evidently, their philosophical respondents. I have named Leibniz for the first. The theory of the general will in Rousseau seeks the generic or 'whichever' [*quelconque*] point upon which to found political authority. All of classical metaphysics conspires in the third, even in the mode of communist eschatology" (314).

Thus the transversal orientation shatters the harmony of the other paths, bringing each one in contact with the unthought form behind its own "reflection" of ontology. Its insistence on *reflecting the reflection,* dialecticizing its specular content, is the mark of what Badiou, in his *Théorie du sujet,* terms "the materialist reversal of materialism" (TS 193). It is this reversal that ultimately separates Badiou (minimally) from Parmenides and Plato even as he lauds their exemplary status and defends philosophical Platonism against the ideology of mathematical "platonism." The unavoidable constraint of materialism, on Badiou's definition, lies in the refusal to accept a *final* resolution of the metaontological impasse: "The reflection makes a metaphor of the fact that thinking and being are the same thing. To which Engels adds—asymptotically—that they are the same thing to within a trifle [*à quelque chose près*]. A trifle which the process of knowledge [*connaissance*] postpones to infinity as its remainder" (TS 212). Each orientation of thought is brought forward through its concretization, its linkage to mathematical ontology, yet these concretizations reveal their full infrastructure *only asymptotically*. However, this suspensivity inherent to thought no more vitiates the priority of the decision than the existence of *longue durée* philosophical trends corresponding to the metamathematical content of the orientations tells against the epochality of the revolution: the specifically mathematical form of each concretization offers an essential, but never *final*, vantage point from which to assess the structure of the orientations of thought in their totality. These points of transition between philosophy and the ontology immanent to ZFC appear as ineluctable moments of scission, delimited by the choice to add (or not to add) axiom candidates to ZFC:

> To the first orientation corresponds the doctrine of *constructible* sets, created by Gödel and refined by Jensen. To the second, the doctrine of *generic* sets, created by Cohen. To the third, the doctrine of *large cardinals,* to which all the specialists of set theory have contributed. In so doing, ontology proposes the schema of appropriate sets as the *substructure of being* of each orientation. The constructible orientation unfolds being from the configurations of knowledge. The generic, with its concept of an indiscernible multiple, makes it possible to think the being of a truth. Large cardinals approximate the virtual being demanded by theologies. (EE 314)

The "doctrine of constructible sets" appears when $V = L$ is supplemented to ZFC. The "generic" orientation does not add any axioms to ZFC, but contents itself with proving relative results using extensions of the method—"forcing"—created by Cohen to prove the equiconsistency of ZF + ¬CH and ZF + ¬AC with ZF. The "prodigal" orientation depends on the addition to standard set theory of what are known as large cardinal axioms (LCAs): axioms independent of ZFC that posit the existence of cardinals high in the set-theoretic hierarchy that differ qualitatively from those, like $\aleph_0$, $2^{\aleph_0}$, and $\aleph_\omega$, familiar to Cantor.

Combining the different moments of the analysis offered in meditation 27, it is possible to produce a schematic diagram of the four orientations of thought (see figure 1). The focus of my reading is on Badiou's analysis of the first ("grammatical"/constructivist) orientation in meditations 28–30 and its relation to $V = L$. Yet it is not possible to consider this tack independently of the third ("prodigal") path, for the theory of large cardinals provides an essential correlate to the crucial notion—alluded to at the end of part 1—that $V = L$ is limitative relative to alternative models of the hierarchy that could be formed on the basis of the intuitive set-notion.

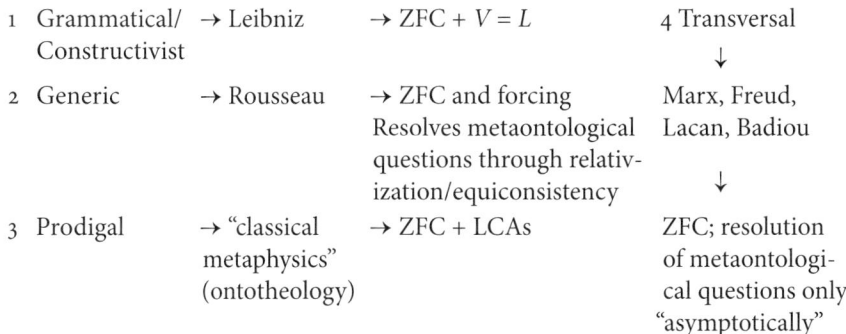

Figure 1. The four orientations of thought.

2.2

Gödel's sense that $V = L$ expresses a "minimal" property might be said to express a concept of "horizontal" limitativity: if $V \neq L$, then at some stage α, $\wp(V_\alpha)$ will be a proper superset of the definable subsets of V_α, causing $V_{\alpha+1}$ to be "wider" than the corresponding stage $L_{\alpha+1}$. However, this "horizontal" limitativity is not the sole relevant sense in which the Axiom of Constructibility constrains the set-theoretical universe. In 1961, Dana S. Scott proved that $V = L$ is "vertically" limitative relative to a type of large cardinals, whose existence cannot be proved in ZFC, called "measurable cardinals": if there exists a measurable cardinal, then $V \neq L$. To understand the implications of this result for the structure of the set-theoretical universe, it is first necessary to give a brief explanation of the basic concept behind the LCAs and their relation to ZFC.

The simplest large cardinal axiom is the least powerful, the axiom of inaccessible cardinals.[43] Inaccessibles can be defined as follows: the cofinality of a cardinal κ is the smallest cardinal ξ such that κ is the sum of ξ many cardinals, each of which is less than κ. A cardinal is called *regular* if it is equal to its own cofinality—if it cannot be built up from the union of a smaller number of smaller cardinals. $\aleph_0$ is regular, as is every transfinite successor cardinal; but a $\kappa > \aleph_0$ is termed inaccessible if it is regular and has the property of being a strong limit (which means that κ is *not* a successor of any cardinal and for every $\lambda < \kappa$, $2^\lambda < 2^\kappa$). Rendered in more informal language, a cardinal is inaccessible if it cannot be reached from below by any combination of the successor (from $\aleph_\alpha$ to $\aleph_{\alpha+1}$) and power-set (from $\aleph_\alpha$ to $2^{\aleph_\alpha}$) operations. (As is to be expected from this definition, if κ is an inaccessible cardinal, it has the property of being the κth aleph, but the converse is not always true.)

It is not possible to prove or disprove in ZFC the existence of an inaccessible cardinal; thus "there exists an inaccessible cardinal" (INAC) is the smallest LCA that extends ZFC. (For reasons having to do with Gödel's incompleteness theorems, ZFC + INAC cannot be proved relatively consistent to ZFC, as could ZFC

+ GCH. However, it is generally considered unlikely that inconsistency threatens INAC, or even much stronger assumptions about the existence of large cardinals.) INAC extends ZFC on the basis of a primary decision, much as the axiom of infinity extends finite set theory; expanding on this comparison, the set theorist Thomas Jech notes that the "inaccessible cardinals owe their name to the fact that they cannot be obtained from smaller cardinals by the usual set-theoretical operations. ... In fact, $\aleph_0$ has this property too. Thus we can say that in a sense an inaccessible cardinal is to smaller cardinals what $\aleph_0$ is to finite cardinals. This is one of the main themes of the theory of large cardinals."[44]

However, this analogy between $\aleph_0$ and the first inaccessible is, like the medieval theologian's *analogia entis*, traversed by an irrevocable trace of differentiation; in order to function *as an analogy*, it must constantly draw attention to that within it which is resistant to univocity, that which fails to come to full expression in the name it accords to its terms: the ultimate object that hovers on the edge of apophasis. INAC expresses, in Badiou's terms, a primary ontological claim dependent on a "decision" (EE 344), yet this decision carries with it an exorbitance that threatens to reduce the internal structure of the hierarchy by literalizing the *analogon*: "[T]he cardinal ω_0 is in truth this limit one-step-more that is the toppling of the finite in the infinite. ... If there were another regular limit cardinal, it would relegate the infinite cardinals, in comparison with its supereminence, to the same rank as that held by finite numbers in comparison with ω_0. It would operate a sort of 'finitization' of the preceding infinities ..." (490–91). Even more problematically, the notion of inaccessibility is not merely an extension of the axiom of infinity, but is itself *generative* in that it can easily be extended to yield still stronger LCAs: from inaccessibles one passes to hyper-inaccessibles (cardinals which cannot be reached "from below" through the *inaccessible* series), then to hyper-hyper-inaccessibles, n-hyper-inaccessibles for (finite or transfinite) ordinal n and so on. The inaccessibles and their analogues are immense by the standards of all conceivable needs of practical mathematics, but set theorists nonetheless consider them to be "small" large cardinals. The measurables, by contrast, first postulated by Stanislaw Ulam in 1930, are the classic examples of "large" large cardinals—although contemporary research in set theory focuses on a menagerie of even bigger and stranger types (Woodin, Shelah, supercompact, huge, superhuge, and so on).

For Badiou, this intricate proliferation evinces the other edge of the analogy between the LCAs and the "original" axiom of infinity: "The theory of 'large cardinals' has continually been enriched by new monsters. Each must be the object, if one wishes to ensure its existence, of a special axiom. Each seeks to constitute within the infinite an abyss comparable to that which separates the first infinity, ω_0, from the finite multiples. None achieves it, exactly" (EE 344–45). Because it is ultimately bound to an open-ended set of alternatives, the prodigal temptation cannot definitively resolve the aporia to which the triptych of orientations testifies; in *Théorie du sujet,* Badiou goes so far as to compare it to the "nationalist, martial, and imperial 'great plans' through which the bourgeoisies launch a counterblast to popular movements and crises" (TS 286). In *L'être et l'événement,* by contrast, he offers a much more favorable analysis: even if the LCAs cannot by themselves provide a solution to the impasse (the fact that no LCA yet proposed determines CH is presumably a contributing factor to Badiou's judgment), the drive to transcendence motivating their introduction nonetheless contains a certain "heroism," which permits an internal critique of the constructivist orientation—*even as the temptation toward the "grammatical," of which V = L is the insignia, holds in check the potentially theological trajectory of the LCAs.* "From my point of view," he writes, "which is neither that of the power of language (whose indispensable ascesis I recognize) nor that of transcendence (whose heroism I recognize), there is a certain pleasure in seeing how each of these paths permits a diagnostic on the other" (EE 344). The example Badiou gives of this "diagnostic" is the theorem mentioned above: if a measurable cardinal exists (a hypothesis we will designate by MC), then $V \neq L$.

Measurable cardinals are difficult to define, but even a non-rigorous treatment can offer a certain intuitive motivation for Scott's result, mentioned at the beginning of this section, that the existence of a measurable cardinal implies $V \neq L$. A (nontrivial) measure on x is a function $\mu(a)$ from $\wp(x)$ into $[0, 1]$ such that $\mu(x) = 1$, $\mu(z) = 0$ for all $z \in x$, and $\mu(b_1 \cup b_2) = \mu(b_1) + \mu(b_2)$ if b_1 and b_2 are disjoint. Heuristically, a measure on sets of reals can be thought of as a generalization of the notion of the length of a line segment: a single point (or a countable set of points) has measure zero, the entire segment has measure one, and two disconnected pieces of the segment have a total measure equal to the sum of their individual measures. (Counterintuitively, a non-denumerable set of points can also have measure zero, and there is no measure on $\mathbb{R}$ that is both applicable to *all* subsets and is of the type, known as Lebesgue measure, that preserves the natural properties of length.)[45] In a generalization of the union property, a measure on x is termed κ-additive for some cardinal κ if for every family f of less than κ mutually disjoint subsets of x, the measure of the union of the members of f equals the sum of the measures of the members of f. A measure on x is two-valued if, for all $a \in \wp(x)$, $\mu(a) = 0$ or $\mu(a) = 1$. A measurable cardinal is defined as a cardinal $\lambda > \aleph_0$ for which there is a two-valued λ-additive measure on x for some set x of cardinality λ. If they exist, measurable cardinals are extraordinarily immense: the first inaccessible cardinal cannot be measurable, nor the first hyper-inaccessible, nor the first n-hyper-inaccessible for any n that is not itself measurable; if λ is the first measurable cardinal, then there are λ inaccessibles below it, and λ hyper-inaccessibles, and so on. Indeed, measurable cardinals are so large that any attempt to formulate "λ is a measurable cardinal" in the language of set theory runs up against the limits of what can be described in first-order (and, in fact, second-order) formulas; in the jargon of the discipline, measurable cardinals have very strong indescribability properties.[46] Indescribability properties as such are not a perfect indicator of size; there are many cardinals of much higher levels of inaccessibility below the first measurable. However, the fact that the formula "λ is a measurable cardinal" greatly outstrips the simple formalizable properties by means of which the Df operation—and, through its mediation, the hierarchy of L—were established offers at least an analogical ground for finding Scott's theorem plausible.[47] (In fact, it was widely assumed before Scott's proof that $V = L$ would ultimately be found to be limitative relative to sufficiently strong LCAs.)[48]

2.3

The existence of a measurable cardinal thus implies the existence of a nonconstructible set—a set resistant to the explicit definability requirements encoded in the definition of the L hierarchy: "The constructible universe *decides,* itself, on the impossibility of being for certain transcendent multiplicities. It restrains the infinite prodigality of presentation" (EE 345). This tension between the first and third orientation lies at the center of the argument within mainstream philosophy of mathematics about what can be known, intramathematically, about the kind of object the set-theoretical hierarchy is. But Scott's result, in and of itself, seems to move us no closer to a resolution of the epistemological impasse: is the fact that MC implies $V \neq L$ an argument for $V \neq L$ (based on a prior intuition that measurables seem plausible)—or is it an argument against MC (based on a prior intuition that $V = L$ seems to instantiate the "intended model" of the hierarchy)? For the later Gödel, the first of these options would be the case, but this can only amount to contributing evidence, a supplement to and not a replacement of primary mathematical intuition. For Penelope Maddy, on the other hand, there is no sharp line between this sort of *extrinsic* evidence and the *intrinsic* evidence that comes from the desire to reject the "horizontal" limitativity of the definable. On her analysis, both types of evidence appear gradually through the process of testing a model against its consequences, in the light of a set of background maxims that govern mathematical practice. These maxims are not to be justified foundationally, but through a "naturalism" inspired by Quine's "naturalized epistemology"—although she rejects Quine's reduction of mathematics to the handmaiden of the physical sciences (and his consequent scorn for higher set theory), insisting instead on the autotelism of mathematical practice and its responsibility for constructing its own epistemology. The two maxims Maddy discusses at length in her work go by the names "UNIFY" and "MAXIMIZE." The former compels the mathematician to seek a single, coherent theory explaining as much as possible: the latter, on Maddy's account, means a maximization over *structures* rather than a maximization over entities:

> If mathematics is to be allowed to expand freely in this way, and if set theory is to play the hoped-for foundational role, then set theory should not impose any limitations of its own: the set theoretic arena in which mathematics is to be modeled should be as generous as possible; the set theoretic axioms from which mathematical theorems are to be proved should be as powerful and fruitful as possible. Thus the goal of founding mathematics without encumbering it generates the methodological admonition to MAXIMIZE. And, given that set theory is out to provide models for all mathematical

objects and instantiations for all mathematical structures, one way in which it should MAXIMIZE is in the range of available isomorphism types.⁴⁹

For this reason, the limitativity of $V = L$ is to be understood primarily as restrictiveness relative to isomorphism types, under the overarching constraint of consistency expressed by UNIFY. "[F]aced with alternatives like $V = L$ and MC," Maddy writes, "the easiest way to MAXIMIZE would be to adopt both theories, to use whichever happens to be most useful in a given situation. But UNIFY counsels against this course."⁵⁰ The second best course, then, is to choose an axiom system that does not restrict instantiation of the "missing" isomorphism types while allowing lesser-included *models* equivalent to those of the restrictive theory. ZFC + MC accomplishes this; although it implies $V \neq L$, L does not "disappear," but retains its properties and can be studied on its own (in fact, because L is "absolute," the sentence "$V = L$" holds relativized to L in ZFC + MC—or any other model of ZFC—even though it does not hold in V).⁵¹

These arguments, coupled with the "attractive" character of the theory ZFC + MC "in [its] own right,"⁵² combine to provide Maddy with good "naturalistic" grounds for believing $V \neq L$—grounds that do not stand or fall along with mathematical intuition, grounds whose justificatory process "turns away from metaphysics and toward mathematics."⁵³ Yet the strength of Maddy's analysis—its focus on the "maxims" governing the production of mathematical knowledge rather than the philosophical demand to reintegrate mathematical knowledge within a foundationalist epistemology—is also its limitation. Maddy taxes the later Wittgenstein, perhaps the most intransigent foe of pure mathematics and its platonist (but not Platonist) justification, with failing to explain fully "the final question: what drives mathematicians to platonism?"⁵⁴ Her own analysis, however, encounters a similar problem: even if she has demonstrated that an "anti-constructivist" (in Badiou's sense) orientation is epistemically justified in intramathematical terms, she has explained neither the epigenesis of the constructivism/anticonstructivism dualism itself nor the way in which the resolving "maxims" connect to the more general structure of mathematical practice. The true question, one can fairly assert, is the one she never poses: what drives mathematicians to maximalism?

By contrast, this question is at the core of Badiou's analysis of $V = L$. The precept of maximization derives its authority not from within mathematics, but from the limit-point between mathematics and metaontology:

> The decision to accept only the existence of constructible multiples is thus without risk. So long as one keeps to the classical Ideas of the multiple, no counter-example can arrive to ruin its rationality. The hypothesis of an ontology in submission to language—and thus of an ontological nominalism—is irrefutable. ... The major sets of active mathematics (integers, real and complex numbers, functional spaces, etc.) are all constructible.
>
> Is this enough to convince one whose desire is not only to advance ontology (hence, to be a mathematician) but to think ontological thought [*de*

penser la pensée ontologique]? ... The mathematician, who never *encounters* anything but constructible sets, doubtless possesses also, latent, this *other* desire—and I observe the sign of this in the fact that, in general, he recoils from holding the Axiom of Constructibility, even though it is homogeneous to every reality he manipulates, to be an axiom in the same sense as the others. (EE 336)

For Badiou, the mathematician's desire for maximality arrives from outside the space of that which can be encountered and utilized, manifesting itself first as a negative and "latent" trace: because neither "there exists a nonconstructible set" nor "every set is constructible" can be a theorem of ZF alone, the very intractability of the imputed excess that constructibilism denies, "the 'whatever,' the unnamable part, the linkage without concept" (EE 319), serves to anchor it as the point of orientation for the ontological *conatus*. Here Lacan's contribution is crucial: desire is not a positive relation to a pregiven entity, but appears "in the margin ... that demand ... opens in the form of the possible failure that need can bring, of not having universal satisfaction."[55] Desire always operates in the shadow of the law, and $V = L$ is the legalistic gesture *par excellence*, the conversion of the very language from which the definability property is produced into a "legal filter" (318) operating on the universe.

Within this dialectic of (mathematical) law and (metaontological) desire appear, in relief, the two signal traits of the constructivist orientation: *the primacy of language* and *the exclusion of the event*. "In its essence," Badiou writes, "constructivist thought is a logical grammar. Or, more precisely, it makes language prevail as the norm concerning that which it is acceptable to consider, in representations, as one-multiples" (318). Constructivism restricts ontology by tying the scope of quantifiers to a fundamentally logico-linguistic principle: "if one says 'there exists,' this must be interpreted as 'there exists a term named in the situation'; and if you say 'for all,' this must be interpreted as 'for all of the terms named in a situation'" (318). No term can be represented (which, in Badiou's idiom, simply means to be counted as part of a multiple under the inclusion relation) unless it is picked out by a linguistically definable property; thus "the state is programmed to recognize as a part, of which it assures the counting, only that which the resources of the situation themselves allow to be distinguished. The central principle of this type of thought is the Leibnizian principle of indiscernables: two things cannot exist of which it is not possible to mark the difference. Language is valid as a law for being in that it will hold what it cannot distinguish to be identical" (313).

Here Badiou's argument draws on a rhetorical slippage which, at first sight, seems to leave him open to a charge of paralogism: "language" is used to mean both language in general, including natural language, and the specific first-order theory in which ZF is formulated and to which the definability function, and by extension the hierarchy L, refer. In part 3, I shall discuss this slippage at greater length, in connection with Badiou's reading of Leibniz; for the moment, however, it is crucial to note that, from the philosopher's standpoint, this distinction is entirely secondary: formal language cannot be fully purified of its inracination within the signifying system *generaliter*, and the collision of $V = L$ with the limits of the linguistic is consequently a subspecies—albeit the most important, because the closest to the ontological core—of the crisis in the *grammatical orientation* itself. Badiou's opponent might claim that arguing from the limitativity of $V = L$ to the limitative character of linguistic definition in general is specious, for there are many ways of formulating the properties of nonconstructible sets meaningfully outside the formalism of first-order set theory.[56] But, for Badiou, this objection itself partakes of the grammatical orientation, inasmuch as it assumes that the limitations of representational systems can be studied in terms of mere formalism, with natural language invariably assumed to be both the reliquary of that which is inexpressible in a given theory and the unquestioned metasyntax in which discourse on the limits of logic itself is to be couched. Instead, he argues, the path of analysis must progress from the exemplum of $V = L$ beyond the problem of definability in ZFC to the question of the motivation that subtends the very problem of the "grammatical," which then becomes the ultimate frame within which the "intramathematical" claims against constructibility can be seen as meaningful.

This *mise-en-parenthèses* of the specificity of ZF's idioms relies on a strong conception of the univocity of language as "the mediation of complete interiority to the situation" (EE 318); beyond the *factum linguarum,* the diversity of languages attested to in the presentation of diverse situations, lies the problem of "language" itself (always interpreted to mean *grammaticized* language), and its inability to "represent" the condition of possibility of its very presentative structure: the event.[57] Thus, Badiou writes:

> Moreover, in the constructivist vision of being—and this is a crucial point—*there is no place for the taking-place* [l'avoir lieu] *of the event*. One might be tempted to say that it coincides in this respect with ontology, which forecloses the event, and declares thus its appurtenance to that-which-is-not-being. But this would be nonetheless too narrow a conclusion. Constructivism does not need to *decide* on the non-being of the event, because it doesn't have to know of its undecidability. Nothing here asks for a decision relative to a paradoxical multiple. In fact, it is essential to constructivism (it is its *total* immanence to the situation) that it conceive neither of self-membership, nor of the supernumerary, thereby holding outside of thought the entire dialectic of event and intervention. (320)

Here Badiou amplifies a theme first adumbrated in *Théorie du sujet*: the organization of the constructible hierarchy—and, in particular, the restriction of the purely decisionistic character of certain key ZFC axioms by $V = L$—means that the constructivist orientation is essentially "antidialectical" (TS 284). Dialectic is only possible where the event is impressed, spectrally, on a situation without allowing itself to be mapped in terms of that situation: because the event does not exist, but is "separated from emptiness by itself" (EE 203), it marks the point where the element-relation is sublated: both "the event belongs to the situation" (202) and "the event does *not* belong to the situation" (203) are hypotheses induced by the impinging of the evental "ultra-one," irreconcilable *Denkbestimmungen* whose ultimate resolution must be not ontological but extra-ontological.

2.4

For this reason, the matheme of the event finds no place within the set-theoretical universe: every event is constitutively an element of itself, but the Axiom of Foundation, which states (in its class form) that every nonempty class A has some element x such that $x \cap A = \emptyset$, proscribes the existence of self-membered sets in V.[58] Thus "the axiom of foundation de-limits being by the interdiction of the event" (EE 212); for this reason, "with the event, we have the first concept *exterior* to the field of mathematical ontology" (205).

The Axiom of Foundation (also called the Axiom of Regularity) is, in Jech's formulation, "irrelevant for the development of ordinal and cardinal numbers, natural and real numbers, and in fact all of ordinary mathematics."[59] Its exigency derives, as Badiou remarks, from *metaontological* considerations: introduced by Zermelo in the weak form $(\forall x)\, x \notin x$ in 1906 and strengthened by Dimitri Mirimanoff in 1917, it blocks Russell's paradox preemptively by insisting that every set must have a member that is minimal on the $\in$ relation: not only self-membership ($x \in x$) but infinite downward chains ($\ldots \in x_n \in x_{n-1} \in x_{n-2} \in \ldots \in x_1 \in x_0$) and cyclic membership structures ($x_0 \in x_1 \in \ldots \in x_n \in x_0$) are forbidden.[60] This is not the only means to block Russell's paradox; in fact, the mathematician Peter Aczel has created a completely workable set theory that allows for non-well-founded sets by replacing Foundation with the "Anti-Foundation Axiom" (AFA). However, as Maddy notes, ZF − Foundation + AFA does not instantiate any isomorphism types not present in ZF, and "[t]o date, models of AFA are constructed inside models of ZFC."[61] But Foundation also garners support because it expresses the kernel of the iterative conception of the set-theoretic hierarchy; Foundation enables the proof that every set is a member of some V_α.[62] By contrast, a set theory based on $V = L$, because it *begins* from the hierarchical construction of the L_αs, can forego this step; from ZF − Foundation + $V = L$, Foundation can be proved as a theorem.

This, on Badiou's analysis, offers a final argument against the constructible orientation. Ontology itself is shadowed from outside by the "paradoxical multiple" that it must *decide* to eliminate; this decision opens toward a realm of non-being as other-than-being, as that which cannot be *named* in set-theoretical ontology, and Foundation is the paradoxical "name" of this unnamability. Because, for Badiou, this "a-normal" is itself "history" (EE 194), which "does not exist" (196), ontology attests negatively to the exorbitance of its own historicity in its choice of Foundation as the imposed resolution of the impasse of the "ultra-one": "historicity is presentation at the punctual limits of its being" (197). By contrast, within the constructible orientation, historicity is reduced to that which is preprogrammed *within* being—in other words, that which is nameable in the situational structure of the hierarchy: "[i]n the constructible universe, it is necessary (and not decided) that the event does not exist.

This is a difference of principle" (337). Inside the constructivist orientation, history is reduced to change; but this change is, in truth, only pseudo-change, the specious offering brought forth by ideology of *development*:

> The event, inconstructible, is not. Exceeding the immanence of language to the situation, the intervention is unthinkable. The constructive orientation *builds* an immanent thought of the situation, it does not *decide on* its occurrence.
>
> But if there is neither event nor intervention, how can the situation change? The radical nominalism enveloped by the constructivist orientation of thought does not rebel at all at having to declare that a situation does not change. Or rather—what it calls the "change" of a situation is merely the constructive deployment of its parts. The *thought* of the situation evolves, from the fact that the exploration of the effects of the state brings to light new connections, linguistically controllable but previously unnoticed. *That which supports the idea of change is in reality the infinity of language.* (321)

This passage, more than any other, offers the clue to Badiou's historicization of the constructivist orientation and his repeated invocation of the name of Leibniz—a gesture that, because it is fundamentally *evental*, presupposes the very "transversal" critique of the ontological triptych prepared and strengthened by the *intramathematical* arguments against $V = L$. When the primacy of language is conjoined to the reduction of historicity, the constructivist ideology (which Badiou sees as the dominant mode of contemporary thought, with representatives as far afield as Wittgenstein, Lyotard, and Heidegger [MP 77; CT 121]) merely replicates the twin pillars of Leibnizian rationalism: the primacy of language conceived as *characteristica universalis* and the combinatorial metaphysics of possibility that justifies the actual, via theodicy, as "the best of all possible worlds." Thus and here Badiou is strikingly close to the insights of Deleuze—Leibniz's "baroqueness" is an index not only of *his own* contemporaneity, but a mode of access to the historicity of contemporaneity itself.[63] Internally, each individual manifestation of the constructivist *Denkstil* (the set-theoretical argument for $V = L$, the masterpiece of seventeenth-century thought that is Leibniz' system, and the contemporary "linguistic turn") is almost impregnable, yet the transversal orientation, by bringing these differing incarnations together in spite of themselves, exposes the limitations of that which subtends all of them. In tracing the congruity of these various moments, sounding out the various ways in which their architectonic seeks after the liquidation of the event, Badiou's thought attempts to *produce an event from within them*—to refract the non-event, paradoxically, into a *new* event. This event—organized through the Cantorian revolution, which coalesces the historical structure of earlier (rationalist) philosophy—is itself the true subject of meditations 26–30 of *L'être et l'événement*; it is nothing other than the crisis of contemporary Continental philosophy, within which Badiou's text seeks to intervene.

3 The Revolution and the Restoration of All Things: Meditation 30, Leibniz, and History

3.1

Yet it is by no means clear that the three nexuses of Badiou's attempt to reinscribe the historicity of the constructivist orientation within its set-theoretical concretization, bringing forward the subjacent assumptions governing its relation to the "impasse of ontology" (EE 311), all succeed in the context of his larger project. A full treatment of this problem is beyond the scope of this article; here I intend to focus solely on Badiou's reading of Leibniz in meditation 30. The argument offered in that chapter centers on the claim that the two keystones of Leibniz's philosophy—the principle of non-contradiction and the principle of sufficient reason—"guarantee … [the] submission [of being in general] to language," providing an "ontological foundation" that holds in check the expansive imaginings of the late metaphysics: "the thesis that I propose is that Leibniz could demonstrate the most implacable inventive liberty, once he had *assured* the safest possible ontological foundation, the most controlled [*maîtrisé*], which is the one that accomplishes, to the last detail, the constructivist orientation" (349).

It is not my purpose to claim simply that Badiou has misread the great seventeenth-century thinker; meditation 30 is not intended to be a work of historical scholarship, and any inaccuracies in its reconstruction of Leibniz's thought will be of little more than anecdotal importance unless they can be shown to relate substantively to Badiou's larger project. Instead, I suggest that the *symptomatic* reading of Leibniz that Badiou proposes encounters serious problems precisely because it occults a tension internal to the notion of "constructivism" for which the typologies offered in *L'être et l'événement* cannot fully account. It was pointed out in section 2.3 that Badiou's critique of the constructivist orientation relies on a unitary notion of grammaticized language that subtends both the formal "language of set theory" and the system of predicates that can be ascribed to subjects within a natural language. Constructivism is marked by the attempt to *actualize* this unity, building better and better "total" languages, but the critique of constructivism must also take it as its starting point. The transversal orientation does not try to find an excess beyond formalizability in a non-formal language—to do so would be to fall prey to the "poetic" temptation, which Badiou considers to be of a piece with the linguistic turn—but rather to reassert the primacy of a connection between ontology and historicity that cuts across the entire logic/language nexus.[64] In his recent *Court traité d'ontologie transitoire,* Badiou offers the tantalizing suggestion that category theory—in which distinct set-theoretical and logical systems can be theorized within certain extremely general notions of structure and morphism—may provide a means to this end. However, his argument does not fundamentally alter the basic schema propounded in *L'être et l'événement,* for the merit of category theory (as Badiou sees it) is precisely that it offers not a deformalization of language, but *a degrammaticization of logic*: logic is no longer "a formalization, a syntax, a linguistic apparatus [*un appareillage langagier*]," but rather "a mathematized description of possible mathematical universes, under the generic concept of the *topos*" (CT 134–35). The mode of apparition of the thing called grammar, which makes possible "the mathematization of logic" (CT 119), is rejected as a possible guiding principle for philosophical methodology, but it is still not fully clear why the grammatical should be directly coextensive with the problem of "language," or why it should be possible to reach an understanding of the variegated tapestry of metaontology only by first attesting, and subsequently turning away from, the privilege of grammaticality that the ideology of V = L itself—the proximate object of transversal critique—reifies.

It is thus of primary importance to determine whether the coupling of logic to a combinatorial notion of grammar is a necessary feature of any attempt to think ontology by way of language. Since Badiou finds in Leibniz the very archetype of the triple imbrication of language, logic, and grammar, the herald of the project of a "pure logic, the ideal and transparent language on which Leibniz worked from the age of twenty onward" (EE 350), the search for a counterexample to this equivalence within the Leibnizian corpus itself—a point at which the "constructivist" determination to approach the metaphysical structure of the world through language would yield an *expansive,* rather than a *limitative,* ontology—is of more than merely philological interest. I contend that at least one Leibnizian text offers precisely such a counterexample: the second version of a fragment written in 1715 in connection with a series of letters to the theologian Adam Theobald Overbeck, entitled "Ἀποκατάστασις"—a shortened form of the theological term ἀποκατάστασις πάντων, the restoration of all things.[65] It is unlikely that Badiou was aware of this text, first published in 1926 in a relatively obscure collection of Leibniz's historical writings, at the time he wrote *L'être et l'événement*; nonetheless, it offers a particularly lucid perspective on the mathematical infrastructure behind the "implacable inventive liberty" (EE 349) whose existence Badiou is obliged to admit within the space of Leibniz's late system. As such, it can provide a focal point for a critique of the interpretation of constructivism offered in *L'être et l'événement*—a critique rendered all the more striking by the fact that the *first* draft of Leibniz's text, which bears the full title "Ἀποκατάστασις πάντων" and was not published until 1991, presents a strictly limitative combinatorial vision of history that corresponds exactly to Badiou's vision of the Leibnizian subject, its position foreordained by the linguistic foundation of the *principium reddendae rationis* and its temporal structure reduced to "a practical tautology, a reiteration of its difference" (EE 357). In the gap separating the first and second versions of the "Ἀποκατάστασις," a new vision of the event opens; this non-Badiouian event is not grounded in "what-is-not-being-qua-being" (EE 211), but rather allows the disclosure, through language, of the metastructure within being that is language's own non-grammatical, non-calculable condition of possibility.

Badiou's resistance to this conception, which determines his entire reading of Leibniz, depends both on his specific notion of the relationship between philosophical language and the event and on his interpretation of the historical embedding of (mathematical) ontology. The Badiouian event, in its "supernumerary" (EE 199) character of not being a be-ing (*étant*), opens up toward those extraphilosophical truth-processes, tangential to the space of ontology, through which philosophy operates. For this reason, Badiou's exemplary events are religious and political: Saint Paul's "second beginning" of Christianity (TS 143), the Pascalian "provocation" (EE 238), and the great political revolutions of modernity, from July 1789 to the "antisystemic" moment of May 1968, traverse the pages of all his mature works.[66] In the very moment that it supplements philosophy with antiphilosophy, that *Doppelgänger* with respect to which philosophy "should always think as closely as possible,"[67] the event also reorganizes the temporal order, making possible the ingress of historicity. History, as such, does not exist (TS 110; EE 196), because if it did, it would appear as a natural totality; but Badiou defines "the historical" as precisely "that which is ... determined as the opposite of nature" (EE 194). The anti-natural effect induced by the event on the temporal sequence is what marks the kinship of religious fidelity and political transformation, as a comparison of Badiou's analyses of the French Revolution and the "Christ-event" demonstrates:

> Consider the syntagm "French Revolution." What must one understand by these words? One can certainly state that the event "French Revolution" unifies everything that makes up its site, i.e., France between 1789 and, let us say, 1794. ... The historian ultimately includes in the event "French Revolution" everything that the era delivers in the way of facts and traces. From this tack—which is the inventory of all the elements of the site—it is still possible that the one of the event should decompose until it is no longer, indeed, anything but the always infinite enumeration of gestures, things, and words that coexist with it. What gives this dissemination a stopping point is *the mode in which the Revolution is an axial term of the Revolution itself,* that is, the way in which the consciousness of time—and the retroactive intervention of our consciousness—filters the entire site through the one of its eventual qualification. (EE 201)

> [T]he resurrection ... is not, even in Paul's view, of the order of a fact, falsifiable or demonstrable. It is a pure event, the opening of an epoch, a change in the relations between the possible and the impossible. ... Unlike a fact, the event is measurable only according to the universal multiplicity whose possibility it prescribes. In this sense it is grace, and not history. (SP 47–48)

> For Paul, in contrast [to Pascal], it is precisely the absence of proof that compels the faith which is constitutive of the Christian subject. Concerning prophesies, the fact that the Christ-event is their realization is practically absent from the totality of Paul's preaching. The Christ is quite precisely incalculable. (SP 53)

Paradoxically, the event is "grace, and not history" *precisely insofar as it historicizes the temporal continuum,* remaining a foreign presence irrupting within time, a *punctum* inassimilable to the (quasi-physical) sequential ordering of a manifold. Here "grace and not history" means as much as "historicity and not nature." These terms, exceeding the specifically theological register invoked in Badiou's reading of Paul, provide a shorthand for a general theory of the modal character of historicity: the event is the point at which the possible manifests itself, in the excess of its grace, *as possible*. For Badiou, the non-eventual possible—the combinatorial possible of the "possible world"—is in reality merely a diminished mode of the actual. A "change in the relations between the possible and the impossible" occurs only when the possible reveals itself as truly (eventally) possible, as something more than a grammatical reordering of that which exists or a catalogue of elements in a well-founded multiplicity.

The primacy of this punctual structure for Badiou's model of the event offers a crucial insight into his *Auseinandersetzung* with the sage of Hanover, for it was Leibniz, more than any other of the great early modern thinkers, who believed that the concordance of nature and grace was to be explained *philosophically*—and, moreover, it was this very problem that motivated his conception of possibility as a combinatorial rearrangement definable in terms of possible worlds. The famous allegory at the end of the *Théodicée*—in which the goddess Pallas shows the dreaming Theodore the hierarchy of worlds, represented as rooms in the temple of Jupiter, from which the god must choose—is the most elegant description of Leibniz's full vision, but the connection to his theory of nature and grace is summed up with more concision in a passage from the 1714 *Principes de la nature et de la grâce, fondés en raison*: the "most perfect state, formed and governed by the greatest of Monarchs" possesses "as much virtue and happiness as is possible … not by a disturbance [*dérangement*] of nature, as though that which God prepares for souls were to trouble the laws of bodies, but by the very order of natural things, in virtue of the preestablished harmony of all time between the Reigns of Nature and Grace, between God as Architect and God as Monarch, in such a way that nature itself leads to grace, and grace perfects nature in making use thereof."[68] Badiou's interpretation depends on demonstrating that this grace is essentially non-eventual and non-historical, that, precisely insofar as it can be determined through a theoretically calculable algorithmic expansion of possibilia, "digested … into worlds"[69] as Pallas states in Leibniz's allegory, this grace is no grace at all, but merely the logical consequence of a "continuous" presentation, "which does not tolerate interruption or the beyond-one [*l'ultra-un*]" (EE 353). It is only in this way that the essentially limitative character of Leibniz's "constructivism" can be guaranteed; the project of meditation 30 is to connect the different elements of the Leibnizian system in a way that supports this theory.

3.2

The specific mode in which Badiou pursues this project is strongly dependent on the sections of the Leibnizian corpus that Badiou chooses to analyze; throughout meditation 30, he juxtaposes the late metaphysics, represented by a number of short texts named in a footnote (531), with the never-completed enterprise of the *characteristica universalis*—the "ideal and transparent language on which Leibniz worked from the age of twenty onward" (350). Although the connection between these two projects is not *prima facie* obvious, Badiou's decision to make a claim for their essential congruence is far from arbitrary; in fact, it is prefigured by the very *longue durée* pattern in the history of logic that the transversal critique of constructivism seeks to locate synthetically. It is no coincidence that the fragments of the *characteristica universalis* appear as a matrix-text in modern philosophy at almost exactly the same time as Giuseppe Peano developed the logical symbolism that would be necessary to the progress of the Cantorian revolution. Louis Couturat, the first great twentieth-century editor of Leibniz, was motivated to seek out the Hanover Archive after meeting Peano's student Giovanni Vacca at the August 1900 International Congress of Philosophy in Paris—a meeting which would have momentous importance in the development of analytic philosophy, for it was there that Bertrand Russell first encountered Peano's formal logic.[70] The texts that Couturat found would cause him to rewrite much of the text he was composing on Leibniz's logic, using the *characteristica universalis* as the keystone in a "panlogicist" interpretation of the entire Leibnizian system.[71] This analysis was prefigured, however, by Russell's lectures on Leibniz given at Cambridge in 1899, which were in proof at the time of the Paris Congress.[72] Russell's and Couturat's writings set the parameters of the twentieth-century logicist interpretation of Leibniz's thought; among other things, it was their work that lead to a reconsideration of the text written by Leibniz at the age of twenty to which Badiou alludes—the *Dissertatio de arte combinatoria* of 1666.[73] In this treatise, Leibniz attempted to ground syllogistic in a theory of the possible combinations of arbitrary entities, which could be associated with simple concepts; by the following decades, however, his project had expanded to one of giving an absolutely general mode of formalization, a *characteristica generalis* underpinning the *mathesis universalis*. This universal formal language, a "cabala of the learned"[74] (*cabala sapientium*), would allow all philosophical disputes to be resolved by means of mere calculation, as Leibniz claimed in a famous letter of 1679: "I will say, in a few words, that this characteristic would represent our thoughts truly and distinctly. ... I will say here only that, because what we know is either reasoning or experience, it is sure that, hereafter, all reasoning in demonstrative or probable matters will demand no more skill than a calculation in algebra …."[75]

Following the exegetes of the logicist tradition, Badiou interprets this Leibnizian imperative—"*calculemus!*"—as the foundation from which the principle of sufficient reason is to be explicated. The need to calculate is inextricably bound to the limitativity of the constructivist orientation: calculation is always calculation on a defined combinatorial set, whose limits are always given by the language(s) of its formalization(s): "The logicism of Leibniz is an ontological postulation: every non-contradictory multiple desires to exist" (350). To be in the most general sense is to be possible—to be in one of the infinite aggregation of possible worlds from which God chooses the best—and all possibilia "tend toward existence" (350); but to be possible is nothing more or less than to possess a catalogue of noncontradictory predicates representable in a language. Moreover, the principle of sufficient reason, which reigns over the (non-eventual) mode of transition from possible to actual, is itself inscribed within the total system of formalization: in its asymptotic limit, an absolutely adequate infinitary language would manifest perfectly—in fact, would simply *be*—"the distinct knowledge of everything" that "God alone has."[76] Within the space of Badiou's reading, this equivalence is used to justify an extraordinary series of extensional equivalences for the term "God"—as though, to emphasize the indissociability of ontological limitativity from grammatical form, the origin and cause of all things, the principle behind the *principium reddendae rationis*, must itself suffer an ever more extensive process of predicative confinement: "being-presented, infinitely multiple, has its ultimate reason in a limiting term that is God"; "God is the reason for the ... series [of presented multiples]"; "God designates only the *space of these laws of the nameable*"; "God is the constructibility of the constructible, the program of the World"; "Leibniz is the principal philosopher for whom God is the language that is taken to be complete" (351).[77] For Badiou, Leibniz's metaphysics is less an onto-theology than an ontotheo-logic: the "constructibility of the constructible" is conditioned by a λόγος itself equivalent to that which can be *determined* through a formal process.[78] This λόγος is the ultimate kernel of grammaticizable language; legible in Leibniz's first, rough attempts at the *characteristica* are the traits that would culminate, two and a half centuries later, in the formal logic of set theory and the ontology that seeks to actualize that logic as a delimiting structure—the orientation expressed by $V = L$. It is this "ontotheo-*logic*"—at the opposite pole of thought from the "onto-*theo*-logy" of the expansive orientation of thought—that accounts for the exemplarity of the Leibnizian *démarche*; much as the thin hatch-lines and taut contours of Poussin's Roman sketchbooks manifest the governing logic of Classicism far better than the polychrome tableaux that succeeded them, the fragmentary and repetitive drafts of the *elementa calculi* attest to a perspectival structure rendered almost imperceptible by the meticulously ordered arborescence of Gödel's constructive set theory: "The logical nominalism of Leibniz is of a superior essence: it makes being and the name coincide only as far as the name is, in place of the complete language named God, the effective *construction* of the thing" (354).

This asymptotic perfectibility is the key to the exclusion of the event from the constructivist *Denkstil*: the seemingly evental surface of human language, whose finitary and incomplete presentation of predicates allows the illusion of an unmotivated *clinamen*, vanishes in the limit: "there is no event, because everything that happens is locally calculable and globally placed in the series of which God is the reason" (353).[79] This interpretative leap, however, depends on Badiou's strong reading of the principle of identity of indiscernibles: *for the constructivist, no event can happen, because the event would require God to choose between indiscernibles—to make history "happen" by way of a rupture, an irreversible change which destroys the symmetry between two otherwise indifferentiable states of affairs*. The identity of indiscernibles must hold not only between objects within the combinatorial collection of a possible world, but throughout the preprogrammed hierarchy of worlds, past, present, and future, from which God "selects" (in an act that is, for Badiou, the very negation of a choice) the best:

> For us, the most striking example of this power from which nothing thinkable can subtract itself is the principle of indiscernibles. When Leibniz as-

serts that "in nature there are no two real, absolutely indiscernible beings," or, even more strongly, that (God) "will never choose between indiscernibles," he has an acute awareness of the stakes. The indiscernible is the ontological predicate of an abutment of language. The "vulgar philosophers," who, Leibniz repeats, think with "incomplete notions," thus according to an open and poorly made language, go awry when they think that there are different things "solely because there are *two*." If two beings are indiscernible, language cannot separate them. A sundering [*désappariement*] with respect to reason, whether logical or sufficient, the pure "two" would introduce nothingness in being, because the one-of-the-two, remaining in-different to the other for every thinkable language, could not be qualified with respect to its reason-of-being [*raison d'être*]. It would be supernumerary with regard to the axioms, an effective contingence, "in excess" in the sense of the Sartre of *Nausea*. And because God is in reality the complete language, he cannot support this unnamable in-excess [*cet en-trop innommable*], which is the same as saying that he could neither think nor create a pure "two"; if there were two indiscernibles, "God and nature would act without reason in treating one differently from the other." God cannot tolerate the nothingness that is the action without name. He cannot lower himself to the "*agendo nihil agere* because of indiscernibility."

The indiscernible, the whatever [*le quelconque*], the unpredictable, is properly that around whose exclusion the constructivist orientation of thought is built. If every difference is an attribute of language and not of being, then *presented* in-difference is impossible. (352–53)

Badiou's analysis in this passage draws primarily on one of Leibniz's responses in his correspondence with Samuel Clarke in 1715–16, but he depends on a very subtle decontextualization to permit his argument to go through: in the letter itself, Leibniz's claim is that "in nature there are not two real, absolutely indiscernible beings, because if there were, God and nature would act without reason, in treating one differently from the other."[80] But "real, absolutely indiscernible beings" refer clearly to actual material beings, for Clarke's objection was that the principle of the identity of indiscernibles would prevent God from creating "any matter at all," since "the perfectly solid parts of all matter, if you take them of equal figure and dimensions (which is always possible in supposition) are exactly alike."[81] Leibniz states that the impossibility inscribed in the principle is not a *pure logical* impossibility, but an impossibility of *actuality*; it holds by virtue of the principle of sufficient reason over the space of *that which exists*: "When I deny that there are two precisely similar drops of water, or two other indiscernible bodies, I do not say at all that it is absolutely impossible to posit such; but that it is a thing contrary to divine wisdom, and consequently does not exist."[82] Badiou's expansion of the principle beyond this formulation is not *prima facie* implausible (on one reading, for instance, it can be used to explain Leibniz's famous denial of transworld identity).[83] It is, however, overdetermined by his need to interpret the constructivist orientation restrictively: if an eventual change based on a choice between indiscernibles were possible *between* worlds, or between disjoint phases of a world, then the divine language would not be bound by the pure grammatical constraint of definability; in this case, the "extra-grammatical" logic of the divine would represent not a limitative, but a maximizing, principle. In order to be truly eventual, however, this change would make the system of possible worlds something other than the neat hierarchy that Pallas displays to her visitor in the *Théodicée*; the method through which possibilia are "digested" into possible worlds would remain opaque, irreducible to the linguistic representation of any one world—even though it would be through those representations alone that the "grace" of its production would be legible to the human intellect. For Leibniz, this "legibility" is precisely what it means for a language to be "language": when Pallas shows Theodore the history of a (possible) world and the history of Sextus Tarquinius within that world, it is in the form of a book:

> Theodore saw all his life as though at a glance, and as if it were in a theatrical representation. There was a great volume full of writing in this apartment; Theodore could not keep himself from asking what it meant. It's the history of the world which we're visiting now, the goddess told him; it is the book of its fates [*le livre de ses déstinées*]. You saw a number on Sextus' face, look for the place in the book that it marks. Theodore looked for it, and there he found the history of Sextus in a more extended form than the one he had seen in summary. Put your finger on whichever line you please, said Pallas, and you will, in fact, see represented in all its detail what the line marks out in general. He obeyed, and saw all the particularities of one part of Sextus' life appear. They went to another apartment, and there was another world, another book, another Sextus ....[84]

Are these "books" bound by the identity of indiscernibles in the same way that events in a single world are? If this must be the case, then Badiou's reading is correct, and truly eventual transition is excluded from the Leibnizian system from the start. If another interpretation is possible, however, then an event remains possible *between the signs of the universal language*: the script in which fate is written, less a collection of characters than a flowing line, remains open to something beyond the simple restrictivity of the "grammatical orientation."

3.3

It is precisely this flowing script, in which the continuum passes into the event and vice versa, that the second version of the "Ἀποκατάστασις" text adumbrates. The formalization of the encyclopedia is only the obverse of the Leibnizian system; in its hidden face, ontotheo-*logic* ceases to exclude the event, but rather makes it into the ultimate horizon of linguistic inquiry: language announces itself as the sole mode of presenting that which is, under the law of calculation, but at the same time orients itself as a totality toward that which lies beyond any presentation of discernable multiples. Language itself becomes not grammatical but eventual, and thus demands its own historicization; history is that which happens in the properly ungrammaticizable space opened up between combinatorial moments, a space that cannot be presented, but makes possible the "constructive" and combinatorial formalism through which alone the truths of logic and metaphysics can be grasped. The "Ἀποκατάστασις" renders visible a "transversal" punctum already latent in the play of finite and infinite upon which formalization opens: beyond the dialectic among the orientations of thought, there is a dialectic within the constructivist orientation that sculpts in advance the path of the historicization that the second-order critique of mathematical philosophy represented by the transversal attitude claims to perform, *après coup*, through its interrogation of ontology; this dialectical point, very different from the Badiouian event, is the καιρός at the centre of Leibniz's radical ontotheology.

The perspective taken by the "Ἀποκατάστασις" text is inscribed in the title itself, which concentrates a millennium and a half of theological speculation, ranging from the officially suspect to the frankly heretical, in a single Biblical quotation. "Ἀποκατάστασις πάντων" derives from an enigmatic phrase in the Acts of the Apostles, in which Christ is spoken of as the one "whom heaven must receive until the times of the restoration of all things [ἄχρι χρόνων ἀποκαταστάσεως πάντων], which God has spoken of through the mouths of all his holy prophets from eternity [ἀπ' αἰῶνος]."[85] There is still little agreement among exegetes as to how exactly this formulation should be taken; the difficulty is not only doctrinal but conceptual, for—belying the famous Pauline dismissal of Greek philosophy—the word ἀποκατάστασις is in fact a technical term taken from Stoic physics, designating the eternal return of events, states, and beings. Its sense is preserved in a fragment from the late fourth-century author Nemesius:

> The Stoics say that when the planets return [*forms of* ἀποκαθίστημι *throughout*] to the same celestial sign, in length and breadth, where each was originally when the world was first formed, at set periods of time they cause conflagration and destruction of existing things. Once again the world returns anew to the same condition as before; and when the stars are moving again in the same way, each thing which occurred in the previous period will come to pass indiscernibly. For there will again be Socrates and Plato and each one of mankind with the same friends and fellow citizens; they will suffer the same things, and put their hand to the same things, and every city and village and piece of land return in the same way. The return of everything [ἀποκατάστασιν τοῦ παντός] occurs not once but many times; or rather, the same things return infinitely and without end [εἰς ἄπειρον καὶ ἀτελευτήτως]. The gods who are not subject to destruction, from their knowledge of this single period, know from it everything that is going to be in the next periods. For there will be nothing strange in comparison with what occurred previously, but everything will be just the same and indiscernible down to the smallest details.[86]

The reference to a time "when the planets return to the same celestial sign" probably draws on the doctrine of the "perfect year"—the ultimate cycle of the heavenly bodies—from Plato's *Timaeus*; in any case, whether or not the Stoics had the connection in mind, this was the matrix through which the early Christian writers interpreted the notion of the eternal return in their exegeses of the biblical ἀποκατάστασις.[87]

This was the philosophical subtext that rendered the theory of the ἀποκατάστασις threatening for Christian orthodoxy—to such a degree that the term "apocatastasis" appears to this day in theological lexica less often in the context of New Testament eschatology than as the formal name for one of the most persistent of heresies: the claim, associated in various forms with Clement of Alexandria, Origen, and Gregory of Nyssa, that salvation will be universal and Hell empty at the end of time. In purely formal terms, the connection between this idea and the Classical doctrine of eternal return seems anything but perspicuous: according to Numenius, the Stoic return occurred ἀτελευτήτως, without an end or τέλος, whereas the entire logic of Christian theology is centered on the determination of a τέλος, closure to the temporal order in which—to use the Pauline phrase favored by the apocatastasists of the early church—"God would be all in all."[88] However, at a deeper level, the linkage of apocatastasis as reiteration and apocatastasis as perfection serves to disclose a fundamental ambiguity in the concept of the ἔσχατον: the temporal structure that delimits the primitive Christian experience can be apprehended by way of the "incomprehensible" specificity of the messianic moment, or it can be comprehended philosophically—as Heidegger would say—*aus der Zeit selbst*, from the traces it leaves in an ontological structure accessible to reason.[89] It is the first mode of interpretation that dominates Christian orthodoxy; it is also, strikingly, this mode that wholly determines Badiou's interpretation of the "Christ-event" in his *Saint Paul*: this event "attests that God is not the God of Being, is not Being" and thus enables Paul to announce "an anticipatory critique of what Heidegger calls onto-theology" (SP 50). Within the second mode of interpretation, by contrast, the theophanic καιρός attested by the evangelium becomes not an absolute exception to the temporalized structure of the world, but rather its source and focal point: the Christ-event is not the pure mark of a Real without ontological content, but rather the absolute testimony of an ordering present in the world itself, logically if not chronologically equiprimordial with the Incarnation itself. Like Badiou, the apocatastasists emphasized the universality of the Christian kerygma; unlike Badiou, they found the manifestation of this universality not in antiphilosophy—that predication which, aping Gorgias, risks ridicule in trying to speak of "non-beings," τὰ μὴ ὄντα, in "a language where madness, scandal, and weakness supplant knowing reason, order, and power" (50)—but by means of the ratio inscribed in the heart of philosophical systematization itself.[90]

Within this framework, the question of whether there will literally be a reiterative "return" in the Stoic sense is less important than that of the conjunction of past and future *in every moment of* the totality of Being, which ensures that the "beginning"—the state of prelapsarian sinlessness—foreordains and controls the "end." It follows from the very nature of existent being—in its alliance with God—that it seeks irresistibly to regenerate in the fount of its creation; in the words of Gregory of Nyssa, "the perpetual motion of our nature returns again to the good."[91] It would be Origen, however, with whom the doctrine was most clearly identified, and it was "Origenism" that the Council of Constantinople condemned in 543, stipulating that "if someone says … that there will be restoration [ἀποκατάστασιν] of demons or of impious men, let him be anathema."[92] The Council's decision sets in relief the difference between the universalism of the apocatastasists and that which Badiou claims to be genuinely Pauline. For Badiou, it is through hope—conceived as the possibility of the subject's persistence in fidelity to a truth, dependent on the universality of the event—that Paul's repudiation of the "repartitive" model of the Last Judgment is to be understood: "If Paul cannot order hope according to the imaginary of a retribution, besides the fact that he is opposed, in general, to the idea of a 'salary' for faith, it is because the resurrection has no meaning outside the universal character of its operation. Nothing allows one to fix divisions or repartitions, once it is a question of the contingence of grace" (102). By contrast, the true Origenian apocatastasist does not *hope* for the universality of salvation, but reads it off the very logic of temporality itself. If, on occasion, the fathers of the Church were constrained by prudence to admit that they were not *certain* of the doctrine of universal salvation, it was nonetheless always the case that they believed in the existence of a fact of the matter about the question, independent of an attitude of hope: the apocatastasis denotes not a place of subjectivation but a flight beyond the subject into the *ordo saeculorum*—an interpretation of the conjunction of grace and the event in history entirely opposite to that offered by Badiou.[93]

From the Council onward, the theory of apocatastasis became an underground doctrine; after the Reformation, however, it began to reappear in the public works of speculative Protestant theologians. In 1701, the chiliast Johann Wilhelm Petersen anonymously published the first volume of Μυστήριον ἀποκαταστάσεως πάντων, das ist: Das Geheimnis der Wiederbrinugung aller Dinge; it is this work that provided the direct inspiration for the correspondence with Overbeck and the meditations collected in the two versions of the "Ἀποκατάστασις πάντων." Leibniz reviewed the first volume of the Μυστήριον favorably (but without attaching his name or giving explicit sanction to Petersen's theories) shortly after it appeared. In the *Théodicée*, he would make a similarly delicate allusion to the "great and learned work entitled Ἀποκατάστασις πάντων":

> Many pious and even learned—but audacious—people have revived the opinion of Origen, who believes that the good shall gain the upper hand in time, in all things and everywhere, and that all reasoning creatures will ultimately become blessed and happy, even including the evil angels. The book of the *Eternal Evangel,* published recently in Germany, and supported by a great and learned work entitled Ἀποκατάστασις πάντων, has provoked much discussion on this great paradox. … There is a man of intelligence who, pushing my principle of harmony to arbitrary suppositions of which I in no way approve, has made for himself an almost astronomical theol-

ogy. He believes that the disorder present in this fallen world began when the angel presiding over the sphere of the earth, which was still a sun (a fixed, self-luminous star) committed a sin with some lesser angels under his charge, perhaps by rising against the angel of a higher sun; that, at the same time, by virtue of the *preestablished harmony* of the reigns of *nature* and *grace,* and consequently by natural causes having reached a given point, our globe was covered in spots, rendered opaque and forced out of its place, which caused it to become a wandering star or planet, i.e., a satellite of another sun …. On earth Jesus Christ arrived to save man. He is the eternal son of God inasmuch he is the only son, but (according to some early Christians, and according to the author of this hypothesis), having taken up, from the beginning of things, the nature of the most excellent of creatures to perfect them all, he set himself among them; and this is the second filiation, through which he is the firstborn among all creatures. This is what the Cabbalists called *Adam Cadmon.* … When the time of judgment approaches … he will return overtly to take away the just, transplanting them perhaps to the sun, and to punish evil men along with the demons who seduced them; then earth's globe will begin to burn and will perhaps be a comet. … But finally hell will render up its dead, death itself will be destroyed, reason and peace will begin again to reign in the minds that had been perverted. They will feel their error; they will adore their Creator, and will even begin to love him more to the degree that they see the size of the abyss from which they are exiting. At the same time (by virtue of the *harmonic parallelism* of the reigns of nature and of grace) this long and great fire will have purged the earth of its spots. It will again become a sun; its presiding angel will again take his place along with the angels that follow him; the damned men will be, with them, among the number of the good angels; this leader of our world will offer homage to the Messiah, the leader of creatures: the glory of this reconciled angel will be greater than it had been before his fall.[94]

The "man of intelligence" to whom Leibniz attributes this vision has never been identified.[95] However, it is difficult to avoid the temptation to read the passage as Leibniz's own concealed fantasy; the less than overwhelming argument against the apocatastatic vision adduced in the following paragraph does little to dispel this idea: "The vision seemed amusing to me, and worthy of an Origenist; but we have no need of such hypotheses or fictions, in which the mind has a larger share than revelation, and even reason does not entirely find its due, for it seems that there is no principle place in the known universe which merits being the seat of the oldest of creatures, in preference to others, or at least the sun of our system is not it."[96] If we accept this narrative as potentially inscribed within the theory of nature and grace, even though its author claims "in no way [to] approve," then it suggests that the notion of a full temporal order of the actual world presupposed by apocatastasis stands at the edge between eventual and non-eventual transition.

The consuming fire that destroys the earth in this "astronomical theology," recalls the Stoic apocatastasis, but, unlike the "conflagration" reported by Numenius, it fails to reproduce precisely the pristine form of the originally created universe. The terminal state of the universe is only *apparently* equivalent to its beginning state; in fact, not merely Lucifer's glory but the total greatness of the universe must be increased by the fact of having fallen, since if there were no ultimate advantage to be gained from the cycle, a maximally rational and good God would not choose it. Yet, before the fall, the universe *must have seemed from the point of view of its inhabitants* to be completely ordered and fixed in maximal greatness; had the terminal state been conceivable from within the initial state, the rebellious movement of the will essential to Lucifer's fall would have been pre-empted. History thus has as its condition of possibility an illusion in created beings' perceptions of what is possible: the calculus of predicates through which created beings could analyze the field of possible worlds at the time of creation must have failed to differentiate between two states, the state of creation and the state of the end, that were for God nonidentical, causing Lucifer to fail to perceive the ultimate benefit that justifies the mediatory role of his evil—thereby making that evil and its consequent benefit possible. But no new being intervenes in the world during its cycle; even Christ, through whose reappearances the entire cycle is ordered, was always already "eternal," present ἀπ' αἰῶνος in the form of Adam Cadmon. Thus the final state of the universe must be *in some sense* a re-combination of properties of all the beings present in the initial state, but one wholly unfigurable in the optimal language of the original hierarchy: the trajectory of fall and redemption impinges eventually on the universe, participating in the initial situation only at the price of being unrepresentable within it. The transition is only nonevental *from the perspective of the Deity*, inasmuch as he is capable of differentiating the terminal state from the initial state and eternally foreseeing the latter in the former. From this it results that the divine plan is not an asymptotic perfection of the language of created beings, but something fundamentally distinct and discontinuous from it: God is not "a language supposed to be complete" (EE 351), but *that which transcends the incompleteness of every language*. If this is the case, however, then there is no reason to believe that the terminal state represented in the narrative, whose relational ordering after all depends on the temporal beings that occupy it and not on a God who possesses his whole existence "totally and all at once,"[97] is *truly* optimal. Could not the entire cycle begin again, leading to a yet higher "terminal" state, repeated *ad infinitum*—an endless progress, whose openness to the good exceeds the capacity of the language of any cycle, no matter how complete, to describe? It is this question that cuts between the two versions of Leibniz's "Ἀποκατάστασις," written five years after the *Théodicée;* and it is this question that is ultimately decisive for a consideration of the true "limitativity" of the linguistic orientation.

Both versions of the "Ἀποκατάστασις" begin with a description of moments in the history of the world in terms of a combinatorial notion of possibility, coupled directly to a criterion of adequate definability, that exemplifies both Badiou's argument for a "grammatical" tendency at work in constructivism and a finitistic reading of the "books" shown to Theodore in the allegory at the end of the *Théodicée*: "The number of all possible books of a certain length, made up of signifying or non-signifying words [*ex vocabulis significantibus vel non significantibus constantium*], can be defined."⁹⁸ Leibniz's example is a book of 10,000 pages, with 100 lines per page and 100 letters per line—yielding 100,000,000 (10^8) letters in all. The total number N of possible books of this length for a finite alphabet of F characters is $N = F^{10^8}$: Leibniz claims that N (presumably for the Latin alphabet or a similar one) serves as a plausible upper bound to the number of descriptions of states of affairs that have "historical" significance: "Let us posit furthermore that an annual public history of the world [*Historiam publicam annalem orbis terrarum*] can be described sufficiently in a book of such length as to contain 100 million letters: it is clear that the number of possible different public histories of the world, each different from the others, is definite; for each one would yield a new book. … From this it follows furthermore, if it is imagined that the human race will endure sufficiently long in its present state [*in statu qualis nunc est*], anterior public histories must return."⁹⁹ Moreover, precisely the same principle can be applied to the *private* history of each individual: "Let there be thought to be a thousand million men on earth … and let there be assigned, for each man, to every year of his life, in order to describe one year of his life in detail [*minutatim*], a book as long as the one we assign to the public history of a year, that is one formed from 100 million letters."¹⁰⁰ Thus the private histories of all the humans on earth can be described by $1{,}000{,}000{,}000 \times 100{,}000{,}000 = 10^{17}$ letters. "Yet the number of possible works of this size, each different from the others, is finite; indeed, it can be obtained from the number of the combination. Call this number Q."¹⁰¹ Q, of course, can be demonstrated to be equal to $F^{10^{17}}$ for an alphabet of F characters.

On the basis of this calculation, in the first version of the "Ἀποκατάστασις," Leibniz offers an image of the eternal return that amounts to a virtual paraphrase of Nemesius:

> From this it follows thus: if the human species endures long enough in the state that it is now in, a time will come in which even the life of individuals will recur in detail in the same circumstances. For example, I myself—living in a city called Hanover, on the river Leine, working on the history of Brunswick, writing letters with the same meaning to the same friends. For the same argument can be shown with respect to the number Q that we made above with respect to the number N, because there is no difference except of magnitude.
>
> But these things will occur not only once, but more often, and even a number of times greater than any that can be assigned, if the human race lasts long enough. And the Ancients seemed to have such things in mind, who spoke of the Platonic Great Year, even if they did not transmit the reasoning behind their words to posterity; but it seems evident from what they said.
>
> Finally, even if the human race is not to endure forever, nonetheless if we simply suppose that there will always exist minds knowing and investigating the truth, it will follow that one day the minds will reach a point at which truths independent from the authority of the senses or demonstrable theo-

rems already found which do not exceed a certain size (for example of one page if written) will necessarily return, and even more so the short sentences which can be written in only a few words; and it will thus be needed that new theorems to be found grow in length to infinity. And if that happens, necessarily there will be minds of a greater capacity in order to understand such longer theorems.[102]

It is clear that Leibniz's argument, here and in the antecedent paragraph, depends on an elementary error: an infinite length of time might pass by way of infinite repetitions of a subset of the Q possible combinations, with some combinations occurring only finitely many times, or once, or not at all. The most that can be claimed is that, if all combinations are equally likely, then the probability of a given combination appearing more than n times for any finite n approaches one as time goes to infinity. But more important, for the purposes of our reading, is the scission Leibniz operates between the Stoic and the Christian notions of apocatastasis: the absolutely confining character of the language of private histories (which we can call the Q-system) functions to eliminate preemptively the possibility of any improvement in the *visible* situation of the world. A truly unending and irreversible improvement could only occur *hypothetice* in the expanding intellects of transhuman beings, if some such should come to exist; but none of the theorems proved by transhuman intellects could be comprehended within the combinatorics of the Q-system, which is perfectly closed on itself. The possibility of a transhuman intellect—*and by extension, a transhuman language*—is thus eliminable, just like the realm of non-constructible sets for the proponent of $V = L$, on the grounds of a minimalization maxim. The realm of "truths independent of the authority of the senses"—those of which the *characteristica universalis* is ultimately intended to be the organon—does not admit of anything radically nonconstructive; at most it admits of a constructive succession, expanded beyond the minds of a single species, in the form of a sequence of ever-larger finitary languages. To this realm can be opposed merely the space of "sensible truths," which can be "varied to infinity" precisely because they *do not signify*:

> But the sensible truths, or those which attest not to reason but to experience, can be varied to infinity [*variari possunt in infinitum*] although they would not become any more prolix [*etsi non fiant prolixiores*], because the senses are composed of a confusion of perceptions, which can be varied in an infinity of ways in conserving their brevity [*infinitis modis variari potest salva brevitate*], for there can be an infinity of species of living things, sensations, sensible qualities; it is different in theorems or in truths which can be known adequately or by a perfect demonstration.[103]

Here the opposition that Leibniz deploys exemplifies the claim made at the beginning of meditation 30: even if—in the phrasing Badiou quotes from the *Monadologie*—"every portion of matter can be conceived as a garden full of plants, or a pond full of fish," it is nonetheless the case that this profusion depends on "the safest ontological foundation, the most controlled": a total "submission to language" (EE

349).¹⁰⁴ The panoply of sensibila can never *happen historically,* because they can never be recorded; they can never impinge eventally on the temporal deployment of the universe, nor alter anything within the combinatorics of a language interpretable in a fixed grammar—thus temporal deployment is reduced to language, and language to grammaticized characters, to the total exclusion of the event.

In the second version of the "Ἀποκατάστασις," however, this limitative vision of language is precisely what Leibniz eschews, correcting in the process his analytical error about the necessity of infinite return:

> But, nonetheless, one cannot demonstrate by calculation alone that Leopold I or Louis XIV or I or another individual will return precisely, because if some other [histories] repeat more often, it is not necessary that all repeat.
>
> Because it is established nonetheless for metaphysical reasons that the present is pregnant with the future, it can be judged that, one century returning sufficiently exactly, many others will also return sufficiently exactly, since it is agreed that, the same returning causes occurring, the same effects will occur.
>
> Yet, even if an earlier century returns as far as objects of sensation or the things that can be described in books are concerned, it will nonetheless not return wholly in relation to all things [*omnino quoad omnia*]; for there will always be distinctions [*discrimina*], even if imperceptible and incapable of being sufficiently described by any book, for the continuum is divided into an actual infinity of parts, and in each part is a world of an infinity of creatures which can be described by no book whatever. To be sure, if the world consisted of atoms, all the atoms would return precisely in the same collection, as long as new atoms were not admixed from outside; as if one of the worlds of Epicurus were supposed to be separated from others by interworlds [*intermundia*]. But such a world would thus be a machine that a creature of finite perfection could perfectly know, and this has no place in the true world.
>
> And for this reason it may happen that things progress for the better, little by little, albeit imperceptibly [*res paulatim etsi imperceptibiliter in melius proficerent*], following the revolutions.¹⁰⁵

Here, in contrast to the first version, the structure of the endless cycle itself organizes an excess over what can be shown by "calculation alone": nothing returns *omnino quoad omnia* because the world is not reducible to a combinatorics of atoms, and by extension not reducible to any combinatorics of characters. The distinction between sensibilia and objects describable in the Q-system is displaced, and replaced with a new category; the imperceptible *discrimina* that create the possibility of a progression of world-phases, each separated from the next by an eventual movement that is representable neither in the Q-system *nor in any arbitrarily fine-grained extension of it.*¹⁰⁶ This version of the apocatastatic sequence entirely reverses Badiou's claim in meditation 30: the proliferating monadological landscape of the late metaphysics, where worlds lie inside worlds in an infinity of (nonspatiotemporal) dimensions, is

80 *The Cantorian Revolution*

no longer tamed by the restrictiveness of grammar, but serves to relativize it, demonstrating that no constructive language can contain the panoply of being. Yet this can only occur by a radical reinterpretation of what Badiou describes as "the origin of every orientation of thought: the problem of the continuum" (EE 354).

According to *L'être et l'événement,* the precise balance of infinite divisibility and containment by language in the Leibnizian continuum attests to the precision with which the constructivist orientation is able to exercise its restrictive power:

> One of Leibniz's great powers is that of having rooted his constructivist orientation in what is truly the origin of every orientation of thought: the problem of the continuum. Assuming without concession the infinite divisibility of natural being, he compensated for and restrained what was thereby liberated in excess in the state of the world—in the natural situation—through the hypothesis of a control of singularities, through "intrinsic denominations." This exact balance of the measureless proliferation of parts and the exactitude of language offers us the paradigm of a constructivist thought at work. On the one hand, although the imagination sees only jumps and discontinuities—thus, the denumerable—in the natural orders and species, it is necessary to suppose, audaciously, a rigorous continuity in them, which presupposes that an exactly innumerable crowd—an infinity in radical excess over numeration—of intermediary or "equivocal" species populates what Leibniz calls "the regions of inflexion or heightening." But, on the other hand, this surpassing [*débordement*] of infinity, if one links it to the complete language, is commensurable, and dominated by a single principle of passage which integrates its nominal unity, for "all the different classes of beings of which the assemblage forms the universe are only, in the ideas of God—who knows distinctly their essential gradations—like so many ordinates of the same curve." By the mediation of language, and the operators of the "divine mathematics" (series, curve, ordinates ...), the continuum is tightly closed on the one, and far from being wandering and undetermined, its quantitative expansion assures the glory of the well-made language according to which God constructs the optimal universe. (354–55)

Leibniz's conception of the continuum is one of the most intricate aspects of his philosophy, and his views changed significantly from his first substantive meditations on the subject in a letter to Thomasius in 1669 to the final system.[107] A full interpretation would be impossible here; it is sufficient for the purposes of reading the "Ἀποκατάστασις" to note that, in order to claim Leibniz for limitative constructivism, Badiou must assimilate his notion of the continuum to the post-Cantorian conception of $\mathbb{R}$ as a set equipollent to $\wp(\mathbb{N})$. The "well-made language" through which "jumps and discontinuities" can be shown to be merely epiphenomenal would thus be analogous to a language in which Cantor's diagonal argument can be rigorously propounded, and the early modern problem of *quanta continua*, which Leibniz studied more deeply than anyone else, would be merely a prefiguration of the question of CH as it appeared in the twentieth century. But this interpretation minimizes Leibniz's resistance to the assimilation of the continuum to any numerical multiplicity, even one whose relation to the additive sequence is that of "surpassing." The mature Leibniz rejects not only atoms but any way of controlling the transition from point set to continuum:

> Space, far from being a substance, is not even a being. It is an order, like time: an order of coexistences, as time is an order among existences that are not together. Continuity is not an ideal thing, but what is real is what exists in this order of continuity. In the ideal or continuum, the whole is anterior to the parts, just as arithmetical unity is anterior to the fractions that partition it, which one can assign arbitrarily; the parts are only potential. But in the real the simple is anterior to assemblages, parts are actual and before the whole. These considerations resolve the difficulties of the continuum, which suppose that the continuum is something real, having parts before all division, and that matter is a substance. Thus one must not conceive of extension as a real continuous space, scattered through with points. These are fictions useful to content the imagination, but in which reason does not find its due.[108]

The continuum, for Leibniz, is in no way made up of points: monads, which, as Badiou notes, are sometimes equated to "metaphysical points" (356), are the true substratum of the spatiotemporal extensa that "exist" only illusorily. But this does not mean, as Badiou claims, that the monad is that which can be multiplied over transfinitely to reach the continuum, subjugating the "discontinuities" to the "commensurable" by way of language.

Instead, as the second version of the "Ἀποκατάστασις" suggests, the continuum persists in its incommensurability; its "ideality" is not a simple negation of the real, but a positive quality *in actu* which prevents the adequacy of any linguistic representation: "the continuum is divided into an actual infinity of parts, to such a degree that in each part of matter is a world of an infinity of creatures, which can be described by no book whatever."[109] If it is necessary to find a successor for Leibniz in modern philosophy of mathematics, it may be less the "constructivist orientation" than the intuitionism of Brouwer and Heyting, for whom the continuum was paradoxically best described as a *dis-continuity*, a jump beyond numeration for which no mathematical schema can fully account—"the 'between,' which is not exhaustible by the interposition of new units and which therefore can never be thought of as a mere collection of units."[110] This "between" appears in the space of the "Ἀποκατάστασις" as precisely that kind of jump or discontinuity which Badiou had claimed was tamed once and for all. The transition between cycles of the world keeps open a ruptural (and non-combinatorial) possibility of the event, to be compared to the transition from the continuous harmonic oscillation of a single string to the movement of the divine musician's hand *between* strings:

> In addition, from these things one can conclude that the human race is not always to remain in the same state, for it is not in conformity with the di-

vine harmony that the same string should always move. It is to be believed instead, from reasons of natural congruence, that things must advance for the better either little by little [*paulatim*] or also sometimes by jumps [*per saltus*]. For although they often seem to develop for the worst, this is to be thought of in the way that we sometimes step back in order to jump forward more strongly.[111]

Here the passage from a restrictive ontology of the continuum to an expansive one coincides with the passage from the apocatastasis of the Stoics to the illicit Christian apocatastasis of Origen: by transgressing the combinatorics of the actual, the "divine harmony" shows the way to a progressive divinization of the intellect. The passages that follow this largely repeat the speculative meditations on the transhuman from the first version, but their global sense has changed radically. The properly evental—indeed, revolutionary—character of transition between celestial cycles permits the advent of transhuman cognition to be not something incomprehensible from within a limitative schema but as a pure possibility opened on the "minds seeking and knowing the truth" within each cycle of repetitions: "If this [the advent of new theorems of increasing length] takes place, then it will be necessary that minds which were not yet of a great enough capacity for them, become more capacious …."[112] This progressive opening depends on an event, but one which has no place in Badiou's schema; it does not simply transgress the linguistic, but appears *through language*—through the very expansive process of theorem-construction itself—as the horizon of that within language which is not grammaticizable, that which no sequence of signs, not even the *characteristica universalis* itself, can contain. Thus Leibniz writes, in the last sentence of the second version of the "Ἀποκατάστασις": "And each mind has a horizon of its present capacity with respect to knowledge [*circa scientias*], but no horizon of its future capacity."[113]

3.4

If it is this horizonless future that marks the late Leibniz's ultimate deviation from what Badiou terms the "constructible orientation," it is also here that the properly utopian ambition of the Leibnizian *démarche* becomes patent: the mathematical metaphysics of the continuum, far from merely attesting to the combinatorial structure of the present, opens toward a development "for the better" either "little by little" or "sometimes by jumps"—an oscillation of reform and revolution whose precise trajectory, although in perfect conformity with reason, remains incalculable in advance by the sublunary beings who bear its effects, unspeakable within the space of any grammaticized language.

It is not my purpose to argue that this Leibnizian conception of an "anti-constructivist" historical trajectory—which, even in its most formalized presentation, retains the unmistakable impress of a theodicic project that (at least in positive form) did not survive the epoch of Kantian critique, let alone the ravages of the twentieth century—is or should be a valid model for thinking about the relation of historical time to the continuum today. It may, however, provide a useful triangulation point for Badiou's politico-ontological project—a project in which the question of the continuum's relation to infinite number, that great "mystery of being" (EE 311), is for the first time in postwar French thought elevated to a general governing principle. Badiou's formulation of the problem cannot, of course, be rendered conceptually equivalent to that offered by his seventeenth-century predecessor; the Cantorian revolution stands in the way. But, as meditations 26–30 show, that revolution is itself historicizable, capable of being thought eventally through the critical gesture of the "transversal orientation" without losing its intramathematical force; to do so, however, means thinking through seemingly recondite technical problems—of which the question of $V = L$ is paradigmatic—at once in their formal specificity and in their connection to the classical concerns of the philosophical tradition. That, as I have suggested, the "constructible orientation" thematized in Badiou's critique may ultimately prove an insufficiently specific category for that task, unable to chart fully the curves of Leibniz's own multifarious thought or the *Wirkungsgeschichte* of his logical innovations, does not detract from the ambitiousness and importance of the global project. Not only philosophers working in the Continental traditions, but all philosophers who take seriously the question of the status of mathematics and its relationship to the other classical spheres of concern of philosophy, must ultimately engage with Badiou's contributions. This article is intended merely to suggest a possible path into that fruitful discussion; I claim neither that this path is the only one nor that it is the best one. However, it is clear that, regardless of the path chosen, at some moment every traveler into the labyrinth of Badiou's thought will find herself at a point where further progress is possible only through consideration of set theory. This exigency is in no way to be taken as a claim of esoteric privilege or secret insight; it is instead the marker of Badiou's exemplary commitment to the most rigorous and *exoteric* moment of modern thought—the "mathematico-logical revolution" (EE 8) of Cantor and his successors. ∎

....

1 All translations from foreign-language works, unless otherwise noted, are my own. Badiou's (sometimes idiosyncratic) mathematical notation is always maintained in quotations, although typographical conventions have been made consistent with the rest of the article. [For a list of Badiou's principal texts and their corresponding abbreviations, as well as a note on mathematical notation, see the introduction to this issue.—Ed.]
2 Badiou discusses Hilbert, and his comment, at TS 232.
3 Penelope Maddy, *Naturalism in Mathematics* (Oxford: Clarendon Press, 1997), 209–15. Maddy's ideas are developed in the course of a series of books and articles: "Believing the Axioms I," *Journal of Symbolic Logic* 53 (1988): 481–511; "Believing the Axioms II," *Journal of Symbolic Logic* 53 (1988): 736–64; *Realism in Mathematics* (Oxford: Clarendon Press, 1990); "Does V Equal L?" *Journal of Symbolic Logic* 58 (1993): 15–41; and *Naturalism*. Her ideas change considerably between the earliest articles and *Naturalism*; for simplicity, however, I draw on all of these writings in my presentation of what I take to be her current position.
4 I write "platonist" with a lower-case letter to distinguish the position in modern philosophy of mathematics that combines belief in the mind-independent existence of math-

ematical objects (realism) with the claim that knowledge about these objects is possible through a specifically "mathematical" intuition from the positions on epistemology and ontology held, or presumed to be held, by the historical Plato or his neo-Platonist successors. This distinction is discussed in part 2 of this article.

5   I borrow this particular notion of "epochality" from Kenneth Surin, "The Epochality of Deleuzean Thought," *Theory, Culture & Society* 14 (1997): 9–21.

6   The appendices to *L'être et l'événement* offer a sufficient treatment of these fundamentals, as does the discussion in Peter Hallward, *Alain Badiou: A Subject to Truth* (Minneapolis: University of Minnesota Press, 2003), 323–48. In my discussions, I have made use of the standard summa, Thomas Jech's *Set Theory*, 3rd ed. (Berlin: Springer Verlag, 2002), as well as Azriel Levy, *Basic Set Theory* (Mineola, NY: Dover Publications, 2002) and András Hajnal and Peter Hamburger, *Set Theory*, trans. Attila Máté (Cambridge: Cambridge University Press, 1999), two extremely lucid textbooks. It should be noted that I am not a professional mathematician or logician; I have followed the reference works cited as closely as possible, but any errors that remain are my own.

7   Immanuel Kant, *Kritik der reinen Vernunft*, ed. Jens Timmerman (Hamburg: Felix Meiner Verlag, 1999), A432/B460.

8   Throughout his life, Cantor distinguished with great care the "absolutely infinite" (which he held to be properly predicated only of God) from the "transfinite"; see, for example, the opening passages of the "Mitteilungen zur Lehre vom Transfiniten," originally published in 1887, in Georg Cantor, *Gesammelte Abhandlungen mathematischen und philosophischen Inhalts*, ed. Ernst Zermelo (Berlin: Springer Verlag, 1980 [1932]), 378: "The A[ctual]-I[nfinite] was differentiated [in my earlier essays] in *three* relations [*Beziehungen*]: *first*, insofar as it is realized in the greatest perfection, in a fully independent, extraworldly Being, *in Deo*, where I term it the *Absolute Infinite* or simply the *Absolute*; *second*, insofar as it is represented in the dependent, sublunary world; third, insofar as it can be comprehended by thought *in abstracto* as mathematical magnitude, number or order type. In *both* the latter relations ... I term it the *Transfinite* and most strictly oppose it to the *Absolute*." On Cantor's theology, see Michael Hallett, *Cantorian Set Theory and Limitation of Size* (Oxford: Oxford University Press, 1984), 35–38, as well as the biographical discussion—focusing on Cantor's correspondence with Johannes Cardinal Franzelin—in Joseph Warren Dauben, *Georg Cantor: His Mathematics and Philosophy of the Infinite* (Princeton: Princeton University Press, 1979), 140–48; compare also EE 49–61.

9   Richard Dedekind, *Essays on the Theory of Numbers*, trans. W. W. Beman (New York: Dover, 1963 [1901]), 63.

10 Galileo's famous example was the equipollence of $\mathbb{N}$ ($\{1, 2, 3, ...\}$) with $\{x : \sqrt{x} \in \mathbb{N}\}$ ($\{1, 4, 9, ...\}$). For a discussion of the history of this problem, see Jan Sebestik, "Le paradoxe de la réfléxivité des ensembles infinis: Leibniz, Goldbach, Bolzano," in *Infini des mathématiciens, infini des philosophes*, ed. Françoise Monnoyeur, 179–245 (Paris: Belin, 1992).

11 For the classic presentation of finitism, see David Hilbert, "On the Infinite," in *Philosophy of Mathematics: Selected Readings*, 2nd ed., ed. Paul Benacerraf and Hilary Putnam, 183–201 (Cambridge: Cambridge University Press, 1983); a modern consideration is given in Shaughan Lavine, *Understanding the Infinite* (Cambridge: Harvard University Press, 1994).

12 Dedekind's argument is in §66 of *Was sind und was sollen die Zahlen?* translated in *Essays on the Theory of Numbers*, 64. For the refutation, see Bertrand Russell, *Introduction to Mathematical Philosophy* (London: Allen & Unwin, 1919), 138–40; see also the discussion in Jean-Pierre Belna, *La notion de nombre chez Dedekind, Cantor, Frege* (Paris: Vrin, 1996),

55–56. Badiou discusses Dedekind's argument in NN 53–62.

13 For simplicity, I use throughout the modern (von Neumann/Zermelo) notion of ordinals as transitive sets and take the class of cardinals to be a subclass of the class of ordinals. With the assumption of Choice, this affords an easy definition of cardinal number: the cardinality of a set a, written $|a|$, is just the smallest ordinal α such that α is similar to a. (See Levy, *Basic Set Theory*, 83.) It should be noted that this does not correspond to Cantor's own notion of the distinction among ordinal, order type, and cardinal, but it simplifies the argument considerably.

14 For a discussion of Choice, see Levy, *Basic Set Theory*, 158–59. For historical information, see Ivor Grattan-Guinness, *The Search for Mathematical Roots* (Princeton: Princeton University Press, 2000), 339–40. Badiou discusses Choice in meditation 22 of *L'être et l'événement* (247–55).

15 The best nontechnical treatment of CH and its philosophical implications remains Kurt Gödel, "What is Cantor's Continuum Problem?" in *Collected Works*, ed. Solomon Feferman et al., 2:254–70, (Oxford: Oxford University Press, 1986–), discussed in section 1.3 below.

16 Abraham A. Fraenkel, "The Notion 'Definite' and the Independence of the Axiom of Choice," in *From Frege to Gödel: A Source Book in Mathematical Logic, 1879–1931*, ed. Jean van Heijenoort, (Cambridge: Harvard University Press, 1967), 284–301. In effect, Zermelo constructed a model of his system that satisfied ¬AC, although he did not use this terminology. In 1963, using the same forcing technique with which he proved the independence of CH, Paul Cohen would construct a model of ZF + ¬AC, firmly establishing the axiom's independence.

17 The fullest version of the proofs is presented in Kurt Gödel, "The Consistency of the Axiom of Choice and of the Generalized Continuum Hypothesis with the Axioms of Set Theory," in *Collected Works*, 2:33–101. Much more readable modern treatments are given in Levy, *Basic Set Theory*, 289–91; Jech, *Set Theory*, 174–200; and Joseph R. Schoenfield, *Mathematical Logic* (Nantick, MA: Association for Symbolic Logic, 1967), 270–81.

18 To be exact, Gödel's proof was not couched in ZF but in what is known as Bernays-Gödel (BG) set theory, which allows explicit reference to proper classes in its syntax. However, BG can be shown to be a conservative extension of ZF, making the distinction unimportant for our purposes. See Robert M. Solovay's introduction to Gödel's "The Consistency of the Axiom of Choice," in *Collected Works*, 2:5. On models, see Jech, *Set Theory*, 156–72, and the excellent short discussion in George S. Boolos, John P. Burgess, and Richard C. Jeffrey, *Computability and Logic*, 4th ed. (Cambridge: Cambridge University Press, 2002), 137–52. It should be noted that L is technically the "universe" of the interpretation in question; the full interpretation also includes a function mapping the variables, constants, and predicates of the formal language in which the axioms of ZF are stated to the elements of the universe. Because the language of set theory has only one nonlogical predicate, $\in$, the interpretation function is essentially just the relativization of the quantifiers $\forall$ and $\exists$ to the universe of the interpretation. For simplicity, I will use the word *model* and the symbol L to refer both to the constructible universe and to the full interpretation $(L, \in)$, which Gödel termed Δ in his original paper.

19 I follow the treatment in Levy, *Basic Set Theory*, 290, and Frank R. Drake, *Set Theory: An Introduction to Large Cardinals* (Amsterdam: North-Holland, 1974), 127–28.

20 For the philosophical justification of this "image" of V, see George Boolos, "The Iterative Conception of Set," in *Philosophy of Mathematics* (cited in note 11), 486–502.

21 These presentations are excerpted in *Philosophy of Mathematics*, 41–65.

22 Technically, the position presented here is a particularly strong version of formalism sometimes called "if-thenism." For other positions that respond to some of the problems with if-thenism, see Maddy, *Realism in Mathematics*, 24–28.
23 L. E. J. Brouwer, "Intuitionism and Formalism," in *Philosophy of Mathematics*, 80.
24 Ibid.
25 Ibid., 84.
26 Ibid., 86.
27 Gödel, "What is Cantor's Continuum Problem?" (cited in note 15), 260.
28 Ibid., 268.
29 Levy, *Basic Set Theory*, 291. This sentence is quoted by Badiou in EE 347–48. To the best of my knowledge this problem is still unsolved.
30 Gödel, "The Consistency of the Axiom of Choice" (cited in note 17), 27; Maddy, *Naturalism in Mathematics*, 82.
31 Maddy, *Naturalism in Mathematics*, 82–83; see also the more complete discussion, referred to in a footnote to *Naturalism*, in Maddy's "Believing the Axioms I," particularly 495–98.
32 Gödel, "What is Cantor's Continuum Problem?" 264 (emphasis added).
33 Ibid., 262n23.
34 The caveat is necessitated, of course, by Russell's Paradox; for an analysis of what is meant by "large" in the realm of proper classes, see Hallett, *Cantorian Set Theory and Limitation of Size* (cited in note 8), particularly 165–223.
35 Gödel, "What is Cantor's Continuum Problem?" 259n14. Maddy discusses this footnote, and gives quotations from other set theorists on the iterative conception of set for comparison, in *Naturalism in Mathematics*, 84.
36 In an exemplary recent article, Étienne Balibar offers a reading of Badiou's work that emphasizes the central position of the concept of truth in his project; see "'Histoire de la verité': Alain Badiou dans la philosophie française," in *Alain Badiou: Penser le multiple*, ed. Charles Ramond, 497–524 (Paris: L'Harmattan, 2002).
37 Martin Heidegger, *Identität und Differenz* (Stuttgart: Neske, 1957), 14–16.
38 Gödel, "What is Cantor's Continuum Problem?" 268, quoted by Badiou at CT 101.
39 It should be noted that, for all the fidelity of Badiou's reconstruction to Socrates' statement in the *Meno* that "the truth about what there is [ἡ ἀλήθεια ... τῶν ὄντων] is in our soul from eternity [εἰ ἀεί]" (86B), it is surely less representative as an expression of the middle Plato's thought on mathematics as a whole. In *Republic* VI, for example, geometry is said to be "thought [διάνοια] ... but not understanding [νοῦς]" (511E), a distinction which is correlate to a certain hypotheticality induced by the separation of the ἐπιστήμη from its objects. Needless to say, in late Plato, the situation is complicated further by the objections raised against the theory of Forms in the *Parmenides*. See, in general, Paul Pritchard, *Plato's Philosophy of Mathematics* (Sankt Augustin: Akademia Verlag, 1995). My translations of Plato draw on John Cooper's edition of the *Collected Works* (Indianapolis: Hackett, 1997), with modifications; the Greek is taken from John Burnet's edition (Oxford: Clarendon Press, 1900–1905).
40 On the history of the *res* and related terms, see Jean-François Courtine, *Suarez et le système de la métaphysique* (Paris: Presses Universitaires de France, 1990).
41 It should be noted that this very formulation of the problem excludes the intuitionist position from the outset, as is made clear by the very next sentence: "This abyss is no other," Badiou writes, "than the one that separates ω_0, the infinite denumerable domain of finite numbers, from the set of its parts, $\wp(\omega_0)$, which alone is capable of fixing the quantity of

points in space" (EE 311). For Brouwer and his followers, $\wp(\omega_0)$ does not fix the quantity of points in space; it fixes nothing at all because it *means* nothing at all; and its scriptibility proves only that Cantorian set theory is powerless to descry the "abyss." Badiou's failure to address the challenge of intuitionism remains one of the signal limitations of his work on philosophy of mathematics; a full analysis of this question would be of great importance, but cannot be undertaken here.

42 Badiou uses "constructivism" in a somewhat nonstandard sense; the term normally refers to a subspecies of intuitionism. The nonce word "constructibilism" would be less confusing as a designation for the "grammatical" orientation, since it correlates to ZFC + the Axiom of Constructibility, but here I will follow Badiou's usage instead.

43 As is standard, I use inaccessible without qualification to mean "strongly inaccessible." On inaccessibles in general, see Levy, *Basic Set Theory,* 138–41 and Jech, *Set Theory,* 32.

44 Jech, *Set Theory,* 58.

45 For a much fuller treatment of the concept of measure, including a discussion of the connections between extensions of Lebesgue measure on $\wp(\mathbb{R})$ and measurable cardinals, see Noa Goldring, "Measures: Back and Forth Between Point Sets and Large Sets," *Bulletin of Symbolic Logic* 1, no. 2 (1995): 170–88.

46 To be precise: the first measurable cardinal is describable by a Σ_1^2 formula in a *third-order* language—a formula of the type $(\exists X)\,\varphi$ where X ranges over third-order variables and the quantifiers in φ range over variables of no more than second order. See Drake, *Set Theory* (cited in note 19), 283.

47 My presentation of measurable cardinals follows Levy, *Basic Set Theory,* 342–56, and Drake, *Set Theory,* 173–85.

48 See Maddy, "Does V Equal L?" 15.

49 Maddy, *Naturalism in Mathematics,* 210–11 (footnotes omitted).

50 Ibid., 211.

51 Badiou gives a brief treatment of absoluteness in EE 334–36; for more details, see Jech, *Set Theory,* 163–65 and 187–88.

52 Maddy, *Naturalism in Mathematics,* 231. My presentation simplifies Maddy's claim somewhat; in fact, most of her discussion treats not MC but the weaker hypothesis "$0^\#$ exists." $0^\#$ is a particularly important nonconstructible set, but one whose exact definition is extremely technical; see *Naturalism in Mathematics,* 76, for a rough outline. MC implies that $0^\#$ exists and, of course, the existence of $0^\#$ implies $V \neq L$, so the essential structure of Maddy's reasoning is preserved even without considering her independent arguments for the existence of $0^\#$.

53 Ibid., 233.

54 Ibid., 169.

55 Jacques Lacan, "Subversion du sujet et dialectique du désir," in *Écrits* (Paris: Éditions du Seuil, 1966), 814.

56 To use the most obvious example, "$0^\#$" (see note 52) is a referring term in a natural language that picks out a unique entity for which there is no identifying formula in first order ZFC. It should be noted that, although Badiou does not make reference to this example, a famous paradox suggested to Bertrand Russell by the Oxford librarian G. G. Berry proves that even natural language, outstripping every formalization in its capaciousness, finds itself descriptively impoverished in comparison to the field of the multiple. Consider the property of being a positive integer not nameable in under eleven words; the set of all numbers with this property must have a least element; yet this number is itself named, in

only ten words, by "the least positive integer not nameable in under eleven words." The "least positive integer not nameable in under eleven words" is thus, despite its appearance, not a referring term; and, although it is surely the case that not all positive integers are nameable in under eleven words, the least member of that company remains uncapturable by its description.

57 On the notion of the *factum linguarum*, see Jean-Claude Milner, *Introduction à une science du langage* (Paris: Éditions du Seuil, 1989), 41–45. The problem of the relation between languages and "language as such" has been the object of much discussion in recent Continental philosophy; for a summary, see Daniel Heller-Roazen, "Language, or No Language," *Diacritics* 29, no. 3 (1989): 22–39. Badiou's perspective is, however, unique, both in the privilege it accords to formal languages and in its resistance to "grammatical" and "theological" approaches to the extralingual.
58 On Foundation and its various forms, see Levy, *Basic Set Theory*, 68–75.
59 Jech, *Set Theory*, 63.
60 On the history of the Axiom of Foundation, see Maddy, *Naturalism in Mathematics*, 61–62, which amplifies on the earlier "Believing the Axioms I," 484; see also, for a clear presentation of $\in$-minimality, Jech, *Set Theory*, 63.
61 Maddy, *Naturalism in Mathematics*, 61; see also her discussion of AFA at 216–17 in the same work.
62 For the proof, see Jech, *Set Theory*, 64–65.
63 See Gilles Deleuze, *Le pli: Leibniz et le baroque* (Paris: Éditions de Minuit, 1988).
64 See Badiou's comments at CT 122–23.
65 Both versions are edited magisterially by Michel Fichant in G. W. Leibniz, *De l'horizon de la doctrine humaine / Ἀποκατάστασις πάντων (La Restitution universelle)* (Paris: Vrin, 1992); all references to the texts, introduction, notes, and afterward in this volume are cited as *De l'horizon/Apokatastasis* in subsequent notes. I am greatly indebted to Marwan Rashed of the Centre National de la Recherche Scientifique (Paris) for bringing these texts to my attention and for many illuminating comments on the differences between the two versions.
66 For the interpretation of May 1968 within a *longue durée* perspective on which I draw here, see Giovanni Arrighi et al., *Antisystemic Movements* (London: Verso, 1987).
67 Alain Badiou, "Politics and Philosophy," *Angelaki* 3, no. 3 (1998): 124, quoted in Hallward, *Badiou* (cited in note 6), 22.
68 Leibniz, *Principes de la nature et de la grâce*, §15, in *Die philosophischen Schriften*, ed. C. I. Gerhardt (Hildesheim: Olms, 1962 [1875–90]), 6:605.
69 Leibniz, *Théodicée*, III, §414, in *Die philosophischen Schriften*, 6:362.
70 See Couturat's introduction to Leibniz, *Opuscules et fragments inédits* (Hildesheim: Olms, 1961 [1903]), i: "Our work on the *Logic of Leibniz* was almost finished (or so we thought, at least), when we had the pleasure of meeting M. Giovanni Vacca at the International Congress of Philosophy (August 1900) … who had consulted, one year earlier, Leibniz's manuscripts preserved at Hanover, and had extracted therefrom a few formulas of Logic inserted in the *Formulaire de Mathématiques* of M. Peano." Cf. Couturat's comments in *La logique de Leibniz d'après des documents inédits* (Hildesheim: Olms, 1985 [1901]), ix–xi. On the Paris Congress, see Grattan-Guinness, *The Search for Foundations* (cited in note 14), 290–94.
71 See Couturat, *La logique de Leibniz*, particularly 176–278.
72 Bertrand Russell, *A Critical Exposition of the Philosophy of Leibniz*, 2nd ed. (London: Allen and Unwin, 1937), v.

73 The text of the *Dissertatio de arte combinatoria* can be found in Leibniz, *Die philosophischen Schriften*, 4:27–104; for a modern reconstruction, see Hidé Ishiguro, *Leibniz's Philosophy of Logic and Language* (London: Duckworth, 1972), 35–51.
74 Leibniz, *Die philosophischen Schriften,* 7:49.
75 Ibid., 4:295–96. For an English translation of the whole letter, see G. W. Leibniz, *Philosophical Essays,* trans. Roger Ariew and Daniel Garber (Indianapolis: Hackett, 1989), 239–40.
76 Leibniz, *Principes de la nature et de la grace,* §13, in *Die philosophischen Schriften,* 6:604.
77 On the principle of sufficient reason, see Martin Heidegger, *Der Satz vom Grund* (Stuttgart: Neske, 1957), particularly 63–75, and now Vincent Carraud's exhaustive *Causa sive ratio: La raison de la cause de Suarez à Leibniz* (Paris: Presses Universitaires de France, 2002).
78 By contrast, for Heidegger (to whom the rebirth of the Kantian term "ontotheology" as "onto-theo-logy" or "onto-theo-logic" is due), the language that presents Being as the *summum ens* in the metaphysical tradition contains, from its incipience, the possibility of surpassing—however incompletely—the λόγος αποφαντικός toward the *spekulativer Satz*. See Martin Heidegger, *Hegels Phänomenologie des Geistes,* in *Gesamtausgabe* (Frankfurt am Main: Klostermann, 1972–), 31:141; on ontotheology more generally, see Olivier Boulnois, "Heidegger, l'ontothéologie, et les structures médiévales de la métaphysique," *Quaestio* 1 (2001): 379–406.
79 For a discussion of the aleatory structure of the *clinamen* with interesting connections to Badiou's theory of the event, see Jacques Derrida, "Mes chances: Au rendez-vous de quelques stéréophonies épicuriennes," *Cahiers confrontation* 19 (1988): 19–45.
80 Leibniz, 5th letter to Clarke, §21, in *Die philosophischen Schriften,* 7:393.
81 Clarke, 4th objection to Leibniz, §§3–4, in *Die philosophischen Schriften,* 7:382 (orthography modernized).
82 Leibniz, 5th letter to Clarke, §25, in *Die philosophischen Schriften,* 7:394–95.
83 This question is discussed at length in Leibniz's famous correspondence with Arnauld (*Die Philosophischen Schriften,* 2:11–138; see particularly 37–51). For an interpretation that would not necessitate a "counterpart theory" (in which direction Badiou's reading tends), see Robert M. Adams, *Leibniz: Determinist, Theist, Idealist* (Oxford: Oxford University Press), 53–57.
84 Leibniz, *Théodicée,* III, §415, in *Die philosophischen Schriften,* 6:363–64. My translation draws on the text of Jacques Brunschwicg's edition of the *Théodicée* (Paris: Garnier-Flammarion, 1969), 361, which, as Fichant notes (*De l'horizon/Apokatastasis,* 191), corrects an important error in Gerhardt's edition. For an extraordinary reading of the allegory, see Peter Fenves, *Arresting Language: From Leibniz to Benjamin* (Stanford: Stanford University Press, 2001), 53–73. It was through a conversation with Fenves that I was first alerted to the connections between early modern philosophy and set theory; I am indebted to him for this and for many other insights, without which this article would never have been conceived in its present form.
85 Acts 3:21. As always, the rendering of αἰών is vexed; the Vulgate translates it by *a seculo,* Luther by *von der Welt an*.
86 Nemesius 309,5–311,2 = *SVF* 2:625, trans. A. A. Long and D. N. Sedley in *The Hellenistic Philosophers* (Cambridge: Cambridge University Press, 1987), 1:309 (very lightly modified); the Greek text is given in 2:306–7. Fichant discusses the Stoic doctrine of eternal return in *De l'horizon/Apokatastasis,* 177, giving Nemesius in Duhem's translation.
87 *Tim.* 39C; on the connection with the Stoics, see Fichant's notes to *De l'horizon/Apokatastasis,* 176. The crucial precondition for this idea is the properly philosophical notion of time as a "moving image of eternity" (εἰκὼ κινητόν … αἰῶνος) in *Tim.* 37D; on the history

and sense of this phrase, and its importance for Western thought, see Rémi Brague, *Du temps chez Platon et Aristote: Quatre études* (Paris: Presses Universitaires de France, 1982), 11–71.
88 1 Cor. 15:28.
89 See Martin Heidegger, *Der Begriff der Zeit* (Tübingen: Niemeyer, 1995), 6. For an analysis—at odds with Badiou's—of what the experience of finite time would mean in Paul, see Giorgio Agamben, *Le temps qui reste: Un commentaire de l'"Épitre aux Romains*,*"* tr. Judith Revel (Paris: Payot, 2000). I am indebted to both Peter Fenves and Jean-François Courtine for directing my attention, at different times and in different ways, to the importance of St. Paul and Augustine in the development of Heidegger's notion of temporality.
90 On Gorgias, Plato, and non-being, the essential work is Barbara Cassin's extraordinary *L'effet sophistique* (Paris: Gallimard, 1995).
91 Gregory of Nyssa, *De hominis opificio,* 21; PG 44:232c. For a French translation, see *La création de l'homme,* trans. J. Laplace and J. Daniélou (Paris: Le Cerf/Sources Chrétiennes [SC 6], 1943).
92 Henrich Denzinger, *Enchiridion symbolorum definitionum et declarationum de rebus fidei et morum/Symboles et défintions de la foi catholique,,* 37th ed., ed. Petrus Hünermann, trans. Joseph Hoffman (Paris: Éditions du Cerf, 1991), no. 411. For Origen's analysis, see his *De principiis* I, 6, 2, GCS 22:79–80; and compare Clement of Alexandria, *Strom.* VII, X, 56:3–6, ed. Alain Le Boulluec (Paris: Le Cerf/Sources Chrétiennes [SC 428], 1997), 180–83, who goes so far as to claim that the justified will be "called gods." The literature on apocatastasis is extraordinarily vast; for a brief survey, with references to all the cited texts and many others, see Brian E. Daley, "Apocatastase," in Jean-Yves Lacoste, ed., *Dictionnaire critique de la théologie,* 2nd ed. (Paris: Presses Universitaires de France, 2002), 70–72, as well as the analysis in Fichant's afterword to *De l'horizon/Apokatastasis,* 172–78.
93 Paradoxically, Badiou is here closer to the position of the modern Catholic Church—which has endorsed, largely through the influence of the German theologian Hans Urs von Balthasar, the legitimacy *of a hope for universal salvation* whilst denying the possibility of certain knowledge on the matter. For a succinct summary and critique of Urs von Balthasar's position from an orthodox Catholic point of view, see Avery Dulles, "The Population of Hell," *First Things* 133 (May 2003): 36–41.
94 Leibniz, *Théodicée,* I, §18, in *Die philosophischen Schriften,* 6:111–15. The full title of Petersen's work, along with a discussion of Leibniz's relation to the theologian, is given in Fichant's introduction to *De l'horizon/Apokatastasis,* 20–24; a translation of Leibniz's review appears at 94–97.
95 See Brunschwicg's note to his edition of the *Théodicée* (cited in note 84), 468.
96 Leibniz, *Théodicée,* I, §18, in *Die philosophischen Schriften,* 6:113.
97 See the definition of Boethius, decisive for the entire ontotheological tradition, in *Cons.* V. 6. 9–11: "Aeternitas igitur est interminabilis vitae tota simul et perfecta possessio."
98 Leibniz, *De l'horizon/Apokatastasis,* 60. In rendering Leibniz's Latin, I have benefited throughout from comparison with Fichant's excellent facing-page translation.
99 Ibid., 60–62.
100 Ibid., 62.
101 Ibid., 62–64.
102 Ibid., 64.
103 Ibid., 64–66.
104 Badiou's quotation is from *Monadologie,* §67, in *Die philosophischen Schriften,* 6:627.
105 Leibniz, *De l'horizon/Apokatastasis,* 72.

106 Compare Fichant's exegesis of §415 of the *Théodicée* on the basis of the second version of the "Ἀποκατάστασις" in *De l'horizon/Apokatastasis,* 191: "The descent in detail is in principle without end: from the theatre to the book, from the book to the line, and on to just as many representations, ever finer, encased to infinity, whose minuscule differences can always be developed." A full reading of the "Ἀποκατάστασις" would require a formalization of Leibniz's notions of finitary and infinitary languages, and an analysis of his arguments against total describability in comparison with the theory of metalanguages and models in modern logic. I intend to undertake this task in a forthcoming set of essays, of which section 3.3 of this article offers a heuristic outline. It should be noted that the paragraph opposing sensibilia and theorems reappears at the very end of the second version; the distinction, however, is clearly subordinate to that between describable and non-describable *distingua,* and it is difficult to anticipate how Leibniz would have reconciled the two had he finished the fragment.

107 See the collection of texts in G. W. Leibniz, *The Labyrinth of the Continuum: Writings on the Continuum Problem, 1672–1686,* ed. Richard T. W. Arthur (New Haven: Yale University Press, 2001), and Arthur's indispensable introduction, particularly xxxvii-lxi. A translation of the letter to Thomasius is given in this edition at 337–39.

108 Leibniz, *Die philosophischen Schriften,* 3:622–23.

109 Leibniz, *De l'horizon/Apokatastasis,* 72.

110 Brouwer, "Intuitionism and Formalism" (cited in note 23), 80.

111 Leibniz, *De l'horizon/Apokatastasis,* 74.

112 Ibid.

113 Ibid. The concept of the "horizon" is explored at length in the other pieces collected in Fichant's edition; see also the postface, 140–44.

DOMESTIC ANIMALS.

THE ELEPHANT.

Topography and Structure

Jason Barker

> "To Real Being we go back, all that we have and are; to that we return as from that we came."
> [*Plotinus*, The Enneads]

> "There is no compulsory beginning in philosophy, philosophy does not begin with a beginning that would also be an origin. Philosophy jumps onto a moving train ..."
> [Louis Althusser, "*The Subterranean Current of the Materialism of the Encounter*"]

In this essay I shall set out from the premise, contrary to those anglophone commentators who would diminish the consistency of theory in the aftermath of May 1968,[1] that the modernist reinvention of philosophy that took place in France during the 1960s extends into the following decade and beyond.[2] It is a defining feature of this intellectual sequence to resist being seduced by intellectual fashions, or to renege on principles designed to absorb the discrepancies of political conjuncture. Political affirmation, not negation, characterizes the work of Alain Badiou in this period, who, undaunted by the "crisis of the Left," sets to work—as do Louis Althusser, Guy Lardreau, and Christian Jambet—on a revolutionary ontology.[3] Although I have already outlined the historical dimensions of Althusser's influence on Badiou's thought elsewhere,[4] here I shall present what I regard as the most acute theoretical challenges to Badiou's politics, or "metapolitics," with reference both to Althusser and, somewhat ironically, to Neoplatonism.

I

The distinction between Badiou's thought and Althusser's is arguably centered on the question of Marxism. Althusser's fidelity to the PCF was certainly not shared by Badiou—nor by Lardreau and Jambet for that matter—for whom political clarity could only be attained outside the confines of the party apparatus. Today, Badiou is able to declare with confidence that "*Marxism doesn't exist*," and that politics must therefore proceed "without party" (AM 67, 138). However, Badiou's repudiation of Marxism, along with its presumed philosophical status, would appear to stem from a rival political trajectory. Up until at least 1982 in Badiou's case and for at least as long in Althusser's, both adhered to versions of Marxist-Leninist philosophy.[5] However, since 1988 and the publication of *L'être et l'événement*, Badiou's philosophy has been divorced from all traces of political theory and political science. For Badiou, philosophy is no longer *named* "Marxist." Political militants are quite capable of thinking through the implications of their own practice, of "thinking political novelty effectively" (AM 71), without resorting to orthodoxy. Politics has no tradition to uphold: it simply generates truths; whereas, for its part, "philosophy" involves their non-partisan or purely eventual seizure (AM 64–65).

This strict division between politics and philosophy provides no space for economic determination as such. Let us presume that "Marxism" is defined by a minimal degree of economic determination. Its structuring framework will then involve the action of the economic base on the superstructure, and the "reciprocal action" of the superstructure on the base. Thus the topography[6] peculiar to Marxism consists in a determinate relation of two levels. From this perspective the task of Marxism, including the force of its politics—which always implies a certain *intellectual* effort—is to comprehend the full extent of the efficacy of economic processes, their hold over society, the masses, individuals, and the "relative autonomy" of social practices.

What Badiou is able to contribute today to Marxist topography would, on this basis, appear to be negligible. However, let me suggest as a working hypothesis[7] that Badiou's thought may in fact be broadly compatible with such topography, even if the qualitative nature of capitalist society *as such* remains on this reading an "indifferent singularity" (SP 10).

II

First of all let us set out the key features of Badiou's philosophy (in what follows I shall be dealing with the structures, or structural *conditions*, of his philosophy). Badiou takes for granted that the liberal economy, in the form of "Capital unchained," "is neither measurable nor fixed" (AM 164). The absolute "superpower" of the State means that there is no determinate relation between base and superstructure. What is presupposed in this (non-)relation is instead the indeterminacy of statist excess, or the mundane re-presentation of public space. For Badiou, it is politics that breaks the cycle of the everyday through its determination of the "event" which springs up, haphazardly and without warning, in a given social sphere, e.g., a factory. Henceforth the task of politics is not to seek any sort of bipartisan "mediation" between those representing the bosses and those representing the workers, but to create an autonomous space free from all representation as such. In more precise social terms the aim of politics is to drive society, as a whole, toward the absolute autonomy of its superstructures. There are no "grounds" for radical action because politics is opened up in the aftermath of what is unforeseeable and which cannot be predicted through a knowledge. There is no anticipatory dimension, of would-be prophetic communism, to what goes on politically anymore. However, the question I want to pose here is the following: despite its singularity does the event of politics imply a much more determinist (more globalizing) structural framework than one might otherwise imagine?

In *Peut-on penser la politique?* a text dating from 1985, the impulse for political events is not unprecedented. The concept of the event that emerges in Badiou's later work is a little different to the one introduced here. Firstly, the axioms setting out the structural conditions for political engagement are not the ZF axioms, although they do include terms that re-emerge in the later writings, viz.: "counting as one," "intervention," "interpretation," "fidelity," "void," etc. Secondly, its structural locale is the so-called "*pre-political situation*" wherein "a failure in the regime of the One is discernible" (PP 76). Ordinarily speaking, as a matter of fact and necessity, pre-political unity prevails. Despite their respective differences, in the factory-place "unions," "workers," and "bosses" all operate as one, i.e., as a corporate entity. However, there comes a point in any situation when its structure fails to accommodate an underlying and hitherto indiscernible tension, e.g., racial discrimination. This is the structural contradiction, or what Badiou names "void," that unleashes antagonism in the situation, thereby splitting it in two (PP 77–78).

From this point onwards the apathy of the pre-political situation gives way to the intervening *force* of politics proper. Politics is what "propagates [the event] beyond the pre-political situation. This propagation is never a repetition. It is a subject-effect, a consistency" (PP 77). Overall, what we have here is the following sequential distinction:

- Firstly, the pre-political situation in which what is *not* given, i.e., the event, is nonetheless indexed by a failure in the regime of the One, thus giving rise to the unrepresentable figure of Two.

- Secondly, after the event, the intervention that affirms this Two, thus liberating politics from the sphere of the representable.

Politics, although marked by this split in the social bond, the anomie of this Two, nonetheless presumes a pre-political situation—a state of nature prior to the fall—which beckons its return. For politics is the reversal as much as the elimination of historical contradiction. What especially stands out here is the *circularity* of the structure. "The event is not given," Badiou confirms, "for the regime of the One is the law of all donation" (PP 77). However, the event does indeed return to itself in the sense that what is affirmed "after the event" is the evental scission that brings about the Two in the first place, i.e., *from within* the pre-political situation. Granted, and we repeat, politics is not a "repetition." It is a "subject-*effect*, a consistency." But can the event be conceived, somewhat improbably, as that which is *already* given and, dare I say it, "ever pre-given"? Otherwise put, is the event—which is the only true (ultra-)one multiple there is—thinkable as an overdetermined structure?

III

Of course, *L'être et l'événement* posits the *duality* of being as that which is mathematically formulizable on the one hand, and the event as that which cannot be thought or inferred from the givens of the situation-counted-as-one on the other. Although there are social multiplicities (the proletarian, bourgeois and statist typologies of being; EE 121–28), they are the predicative conditions of situations as such and remain indifferent to the singularity of what people think. People's thought can only be gauged after the event by way of a political truth procedure which measures the shortfall between what is and what took place, between the realm of being on the one hand and the political event on the other. Thought emerges from within this interim.

The corollary of this theory is that nothing we know can prepare us for events or account for the type of subjects they inspire, which in any event defy representation. "Political equality," Badiou says in *Abrégé de métapolitique*, "is not what we desire or plan; it is that which, fuelled by the event, we declare to be here and now, and not something that *should* be." Furthermore, "political statements bearing truth spring up in the absence of any statist and social order" (112, 114).

Now, in order to break politically with the realm of the given, the structure, the situation-counted-as-one, Badiou endorses Hegel's separation of politics from civil society and its private sphere of needs.[8] This is reaffirmed in *L'être et l'événement* through the axiomatic distinction between situation and state of the situation whereby the latter merely re-presents the class-bound, seemingly "natural" interests of individuals (EE 123–24). For Badiou real politics, unlike "the political," is not "an objective datum, even invariant, of universal experience" (AM 19). However, the distinction is problematic. I quote Althusser in this respect:

> In the concept of the sphere of needs, economic facts are thought as based in their economic essence on human subjects who are a prey to "need": on the *homo oeconomicus*, who is a (visible, observable) given, too .... *The peculiar theoretical structure of Political Economy depends on immediately and directly relating together a homogenous space of given phenomena and an ideological anthropology which bases the economic character of the phenomena and its space on man as the subject of needs (the givenness of the* homo oeconomicus).[9]

For Althusser, the separation attains mythic status in "political economy." I quote him again:

> ... e.g., in concepts as ambiguous as economic "rationality," "optimum," "full employment" or welfare economics, "humane" economics, etc. The same anthropology which serves as the original foundation for economic phenomena comes to the fore as soon as there is a question of defining the

meaning of these phenomena, i.e., their *end*. The homogenous given space of economic phenomena is thus doubly given by the anthropology which grips it in the vice of origins and ends.¹⁰

Althusser sets out the ramifications of (the ideology of) classical anthropology in the economic spaces of consumption, distribution, and production. Their structural arrangement can be summed up briefly as follows. In the realm of consumption, for instance, "*individual consumption*" is only the ideological effect of the "*productive consumption*" which *induces* human needs. For Althusser consumption is not, and can never be, economically satisfied. Individuals under capitalism cannot be said to be following through any natural predisposition to satisfy their immediate interests when, for example, they purchase their food from the supermarket. The social relation by which human beings satiate appetite or regulate their bodily functions is not universal, or at least is subject to no *economic* (i.e., quantitative) norm. Indeed, regional disparities in consumer wealth result from the successful *reproduction* of such favorable economic and social conditions as low inflation, low interest rates, a pliant labor market, etc., rather than from anything remotely resembling a "free market." It is not difficult today to see why such reproduction might be deemed more than a purely economic imperative, especially for those third world countries where State sovereignty extends only so far as the national debt, or the level of public/private investment, or consumer borrowing allows. What we cannot help but notice is, thus:

1. The *doubling* of the structure. Althusser's topography accounts both for the production of the objects of individual consumption as well as the reproduction of the conditions of production themselves.

2. The *circularity* of the structure. In effect, reproduction comes first because it induces consumption not on the basis of any given set of conditions, or in response to the objective needs of a population, but under *variable* conditions of economic productivity and growth on a global scale. "Uneven development" ultimately dictates who consumes, where and when, and under what conditions. The effects of this "development" may be catastrophic or revolutionary for this or that population, but they do not correspond to any uniquely political imperative. Quite the reverse in fact: what is unique is politics' re-presentation of the event in its overdetermined complexity. For example, considered in its relative political isolation, Russia in 1917 was a "backward" country where conditions were least favorable for revolution. However, in reality the Russian Revolution is a precise expression of the capitalist *project* as a whole, i.e., its "advancement."¹¹ The structure (of overdetermination) is reaffirmed in ever more "backward" countries: China, Vietnam, Kampuchea, etc. Here then the structure is, globally speaking, "ever pre-given." It is not a regional anomaly, or mere contingency, which finally promotes political

subjects from the lower order of economic necessity. Politics is not, strictly speaking, a happening, for "happening," as Plotinus says, "belongs only to the multiple where, first, existence is given and then something is added."[12]

Nothing *happens* politically. The structural conditions for politics, for *real* political practice to take place, depend upon a true conception of social structure, a question to which we shall return. On the basis of the aforementioned circularity it seems that unless we attend to the proper articulation of this structure, which concerns the elevation of complex multiplicity into simplex unity—from infinity to the One under the aegis of Two in Badiou's numerical terms (AM 166)—political practice risks descending workers' struggles to the petty competitive rivalries of consumers in a market economy. We witness this behavior today, e.g., in the "outsourcing" of the service sector to India and south-east Asia, to which Western syndicalists respond "in their members' interests" with their racist clap-trap and management-speak.[13] Such instances of corporate privilege and economic protectionism provide the new challenge to think through the global vectors and placements of politics. For political unity cannot be sacrificed on the grubby domestic altar of "compound" interest.

Now, I am not proposing that the economic structure, in its unending circularity, should assume the status of some kind of ultra-event. This would be to forget the important inroads that Badiou has made in re-thinking *singular* instances of politics, i.e., instances that remain indifferent to prevailing economic conditions. Today capitalism could hardly be seen as the sole, albeit negative, source/target of political practice, even despite the tenacious rise of so-called "anti-capitalism." The leviathan manifestations against the war in Iraq roundly disqualify this idea. However, the question remains as to how the supposed *indifference* of singular politics vis-à-vis the capitalist logic of surplus value may result in social *antagonism*.[14] This question highlights the fact that Badiou's truth criteria, in being localized within one procedural domain (e.g., politics), are of necessity incommensurable with those in another (e.g., science). There is no political science for Badiou. Consequently the singularity of the event and its successive political determination through its own truth procedure is *under*-determined. In other words it is governed by the unforeseen encounter or subjective actualization of what is, nonetheless, always already an overdetermined situation, an ever-pre-given structure. On the one hand we have the local-situatedness of evental underdetermination, while on the other we have the global-systemicity of evental overdetermination. The problematic of antagonism is thus crisscrossed by the disjunction/conjunction of singularity/totality.

A further expository remark is called for here. In setting out questions of topography and structure we must avoid falling back on Wallersteinian systems theory.[15] If we do, then we lose the thread of the rigorous egalitarian axiomatic of Marxism. A revolution is not a systemic fact. Our task instead is one of *thinking* the structural overdetermination of capitalist economy. This will involve, firstly, rejecting any suggestion of the prophetic communism attributable to Marx (PP 105). Overdetermination, or "determination in the last instance," does not defer real politics into the future. There is no "democracy to come." Time, as Plato says, is only the *image* of eternity, after all.

That being said, we must equally avoid the temptation to reintroduce transcendence into politics by way of some minimally specified set of criteria. This may in fact be Badiou's recourse in advancing the concept of the event site as nondescript "place" for the practice of political novelty.[16] Granted, novelty is not prescribed and results only from a rare subtraction of *doxa* from indifferent multiplicity. Moreover, the place and its mode of determination is topological, not geopolitical (politics has no being-in-the-world). But one might wonder in passing what minimally specified criteria for novel (re)invention can avoid being underwritten by the law of general equivalence and by the lender of the last resort?[17]

We already know that every capitalist deterritorialization is backed by its reterritorialization in "new" form. What the political process thus has to contend with is, by definition, the passage through an overdetermined complex of economic, ideological, legal, etc. relations in order to grasp the *unique* overdetermination of society as *one* whole. In this respect the prospect of political autonomy or "separation" may be completely premature and, in certain instances, quite literally suicidal. The Palestinian situation provides the obvious example here. What "Palestine" repeatedly represents as a political signifier is the psychognostic attempt to abstract political subjectivity from ideological and repressive State apparatuses. In giving up on the path of novel antagonism in favor of reactionary voluntarism, militants hell-bent on "jihad" permit social anomie—the question of Two—to be exploited by a State which then binds it to the "security question," thereby neutralizing the antagonism in the name of the now discredited "two state solution for peace" (recently raised from the dead in the form of the U.S.-Israeli "road map") which in reality serves only to justify the accelerated annexation of the occupied territories. In this context the name "Palestinian" is unable to avoid overbalancing into the domestic legal category of "non-Jew." "Palestine" is thus an overdetermined complex overdetermined *in the last instance* by the vector of U.S. military-industrial aid.[18]

These cursory observations strike us as imperative for thinking the univocity of "Palestinian struggle." They suggest a Palestinian problematic which, instead of being purely political, is the overdetermined complex of which politics is but one of the levels of the structured whole. The complex is ever-pre-given, which means that *there is nothing "in"*[19] *the political place apart from its articulation with the other ideological, legal, and economic places*. Therein politics assumes the status of "The impartible Idea" which, as Plotinus has it,

> gives nothing of itself to the Matter; its unbreaking unity, however, does not prevent it shaping that multiple by its own unity and being present to the entirety of the multiple, bringing it to pattern not by acting part upon part but by presence entire to the object entire.
>
> The elements in their totality, as they stand produced, may be thought of as one spheric figure.[20]

Whence exists politics in its singular relation to the structured whole.

But what precise connections can be made between Althusser's overdetermination and Badiou's underdetermination of political events? Isn't a theory that would appear to think through *specificity*, i.e., a combination of practices, flatly opposed to politics as *singular* thought? Doesn't the overdetermination of the structure, which is what the economy ultimately is for Althusser, block the singularity of a political event by merely re-presenting it? Not at all. Overdetermination, since it is determination *in the last instance*—whose "lonely hour never comes"—is not economism. Marx and Engels both knew perfectly well that, left to their own devices, economic "contradictions" bring us no nearer to socialism. However, this by no means leads us to conclude, as Badiou does at the other extreme, that political events are therefore historically contingent. Events, it might be said, have always already happened, are ever-pre-given. Their *seeming* contingency is pre-conditioned through (understanding) the structure in dominance, e.g., politics. In more Badiouian terms we might say that the law of donation (of the One) composes the pre-political situation to which the subject returns, "after the event,"[21] in order to attend to its scission. This is what we mean by *circularity*. Because the propagation of the event is a subject-effect—a consistency, not a repetition—politics regains its singularity as the structure in dominance by coming to re-present the combination which, as Plotinus says, is (in the lower order of being) mere unity in diversity. Politics, in rising out of this material complex, must instead grasp the unity of the simplex Itself, the supreme One of that which politics is in essence.

What the Althusserian complex-articulation enables us to grasp, then, is the "global restructuring of the whole on a qualitatively new basis."[22] This it does by way of three forms of political contradiction conceived as our three hypostases: non-antagonism, antagonism, and explosion. Whereas we might say that the figure of the One is, for Badiou, as far as the political process can go (politics passing from infinity to the One under the aegis of Two), for Althusser the One is (always already) there at the beginning. A political antagonism is displaced under indeterminate conditions and condensed in a "revolutionary explosion" at the precise moment when social contradictions fuse together in one, in this case through the political structure in dominance. But the One is also at the end. "Revolutionary explosion" is for Althusser not the appearance of an open contradiction as it is for Badiou, but the "moment of unstable global condensation inducing the dissolution and resolution of the whole."[23] In other words, revolution stands at the crossroads of the beginning/end of the political process. Better still: revolution is the political opening/closing—its "circular." It is politically ambivalent, possessing the same kind of status that Althusser claimed for philosophy, viz., the re-presentation of politics with the sciences. Doing philosophy requires that one practice it correctly.

IV

Badiou has recently tried to claim that Althusser moved in his later work towards a theory of the political subject rather than the ideological subject with which we are more familiar. In light of the above it would seem that the primary question is not whether we can distinguish between subjective processes and the subject, or think subjectivity "without" a subject,[24] but whether the separation of politics from ideology can, today, be made in quite the way Badiou wants. Obviously we are living through a time, in the aftermath of yet another "so-called revolution,"[25] when politics is frustrated, and in most cases completely suspended, before it begins. But if this is the case then it seems to mark the *displacement* of politics from the social stage. Obviously politics needs to be brought back there. But this return is a complex multiplicity. It involves the recognition that these displacements, these fictions that spirit away antagonism in the name of "security" or "freedom" or "democracy" are not purely political. They assume the form of social statements that are two-faced, rather than universal, in their mode of address. "You can't buck the market," which was Margaret Thatcher's infamous declaration on the necessity of systemic capitalist crisis, serves as a particularly good example, to my mind, of the type of displacements at stake and that political practice needs to face up to today. It emanates from a specific conjuncture, always unpredictable in its continental drift, and subtending real shifts of global capital and surplus value. It displaces politics, it brings about subjective displacements, across time and space. It spirits away the subjects of political process at the precise moment of systemic crisis, like the (w)holes[26] in the space-time continuum, as depicted in Terry Gilliam's film *Time Bandits*. At the moment of truth, the subjects fall through a (w)hole only to wind up somewhere else, isolated, on the margins of history.

The Palestinian situation is the obvious example, it seems to me, of the way in which political displacement evacuates everything (and anything it can lay its hands on) from the event site in order to make it work elsewhere in the name of global security, the "war on terror," etc. We have already highlighted the "two state solution for peace" in this respect—a "peace" whose supreme correlate is the nuclear bomb. But other examples are emerging. The current alleged U.S. military strategy whereby terrorist suspects are "rendered," i.e., extradited to hostile countries in order to undergo forms of interrogation that could never be officially sanctioned in freedom-loving democracies, provides a perfect illustration of such displacement. Under this regime, subjects are stripped of their citizenship along with any last vestige of their human rights and processed like sacks of commodities: thrown aboard a military aircraft in country x, flown halfway across the globe, kept in detention, tortured, then shipped on to country y, *ad infinitum*. Today political displacement is proceeding in ways that require us to face up to the capital-military-industrial complex's multiplication of legal black (w)holes. In places like "Palestine," politics is no longer there, it's operating somewhere else. However, this somewhere else is by no means the "other scene" of politics, either in the sense of its underlying ideological raison d'être (global economic processes, capitalism) or of its psychopathological alter-ego (the public repository of repressed desires: nationalism, racism, classism).[27] The displacement of politics must not be mistaken for its deferral, since ultimately displacement is an integral part of the political process—the very fabric of its relative endurance and deviations, ebb and flow—*as singularity*. Politics will always mark a passage *through* the complex social (w)hole despite the specters and phantasms we run into along the way. In Badiouian terms this passage would correspond to the militant's pursuit of the *vanishing point* of the event even if such political determination brings us into direct conflict with the event's simulacra, or its *void* multiples.²⁸ The pursuit is perilous since the traversal of the site is forever threatened by imminent displacement and the unexplained disappearance of subjects.²⁹ Bringing politics about requires us to step back and grasp these displacements, the question of where they end up, or at what point—how and why—they exit the social stage at least. This is by no means to say that we can predict the accompanying condensation. But what we can say is that political displacement marks the beginning of the process that we are already in, which, despite going round in circles, is still always the beginning of the end for the old world. ∎

....

1   See, e.g., Peter Dews, *Logics of Disintegration* (London: Verso, 1987).
2   Admittedly this never was a consistent theoretical project, "anti-humanist" or otherwise, of the type proposed by Luc Ferry and Alain Renaut in their *French Philosophy of the Sixties: An Essay on Antihumanism*, trans. M. H. S. Cattani (Amherst: University of Massachusetts Press, 1990). However, it is my task to argue here that the reinvention in question is certainly no less diminished in the aftermath of a would-be political event, viz., May 1968. As Badiou would argue, the event is always the inconsistent point from which a knowledge is composed.
3   See Alain Badiou, *Théorie du sujet* [TS; for a list of Badiou's principal texts and their corresponding abbreviations, see the introduction to this issue.—Ed.]; Guy Lardreau and Christian Jambet, *L'ange* (Paris: Grasset, 1976); Louis Althusser, *Sur la philosophie* (Paris: Gallimard, 1994) and *Écrits philosophiques et politiques, Tome 1* (Paris: Éditions Stock/IMEC, 1994). For an excellent reading of Althusser's "aleatory materialism," see Wal Suchting, "Althusser's Late Thinking about Materialism," *Historical Materialism* 12, no. 1 (2004): 3–70. See also Alain Badiou, "Qu'est-ce que Louis Althusser entend par 'philosophie'?" in *Politique et philosophie dans l'oeuvre de Louis Althusser*, ed. Sylvain Lazarus, 29–45 (Paris: Presses Universitaires de France, 1993).
4   Jason Barker, *Alain Badiou: A Critical Introduction* (London: Pluto Press, 2002).
5   See Jason Barker, "The Topology of Revolution," *Communication and Cognition* 36, no. 1/2 (2003): 61–72.
6   The definitive outline of Marxist topography is provided in the essay "Contradiction and Overdetermination" in Louis Althusser, *For Marx*, trans. Ben Brewster, 89–128 (London: Verso, 1996). See also Althusser's "Ideology and Ideological State Apparatuses" in *Lenin and Philosophy*, trans. Ben Brewster (London: New Left Books, 1971), 134–36.
7   A version of this paper was first presented at the *Atelier Badiou* at the Université de Paris-VIII on 30 May 2003. It was subsequently revised and presented at *Badiou's Ethics and Subjectivity*, the one-day conference held at London Metropolitan University on 15 December 2003. The present article has taken in further, more systematic changes.
8   PP 20; see also "One Divides into Two," available at: http://culturemachine.tees.ac.uk/Articles/badiou.htm, and *Le Siècle*, passim.
9   Louis Althusser and Étienne Balibar, *Reading Capital*, trans. Ben Brewster (London: Verso, 1979), 162.
10 Ibid., 163.
11 Althusser, *For Marx*, 207. The idea that Marx's theory of social revolution is disproved on the grounds that Russia in 1917 was an "underdeveloped" peasant economy is patently absurd not just in metaphysical terms, but by the very criteria of monetarist economics, a

fact borne out today by the Latin American and other "regional" subjects of dollarization. The dyad first/third world (or center/periphery in Wallersteinese) has lost any analytical relevance it once had to "political economy."

12 Plotinus, *The Enneads*, trans. Stephen MacKenna (London: Penguin, 1991), VI.8, 8.
13 The response of British labor unions such as Amicus to the outsourcing practiced by UK firms has been to campaign against it, although not through the promotion of international solidarity between workers against capital. Instead, Amicus accepts "offshoring" as the inevitable result of "technological progress" and encourages government to take "regulatory measures" in order to win back the "competitive edge" of the UK workforce. See Amicus, "Offshoring Campaign" available online at: http://www.amicustheunion.org/main.asp?page=219.
14 See Alberto Toscano, "From the State to the World? Badiou and Anti-Capitalism," *Communication and Cognition* 37, no. 1/2 (2004), forthcoming.
15 World-systems theory draws on historical sociology grounded in empirical research. Immanuel Wallerstein, its leading proponent, posits capitalism as one giant integrated system which begins in the sixteenth century and, in traversing historical periods of economic "expansion," "stagnation," and "crisis," operates a division of labor "deprived of a unique political structure." For an excellent introduction to the key ideas see Rémy Herrera, "Les théories du système mondial capitaliste," in *Dictionnaire Marx Contemporaine*, ed. J. Bidet and E. Kouvelakis, 201–21 (Paris: Presses Universitaires de France, 2001). Working paper version available online at: http://matisse.univ-paris1.fr/doc2/mse076.pdf.
16 For Badiou's discussion of the event site, see EE 223–33; for his endorsement of Sylvain Lazarus's theory of political "places [*lieux*] of the name," see AM 35–66.
17 The lender of the last resort (LOLR) is a financial institution, usually a central bank, that provides loans to commercial banks during periods of financial liquidity, thereby immunizing them against the adverse effects of social crisis, civil emergency, revolution, etc.
18 On the Israel-Palestine conflict see also "When the two-state solution is no longer viable," available online at: http://www.bitterlemons.org/previous/bl160603ed23.html#is2.
19 See note 28.
20 Plotinus, op. cit., VI.5, 8–9.
21 From Lucretius to Hegel, the event escapes all reason. But we assert that there is no desire above the law. "Circulation is ever pre-determined, there is not circulation and then the rule, there is only a rule of circulation. Indeed, incest desire doesn't pre-exist the law, the prohibition. It is the prohibition that constitutes the 'sexual act' as such in rendering it impossible." Lardreau and Jambet, op. cit., 30.
22 Althusser, *For Marx*, 216. A note of caution, however. Any *qualitative* restructuring of society as "whole," or totality, passing by way of the constitution of "revolutionary" or "socialist" administration, would not amount to the higher principle itself. Instead it would make such a society *dependent*, from the economic perspective, on the *movement* of global capital: decline in international reserves, collapse of capital investment, etc. Paraphrasing Plotinus, we say that the God of the people never was the All (v.5, 12); paraphrasing Freud, we say that the love of all leads to psychic turmoil and, ultimately, civil unrest. Sigmund Freud, *Civilization and Its Discontents*, trans. James Strachey (New York: W. W. Norton, 1961).
23 Althusser, *For Marx*, 216.
24 See AM 67–76.
25 Although 1968 is today interpreted, like 1848, as a revolutionary failure, for Badiou the former stands out as the ultimate figure of *mass* politics; cf. AM 77–87.

26 I coin this term since every social *whole*, every presumption of totality, belies a *hole* in being through which the prior unity of the Absolute Good falls.
27 See Étienne Balibar, *Politics and the Other Scene*, trans. Christine Jones et al. (London: Verso, 2002).
28 Over and above admitting being "on the edge of the void," $\alpha \cap \beta = \varnothing$, a void that is "universally included" in every situation, Badiou also admits a co-belonging of the event to itself, $e_x \in e_x$. In the case of the event site bordering a potential happening, multiples *in* the site cannot be presented there, since nothing is presented on the edge of the void except the *name* of the void. However, in the case of the event itself, what is *in* its site is equally *of* it, and so free to transgress what would otherwise be (the) void, i.e., barred from being, in an antagonistic situation. For Badiou, this is the precise moment when totality gives way to singularity, when "the event impedes its *total* singularization through the belonging of its signifier to the multiple that it is" (EE 203). What politics as pure multiplicity, presentation of presentation, would thus imply is no longer the *passage from* infinity to the One, but the countable infinity *of* the one itself: the circularity of the structure. This is what Badiou calls "ultra-one," or the point that defies every limit and restriction of totalizing, overdetermined categories—"nation," "race," "class," "people," etc. Crucially, however, for Badiou politics is what *decides* whether the event belongs to its site or not, the event cannot verifiably belong there without the trial of inquests.
29 The logics of appearance, which would also involve the "being-there" of politics, is dealt with in Badiou's forthcoming *Logiques des mondes*. In the meantime, see his "Being and Appearance," "Notes Toward a Thinking of Appearance," "The Transcendental," and "Hegel and the Whole" in TW 163–231.

Nothing but a Truth: Alain Badiou's "Philosophy of Politics" and the Left Heideggerians

Oliver Marchart

Badiou's work constitutes one of the rare examples in current theorizing of a post-foundational philosophical *system*—and there is hardly a contradiction here between a post-foundational stance and systematic philosophy. For Badiou, true philosophy is always systematic, yet it is not systematic in the sense of being centered around a keystone: "if by 'system' you mean, first, that philosophy is conceived as an argumentative discipline with a requirement of coherence, and second, that philosophy never takes the form of a singular body of knowledge but, to use my own vocabulary, exists conditionally with respect to a complex set of truths, then it is the very essence of philosophy to be systematic."[1] The aim of this essay is not, of course, to give an exhaustive account of Badiou's system. What I will try to do is to trace Badiou's attitude to and his role within current political philosophy. This is not an easy task, since Badiou aims at nothing less than the *destruction* of political philosophy. For Badiou, it is a fundamental imperative for contemporary thought to "finish with political philosophy." However, what I will claim is that Badiou's work can legitimately be located within a group of post-foundational theorists which, for lack of a better name, I call the *left Heideggerians* in current political philosophy.[2] This group is held together by a particular "family resemblance": the employment of the conceptual difference between *politics* and *the political*, or between "la politique" and "le politique"—a political descendent, I hold, of Heidegger's ontological difference. One could even think of proposing the thesis that what is called in Heideggerianism the ontological difference is mirrored conceptually in the field of current post-foundational political theory in form of the difference between the concept of politics and the concept of the political.

While versions of this difference in fact can be traced back to Carl Schmitt and, in France, to Paul Ricoeur, it was the *Center for Philosophical Research on the Political*, founded by Philippe Lacoue-Labarthe and Jean-Luc Nancy, which between 1980 and 1984 turned out to be the location for the most intense and influential re-elaboration so far of the notion of the political, respectively the difference between politics and the political. The way Claude Lefort and Jacques Rancière, but also Badiou himself, framed their own versions of the political difference (often in contradistinction to Nancy and Lacoue-Labarthe's version) was certainly influenced by the debates at the Center. This diverse and yet related set of theoretical approaches within "left Heideggerianism" all share a series of family resemblances: they are, in one way or another, *contingency-theories*; they share a strong notion of *the event*; they grant a crucial role to political division and *antagonism*; they, of course, all deny the possibility of a *final ground* of the social, and still are grounded on their own variants of something like the ontological difference (as the abysmal *absencing* of ground). Even as they are sometimes highly critical of one another, these approaches, I submit, are far from being incompatible, given their common belonging to the "family" of post-foundational theories. As in most families, not all members feel dearest affection for the others all the time, yet this does not mean that they were not part of the family.³ Their different positions also determine the way in which the political difference is framed: while Nancy and Lacoue-Labarthe work from the viewpoint of deconstruction, Claude Lefort's work is deeply influenced by Maurice Merleau-Ponty, Rancière's work more or less secretly draws on Foucault, and Alain Badiou's work can be read as an Althusserian-Lacanian (critical) contribution to the topic. In the following I will try, through a systematic presentation of Badiou's political thought, to illustrate the extent to which the latter is actually in line with the group of post-foundational family resemblances outlined above (contingency, event, conflictuality, groundlessness)—notwithstanding Badiou's rather misleading self-representation as an anti-Heideggerian, *anti*-post-foundational Platonist.

Admittedly, as such a self-proclaimed new Platonist, Badiou stands at the most extreme point of the spectrum of post-foundational theory. Some would even say he holds an *antagonistic* position with respect to most other social post-foundationalists. Peter Hallward, for instance, goes as far as claiming that "Badiou's mature work provides the most powerful alternative yet conceived in France to the various forms of postmodernism that arose after the collapse of the Marxist project."⁴ In the same fashion, Jean-Jacques Lecercle claims that Badiou's position of a *Platonism of the manifold* "is a lonely place, as he opposes everything continental philosophy of the post-structuralist kind has been about."⁵ However, this may only seem so if we take Badiou's declarations at face value. A closer look will reveal that Badiou's Platonism—supposedly standing in radical opposition towards anything post-foundational—is a Platonism of the most peculiar kind. There is a strong element of provocation involved. Badiou's self-styled Platonism should thus be taken as *strategic coquetry* following from a serious intent, or simply as "*serious* coquetry": "Our century is fundamentally anti-Platonist. So there's an element of coquetry in calling yourself a Platonist, which I am, profoundly."⁶ How can one be profound and coquette at the same time? I hope that the following will show that there are many more similarities between Badiou and his adversaries, the modern "sophists" (including theorists like Lyotard, Derrida, Lacoue-Labarthe, and Nancy), than there are incompatibilities.

Against Political Philosophy as a Philosophy of the Political

Let us start by considering the premises upon which Badiou's attack against political philosophy is based. From the point of view of the political difference, it is of importance that Badiou relates the category of *the political* [*le politique*] precisely to "traditional" political philosophy while retaining the category of *politics* [*la politique*] for his own intellectual enterprise. For Badiou, political philosophy describes a program by which politics is "reified" into an invariably and objectively given of universal experience, i.e., the political, and eventually consigned to the realm of ethical norms (AM 19).[7] In the classical tradition of political philosophy, politics was subordinated to a normative evaluation and quest for the "good State"—it was thus subordinated to questions of the legitimation of sovereignty. The political philosopher will turn out to be the beneficiary of that process in three ways: first, s/he will be the analyst of the brutal and confused empiricity of real politics; second, s/he will be the one to determine the principles of a "good" politics or polity which are in line with the exigencies of ethics; and third, s/he can avoid the risk of becoming the militant of a truth-related political process (engendered, for Badiou, by the intervention of thinking/acting) by withdrawing to the non-activity of *judgment*. Thus, politics no longer describes, as it does for Badiou, the subjectivizing truth-processes of militants, but is reduced to "free judgment" and the exchange of opinions within a public sphere (AM 20).

It is Hannah Arendt who serves as Badiou's main target and stand-in for political philosophy at large, since for Arendt truth is not a category of the political sphere. Accordingly, from Badiou's point of view, this implies that "'politics' is neither the name of a thinking (if one agrees that every thinking, where its philosophical identification is concerned, is linked in one or the other way to the theme of truth) nor the name of an action" (AM 20). A political philosophy which advocates the plurality of opinions by excluding the notion of truth is devoted, in the last instance, to the promotion of the particular politics of parliamentarism. Behind the abstract notion of *the political* we thus find *a particular politics*, the politics of parliamentarism ("talking about 'the political' here means masking the philosophical defense of a politics" [AM 25]) legitimated by the notion of pluralism—the plurality of opinions within the public sphere. Against the "ontological" characterization of the political as plurality (of opinions), Badiou makes a stand for the *singularity* of politics. By this he does not mean that there is only one politics, rather he seeks to underline that the effective "plurality" of politics in his sense ("there is no simple plurality, there is only a plurality of pluralities" [AM 31]) is always induced by subjects that are different. Each of them is defined by his/her singular relation to a truth-event and *not* by his/her mutual exchange of opinions under the common norm of pluralism.[8]

Now, today's parliamentary states are, according to Badiou, regulated by three norms: economy, which is why Badiou also speaks about "capitalo-parliamentarism"; the national norm; and democracy as such—constructed as a norm vis-à-vis (including the freedom of opinion, association, and movement) despotism and dictatorship. "Capitalo-parliamentarism," regulated by these norms, does not simply describe a political regime or form of government, but the parliamentary mode of *the state*—which is defined as the particular way in which elements (or sub-sets) are *ordered* within a situation.[9] Obviously, Badiou is highly critical if not inimical to representative democracy in the parliamentary mode. "Democracy" (and, in particular, "Western liberal democracies"), for Badiou—and herein he retains a Marxist point of view—is an intrinsic part and element of capitalism ("it is always entangled in the domination of the proprietors" [DO 31]), in that democracy politically supports and secures the private ownership of the means of production. While history knows other ways of using the term democracy (the Athenian way, the republican way of the French revolution, the socialist-revolutionary way of general assemblies, of workers councils, etc.), in today's propaganda democracy signifies a form of government limited to the party state.[10]

After the collapse of the former party-states of the East, "capitalo-parliamentarism" seems to be the only version of democracy left. Yet the disappearance of the socialist states only covers up the effectual *triumph* of "vulgar" Marxism, the capitalist version of *economism*, by which the absolute and unrivalled primacy of the market is assumed.[11] The pluralism on which Western democracy prides itself only covers up a regime of the One: "We are, politically, under the regime of the One, and not under that of the multiple. Capitalo-parliamentarism is the tendentially unique mode of politics, the only one which combines economic efficiency (hence the profit of the proprietors) with popular consensus" (DO 37). It has become the only way to imagine democracy *and* it is a regime of the One, since "capitalo-parliamentarism" implies the subordination of politics under a single sphere: the state, thus annulling politics proper ("*la politique comme pensée*" [36], as Badiou would have it). Real politics is thus subsumed under and, in the last instance, confounded with the state.[12]

The three "capitalo-parliamentary" normative functions of the economy, the nation and democracy characterize the parliamentary state as *a* politics (*une* politique) that is oriented towards the State. A politics—which is always *particular* and "statist" by nature—must therefore be distinguished from what Badiou calls *the* politics (*la politique*) in general. But what is *the politics*? Before a more detailed outline of "*la politique*" is presented, it should be stressed that Badiou does not proceed via definitions, if by definitions we understand an assertion which would link politics to a particular object. Badiou is entirely against any objectifying approach to politics, since philosophy in Badiou's sense (as thinking) does not have an object: "Philosophy doesn't have an object. The 'political' object in particular does not exist for it" (AM 72). This is one of the reasons why it should not be confused with political theory—which objectifies *la politique* into *le politique*—since "politics [*la politique*], just like philosophy, has no object and is not subordinated to the norm of objectivity" (AM 73). Since there is no object of politics (there is only the militant subject), there can be no definition of politics. Of course, Badiou himself is never tired of providing definitions, but not definitions in the sense of an objective predication, but *axiomatic* definitions that do not refer to any empirically given "object" outside the processes of thinking. And he consequently denounces *political science*, which also "objectifies" politics and reduces an objectless field in which truth can appear to the "extrinsic" object of the party state.[13] In this anti-positivism and anti-objectivism, traits of the Heideggerian criticism of the metaphysics of technology and science are clearly discernible.[14] The corresponding claim is made by Badiou about politics: politics proper must not to be confused with today's "technologized" politics,[15] with the bureaucratic management of the affairs of the State—which is only part of a larger process of technologization and does not enter what Badiou calls truth procedures or the conditions of philosophy.[16]

Politics of the Real

From the viewpoint of politics (*la* politique), both democracy and so-called totalitarianism are figures of the state. What unites liberal, Marxist, and fascist conceptions is their common *suppression* of real politics and its replacement by the complex of state and economy as something which occupies the totality of the visible.[17] Yet the state in itself, while certainly being a term of the *political field*, is *a*-political by nature (PP 108–9). So it is democracy *and* totalitarianism together (and in their seeming opposition) that constitute the terrain for the "apogee of the political [*apogée du politique*]" (PP 17). The Soviet paradigm is built on nothing other than *the political* in the form of the universal pretension of the state, on which the parliamentary democracies are built as well—even though they were long in a position to "hide" behind the more obvious statist façade of totalitarianism. For this reason, the problem starts when democracy and totalitarianism are presented in terms of an opposition. Instead, "democracy and totalitarianism are two epochal versions of the accomplishment of the political [*du politique*] in its twofold category of tie and representation. Our task concerns politics [*la politique*] to the extent that it positions occurrences of un-tying in the order of the irrepresentable" (PP 17).

So, one has to disconnect politics (*la* politique) from the fiction of the communitarian or *social bond* as well as from the fiction of *representation*, that is, from the two main fictions of the political (*le* politique). Where representation is concerned, Badiou makes it more than clear that he is entirely against the representation of anything social (be it the proletariat, the class, or the Nation) within or with the help of politics. His claim is that we have to finish with the representative view of politics. For him, politics does not represent anything, it is a procedure of *irrepresentation*. And it is only to the extent that it escapes the logic of representation that politics touches on *the real* whose "logics" is entirely different: the real works in the mode of the *future antérieur*. Politics, the politics of the real, occurs in the *futur antérieur*: "But the time of real politics is the *futur antérieur*" (PP 107). That is to say, a political subject (say, the proletariat) cannot be represented, because it does not exist in the social prior to its political construction: it is established as a subject only *retroactively* through the very process of faithfully linking up with a truth-event (say, the revolution). Consequently, for Badiou, *real* politics always means politics of *the real* and political organization means "organisation du future antérieur" (PP 109).[18]

In Lacan, of course, the register of the real has to be strictly differentiated from "reality," and hence, for the Lacanian Badiou, the politics of the real cannot be related to the level of empirical facts and social data either. This realm is not the register of politics, but the realm of *the police*, if by police we understand the "amplifier" of the pre-given, that is, the management of already established facts. Police is always the "police of facts" [*police des faits*].[19] A thinking/acting of politics, on the other hand, always must *subtract*[20] itself from the order of being, the state or the police—i.e., from the order of the necessary—and, quite literally, seek to achieve the *impossible*. In order to do this, that is to say, in order to allow the event to occur, one has to leave aside all the facts and be faithful to something which is not a given fact of reality but an evanescent interruption of the real: "The possibility of the impossible is the ground of politics [*de la politique*]. It is massively opposed to everything we are taught today, including politics being the management of the necessary. Politics [*la politique*] starts with the same gesture by which Rousseau clears the ground of inequality: leaving aside all the facts. It is important for an event to arrive to leave aside all the facts" (PP 78).

Again, what is of course incompatible with a true politics that belongs to the register of the real is the notion of the social bond. Politics, like the real, belongs to the order of the *event*, not to the order of the bond (PP 20). Political philosophy, for Badiou, is nothing other than *the fiction of the political as social bond*.[21] It is a fiction because political philosophy, in its search for the *legitimate* bond, inscribes politics into the narrative and linear figure of the novel: the fiction of a measurement, according to a philosophical norm, of the *good* state, or the good revolution (PP 12). The disturbing event of politics is thereby sublimated into the fiction of the political as, on the one hand, bond (or social relation) and, on the other, representation under an authority (or political sovereignty) (PP 15).

The name for the place of all relations is *the social*—which is where all relations of oppression and exploitation are located (PP 19). This implies for Badiou that the social is also the order of *differences*. As such, it belongs, in our words, to the "ontic" level, which is of no importance for Badiou's theorization of the event as that which disturbs and interrupts the ontic. The level of the social is characterized by rites, mores, traditions and beliefs, by imaginary formations such as religions, sexual representations, etc. This level is cherished today by the ideology of multiculturalism. Badiou is not interested in differences as such, because every truth disposes of differences or renders them insignificant. With admirable sobriety he writes: "Every modern collective configuration involves people from everywhere, who have their different ways of eating and speaking, who wear different sorts of headgear, follow different religions, have complex and varied relations to sexuality, prefer authority or disorder, and such is the way of the world" (Ee 27). Badiou remains totally unimpressed where the proponents of multiculturalism would be most fascinated. The reasons for his disinterest should have become clear by now: the infinite multiplicity belongs the level of beings ("ce qui est"), while truth belongs to the entirely different register of the event ("ce qui *advient*"): "Only a truth is, as such, *indifferent to differences*" (Ee 27). One may suspect that once more we encounter in Badiou something like a radicalized notion of the ontological *difference as difference*, his *distinction directrice* between being and event, and Badiou's highly original point, if he were to submit to this Heideggerian vocabulary, would then be that this "radical difference" whose play grounds all ontic differences is precisely what *escapes* the ontic order of differences (thus being indifferent to differences).

By way of recapitulation of Badiou's usage of the notion of politics and the political respectively, one can provisionally encapsulate it in the following formula: politics is what *interrupts* the fiction of the political. It cuts off all representation and *de*-relates all social relations. Politics therefore lies beyond the realm of the *social*. It is exceptional in relation to the social.[22] Such theorization of the political difference is certainly inspired by the debates at the Center for Philosophical Research on the Political. In his *Peut-on penser la politique?* a text which originated at the two conferences in 1983 and 1984 at the Center, Badiou agrees with Nancy and Lacoue-Labarthe that there is a *retrait* or a *crisis* of the political in the moment of the political's apogee. For Badiou, this crisis is shown most clearly by the crisis of Marxism, yet what is at stake is a much larger phenomenon ("the crisis of the political in its entirety" [PP 21], "the planetary crisis of the political" [34]) consisting in the dissolution precisely of representation and of the fiction of the social bond: "What the crisis of the political unveils is that all sets [*ensembles*] are inconsistent, that there is no such thing as France or proletariat, and that, for the same reason, the figure of representation, much like its obverse, the figure of spontaneity, is itself inconsistent …" (13).

The "retreat of the political" *in Badiou's sense* corresponds to a crisis of closed ensembles or sovereignty of the One in general. The text on the back cover of the small book makes it utterly clear: "Thinking politics [la *politique*], first and foremost means refuting the political [le *politique*]: renouncing it as an (imaginary) illusion of 'making One' in the form of identifications (the party, the union, classless society), of a confinable fact, of a reliable prediction" (PP n.p.). What differentiates Badiou from Nancy and Lacoue-Labarthe is his emphatic politicism, indicated by his usage of the political difference with reversed premises: politics does not designate, as it does for Nancy and Lacoue-Labarthe, the order of power and of the police but, on the contrary, the order of truth and the event. However, what is of much greater importance is the fact that, even where he changes the premises, Badiou *retains* the political difference as difference between *la* and *le* politique. It seems that wherever we turn in political "left Heideggerianism," be it to the Lacanian or the deconstructive trajectory, we encounter the need to retain this difference.

A "Politics" of Truth: Equality and Justice

Before engaging with the question of the ethical aspects of Badiou's notion of politics, let us locate the latter in relation to the conceptual framework of his philosophical system:[23] A pre-political *situation* is defined by Badiou as a complex of facts and statements wherein a setback for the regime of the One is discernable and where there is, consequently, an irreducible Two (also described by Badiou as a point of irrepresentability and as an empty set). Badiou calls the *state* or *structure* of the situation the mechanism through which the situation is *counted as one* (as *this* situation) and thus located within the sphere of representation. An *event* must then be theorized as the *dysfunction* of the regime of the One. It is the remainder which cannot be absorbed by this regime and which is always the product of an act of interpretation. What he then calls an *intervention* is constituted by the supernumerary facts and statements by which the event is interpreted as *an event* (and *the political subject* is, far from being the "agent" of all this, the retroactive outcome of an interpretive intervention). That is to say, an event has to be named as an event and its name must not belong to the situation. Politics *is that which, via an intervention, gives* consistency *to the event*.[24]

The last nameable political event, in Badiou's eyes, was the revolution of October 1917. The political events between 1968–1980—the events to which Badiou himself, as a Maoist, adheres—have not yet received their definite name. They remain "obscure" because they call into question the previous protocols of political nomination—but this does not exclude the possibility that they will be named (and thus fixed as an event) many years later. Nevertheless, on a more general level one can specify a series of conditions that have to be met for an event to be designated as political. I would like to mention three. First, the "material" of the event must consist in a collective: "An event is political if the material of this event is collective, or if the event cannot be attributed to anything other than to the multiplicity of a collective" (AM 155). By "collective" Badiou does not refer to a certain *number* of people—collective is not a numerical concept, but is that which is established in the relation of the militants to universality. The truth-event of politics addresses itself to *everybody* who proceeds from the event.[25] Second, as an effect of the collective character of the political event, politics presents the *infinite* character of every situation. A situation is open by definition, it is never finite (in this Badiou dismisses the Heideggerian theme of finitude and "being-towards-death," but without grounding the situation in anything other than the void of infinity—which means that the result is still *post*-foundational). Emancipatory and egalitarian politics—and for Badiou, every politics worth that name is egalitarian and universalistic—immediately convokes this infinity of the situation. Third, if we define the *state of a situation* as the power to count the sub-sets of the situation as one, thereby making representable the situation as *this* situation, then it follows that such politics of infinity must be directed *against* the power which, by way of making it countable, would otherwise "close" the situation and render it finite. Thus, true politics always triggers operations of repression by the state and brings to light the state's excessive power. In this sense, one can say that politics has a *provocative* function.[26]

This kind of thesis implies that the essence of politics is emancipatory. In other words, if true politics is directed against the state by definition, then there is no politics worth the name that is not emancipatory. ("The essence of politics [*la politique*] lies in the emancipation of the collective …" [DO 54].) Now, as was indicated earlier, the "moment of politics"—the moment where the state is confronted with the disruption of a political event—is also the moment of *truth*: political truth only begins on the occasion of rupture and disorder, that is, when "business as usual breaks down for one reason or another."[27] Without a truth-event there is no politics in the strict sense, there is only the rule of the state and of the a-political differences of the social: "The vast majority of empirical political orientations have nothing to do with truth, as we know. They organize a repulsive mixture of power and opinions. The subjectivity that animates them is that of the tribe and the lobby, of electoral nihilism and the blind confrontation of communities."[28] Yet such a truth-event, for Badiou, has certain implications for the normative or perhaps philosophico-"ethical" level of emancipatory politics, since it is closely connected to the interrelated concepts of *justice* and *equality*.

Badiou calls justice "the name by which a philosophy designates the possible truth of a political orientation."[29] It is important to note that justice is one of philosophy's *names* for a truth event: it is a philosophical designation, rather than concrete political program.[30] Justice can also serve as a good example for the extent to which the Badiouian concepts intermesh. If the truth-event is defined by its disruptive quality and justice is one of the philosophical attributes of truth, then justice too occurs in the anti-statist and anti-social form of disruption: "Justice, far from being a possible category of state and social order, is the name which designates the principles at work in rupture and dis-order."[31] Such an approach entails an entirely anti-essentialist understanding of justice. Justice is not defined by any predicate or a positive content ("the just"), but only occurs in the "negative" or un-defined moment, in which the social bond disintegrates: "We have too often wished that justice find the consistency of the social tie, while it can only name the most extreme moments of inconsistency."[32]

What was said about justice must therefore also be said about what Badiou calls the *equalitarian political maxim*: equality is a completely "negative" concept in the sense of not being grounded in the positive substance of a common good; nor should equality be instituted with respect to any positive reference: the only reference possible is the *non*-reference to the state of the situation, to the principle of classification and order.[33] For the same reason, equality cannot be defined: one must not turn equality into a positive program or an egalitarian policy (at least, such a policy would be exactly that, a policy, and not politics in Badiou's sense). So, in sum, equality does not refer to anything objectively given or to any concrete goal we have to achieve: "it is in no way a social program. It has, moreover, nothing to do with the social. It is a political maxim, a prescription. Political equality is not what we want or plan, it is what we declare under fire of the event, here and now, as what is, and not what should be."[34] The effect of the equalitarian axiom related to a truth-event will rather be, as in the case of justice, "to undo the ties, to desocialize thought, to affirm the rights of the infinite and immortal against finitude, against Being-for-death."[35] Justice and equality are thus interrelated concepts where justice "is the philosophical name for the equalitarian political maxim,"[36] and the politics of emancipation which imposes an equalitarian maxim, for Badiou "is a thought in act."[37]

If equality is nothing that "exists" in the social world, but is rather an axiom of thought that works as a *prescription,* that is to say, if it is defined by Badiou as *an ethical maxim,* it eventually appears that it is impossible to talk about real politics (as a politics in which truth, justice and equality are inextricably linked) without having to enter the register of the *ethical* at the same time. Indeed, Badiou's whole system, despite its apparently "pure" mathematical inclinations, seems to be evolving towards a generalized ethics.[38] What we encounter in Badiou is an ethics of truths (and, in the political sphere, of equality), which derives from a Lacanian ethics of the real based on the *possibility of the impossible*.[39] Such an ethics of truths escapes the order of the symbolic by definition. Since the truth-event belongs to the order of the real, it cannot be mediated or communicated. Therefore the ethics of a truth cannot be an ethics of communication: "It is an ethics of the Real, if it is true that—as Lacan suggests—all access to the Real is of the order of an encounter" (Ee 52). In other words, while the event cannot be communicated, it can be *encountered*. Hence, one of Badiou's reformulations of his ethical imperative: "Never forget what you have encountered!" (Ee 52). Never forget what you have encountered. Or, in the shortest version: "Keep going!" [*Continuer!*] (Ee 52).[40]

"*Continuer!*" is the formula of fidelity. Continue in being faithful to the event! Badiou's ethics is centered around the general principle of faithfully continuing a truth-process.[41] A political organization of militants (i.e., the subject in the field of politics) is nothing but the collective product of a process of fidelity towards an event (PP 77). The reason why an ethical (if not religious) term like *fidelity* is so important within the framework of Badiou's system lies in the fact that it functions as the main operator of *subjectivation*: there is only a subject if there is a process of fidelity—if a subject through his/her fidelity gives consistency to an event. We remember: an event for Badiou is defined as a supplement to a given (ontic) situation of multiple beings, and while the former is connected to the notion of truth and to the real, the latter is always restricted to the realm of opinions. *Subjectivation* occurs only if a *decision* is taken to be faithful to the event against the world of pre-established rules and opinions. Such fidelity creates a rupture within a given situation: a rupture that belongs to the Lacanian order of the real (as something that disturbs the symbolic "order of things"). At the same time, *a truth* is produced in the situation. One more definition of "truth" would thus be the following: "I shall call 'truth' (*a* truth) the real process of a fidelity to an event: that which this fidelity produces in the situation" (Ee 42). A truth is produced by the decision of a subject to remain faithful to an event. What is important to understand, however, is the *retroactive* logic of subject-formation: the subject only exists to the extent that it actively declares his/her fidelity to the event—it *does not precede* the event: "I call 'subject' the bearer [*le support*] of a fidelity, the one who bears a process of truth. The subject, therefore, in no way pre-exists the process. He is absolutely nonexistent in the situation 'before' the event. We might say that the process of truth *induces* a subject" (Ee 43). At no point in this circular relation between subject, decision, and event do we encounter something of the sort of a ground or Archimedean point. And of course, fidelity is always "optional," never necessary. It consists in an ungrounded decision (a decision for the truth-event), which is grounded only on undecidability and uncertainty (Ee 68). As a result, there always remains the possibility of *treason*—of non-continuation.

The Grace of Contingency

Badiou's key concepts—fidelity, truth, infinity, universality—seem to give to his philosophy a somewhat Christian ring. Is there a secret, or not-so-secret, Christian model, upon which Badiou's atheistic philosophy relies to some extent? His little book on Saint Paul and the foundation of universalism seems to point in this direction. Badiou, as a matter of fact, dates the birth of Western universalism (to which Badiou himself still subscribes) to early Christianity. While it is not an original idea to associate universalism with Christianity, Badiou gives it an interesting twist by retracing the foundational moment of universalism to the Pauline intervention—and it should not surprise us that, from Badiou's point of view, Paul in many ways had a similar role for Christianity that Lenin had for Bolshevism. This intervention consists in Paul's "emancipation" of Christianity from all particular or "communitarian" traditions of both Jews and Gentiles. (For instance, he spoke out against circumcision as a rite by which a particularist link would be retained between Christianity and the Jewish religion; such particularist link, in turn, would exclude the non-circumcised Gentiles from Christian universality). The Pauline universality is empty in the sense of being beyond the level of cultural or religious particularisms and social differences. Every particularity can constitute a potential stumbling-block, as true universality must be *for all*—which is the maxim of universalism: "The One is only insofar as it is for all: such is the maxim of universality when it has its root in the event" (SPe 76).

As Badiou maintains, the source of such "empty universality"—since it is not a certain particularity[42]—can only be evental. In other words, in Badiou there is a necessary co-belonging of the One, of universality and singularity, since the correlate of an event can never be a certain particularity, it must always be the universal (in Paul, all of humanity including former Jews and Gentiles) and the singular of the event. In Paul's case, the event consists in nothing other than Christ's death and resurrection.[43] Once more Badiou detects a certain similarity between the exemplary modern model of an event—the revolution—and the Pauline model: The resurrection of Christ in its evental aspects ("Christ is, in himself and for himself, *what happens to us*" [SPe 48]) has *the same structure as modern revolutions*: it is a political truth procedure ("a self-sufficient sequence of political truth" [48]), which disrupts the previous discursive regime. It is an event in the strict Badiouian sense of the term and, as such, belongs not to the realm of the particular, but to the realm of the singular-universal. For this reason, the universal-singular event of Christ is of a completely different order than the *historical person* by the name of Jesus, who belongs entirely to the realm of the particular:

> For Paul, the event is certainly not the biography, teachings, recounting of miracles, aphorisms with a double meaning, of a particular individual: to wit, Jesus. ... What the particular individual named Jesus said and did is only the contingent material seized upon by the event in view of an entirely different destiny. In this sense, Jesus is neither a master nor an example. He is the name for what happens to us universally. (SPe 60)

The imperative of the event eclipses all circumstantial elements of the situation. Paul does not refer to the life and miracles of Jesus, not even to the time-bound "contents" of his teachings—all that counts for Paul is the event itself, that is, Christ's death and resurrection; "The rest, all the rest, is of no real importance. Let us go further: the rest (what Jesus said and did) *is not what is real in conviction, but obstructs, or even falsifies* it" (SPe 33). An event never draws its force from its impressive miraculousness. It does not "convince," in other words, because it is glorified or elevated to the mystical level of the ineffable (called by Badiou the "discourse of non-discourse"). Since such fascination of the unsayable would be an indicator of obscurantism rather than truth, it bars or masks the event rather than disclosing it. It draws its force only from the *declaration* of a truth by which the militants *subjectivize* themselves vis-à-vis that event: "Genuine subjectivation has as its material evidence the *public declaration* of the event by its name …. It is of the essence of faith to publicly declare itself. Truth is either militant or it is not" (SPe 88). So the only force of such a declaration lies *in the declaration itself*, not in anything "beyond" or "outside" itself: there is no source of machinations behind the scene, from which the declaration could be supported. The declaration of a truth-event is not in need of a David Copperfield, nor is it in need of a Meister Eckhart: "The declaration will have no other force than the one it declares and will not presume to convince through the appeal of prophetic reckoning, of the miraculous exception, or of the ineffable personal revelation" (SPe 53).

The truth-event of Christ and its relation to the Christian subject thus once more exemplifies the retroactive structure of such a declaration: the Christian subject does not exist before the event of Christ's resurrection is declared. To put it differently, the declaration of the event by the subject is logically prior to and constitutive of the subject itself. Truth, then, is entirely *subjective* in that it only consists in the declaration of the subject's conviction with respect to the event. No objectivity of the law, of customs, of the "state of the situation" touches on the nature of truth: "A truth is of itself indifferent to the state of the situation, to the Roman State for example" (SPe 15). It has to be subtracted from the sub-sets describing that state, which implies that the respective subjectivity stands at a necessary distance—corresponding to the subtraction—from the state. But what exactly is the nature of the *relation* between subject and event? Since truth is not a "passive" illumination, but an "active" and ongoing *process* of declaration, the category of *fidelity* becomes crucial. It describes, as it were, the *mode of relation* between subject and event (and it is noticeable that this constitutes an *ethical* mode). Badiou's own translation of the three central notions of Christian "faith" bears on the category of fidelity: the notion of *pistis* is translated by him as conviction (and not only faith, as it is usually translated), the notion of *agape* is translated as love[44] (not charity), and *helpis* (generally translated as hope) is now framed by Badiou as certitude.[45] The Christian categories are thus modernized and, to a certain extent, politicized by Badiou.

Yet the most spectacular modernization of a Pauline category is to be found in the post-foundational re-framing of "grace" as a figure of contingency. The event (of Christ's death and resurrection) *is grace*—it is not foreseeable nor calculable, and it cannot be subject to proof. The phenomenon of grace therefore derives directly from the *incalculability* of the event: "For Paul, the event has not come to prove something; it is pure beginning. Christ's resurrection is neither an argument nor an accomplishment. There is no proof of the event; nor is the event a proof" (SPe 49). The event does not prove anything nor can it be proven in turn (it can only be axiomatically declared), since it is of the order of *the incalculable*: "Christ is precisely incalculable" (50). So, if it cannot be calculated, it must have the nature of a gift.[46] It is then a matter of grace whether or not we are touched by an event. Subjects are constituted by the eventual grace:

> The pure event is reducible to this: Jesus dies on the cross and is resurrected. This event is "grace" (*kharis*). Thus, it is neither a bequest, nor a tradition, nor a teaching. It is supernumerary relative to all this and presents itself as pure givenness. As subject to the ordeal of the real, we are henceforth constituted by eventual grace. (SPe 63)

Badiou calls for a *materialism of grace* based on the event (which is called by Badiou "notre matérialisme de la grâce" [SPe 85]). And if we understand "grace" as a figure of contingency, he calls for nothing other than *a materialism of contingency*.[47] So, what Badiou says about one of Paul's main teachings could equally be said about the post-foundational exigency of contingency: "We are no longer under the rule of law, but of grace" (74). We no longer live under the law, we are subjected to contingency. Law, according to Badiou, is always predicative, particular, and partial, and it always belongs to the order of the state (by which, as we saw, Badiou understands that which denominates and controls the parts of a given situation), while the eventual truth is beyond number, predicate, and control (80).[48] Grace, on the other hand, "is the opposite of law" (77).[49] It is a *post*-foundational category that subverts the foundations of the law and the state. Yet it is far from being entirely *anti*-foundational. He is not at all interested in erasing all figures of foundation. On the other hand, however, it would be misleading to call his theory, as is sometimes done (even by himself), foundational: a ground is maintained but it is the ground of contingency. For Badiou, a subject has to be *founded* indeed, but it is founded upon *grace*, that is to say, upon contingency: "this foundation binds itself to that which is declared in a radical contingency" (77).[50]

Evil as a Figure of Foundationalism

If it is true that Badiou's philosophy secretly relies on the Christian paradigm as its model (or one of its models), one can expect to find a conceptual role for what is in Christianity the function of *evil*. And I submit that while grace is constructed as a figure of contingency, *evil* in Badiou is in fact presented as a figure of essentialism and foundationalism. Evil is, in our own terms, the attempt at *grounding the ungroundable*. This claim can easily be substantiated, if we remember the way in which Badiou's post-foundationalism is systematically constructed. The place from which the event occurs is the place of the void of a given situation. What serves, in Badiou's system, as the absent ground of a situation is hence conceptualized by him according to the figure of the *void*.[51] Together with the event, this grounding void is *named*. The event that, for instance, Karl Marx signifies for political theory consists in his naming of the proletariat as the foundational yet disavowed void of bourgeois society ("For the proletariat—being entirely dispossessed, and absent from the political stage—is that around which is organized the complacent plenitude established by the rule of those who possess" [Ee 69]). So every situation is founded upon something that it excludes: the void.

This is where evil may enter the scene: *terror* (and what Badiou calls the *simulacrum* of a truth-procedure) occurs where it is not the void of a situation that is convoked by an event, but the *plenitude* of that situation. The Nazis for instance, by mis-naming their absolute community as a national-socialist "revolution," presented the void of the previous situation as plenitude. In such case, the void is filled with a substance (the simulacrum of an "event-substance"), let's say the substance of the totality of a people. The result is a closed particularity of, for instance, "the Germans" or "the Aryans." To remain faithful to such a *simulacrum* will eventually lead to war or massacre. So one can speak about a simulacrum of the truth-event, if what is convoked is "not the void but the plenum." If, in such fashion, *substance* is put on the political agenda, a given community will become closed and "always approaches this kind of racial, biological, or territorial conception"[52] of the plenum. In the words of his commentator Jean-Jacques Lecercle: "If the celebrated 'event' is not a hole in the situation but an already existing (and discernible, and nameable) aspect of it, we have not a process of truth but a *simulacrum* of truth."[53]

Here, Badiou introduces into his system a term that is complementary to the void, calling it the "unnamable point" of a situation. While the disavowed void *must be named, if an event is to occur*, the "unnamable point," as one might suspect, is precisely that which must *not* be named in a situation. Every truth procedure implies such a "limit case," a point that must remain without name. Where the truth-procedure of politics is concerned, Badiou argues that the unnamable point is "community" in a substantialized sense: "In order for there to be emancipatory politics, it is absolutely necessary that the substantiality of the community remain unnamable. ... To every generic procedure I attach a limit, a term I call its 'unnamable point.' More and more, I am tempted to think that in emancipatory politics the community in a racial or biological sense is strictly an unnamable point. In order for politics to remain emancipatory, the community must not be named as such."[54] The unnamable of a truth-procedure relates to the Real in being the *symbol* of that which must escape symbolization. Yet, the unnamable should not be confused with the Kantian thing-in-itself, as it is, in principle, communicable (it does not constitute a limit to communication as such); rather, it is the *symbol* of the pure Real of the situation. And, as Badiou makes clear, in the case of politics, it is the substantial community or the collective that is the unnamable, since every attempt at politically naming the community leads into disastrous evil.[55] This has implications for the notion of truth, which must never assume total control over a given situation. Truth is *non-total* in that it must respect the unnamable point:

> In connection with the unnamable, evil takes the form of the idea that a truth can be total, that a truth is not just a subset of the situation but can

englobe the entire situation, ignoring the points that must remain unnamable. When a truth is forced beyond its unnamable point, the consequences are necessarily ruinous, even criminal. ... In seizing truths, philosophy may come to consider the sole, synthetic source of all possible truth. Once it dominates, directs, or subsumes, it can constrain truths to make claims to totality, breaking their limits, smashing their unnamable points. When philosophy articulates its seizing of truths in the form of identity or fusion, it exposes us to disaster.[56]

Critique and Conclusion

By *both insisting* on a notion of ground or truth *and simultaneously detotalizing* it, Badiou definitely locates himself within the ambit of post- rather than anti-foundational theories (not to mention foundationalist theories). His "philosophy of politics," however, leaves open a couple of troubling questions. It will not be possible within the remaining space of this article to discuss these questions *in extenso*, which is why I will restrict myself to just raising one or two, thus opening a space, hopefully, for further debate.

Above all, one might wonder whether the Badiouian politics of the immediate and unconditional can still reasonably be called a politics—or whether one should not rather speak about an *ethics* in the first place. To establish a whole political theory around the notion of *fidelity*, as he does in his *Ethics* and his *Saint Paul*, privileges an ethical perspective on politics. Thus, political action becomes an ethical, even quasi-religious effort at *remaining faithful* to a specific event through one's thinking and acting. In that way, politics—but not only politics; also science, love, and art—is subordinated to the overarching imperative to *continue!* whereby ethics (and not mathematics or set theory) silently assumes the role of a *prima philosophia*. Surprisingly then, if this is the case, Badiou's small book on ethics will turn into the cornerstone of his whole "system." Be this as it may, it certainly has consequences for our view of politics, for a rigorous and uncompromising ethics of the unconditional is entirely at odds with our political reality. By grounding his political theory on the unconditional (the "real"), Badiou steps out of the Machiavellian moment of the *conditioned*, that is, of power and strategy. But how shall we imagine a purely "ontological" politics of the real, completely emptied of any "ontic" content or context of political reality? To be sure, Badiou will always maintain that every politics occurs in a specific situation, but this implies that politics will always take place on an uneven "ontic" terrain and not only in relation (of "fidelity") to a truth-event. In other words, it does not take place on the vertical axis between the militant subject and the event alone, but also on a horizontal axis, that is, between a multiplicity of struggling actors (or subjects), all placed in different positions on an uneven, non-transparent, and power-ridden terrain. If this is the case, politics will always be tainted by compromise, strategy, and a necessary political realism in the Machiavellian rather than the Lacanian sense. In politics, to put it in the language of political science—which surely remains foreign to Badiou, but here at least draws on an expression of Badiou's early master Sartre—we will always be confronted with a "dirty hands" problem. In Badiou, however, we will search in vain for a theorization of actual "ontic" politics. He does not tell us how we are supposed to enact a "politics of truth" on an always uneven and compromising terrain. Since in the so-called real world, politics cannot simply be about fidelity—as this would imply the exclusion of any dimension of strategy—one could argue that there is a significant danger that such expulsion of the strategic might very well lead to an expulsion of politics *per se* in favor of the most radical form of *Gesinnungsethik*.[57]

Isn't there a danger that such *ethical* "politics" will eventually lead to a moralizing and self-righteous attitude, since it does not acknowledge the dirty hands problem (the fact that one's own politics will always be less than pure, less than perfect, less than ethical)? Wouldn't such ethicization of politics prove to be politically disabling? From a more realistic point of view regarding politics—for instance from Laclau and Mouffe's Gramscian (and in this sense Machiavellian) point of view[58]—one would arrive at the very different conclusion that there can be no such thing as a pure "politics of the real" (at most there could be an ethics of the real, while politics always takes place on the level of reality), nor can there be, as Badiou seems to suggest, a politics of a *singular universal*. In the latter case, once more, the universal would be emptied of all particular content, but this again is only conceivable if we remain on a purely "ontological" level. As soon as we take into account the necessity of *ontically* actualizing such politics, we will find that politics can only consist of a constant *negotiation* between the particular and the universal, rather than of the incantation of a seemingly pure universality.[59]

Interestingly, Badiou is not the only one among the left Heideggerians who conceives politics in ethical terms. In fact, this is one of the most striking "family resemblances" among them (with Laclau/Mouffe and Claude Lefort as noticeable exceptions). And it constitutes a point of convergence between Badiou and his rivals, the deconstructive "modern sophists," including Derrida and Nancy/Lacoue-Labarthe. With them he shares a tendency to *ethicize* politics, which makes both paradigms seem rather remote sometimes from the our actually existing political world of compromise and alliance-building. The difference between both paradigms has to be located on another plane though: while in the Judeo-messianic model of Derrida the event is an event-to-come, in Badiou's Christian messianism the event *has already occurred*, and while we now wait for it to return it essentially remains an event of the past. Or, to be more precise, the event to which Badiou's militant subject pledges allegiance is one that *will have occurred in the past* as soon as the subject declares his (in Badiou always *his*) fidelity to it. One might say that this difference is negligible, as in both cases—the case of deconstruction that draws on the model of Jewish messianism, and the Lacanian Badiou drawing on a model of Christian messianism—the event will anyway have to be actualized *in the present*. However, the difference will not only be one of philosophical "style" or "temperament" since in practice too it might make a difference whether I orient myself towards the always receding horizon of an event-to-come or to a potentially namable event of the past. In the latter case, my actions may indeed be directed by a firm fidelity and certainty (eventually verging on dogmatism), while in the former—where the very coming of the event remains uncertain—a more cautious or skeptical attitude may be more likely. Strikingly, however, deconstructivists and Lacanians alike tend to frame our relation towards the event in exclusively ethical terms, that is, in terms of either an infinite *responsibility* towards the other-as-other, respecting the promise of an event-to-come, or an infinite *fidelity*.

Of course, there is no point in playing the arbitrator, precisely *because* in order to arrive at a political theory proper one would have to leave the very terrain of ethics, thus in a certain respect stepping outside the plane of either theoretical paradigm. I nevertheless would like to underline the great benefit of Badiou's stance: by radicalizing most post-foundational concepts (event, contingency, etc.), which constitute the family resemblances of left Heideggerianism, he sharpens our view and presents us with a clear and distinct version that, in this respect, is without comparison. His work could thus be understood as a thought experiment in which post-foundationalism is stressed to the extreme—and yet I hold that Badiou, despite all "serious coquetry" with Platonism and Saint Paul, does not at any point cross the line towards foundationalism and essentialism. ∎

....

1   Alain Badiou, "Being by Numbers," *Artforum International* 33, no. 2 (October 1994): 85.
2   It might perhaps come as a surprise that Badiou is located within the Heideggerian camp, as most often he is presented and presents himself as a sort of anti-Heideggerian. As I hope some of the Heideggerian themes in Badiou will become apparent through the course of this essay, may it suffice to point out the most obvious line of filiation: Badiou's choice to entitle his magnum opus *Being and Event* (*L'être et l'événement*) can clearly be understood as a reference to his early mentor, Jean-Paul Sartre, and his major work, *Being and Nothingness*. Yet Sartre himself, who belonged to the first generation of French Heideggerians, was of course alluding to Heidegger's *Being and Time*. It goes without saying that neither in the case of Sartre nor in the case of Badiou is it an arbitrary choice. What remains at or always—to use a Lacanian phrase—returns to its place in this series of titles is *Being*, while the second term in the respective title then indicates the very perspective through which being (or be-ing) is approached. In Badiou's case, it is the notion of event that in itself bears a deeply Heideggerian mark.
3   I'm well aware of the fact that the "family" metaphor is highly problematic. If I retain it, I do so because I would like to stress the aspect of "family resemblances." Even as these resemblances are presented here in comparative fashion, to stress their nature as resemblances implies underlining that they do *not* constitute *identical* features. What is more, the notion of family resemblances allows us to avoid the rather too rigid concept of "paradigm" since *post*-foundationalism, rather than constituting a paradigm of its own—a counter-paradigm vis-à-vis foundationalism—emerges in the fissures of the collapsing paradigm of foundationalism.
4   Peter Hallward, "Generic Sovereignty: The Philosophy of Alain Badiou," *Angelaki* 3, no. 3 (1998): 88.
5   Jean-Jacques Lecercle, "Cantor, Lacan, Mao, Beckett, *même combat*: The Philosophy of Alain Badiou," *Radical Philosophy* 93 (January/February 1999): 7.
6   Badiou, "Being by Numbers," 87.

7   [For a list of Badiou's principal texts and their corresponding abbreviations, see the introduction to this issue.—Ed.]
8   In Badiou's words: "The real plurality is the plurality of politics in the plural [*des politiques*], the plurality of opinions is only the referent of a particular politics (parliamentarism). The essence of politics [*la politique*] is not the plurality of opinions. It is the prescription of a possibility which breaks with what is there." To arrive at this point of rupture does not necessarily exclude debate and "public discussion," but Badiou insists that these are not the only forms of intervention: "Still more important are the declarations, the interventions and the organizations" (AM 34).
9   One can clearly see how political questions are linked to Badiou's general ontology according to which sub-sets are categorized by the state of the situation as elements belonging to this situation. The multiplicity of a set is thus *counted as One* by the state.
10 Badiou is opposed to political representation and delegation of political activity to parties—no matter whether one thinks about a single party or a plurality of parties, it amounts to "parliamentary 'representation,' where the basic protocol is elections and where the place is the system of the State-parties (in the plural) as opposed to the Party-state (in the singular)" (DO 35). When politics is delegated to an order comprising a plurality of parties, Badiou speaks about "capitalo-parliamentarism."
11 What resulted from the dissolution of State-Marxism was a capitalist "Marxism without proletariat" (DO 29).
12 And it is only on the premise of the state's ruin (in the ruins, as it were, of the criminal state of "actually existing" socialism, for instance) that the history of politics—far from ending with the collapse of the Eastern-European regimes—can *commence*: "The ruin of every statist presentation of truth opens that commencement. Everything has to be invented" (DO 56). What also follows for Badiou is that the category of *rights* is not a properly political category but a category of the state. Rights have nothing to do with truth in Badiou's sense, as truth can never be subsumed under a procedural set of rules.
13 Thus, Badiou holds with respect to the work of his collaborator Sylvain Lazarus—but this also describes his own stance: "Since every politics is a singularity, there will not be a definition of politics [*de la politique*]. Every definition relates politics to something other than itself (most often, in fact, to the State), and desingularizes it by way of historicizing it" (AM 56).
14 Badiou ascribes the power of Heideggerian thought to his "suturing" of philosophy to the poem without, however, subscribing to it. (For Badiou, our own epoch needs to "de-suture" philosophy from the poem.) Yet the same move allowed Heidegger to position poetry against positivistic objectification: "The great force of Heidegger consists in having crossed a properly philosophical critique of positivistic objectivity, of the deployment of technology and the forgetfulness regarding the thinking of being, with a profound understanding of what is at stake, through these very questions, in the poem." Alain Badiou, "L'entretien de Bruxelles," *Les temps modernes* 526 (May 1990): 4.
15 Badiou also finds a more conventional notion of technology in Heidegger. While Badiou agrees that we have arrived at "a sort of technological artificialization of the total system of our universe" ("L'entretien," 4), unlike Heidegger in certain moments, he is not prepared to indulge himself in any reactionary or sentimental feelings regarding pre-modern social bonds. What Badiou retains is the Heideggerian distinction between truth and knowledge ("One thus has to distinguish the regime of knowledge from that of truths, herein I agree, and this is a Heideggerian theme" [ibid., 10]), which then is transformed into the Lacanian notion of an *unsymbolizable real* as that which is *subtracted* from language and knowledge.

16 Badiou, "L'entretien," 17.
17 Again, the existence of more than one party in democratic states does not, for Badiou, constitute a significant difference between democracy and totalitarianism. What counts is that today's democracies are centered around a policy of putting into work economic programs and plans around which the mere *appearance* of parliamentary conflicts is structured. One can speak about "mere appearance" because these conflicting programs converge in their acceptance of apparent economic necessities.
18 The tense which political organization implies always comprises the double dimension of its anteriority and its future. It is the intervention of thinking/acting which retroactively—and à propos an event—politicizes a given situation.
19 A fact is something that is already given, which is why it does not have to be retroactively organized. Police builds on the given order and amplifies its facts (PP 96).
20 "Subtraction" is Badiou's *terminus technicus*: "The point where thinking subtracts itself from the State, thus inscribing that subtraction into being, constitutes the very real of a politics [*d'une politique*]" (DO 57).
21 Today it is political economy which has established itself as the ruling fiction of the political.
22 To the extent that politics only emerges in the moment of exception (PP 19), one can suspect a certain structural parallel to Schmitt's argument as to the *Ausnahmezustand*—a parallel Badiou himself would perhaps not concede, even as it would position him close to another, more openly left-Heideggerian thinker: Giorgio Agamben.
23 See also PP 76–77.
24 This, as we will see, has ethical implications, for it is the ethics of a truth which will be defined by Badiou as "*that which lends consistency to the presence of someone in the composition of the subject induced by the process of this truth*" (Ee 44).
25 See AM 156. The thought of politics is universal in being *collective*, that is to say, in being the thought of *all*. This is what distinguishes the generic procedure of politics from the other three generic procedures: a mathematician only needs another mathematician to prove or disprove his/her demonstration, love has to assume only two, and the artist does not in actual fact need anybody. Therefore these truth procedures are aristocratic, according to Badiou.
26 This provocative function allows for politics to measure the power of the state, whose excess otherwise remains hidden and immeasurable (AM 159).
27 Peter Hallward, "Badiou's Politics: Equality and Justice," *Culture Machine* 4 (2002), http://culturemachine.tees.ac.uk/Cmach/Backissues/j004/Articles/hallward.htm.
28 Alain Badiou, "Philosophy and Politics," *Radical Philosophy* 96 (July/August 1999): 29.
29 Ibid.
30 This was the case in the former socialist states: they tried to reify and incorporate justice into a political program. Only through their collapse—or in the disruptive event of their collapse—were justice and equality "freed" from such incorporation: "But these terrorist states were the incarnation of the ultimate fiction of a justice endowed with the solidity of a body; of a justice which had the form of a governmental program. The collapse attests to the absurdity of such a representation. It frees justice and equality from any fictive incorporation. It restores them to their Being, both volatile and obstinate, of thought acting from and in direction of a collective seized by its truth." Ibid., 32.
31 Ibid., 31.
32 Ibid., 32.
33 Badiou, "L'entretien," 24.
34 Badiou, "Philosophy and Politics," 30.

35 Ibid., 32.
36 Ibid., 30.
37 Ibid., 31. In other words, justice as being based on the maxim of equality, is a form of *seizure* (that is, naming) of the event, and thus belongs entirely to the register of thinking/acting: "In effect, justice, which seizes the latent axiom of a political subject, designates necessarily not what must be, but what is. The equalitarian axiom is present in political statements, or it is not present. And by consequence, we are within justice, or we are not. Which also means: the political exists, in the sense that philosophy encounters its thought within it, or it does not. But if it does, and we relate to it immanently, we are within justice." Ibid., 30.
38 It is most likely that Badiou himself would not subscribe to this account, as for him there is no such thing as a general *ethics*, there can always only be an *ethics-of*: "Ethics does not exist. There is only the *ethic-of* (of politics, of love, of science, of art)" (Ee 28). However, seen from a point of view outside Badiou's system, one can detect a generalized ethics not only as a motivating force, but also as the main operational principle behind most of Badiou's concepts or the linking of these concepts—so that I would submit, and I will elaborate on this in the conclusion to this investigation, that Badiou's politics is actually *an ethics*.
39 Such ethics of the real applies of course to all four generic truth-procedures: "The possibility of the impossible, which is exposed by every loving encounter, every scientific re-foundation, every artistic invention, and every sequence of emancipatory politics, is the sole principle … of an ethics of truths" (Ee 39).
40 The imperative implies certain "capacities": One has to be able to discern and distinguish a true event from a simulacrum; one has to be courageous enough not to give in to the status quo and "stop continuing"; and one has to do this with certain reserve—for otherwise one might be carried away towards the extremes of totality. "The ethics combines, then, under the imperative to 'Keep going!' resources of discernment (do not fall for simulacra), of courage (do not give up), and of moderation [*réserve*] (do not get carried away to the extremes of Totality)" (Ee 91).
41 Insofar as the event is an event of *interruption*, one of the versions of the Badiou's categorical imperative reads as follows: "Do all that you can to persevere in that which exceeds your perseverance. Persevere in the interruption. Seize in your being that which has seized and broken you" (Ee 47). To give consistency to the event implies giving consistency to and persevering within the rupture. In other words: Never break with the rupture! (Such a *break* with the rupture would give way to the unhindered continuation of the previous situation and the regime of opinions.)
42 Herein, as we will see, Badiou's system differs significantly from the model of politics proposed by Ernesto Laclau, where every universality is hegemonized by (and therefore based on) a certain particularity. See Ernesto Laclau, *Emancipation(s)* (London and New York: Verso, 1996).
43 Badiou will later distinguish between death (circumscribing the eventual *site* still belonging to the situation) and resurrection (describing the event itself) as two distinct functions. Their relation or linking together, however, is entirely contingent: "For death is an operation in the situation, an operation that immanentizes the eventual site, while resurrection is the event itself …. They are two distinct functions, whose articulation contains no necessity. For the event's sudden emergence never follows from the existence of an eventual site" (SPe 70–71). Badiou eventually defines the event of resurrection as an affirmative subtraction from death.
44 According to Badiou, "love" is Paul's name for fidelity vis-à-vis the event of Christ's resur-

45 It should be noted that there can be no degrees of eventness nor can there be any degrees of truth or faith/fidelity. This goes for Badiou as it goes for his "master" St. Paul: "For him (and we shall grant him this point), a truth procedure does not comprise degrees" (SPe 21).
46 À propos the event, Badiou speaks about a "a supernumerary givenness and incalculable grace" (SPe 65).
47 A materialism, that is, which is based on the event: "Or let us posit that it is incumbent upon us to found a materialism of grace …" (SPe 66).
48 I would like to point out that in the liberal theory of politics, according to Badiou, law is foundational: "The law is restored as that by which philosophy must secure the foundation" (PP 50).
49 To be precise, Badiou counterposes the figure of ground and the figure of contingency within *two* pairs of concepts so that, in the Pauline lexicon, law (*nomos*) is contrasted with grace (*charis*), and work (*ergon*) is contrasted with faith (*pistis*).
50 This, of course, has implications for Badiou's notion of universalism. There can only be a true universality if it is founded upon contingency, the contingency of the event: "Universality is organically bound to the contingency of what happens to us, which is the senseless superabundance of grace" (SPe 81). Out of the contingency of the event, its abundance, multiplicity arises: "It is the event alone, as illegal contingency, which causes a multiplicity in excess of itself to come forth …" (81). It is a universalism of excessive *multiplicity*: "The profound ontological thesis here is that universalism supposes one be able to think the multiple not as a part, but as an excess of itself, as that which is out of place, as a nomadism of gratuitousness. … What is called 'grace' is the capacity of a postevental multiplicity to exceed its own limit, a limit that has a commandment of the law as its dead cipher" (78).
51 In Badiou's words: "What does this mean? It means that at the heart of every situation, as the foundation of its being, there is a 'situated' void, around which is organized the plenitude (or the stable multiples) of the situation in question" (Ee 68).
52 Badiou, "Being by Numbers," 124.
53 Lecercle, "Cantor," 9.
54 Badiou, "Being by Numbers," 123.
55 Terror, as Lecercle comments, "occurs when the supplementary 'point of exception' of truth is taken as all-embracing, when the name of the event claims to name not a hole in the situation but the whole of it, when in the name of truth, by nature singular and incoherent, a 'subject' (the Marxist-Leninist party) forcibly coheres the situation from the excentric point: then terror, as we know, does reign" ("Cantor," 9–10).
56 Badiou, "Being by Numbers," 124.
57 One might argue that the ethical moment of the unconditional and the political moment of the conditioned are not mutually exclusive. Even as one might concede this, it still remains clear that Badiou does not—and perhaps cannot, given his model—theorize the very *nature of the relation* between the ontological and ontic (in fact, there is no "relation": the event strikes as lightning), nor does he provide us with any theory regarding the very workings of politics on the ontic level. The result is that "real politics" is confined to very "rare moments"—an aspect which might prove politically disabling under more ordinary conditions. Not everybody happens to walk a road to Damascus.
58 Ernesto Laclau and Chantal Mouffe, *Hegemony and Socialist Strategy* (London and New York: Verso, 1985).
59 For a theorization of universalism in its relation to particularism, see Laclau, *Emancipation(s)*.

lacanian ink 24/25

Eroticism

By rejecting the assertion of identities associated with cultural studies *lacanian ink* outlines a new philosophical universalism.

Jacques-Alain Miller
Introduction to the Erotics of Time
Gérard Wajcman
The Birth of the Intimate (II)
Marie-Hélène Brousse
A Sublimation at Risk of Psychoanalysis
Massimo Recalcati
The Anorexic Passion for the Mirror
Alain Badiou
Manifesto of Affirmationism
Stuart Schneiderman
The Boy Who Cried Wolf
Slavoj Zizek
The Politics of *Jouissance*
Odradek as a Political Category
Cathy Lebowitz interviews Josefina Ayerza
Jane and Louise Wilson

Jacques Lacan is Lacan Dot Com
http://www.lacan.com
Single issue: $ 20.00
Subscriptions: http://www.lacan.com/form.htm
email: lacink@lacan.com

"I Love (u)":
Badiou on Love, Logic, and Truth

Lindsey Hair

Of each of the four areas identified by philosopher Alain Badiou as allowing a truth procedure to take place—namely, politics, art, mathematics, and love—it is the amorous procedure that has been received with the most skepticism. In his decidedly unromantic speculations on the nature of love, he presents a series of concise mathematical formulae, devoid of all affect or desire, as a means of approaching what has traditionally been foreclosed from precise articulation, cast instead within the realms of poetic mysticism, or retained as a pure Ideal, and as such deemed incommensurable with any mode of expression within the finite, temporal lifeworld. Amused by the reaction such an approach has generated, Badiou quotes one French broadcaster's reproach that it was "intolerable that one would associate austere formulas with the marvelous experience of love."[1] However, it is precisely the question as to how such an experience is brought to representation that leads Badiou to suggest that set-theory, as a methodology of inscribing being *as* being, might nevertheless provide a more rigorous means of delineating exactly which aspects of the encounter between a couple, or as he styles it, the event, might properly be attributed to love, and which remain within the order of desire and narcissistic projection. Given that love is, indeed, an overwhelming experience, it demands a clear-headed rigor to examine the deficiencies of traditional theorizations, and to strip away those elements that make up the context, but do not belong to the same order of being as love proper.

Love as an event hinges upon a contingent encounter between two people, following which there is the naming of this event, or the declaration of love, which joins them within the order of discourse ("I love you"), and the ensuing fidelity to the truth procedure initiated by the amorous encounter: the daily mode in which the pair live out their lives in a sustained interrogation of what the declaration means, both in terms of their own (inter)subjectivities and their manner of experiencing the world. While this might seem a reiteration of more conventional motifs, Badiou reconceptualizes the notion of the traditional "couple" as the "Two," which comprises "one position and another position," nominally designated as "male" and "female," although not biologically gendered. The Two draws on a Platonic conception of number insofar as it is noniterative—the two positions are not simply added together to form a compound concept; rather, the Two is a singular ideal form that is not given to knowledge within the finite realm of the everyday, but is generated piecemeal by the truth procedure undertaken by the amorous pair, such that "under the post-eventual condition that there were Two,"[2] the infinite aspect of love is brought within the compass of representation as what *will have been the case*. In this manner, Badiou upholds the Platonic notion of love as an Ideal, and does not seek to delimit it within the confines of representation; yet given the impossibility of bringing the event to knowledge, he seeks rigorously to delineate *how* we nevertheless experience love within our temporal confines while maintaining the infinity proper to it. Thus, far from compromising the "marvelous experience," the questions Badiou pursues are, first, given the incommensurability of the finite world and the ideal realm of the truth procedure, how is the experience of love nevertheless possible? and second, if, as Lacan suggests "there is no sexual relation," or to state this differently, the two positions of male and female are disjunct, such that their (separate) experiences of the world are likewise inflected according to the laws of sexuation, what then is the nature of the rapport that binds them?

In setting out to answer these questions, Badiou first dispenses with the conventional notions of love, dismissing the fusional concept which, from Aristophanes' fable through to the modern-day search for a soul-mate, proposes the union of the couple as a means of achieving completeness, and its inversion—the contemporary valorization of "difference" which runs the risk, Badiou claims, of fetishizing Otherness. The pessimistic poststructuralist notion that love is a mode of self-deception, serving as a screen to mask the inevitable *lack* of sexual relation is similarly rejected, despite Badiou's incorporation of Lacanian psychoanalytic theory from which this conception is drawn. Indeed, Badiou rejects the traditional notion of love as "relation," arguing that love has little to do with supplying a lack in the other, but can more properly be thought as a "production of truth," jointly undertaken. The experience of love does not produce knowledge of love, nor is it decipherable by all the affects and vagaries attributable to desire—which, indeed, are more properly the scope of the preceding theories. Love, as a truth procedure, is that which punctures knowledge; thus although the experience (of love) itself structures the situation in which the Two operate, it is not given to be thought, nor is it expressed by the pathos of "passion, error, jealousy, sex, and death"—it is not locatable via affect. Thus, all the conventional tropes are of little relevance to a genuine exploration of the experience of love—precisely because love is subtracted from the representational field.

So why then is love a "generic truth procedure" and why should a mathematical operation—the formation of a generic infinite set—afford a more precise understanding of that which, according to Badiou's own definition, is foreclosed from knowledge? The technique of "forcing,"[3] as a means of interrogating that which is incommensurable with the governing order of knowledge (whether this is conceived as a fully constructed set universe, as in the mathematical framework from which the method is drawn or, transposed to psychoanalysis, the Lacanian Symbolic order), allows a flexibility that comprehends and respects the limits of knowledge while nevertheless providing the means of delineating certain aspects of that which insists beyond its boundaries. Since the axiomatic framework of set theory allows the inscription of being as being, it becomes a question of using the limits of these primitive axioms to pose questions as to the constitution of their own boundaries. Further, it allows us to locate aspects of being that, while constitutively foreclosed from representation, nevertheless play a vital role in structuring the situation they supplement.

Since for Lacan psychoanalysis locates love as outside knowledge, Badiou turns to the procedure of forcing to finesse those aspects of the relation that come to make up the fragmentary, finite part of the real of human experience, specifically because it designates a point of mediation between the infinity of the ideal and the imperfection of the lived reality upon which it relies in order to be brought into being. Badiou takes as his point of departure the common element of the rapport that binds the Two, figuring this as the opening of a generic, infinite set that is brought to representation piece by piece according to the questioning of the Two during their daily lives. This sustained interrogation Badiou casts as "fidelity" to the event.

The human subject provides the point of intersection between the infinite generic set (in this instance, "love") and his/her finite spatio-temporal situatedness. This link is performed by a function which he designates as "humanity"—a concept which has little to do with either the biological species (the "human animal") or a subjective/ideological construct: there is no "essence" of humanity prior to the production of truth procedures. Rather, the humanity function is invoked by the irruption of an event that catalyzes, or instigates, the multiple truth procedures which collectively comprise their compossible configuration within a specific time. In designating the humanity function $H(x)$, Badiou leaves open the question as to whether the subject convoked to being by a truth-in-process—the (x)—is already given to be called prior to his/her participation, or whether the participation itself "humanizes." What is evident is that the humanity function $H(x)$ "localizes" the truth procedure; i.e., it allows a portion of the infinite to be brought within the compass of the finite, such that each site of the event forms a potential opening onto the infinite, while providing the situated, finite anchor of a particular encounter—again reminding us that all interrogations of a generic set are partial. To this extent, "humanity" is a potential—or virtual—reservoir, capable of being convoked to being by each and any of the four generic procedures (politics, art, math, or love), and the function H serves as a knot that binds the different truths. It is important to understand that despite being localized, the truth itself remains addressed to all, and is "indifferent to all predicative partition of its support."[4]

In delineating the form of the Two, or the amorous couple, Badiou is careful to differentiate the amorous presentation from its Imaginary representation—the couple—which presupposes the inclusion of a third party or spectator who is excluded from the experience proper, and is therefore witness only to the resulting symbolization and the couple's involvement within the *state* of love or its representation within knowledge. To this end, he posits three axioms:

1 There are two positions of experience (or "There is one position and another position");
2 The two positions are absolutely disjunct;
3 There is no third position.[5]

Drawing on Lacan, Badiou upholds the lack of sexual relation and maintains that the two positions that constitute the Two are radically disjunct, and that their very experience within the shared truth procedure is likewise sexuated and hence differentiated. Given these assertions, it is necessary first to distinguish between (third party) *knowledge* of the couple that is circulated within the symbolic or imaginary realms, and the *experience* of love, which is proper to the Two, and as such outside representation; having established this, we will move on to discuss how the experience of love is predicated upon a rapport that is foundational despite the disjunction of sexuation.

The first distinction rests between love proper and the representational overlay of desire, which Badiou argues is a function of capital and whose influence dictates the imposition of an *artificial* differentiation mx and wx. This distinction has little to do with the being of the sexuated subjects, but is a gendering that operates purely within the order of representation, an "un-cover-up" that legislates the cultural staging of sex roles while obscuring the truth of the dis-conjunction of the sexes. Much as Lacan argues that sexuation is a law that is enjoined upon the subject, and which overwrites the precarious shiftings and uncertainties that characterize the sexual identity as it is present in the unconscious, forcing it, as the price for representation, to subscribe to an (impossible) norm, so too Badiou views the structuring of the consistent multiple,[6] or *state-of-the-situation*, as foreclosing the excess of the inconsistent multiple (what would be the domain of love) in order to preserve and privilege the dimension of desire in which the logic of capital is inscribed.

Love, as an event/encounter, is uniquely able to transgress the governance of the prevailing law of sexuation, remaining incommensurable with the order of representation—it is always "a-cosmic and illegal, refusing integration into any totality and signaling nothing. … [It] delivers no law, no form of mastery …" (SPe 42).[7] Desire, on the other hand, functions as an obfuscating lure that operates via the *law* of sexuation. Both Lacan and Badiou turn to a reading of St. Paul as a means of articulating the relation between the law and sin (or desire). Much as Freud suggests that the Oedipal prohibition is responsible for simultaneously summoning the law into being, and producing desire via the creation of the forbidden object, St. Paul's epistle likewise proposes that the law is retroactively responsible for creating sin—which Lacan then glosses as *das Ding*. To relate this to our discussion of love, we can take the symbolic construction of sex as a law which governs the state of the situation—the everyday context. Within this realm the imposition of the law creates the structure of desire that is commonly mistaken for love, but which remains within the order of representation (Lacan's Symbolic/Imaginary orders). And yet, despite the deceptive overlay of codified sexual difference imposed by the law of capital, there remains only one situation, and a *single* humanity function, which leads Badiou to propose that love allows the Two to nevertheless experience something of the *shared* ground that is concealed by the order of the count-for-one. Although they remain "one and another one," the inquiry reveals that it can be thought that "the situation is exactly as if there has been a One," leading Badiou to assert that "love is the guardian of the universality of the true."[8] Thus, the "amorous generic procedure" interrogates the hypothesis of the Two (while upholding the radical singularity of each of the sexuated positions) through a questioning of the void of their disjunction—a tracing of the space that, following the declaration of love, or the naming of the event, in-separates the two positions, at once marking the truth of the disjunction (bringing it within the realm of representation in the mode of the couple's being-in-the-world) and forming the real of the Two.

The impersonal subject of truth that bears the humanity function (x) is precisely a human animal that takes on the task of subjectivation, and this wager generates the excess element that Badiou links with immortality, and paradoxically "makes Man":

> "some-one" … is simultaneously *himself*, nothing other than himself, a multiple singularity recognizable among all others, and *in excess of himself*, because the uncertain course [*tracé aléatoire*] of fidelity *passes through him*, transfixes his singular body and inscribes him, from within time, in an instant of eternity. (Ee 45)

It is crucial to note that this subject is at a far remove from the gendered *identities* promoted by the logic of capital. In this respect, the encounter does not differentiate between hetero- and homo-sexual couples, nor does Badiou attempt to prescribe the nature of the attraction.

Badiou takes the inscribed structures of desire as his starting point for tracing how the rapport proper to love might be approached. Drawing directly on Lacan's *Seminar XX*, Badiou maintains that the sexual relation cannot be written. Lacan expresses this non-relation via a series of logical paradoxes which suggest that from the male position, the divided subject $\$$ "never deals with anything by way of a partner but *objet a* inscribed on the other side of the bar. He is unable to attain his sexual partner, who is the Other, except inasmuch as his partner is the cause of his desire. … [T]his is nothing other than fantasy."[9] From the side of "woman," whom Lacan claims is "not all," or occupies the structural position that resists universalization, there is a relation to the phallic function (the symbolic male function) which remains inaccessible to those on the male side of the graph, who accede to castration via what Lacan calls the "father function." From this reading of the sexual relation, it is apparent that sex fails to mediate between the two positions, as both sides of the disjunction relate to a function to which their partners have no direct access, despite it being inscribed within their fields.

Although Badiou's theorization remains consistent with Lacan's reading of male desire as predicated upon the *objet a*, which is located on the side of woman, he observes that the encounter is *guided* by the object, but exceeds it, since "it goes straight to that aspect of the object from which the subject draws its little bit of being."[10] Rather than simply figuring as an Imaginary lure, the *objet a* serves as a singularized representation of the desiring subject, insofar as it is the rema(i)nder of the being that was sacrificed in their accession to the Symbolic order. Subject to the laws of representation (or Badiou's law of the count-for-one), the (newly divided) subject relinquishes its claim to singularity at the price of being produced as a speaking, sexuated subject: "being" is forfeited for "signifying." In Lacanian theory, the notion of the *semblant* elaborates the ambiguous role played by the *objet a*. The Other is only ever reached through its attachment to the *objet a*, which lends it its "semblance of being," i.e., the other re-sembles/dis-sembles being insofar as s/he is recognized as bearing the *objet a*. The *objet a* is projected as a "trace" that marks the "being there" of the Other in which it is inscribed. However, since it figures the "little scrap of flesh" of the desiring subject which was sacrificed during the process of separation, rather than serving as a point of *mediation* between the subject and the other, the relation remains within the Imaginary. The failure to posit the being-there of the other to whom the object remains linked as signifier of this primordial attachment leads instead to the projection of an Imaginary figure ("*I'I*")[11] which Lacan suggests is often dressed as a self-image, or narcissistic *semblant*.

The failure of the sexual relation can be read directly through this mis-apprehension, as the object cause of desire is not the Other *per se*, but an aspect of him or her which bears a narcissistic relation to the desiring subject, and which is mistaken as being proper, rather than recognized as a signifier (S_1) or quilting point that bears a trace of the real, but ultimately functions as a screen, distancing the subject from a dangerous proximity to the mythical lost object and the unbearable *jouissance* associated with its recovery. Once again, the supposed point of conjunction with the Other is an encounter with the Same. Despite this, there remains, says Lacan, an intrinsic affinity between the *a* and its "envelope"—the Other as semblance of being is addressed through its endowment with the object cause of desire.

Badiou capitalizes upon this, arguing that the crucial difference is that the attraction *exceeds* the lure of the Imaginary object and draws its impetus from the being towards which it signals. Much as Lacan figures the *objet a* as the "void presupposed by a demand,"[12] or the gap between the material need and the affective component it bears, which fails to be understood or met, Badiou constructs a topology in which the limitation of desire (its narcissistic fascination with the Imaginary aspect of the object) nevertheless opens the space in which the being of the other might be accessed. The structure of desire is such that what one is aware of getting is never sufficient ("that is not it"), and yet, as with supplemental *jouissance* which lies beyond the structure of knowledge, some form of access to the real, or being, can take place, though only "by chance," and this is what Badiou would style an "event" or encounter. The very limitation itself can sometimes serve as the point of torsion that allows the supplementation of the Symbolic/Imaginary orders—the inscription of the limit point designates the topology of a "beyond" that is brought into being by the failure of access.

Badiou retains the narcissistic element as the catalyst of the encounter, and indeed suggests that there is no point at which the "one plus one" of the amorous relation actually meet, hence his insistence upon the disjunction of the sexes. And yet he qualifies this by adding "it is from the being of the subject [this time, the *desired* subject] that the object, as cause of desire, has the singularity of its presentation, and finally the charm of its appearance."[13] The declaration of love, which addresses the other as "you" directly (and not simply the object that s/he bears), is an acknowledgement that despite the object's function as lure, it is the *singularity* of its presentation that founds the amorous event, or to put this differently, it is the manner in which the object is proper to the subject that ultimately generates the attraction, since it speaks to the being that supports the object (i.e., that of the other) and not simply the projection of being that is inferred from the metonymy of the object. The secondary aspect proper to desire (the charm of its appearance) remains in play too, but the supplemental overlay suggests that even though on the imaginary level being is only mistaken and never actually accessed, the mode of presentation of the object opens a different relation to being that belongs to the other, and it is this dual topology that Badiou sets out to explicate in his careful examination of the nature of this disjunct relation.

It is the being of the desired subject that is primary in the encounter insofar as this being serves as support for the particular, or singularized, mode in which the object is brought to presentation, and while this being cannot be directly accessed by the other (who remains destined, on the imaginary level, to project a being-sameness), it nevertheless figures within the rapport as it is this singularity that marks the encounter as an event—or an amorous encounter—and not simply a generalized form of desire. Outlining the pre-given inscription of sexuated desire, and the fact that this entails a lack in coincidence where the object cause of desire is concerned, Lacan states that "[o]ne lack is superimposed upon the other. The dialectic of the objects of desire, insofar as it creates the link between the desire of the subject and the desire of the Other … this dialectic now passes through the fact that the desire is not replied to directly."[14] The fantasized fusional One, or the perfect symbiosis of Same/Other, fails to take account of the mismatched projections of man's "having" the phallus and woman's "being" the phallus, leading each partner essentially to relate to a part of him- or herself. And yet love is in excess of this masturbatory fantasy. Since the rapport of which Badiou speaks is uninscribable (or outside both symbolic and imaginary orders), it remains to delineate the "bit of being" that is drawn from the void of the eventual encounter.

As a starting point, Badiou remarks that it is evident that if a rapport is to exist between disjunct entities, it has to be "anti-symmetrical": "it contains some relation to itself, but such that this relation to itself cannot in any way be an identical relation to the other"[15]—it is not a relation of equivalence. In maintaining the radical disjunction of the sexes, it becomes necessary to introduce a common term to which both sides of the disjunction relate, but one that is essentially empty; thus, Badiou's "segregative thesis" formalizes this such that $[(t \leq M)$ and $(t \leq W)] \rightarrow t = 0$, where that which is common to each of the two positions M and W remains empty: $t = 0$. However, hypothesizing that the non-rapport nevertheless cannot be a pure disjunction, Badiou introduces a non-null term u as the "supposed local mediator of global non-rapport."[16] This element is related to the phantasmatic nature of the object, and while it is "not composed of nothing," it is "absolutely indeterminate, indescribable, uncomposable." This term punctures the non-rapport, becoming a "relational support," but because it is atomic and evades determination, nothing enters into relation with this additional term, or rather, it enters into relation with the void and is the connector via which the amorous subject draws his/her bit of being. Badiou expresses this as follows: $(u \leq M$ and $u \leq W) \rightarrow ([t \leq u] \rightarrow t = 0)$. Thus, both man and woman intersect with the term "u," which Badiou posits as a marker of a point of rapport. This element has no concrete or determinate predicates, which precludes the substantiation of a positive point of mediation or shared attribute on the part of the two sexes. Badiou illustrates his argument by suggesting, ironically, that the list of shared predicates attached to the concept of "humanity" provides a (specious) link between the disjunct sexes, such that the u would stand for "ubiquitous." We have already see the extent to which Badiou's notion of "humanity" radically differs from that of common usage, which remains blind to the impasse of sexual difference and attempts to link the sets of men and women according to shared biological traits and common humanist goals. The intersection Badiou is attempting to theorize is not reliant upon forming a *class* that would make man plus woman countable as a single entity, or couple, but rather is prior to predication and links in the order of being. This term is drawn from the void of the disjunction, an element which punctures the borderline of the symbolic division and in so doing provides the basis of the relational support. Even though Badiou says it "exists," it is constitutively unformalizable.

Returning to our discussion of generic infinite sets, we can understand that Badiou is attempting to think the link between the formalized set universe (Lacan's Symbolic order, Badiou's "state-of-the-situation") and the generic set that "belongs" without being able to be brought fully to representation and included within the set universe. The "wandering" or aleatory element proper to the generic set is approached from a fresh angle through the re-reading of the myth of Aristophanes, such that the hypothesized (re-)union of the sexes does *not* constitute a perfect One (which is the fantasy of desire as supported by the law of Capital); rather, the element that founds the initial rapport remains excluded from the set: $M \cup W \neq 1$. From these complementary axioms, Badiou arrives at a formal understanding of love: "An amorous encounter is what allocates descriptively a double function to the atomic and unanalyzable intersection of the two sexed positions: that of the object, where a desire finds its cause, and that of a point from which the Two are counted, thus initiating an investigation of the sharing of the universe."[17] Thus, approaching the question of the rapport from a psychoanalytic perspective, the unanalyzable, atomic point of intersection is mapped by the function of the *objet a*. As discussed above, the object functions as a lure that both occludes the real of the other (the amorous partner) *and* nevertheless opens a point of access to the other's being via the mode in which the object is brought to presentation in a singular manner. Lacan argues that this surplus *jouissance* is extrinsic to knowledge, and yet is decisive in differentiating the fantasy mode, in which desire is the catalyst ($\$ \lozenge a$), from love, which bears upon being proper, rather than the object. While, per Badiou's first axiomatic schema, the "misunderstanding" of the element founds the rapport and is responsible for the *being* of the Two (insofar as the relation is founded upon this *méconnaissance*), the second schema inverts the trajectory, stating that given the disjunct sexuated positions, the possibility of relation arises through a shared interrogation of this implied element (u), such that each partner instigates a truth procedure that seeks to map out the perimeter of their (sexuated) being via a sustained questioning of the void that "in-separates" them from the Other. Each interrogation is partial, contingent upon the position of the questioner, such that each sex comes to a separate understanding of the (shared) field upon which the rapport rests, based upon its own starting point. It is this that leads Badiou to insist that knowledge is sexuated, yet the truth that it accesses is nevertheless universal: the investigation departs from a finite, contingent, localized stance, but the generic set it addresses is infinite—it is merely its incommensurability with the finite realm (or Symbolic order) that leads to its inevitable sexuated inflection upon being brought to (re)presentation.

These two functions are "knotted" together. Badiou once more borrows from Lacan's engagement with the topology of knots, drawing an analogy between Lacan's description of the intersecting of the three orders of the Imaginary/Symbolic/Real as productive of the central gap wherein the *objet a* is located to suggest how the confluence of the two functions of u can be understood as initiating and sustaining an amorous truth procedure. Relating this back to the everyday, Badiou locates the process of fidelity to the initial declaration of love as those "innumerable common practices" that a couple holds in common, which constitutes their shared mode of being-in-the-world. This is, in effect, a quotidian version of the mathematician's systematic questioning, which brings forth fragments of knowledge concerning the infinite, uncompletable set—the daily decisions as to how to live, which values the couple share, and how they are to achieve their common goals. Just as mathematically there is, by definition, no final, or *universal*, answer that would bring the generic set to determinacy, there can be no knowledge that brings the process of sharing two lives to perfect completeness, or complementarity.

It must be stressed that Badiou is not suggesting that the *u* is ultimately reducible to a series of practical agreements over school districts, politics, and musical tastes—this would return us to the problem of rendering the disjunct parties as a series of shared predicates, thereby forming a *class* of common attributes, much as was ironically posited regarding the possibility of delineating a common "human nature." Rather, the aleatory element remains irreducible and excluded from knowledge:

although the decisions made by the Two in fidelity to the event remain within the Imaginary/Symbolic realms, they are *inflected* by the trace of the real. The *u* resists all determinate predication.

Badiou's detailed use of Lacan, and in particular the schema of sexuation, inevitably lays him open to the same criticisms of phallocentrism and heteronormativity. Countering such charges of normativity, Badiou situates Lacan alongside Foucault and Althusser in contesting the humanist notion of the subject, arguing that the subject of psychoanalysis has "no substance, no 'nature,' being a function both of the contingent laws of language and of the always singular history of the objects of desire" (Ee 6). In many respects this anti-humanist genealogy is shared by a number of gay, lesbian, and queer theorists who draw directly upon Foucault (and Deleuze) to propose an alternative to what are seen as the disciplinary techniques of psychoanalysis. Before considering the implications of these resonances and divergences, I would like to address the question of whether Badiou does conflate heterosexual and homosexual love, and whether the upholding of love as a universal (or "truth") inevitably results in subsuming the specificity of same-sex love to a heterosexual norm. Clearly such a wide-ranging and important discussion can only be touched upon within the present article; it is, however, important to broach the question and hopefully to open the way to more detailed subsequent theorization.

While Badiou's theoretical framework does not preclude homosexual relations from being included in his definition of the amorous Two, and indeed emphasizes that the sexuated subject positions "male"/"female" are radically distinct from the gender identities imposed by social norms and are, as such, open to occupation by all subjects, Badiou is, perhaps, less attentive to developing the implications of a gay or lesbian rapport. Moreover, while it is relatively easy to project a measure of attunement with the work of queer theorists (such as Tim Dean) who retain a (Freudian/Lacanian) psychoanalytic orientation, it is evident that Badiou's approach is antithetical to those embracing a more Foucauldian/Deleuzian framework such as Rosi Braidotti's writings on nomadology and viral politics, or Elizabeth Grosz's theorization of lesbian relations "in terms of bodies, energies, movements, inscriptions, rather than in terms of ideologies, the inculcation of ideas, the transmission of systems of belief or representations."[18] Nor does it sit well with Leo Bersani's use of Laplanche to theorize the role of the object.[19]

In some respects it would be expedient for Badiou to drop the nominal categories entirely and retain the impersonality of the formulation:

> There is one position and another position.
>
> There is "one" and "one," who are not two, the one of each "one" being indiscernible, although totally disjointed, from the other. Specifically, no position-one includes an experience of the other, which would be an interiorization of the two.[20]

This radical alterity excludes both imaginary identification and phenomenological consciousness of the other as "the-same-as-self." If, as Badiou maintains, desire is a lure, then the discussion as to whether homosexual attraction is predicated upon "self-love hospitable to difference" (Bersani) or an identification with, and assumption of, maternal desire is bracketed for the purposes of a discussion of love.[21] The comedy of the sexual encounter remains, for Badiou, a purely masturbatory experience, predicated upon the mistaking of the other for a (lost) part-object. Thus, "however it is sexuated, desire is homosexual, whereas love, even if it can be gay, is principally heterosexual."[22] Love is principally "an investigation of the sharing of the universe,"[23] and as such involves an opening onto alterity. The possibility that "sameness" might also provide an access to this experience is not considered here, as it is equated directly with identificatory narcissism. The nature of the object is not of direct relevance, since it is not the cause of love, only of desire. Elaborating upon its paradoxical status, Badiou claims that love "can neither elude the object cause of desire, nor can it arrange itself there any longer"[24]—as discussed earlier, the object plays a role in bringing the being of the *semblant* to presentation, but this function is in excess of its role as symbolic or imaginary captivation.

In this respect, Dean's elaboration of the role of the *objet a* in gay relationships, suggesting that it "differentiates and proliferates causes of desire to a point that it confounds heteronormativity,"[25] can be easily accommodated to Badiou's framework: any form of object can be mis-taken. One would hesitate to collapse the two theories, however, given Dean's reservations concerning the usefulness of theorizations valorizing sexual difference. Dean writes:

> Critical emphasis on sexual difference, valuable though it has been, tends to reinforce heteronormativity by tying erotic relationality too closely to differences between sexes. ... [T]he psychoanalytic preoccupation with sexual difference often leads to an elision of otherness with difference, such that one's subjective relations to alterity get figured primarily in terms of relations with "the Other sex."[26]

Badiou's project to explore the notion of love as a Thought specifically attempts to exclude all elements of identificatory appropriation, whether imaginary or phenomenological, yet the fragments of experience constructed by the fidelity of the amorous pair remain sexed, despite the fact that the "truth" of the encounter, as participating in a universal, is of course unsexed, and does not fall under the structuring laws of the symbolic. In this respect, in Badiou's topography the space of the rapport exceeds (sexuated) governance, but nevertheless returns to the sphere of (mis)representation and the sexuated disjunction. Thus, it is a question of whether the laws of the state-of-the-situation can be successfully transgressed—and surely this is what Badiou is suggesting as an outcome of the truth procedure, albeit on a local level—or if there are alternative ways to encounter alterity minus the inflection of sexual difference.

Staying with Dean's argument for the moment, we can see how his suggestion that "thinking *sameness* may entail bracketing or demoting sexual difference as an explanatory category"[27] resonates with Badiou's own militant theorization of the

Same and his outspoken attacks on the insidious influence of cultural relativity and the identitarian politics to which it gives rise:

> [S]ince differences are what there is, and since every truth is the coming-to-be of that which is not yet, so differences are then precisely what truths depose, or render insignificant. ... [The Same] is not what is (i.e., the infinite multiplicity of differences) but what *comes to be*. (Ee 27)

At stake in the various theorizations of the Same is the site in which the Same is to be encountered. Badiou's interest in the Same derives from his upholding of the universal nature of truth(s), and thus the subject-as-immortal is the site of de-differentiation, the aspect of the "to come" that is lived out in mindful anticipation during the present, as well as the knotting of the finite and infinite at the site of the encounter. It is this link to the real (or inconsistent multiple) that situates the subject outside the inscription of sexual difference. Dean and Badiou are in agreement in suggesting that "the real represents a zone of undifferentiation—a place where difference cannot exist—because it is devoid of signifiers. ... [I]t betokens a logical space that is equally inhospitable to difference and identity ...."[28]

It is important to note that the contrasting theorization of "sameness" by Leo Bersani hinges on a reading of homosexuality as the dissolving of boundaries between self and other, leading to a mode of relation that bypasses identitarianism, producing instead a "self-love hospitable to difference: misrecognition here is not the fateful error of imaginary specularization, but rather describes the accommodating of difference by sameness and becomes the motive for continuing the search."[29]

Thus the amorous encounter is not predicated on a simple (mis)recognition of complimentary lacks, but precedes from a recognition of and "longing for sameness" that enables what Bersani terms "a loving" relation to difference. Drawing directly on the Foucauldian notion of "self-fashioning," Bersani proposes a more fluid sexual becoming that is not centered around a fixed identity, but focuses instead on an exploration of "sameness," which entails an impersonal projection of the self as already in the world—"[e]very subject re-occurs differently everywhere"[30]—so allowing a mode of communication that traces "new alliances and ... unforeseen lines of force":[31] a trans-personal actualization of the myriad virtual potentialities always already at play within the world. Thus, the same is not a reflexive limitation of desire, but a means of productively embracing difference, a melding of the same that involves original repetition, producing a new form of being. Rosi Braidotti's work radically extends the potential range of mixtures and transformations, arguing for a "viral politics" that replaces the identitarian binarism of sexuation with a dynamic becoming that draws directly on Deleuze's notion of "man's nonhuman becoming."[32] Badiou's protracted debate with Deleuze can be taken as evidence of the incommensurability of these critical positions. Their opposing theorizations of the multiple lead Badiou to claim that, contrary to the creative potentiality promised by the plurality of becomings, or simulacra, generated by the actualization of the Deleuzian virtual, the proliferation of forms merely refers back to the *a priori* governance of a singular, immanent Truth—the truth of/as continuous variation of the Same.[33]

Thus, while it can be said that Badiou's theorization of love as a truth procedure at its pared-down axiomatic minimum (retaining its universality of address) is designedly inclusive of both hetero- and homosexual relation, it is less certain whether it is necessarily *relevant* to homosexual lifestyles and practices. Decrying the adequation of love to either, on the one hand, a mere "sexual adventure" or, on the other, "sublime or platonic love," and insisting instead on the "hard labor" of the shared fidelity, one cannot help but think that Bersani's theorization of the impersonal intimacy of cruising as a "non-masochistic jouissance ... the sign of that nameless, identity-free contact—contact with an object I do not know and certainly do not love and which has, unknowingly, agreed to be momentarily the incarnated shock of otherness"[34] would certainly be dismissed as "sexual adventure," yet Bersani suggests that cruising, as a "training in impersonal intimacy," can be seen as a mode of proper homosexual sociability. Moreover, if indeed "[s]ociability is a form of relationality uncontaminated by desire,"[35] and cruising facilitates a "relat[ion] to that which transcends all relations,"[36] we can see that Bersani is similarly theorizing a rapport that dispenses with the category of intersubjectivity,[37] which raises the question as to how, then, "love" is to be conceptualized. If it does entail a specific, shared opening onto the world, need it entail the enduring fidelity of a truth procedure, or can it equally be found in the brief, serial encounters of cruising? Could it be that Badiou's notion of love is overly inflected by the Christian paradigm he harnesses in his work on St. Paul, putting him at variance with Bersani's call to adopt practices that potentially "require us to elaborate new ethical vocabularies?"[38]

Perhaps at this point it would be useful to determine why love operates as a *truth* procedure. Badiou states that the "philosophical category of Truth is by itself *void*. It operates but presents nothing" (MPe 124)—it is a purely logical category mapping the intersection between philosophy and mathematics/ontology. In distinction, the localized truth*s* relate to four different areas—politics, mathematics, love, and art—and comprise "the multiple, internal to the situation, that the fidelity constructs, bit by bit" (Ee 67–68). As a procedure, Truth operates in two different but complementary ways, which together form a pincer-like approach whereby localized truth*s* are seized. The first methodological "prong" operates via the "rhetoric of succession": a mode of argumentation linked by a series of definitions, proofs, refutations, etc., which ultimately resembles knowledge, but is in actuality constructive. Its goal is not to produce determinate knowledge, but to establish "a category reaching the clarity of its construction" (MPe 125). This branch of the operation can be related to the mathematical exploration of the rapport between the Two. The whole of set theory proceeds from a series of axiomatic assumptions, which in turn enable the self-reflexive exploration of the relation between the completed set universe (the consistent multiple) and the generic infinite sets (the inert inconsistent multiple). Such a procedure undertakes to delineate the boundaries of the given universe by showing the limits of its construction (or put differently, it enables one to posit the inherence of the inconsistent multiple via the logic of subtraction). Viewed from this perspective, Badiou declares that "Truth is the un-known of this fiction" (MPe 125)—the arbitrary, imposed law of the state-of-the-situation is exposed by an investigation of the disjunction wherein the universality of the situation is un-covered-up. Thus, the enduring fidelity to this procedure enables the piecemeal construction of the generic set/infinity of love by the sustained labor of the Two, bringing it partially within the framework of representation. Bersani's theorization works within a different temporal horizon, and while the series of impersonal encounters might likewise be viewed as forming part of an infinite set, so arguably generating a similar opening onto the truth of the disjunction, there is no emphasis on the *to come* of the infinite. Indeed, Bersani's emphasis on "self-*shattering*" is entirely contrary to Badiou's reliance on the materiality of the militant subject of faith to ensure a universality of address.

The second methodological prong of the operation concerns rhetorical strategy: "metaphors, strength of image … it is a matter of indicating the void of the category of Truth *as a limit-point*" (MPe 125). Art is imitated to produce a "subjective site of Truth." Looking again at the generic truth procedure of love, we have already established that alongside the mathematical derivation of the shared element proper to the rapport, we have the function of the object as both lure and metonymic opening onto the being of the amorous partner. While remaining within the field of the Imaginary, and as such functioning as a kind of rhetorical trope, the *objet a* nevertheless works to present a limit at which being, or the real, is accessed: both the being of the desiring subject (its link with the lost object) and the being proper to the desired partner (the singularity of the object's presentation). In this respect, Truth is the "unutterable" of this fiction of art—the unarticulable element that inheres within the field of representation, or what Lacan would style the "stain" of the real.

These two operations comprise the pincers by which truths can be "seized," both in the sense of "capture," "grasping," and also of "astonishment," "being captivated." Each mode approaches the site of truth in a very different manner: the precise, logical argumentation of set theory allows the careful teasing-out of the element foreclosed from traditional accounts of the love relationship—a deliberate "grasping," whereas the structure of fantasy proper to desire entails a specular capture that, despite the illusion of the object as lure, serves to engage the subjects at the level of being—an overwhelming that likewise "seizes" the subject with a "singular intensity." What each mode nevertheless shares is a *subtractive* element—Truth is subtracted from sense, being incommensurable with knowledge, whether logical or poetic.

The methodological trope of the pincers can be re-applied to the logic of the disjunction: although each position within the Two is destined to assemble a different, sexuated knowledge (or veridical truth), the void of the disjunction as the site of their in-separating is "seized" as a result of their joint endeavors. In this sense, love as a thought "is an immanent construction of an indeterminate disjunction, which does not pre-exist it."[39] Despite the eager protests of his detractors, and bearing in mind the limitations discussed above, Badiou does not wish to reduce the experience of love to a series of mathematical formulae, but rather seeks a means of teasing out the site of its infinite possibility from its complex interweaving with the law of desire that structures our everyday lives. That mathematics might paradoxically provide the means to do so is hardly heretical—some of the most famous expositions of love have likewise made use of geometric figures as a means of grasping the topological site of the Two:

> If they be two, they are two so,
>   As stiff twin compasses are two;
> Thy soul the fixed foot, makes no show
>   To move, but doth, if th' other do.
>   [Donne, "A Valediction: Forbidding Mourning"]

Badiou's logical pincers simply provide a keener grip that plucks the rigorous thought of love from the narcissistic clutch of fantasy. Perhaps that is the real source of the complaint? ■

....

1   Alain Badiou, "The Scene of Two," trans. Barbara P. Fulks, *Lacanian Ink* 21 (2003): 43.
2   Alain Badiou, "What Is Love?" in *Sexuation*, ed. Renata Salecl (Durham: Duke University Press, 2000), 266.
3   This draws on the work of Paul Cohen and his introduction of "forcing" as a means of accessing generic infinite sets. Given a set universe of fully constructible sets, the generic set is an infinite, uncompletable set that is not initially included within the basic model, but can nevertheless be posited as *belonging* to the universe as a supplement that resists total incorporation, remaining properly uncountable. Partial access to aspects of the set can be gained by posing a series of questions which allow deductions to be drawn that "force" its unlocatable nature to become (partially) anchored by capturing elements within representation. Because the set is infinite, it can only be interrogated section by section, and the answers derived are based upon these finite fragments about which it is possible to give an answer with a determinate truth value. All questions regarding universal quantifiers are thus bypassed, as the set is by definition uncompletable. See Paul J. Cohen, *Set Theory and the Continuum Hypothesis* (New York: W. A. Benjamin, 1966).
4   Badiou, "What Is Love?" 270.
5   Ibid., 267–68.
6   To conceptualize the separate, but coincident orders of love and desire, we need to have a clear understanding of Badiou's topography of the "situation." The situation, or the lifeworld, is formed from a "consistent multiplicity"—or a multiple that is subject to a law of composition—and an "inconsistent multiplicity"—the excess of the represented situation that was foreclosed via the operation of inscribing the law of the count-for-one. Thus, the imposed law or structure brings the presented situation to re-presentation at the cost of losing part of the initial multiplicity, which inheres as presence that exceeds the boundaries of knowledge within the formed *state-of-the-situation*. Despite these being different orders—of presence and presentation—it is nevertheless evident that there is some degree of contamination between the levels, and it is here that Badiou locates the eventaI site, allowing love to transgress the governance of the prevailing law of sexuation. The event/encounter is precisely an irruption of the foreclosed real (or inconsistent multiple) within the boundaries of the formed situation that shatters the functioning of knowledge.
7   [For a list of Badiou's principal texts and their corresponding abbreviations, see the introduction to this issue.—Ed.]
8   Badiou, "What Is Love?" 274.
9   Jacques Lacan, *The Seminar of Jacques Lacan, Book XX: Encore 1972–1973, On Feminine*

Sexuality: The Limits of Love and Knowledge, trans. Bruce Fink (New York: Norton, 1998), 80.

10. Badiou, "The Scene of Two," 42.
11. Lacan, *Seminar XX*, 92.
12. Ibid., 126.
13. Badiou, "The Scene of Two," 43.
14. Jacques Lacan, *The Seminar of Jacques Lacan, Book XI: The Four Fundamental Concepts of Psycho-Analysis*, trans. Alan Sheridan (London: Penguin, 1979), 215.
15. Badiou, "The Scene of Two," 45.
16. Ibid., 48.
17. Ibid., 51.
18. Elizabeth Grosz, "Refiguring Lesbian Desire," in *The Lesbian Postmodern*, ed. Laura Doan (New York: Columbia University Press, 1994), 77–78.
19. Bersani conceptualizes the object in terms of Laplanche's "enigmatic signifier," whose encounter "re-activates a world in which the subject is nowhere to be found, one of pure otherness. The world has become, again … the enigmatic signifier that sent us, and that appears to be sending us once again, messages we cannot process, or 'metabolize.'" Leo Bersani, "Sociability and Cruising," *Umbr(a)* 1 (2002): 19.
20. Badiou, "What Is Love?" 272
21. Indeed, this move also excludes theories that center on "performativity," as the whole imaginary dimension is likewise foreclosed.
22. Badiou, "What Is Love?" 280.
23. Badiou, "The Scene of Two," 51.
24. Badiou, "What Is Love?" 272.
25. Tim Dean, "Sameness Without Identity," *Umbr(a)* 1 (2002): 35.
26. Ibid., 31.
27. Ibid., my italics.
28. Ibid., 30.
29. Bersani, "Sociability and Cruising," 18.
30. Ibid., 17.
31. Michel Foucault, "Friendship as a Way of Life," in *Ethics, Subjectivity and Truth*, ed. Paul Rabinow, (New York: The New Press, 1997), 136; cited in Bersani, "Sociability and Cruising," 20.
32. Rosi Braidotti, *Metamorphoses: Towards a Materialist Theory of Becoming* (Cambridge: Polity, 2002).
33. See Badiou's *Deleuze: The Clamor of Being*. Badiou argues that the endless multiple becomings, or simulacra, generated by the actualization of the powers of the virtual amounts to a singular, immanent Truth—the truth of/as continuous variation of the Same, thus the subversive freedom it claims does not lead to a bypassing of the restrictions inherent in the construction of identity-as-difference/deviance, but rather traps the subject in an endless repetition of the same, a reproduction, as opposed to a true becoming.
34. Bersani, "Sociability and Cruising," 21.
35. Ibid., 9.
36. Ibid., 21.
37. Ibid., 22.
38. Ibid., 21.
39. Badiou, "The Scene of Two," 55.

How Much Truth Can Art Bear?
On Badiou's "Inaesthetics"

Élie During

In contemporary thought on aesthetics, one distinguishes philosophical alternatives according to their ability or willingness to address two major questions:

1   How much truth can art (still) bear?
2   Is there, strictly speaking, such a thing as art?

The first question, formulated by Alain Badiou, may seem outdated. Nevertheless, if it revisits a very ancient Platonic problem (which Nietzsche still pursued), it does so in order to formulate a new solution. Badiou addresses the question of truth in art (truth effects that art may produce for its own sake) to all contemporary artistic productions (those that define, therefore, the field commonly known as "contemporary art") as well as to the very project of a philosophical aesthetics. In fact, we will see that, beyond the problems particular to the relationship between philosophy and art, this question of truth defines an original intervention in (broadly construed) discourses about art [*pensées de l'art*] including thoughts by critics and artists alike. On this last point, Badiou's philosophy appears to be a war machine positioned against traditional philosophical aesthetics: under the curious term "inaesthetics," he attempts to define a new "nouage," a new "knot" of philosophy and art. This new relationship would neither transform art into a particular application or object of philosophy (a dogmatic or "didactic" stance), nor would it reduce philosophy to the pious role of silent witness or spellbound herald of a revelation specific to art (a "romantic" stance).

The second question, which addresses the validity of art as a category (and the usage of this noun, in the singular, with or without capitals), has been tackled in the past several years by Jacques Rancière. He has attempted to re-inscribe the philosophers' question on aesthetics within the larger context of a "division of the sensible,"[1] where thoughts and practices are distributed and identified as artistic or non-artistic. His reflection was bound to cross and confront Badiou's. The critical question here would be the following: to what extent does Badiou's inaesthetics not re-instate, in spite of itself, a rather traditional philosophical resolve to Art, and consequently a division between art and non-art (a division seemingly challenged, in the past century, by the whole evolution of artistic productions, and this despite modernist mythologies that attempt to give credit to the idea of art's autonomy and specificity)?

Inaesthetics: A Working Definition

But let us return to the first question, focusing on the relationship it presupposes between art and philosophy. What, really, is inaesthetics? Badiou suggests the following definition in the opening pages of his *Handbook of Inaesthetics*:

> By "inaesthetics" I understand a relation of philosophy to art that, maintaining that art is itself a producer of truths, makes no claim to turn art into an object for philosophy. Against aesthetic speculation, inaesthetics describes the strictly intraphilosophical effects produced by the independent existence of some works of art.[2]

In several dense formulas, this definition expresses the essence of Badiou's strategy. Each word matters, beginning with the term inaesthetics itself, a word whose neologism Badiou clearly indicates with the use of quotation marks.

Several remarks will clarify what this all means.

First, inaesthetics defines less a particular discipline or a sphere of philosophical reflection, than a certain *relationship* between philosophy and art, a relationship whose distinguishing trait lies precisely in the fact that it removes philosophy's usual hold over art, a hold that it exerted in different ways under the terms "aesthetics" and "philosophy of art." Philosophy will no longer transform art into its object, or a group of objects to reflect upon. In other words, philosophy will no longer apply to art ordinary processes of judgment, or summon in its name the play of descriptive or normative categories that allow one to identify modes, functions, and values of particular works of art. This judicatory manner of evaluating art always amounts to submitting it to norms that are external to it (notions of beauty, the terrible, or the abject …). This is still true when art becomes a space where norms are emancipated or, as Badiou would say, "a moment of the Subject's dissemination in the history of Truth."[3] By contrast, from the standpoint of "inaesthetics," it will no longer be important to speak the truth of art, or to bemoan its absence. For it will not be a matter of telling the truth *about* art, if that truth is something to be found outside of art, something that does not need to be extracted and unfolded. Instead it will be important to come to terms with the fact that "art *itself* is a truth procedure" (PM 21/9), that it is signaled, therefore, by immanent productions of truth (such as Mallarmé's subtractive operation of the "throw of the dice," or Rimbaud's hallucination and "derangement" of the senses). It should be added that this idea acquires full force when one recalls that for Badiou (as well as for Althusser), there cannot be, strictly speaking, philosophical truth. Philosophy elaborates truth categories by intervening in discourses and practices; philosophy seizes truths, exposes them, and begins by stating that they exist. But "philosophy does not itself produce any effective truth" (PM 28/14).

Under various forms, traditional aesthetics was not only *reflexive* (or judicatory), but also *speculative*, to the extent that aesthetics attempted to recuperate in art's mirror the vague or vivid reflection of its own truths, whether these truths were formulated in the realm of pure theory or, having gone beyond the limits of philosophical reflection, they eventually found refuge in art as an expression of the power of reflection proper to phenomena. Against this speculative relationship between philosophy and art, inaesthetics proposes a "descriptive" relationship, with a very specific meaning: it will be necessary to describe the "effects," for philosophy itself, of the specific processes that art initiates for its own sake. In other words, it will be necessary to deduce, in philosophy, consequences that stem from certain truth processes or procedures immanent to art, identifiable within works or particular artistic configurations. There, beneath the curiously Husserlian or Wittgensteinian vocabulary of description, Badiou's "axiomatic" style is recognizable: one must always know what derives, within the concept, from certain axioms linked to the recognition of "the independent existence" of several exemplary works [*réalisations*]. (Independence is indeed the very essence of an axiomatic proposition: its articulation does not depend on other axioms.) Given Mallarmé, Brecht, or Pessoa, what are the consequences for philosophy? What must be changed in our concepts?

In conclusion, Badiou suggests that the inaesthetic relationship translates into a rarefaction of its object (which, it should be repeated, is not an object in the strict sense). Therefore, one only deals with "certain art objects," which means that inaesthetics will always be *local*, that it cannot claim to speak of art *in general*.

The most striking aspect of this "operational" definition of inaesthetics is, of course, the paradoxical definition of philosophy's task: it is an "intraphilosophical" operation that nevertheless recognizes and in fact lives by truth procedures immanent to art. A curious knot indeed, where the philosophical and artistic coil occurs within art's core, but strictly for the benefit of philosophy. This particular configuration allows Badiou to denounce the speculative arrogance of philosophers and the terrorism that aesthetic theories can exert on the field of artistic reflection. Moreover, Badiou reveals the strictly philosophical nature of the new relationship between art and philosophy, a relationship which is absolutely incompatible with the mere subordination of philosophy to the conditions of art, as can be observed with certain romantics or (differently with Heidegger) when philosophy "sutures" itself to the poem. Even "conditionally," philosophy maintains its starring role. To such an extent that one could say of inaesthetics: art is probably not its business, if it is true that it is not its *object*. In this manner, inaesthetics separates itself from three clearly distinguishable variations of the art/philosophy knot to which we must return: the Platonic or didactic schema, the classical or therapeutic schema, and finally the romantic or hermeneutic schema.

Inaesthetics at Work: The Case of Mallarmé

How does this work in practice? The quote on inaesthetics cited above is meant to be a working definition. It is therefore necessary to put it to work and see how it affects our ordinary apprehension of "some works of art." Mallarmé is often presented by Badiou as an exemplary case of the inaesthetic knot he has in mind. Let us take up this example.[4] The Mallarmé case is exemplary in two significant ways. First, because his "hermetic" poetry (more so than any other) forces philosophy to abandon openly a hermeneutic posture in favor of a particular mode of intervention, which would apply to the set of operations that allow the poem to operate, rather than to the philosophical content or meaning displayed by its characteristic themes: "The poem states what it makes" (TS 99). But it is up to philosophy to show and subsequently make something of this. Furthermore, the name Mallarmé already suggests a method of primary interest for Badiou's philosophy. What, in fact, does the poem bring about? Where does its procedure lie? The answer of course has something to do with the lack, the unnamable absence, but the poet is not content to signal or to suggest, thus to *pronounce* this absence (as such, absence would only be a Mallarméan "theme," and a rather trite one in the end); it produces it through a "subtractive" procedure, one that is best captured in the "enigma" of a double dissolution: that of the object (the referent's sensory presence), and that of the subject (the "elocutory disappearance of the poet", to quote Mallarmé's famous maxim).

Pierre Macherey does a good job summarizing this ordered mechanism, in which Michel Leiris saw "a language that is less about description or storytelling than about engaging certain movements of the mind":[5]

> Mallarmé is not hermetic, in the sense of a well-kept secret that should be exposed. He is just difficult because, as an essential poet, he produces enigmas. These provoke thought, not in order to reveal, at the expense of description, a pre-existing truth, but in order for thought to insinuate itself in the act through which truth arises, through which it is produced, literally, in the form which is precisely that of an enigma and at the limit of non-sense. The secret is therefore what is not secret, because everything that the poem has to say is spread out, thrown about, dispersed, properly spaced out black on white in a constellation that forever becomes (once the dice are cast) his text.[6]

It is therefore incumbent upon the philosopher, not only to work the Mallarméan text in order to extract from its material conditions its ideational event (this is what any reader, philosopher or not, must go through in order to make sense of the poem), but also to prolong this event within a concept, to extract the philosophical consequences orchestrated by the poet in his subtractive procedure. From this point of view, however, the interest in the Mallarmé method is to propose an allegorical staging of the very process of philosophy when it mimics the unfolding and deployment of an Idea. The proverbial opacity of Mallarméan writing stops short, indeed, at the hermeneutic temptation that thinks it can find the poem's key by adding, by delving ever more deeply into the thick layers of multiple interpretations and significations evoked or simply suggested by the poem's material layout. In this game of overbidding, the philosopher would not be able to get something out of it: he has no use for an interpretation that, over a series of analyses and cross checks, would extract a "Mallarmé philosophy": all the poet's *idées fixes* and world vision would no doubt finally find a place, but what would be the point? "This lazy circumvention of the obstacle that drives many to say that the virtue of the enigma lies in its ability to tolerate a hundred tendentious answers must come to an end," says Badiou. "There is no 'polysemantics' with this absolute dialectician [Mallarmé] ..." (TS 92). The poem derives its strength precisely from everything that it *subtracts*, within the closed field of its regulated operations, from the abundance of significations, from the immediate and sensible presence of objects. "This idea is essential: the poem is neither a description nor an expression. Nor is it a painting imbued with the world's extension. The poem is an operation. The poem teaches us that the world is not a collection of objects. The world is not what *objects* to thought. The world's presence is—for the poem's operations—more essential than its objectivity." But this priority of presence must be demonstrated: "To think presence, the poem must work toward an oblique operation of capture" (92). Freed of its ever-renewing compromises with the sensible (or, which is the same, sensible significations), the poem defines a protocol, a mechanism of capture. And what must be captured? Not presence itself, which would immediately transform into an object; not absence, which as the abstract negation of the object still sounds the murmur of presence; but the very movement of disappearance, a dissolution-event that can be captured only obliquely.

"Mallarmé's poem does not ask to be interpreted, nor does it possess any keys. The poem demands that we delve into its operation. The enigma lies in this very demand" (PM 51/29). Like Deleuze, Badiou would be ready to say: "Do not interpret: fabricate [*machinez*]." Admittedly, one would then need to distinguish between two conceptions of the machine as well as of the operation. But this is beyond the scope of this paper. Let us only note the following: what is striking with Badiou, is that the poem's most general operation finds an immediate echo in the type of operations typical of philosophical practice when philosophy occurs conditionally under truth procedures defined by art.[7] Upon reflection, there is nothing surprising to this, since it is philosophy and philosophy alone that attests and prolongs in its own realm the truth procedures immanent to art. In fact, it often seems as if philosophy finds in art simply the effect or local verification of its own operations (those ruled by a theory of the event, for example), even though these operations conditionally exist only in relation to certain truths they are supposed to discern and identify outside philosophy. This strangely embedded situation provides Rancière with an easy target. As we shall see, his point is that despite all claims to the contrary, "inaesthetics" amounts to a restoration of philosophy's traditional hold on matters of art: a "subtractive" hold, if that makes any sense. Paradoxical as it may seem, philosophy's grip on art is firmer than ever when, having renounced the speculative stance altogether, it does not have to "overdo it" anymore. This intuition seems correct, but it remains to be tested against particular cases.

If one agrees that philosophy's proper task is to show that a poem can have something to tell us about what thinking means, then the following would be a typical claim of "inaesthetics": the poem describes nothing, nor does it express anything; it is a machine, a thinking machine. If the commentaries generated by the Mallarmé case have such general value, it is because they define in the clearest manner something like the essence of the "modern poem." The "modern poem" identifies itself with a thought protocol (one sees, by the way, that art has no need for philosophers to begin to think, or to reflect upon itself and its operations). The poem "is not just the effective existence of a thought offered up in the flesh of language," explains Badiou,

> it is the set of operations whereby this thought comes to think itself. The great poetic figures, whether in Mallarmé—the Constellation, the Tomb, or the Swan—or in Rimbaud—the Christ, the Worker, or the Infernal Groom—are not blind metaphors. They organize a consistent *dispositif* in which the role of the poem is to engineer the sensory [*sensible*] presentation of a regime of thought: subtraction and isolation for Mallarmé, presence and interruption for Rimbaud. (PM 37/20)

But whether by Rimbaud or Mallarmé, it is essential that the poem, recuperated by philosophy in its immanent operation, henceforth presents itself as a living allegory of the movement of thought that it orchestrates, or of the form of the event in general. It is not the sensible form of the Idea (be it a fulfillment or a loss), not the sublime descent of the infinite into the finite form of the work (as in the romantic scheme); but rather a mental theater that reveals, by contrast, the sensible in its fundamental inconsistency, as a nostalgic longing for the Idea. It is not a matter of giving meaning in order to elevate and transcend the sensible, but of subtracting something from it: thus, the poem carves out the sensible form recuperated in language and prepares the ground for an ideal event. This is why, of all the examples that Badiou identifies, Mallarmé remains the privileged figure of his inaesthetics. His poems so clearly stage this process that they seem to dispense with philosophical commentary entirely.

The point, of course, is that philosophy can do better than providing a commentary. It is incumbent upon philosophy to find this regulated carving-out that the poem operates, to name its procedure, and most importantly, to unfold [*dérouler*] all its consequences. Because "like every local figure of a truth, [poetry] is also a program of thought, a powerful anticipation" (PM 41/23)—a powerful anticipation that matches an even greater fundamental weakness. In fact, what is this truth, always the same, that the poem produces by its own means? The following: there is no truth of the Whole [*vérité du Tout*] because truth can never give itself "wholly." There is no such thing as "the whole truth." For truth always encounters an internal limit that situates it locally, that prevents it from recuperating itself as the integral truth of that of which it is the truth. Thus truth is subtracted from the reflexive foundation of the Whole in itself. This is the edge of the unnamable, of what Lacan called the "Real." As far as poetry is concerned, this edge is one with language's infinite power, for this infinite power stops short of sensible presence and cannot be properly named—it is therefore the flip side of a weakness. In the end, it matters little what one thinks of this view of truth. What is essential here is to understand in Badiou's own mechanism how philosophy comes to recognize the truth produced by the poem, as the result of an excess of power, which is at the same time a weakness. In this respect, the inaesthetic method has one striking characteristic: it tends to recapture, through the words combined by the poet, the localized effect of a universal truth that the poem itself cannot fully express by its own means, a truth that must somehow be extracted (though not produced or imposed) by philosophical analysis. A strict equivalent of this situation could easily be found in the concept of the "matheme" (one thinks of course of the Gödel example, studied at length in *L'être et l'événement*).

Truth or Truths?

This long and yet schematic setup was necessary to understand better the scope of Badiou's general theses on the aesthetics of philosophers. Obviously, there would be much to say on the relationship, defined by the inaesthetics, between art and its concept on the one hand, and the diversity and dispersion of arts on the other hand. Badiou criticizes the traditional forms of the art/philosophy knot for relying, implicitly or explicitly, on a hierarchy of the arts. From Hegel to Deleuze, one would thus find a classification of the arts according to their greater or lesser ability to demonstrate art's own power. Inaesthetics, on the other hand, does not hierarchize. Hierarchies are generally governed by external rules or criteria, and as we saw, inaesthetics advocates a thoroughly immanent relation between philosophy and art. Does this mean that the attention given to the poem should be considered only secondary, a mere expository device? If Mallarmé's case is exemplary, is it not because language arts are, of all arts, those that most clearly represent the necessity of an inaesthetics in order to formulate aporias of nomination encountered by Badiou's ontological project of a pure multiple? But what about the "impure" arts located in the uncertain realm separating the "pure notion" from sensible presence? Are they secondary? And are they so for essential or inessential reasons? Badiou speaks of dance, theater, and cinema as the "unfixed" arts, those arts where the Idea's temporal becoming or its simple *passage* is played out (in the theatrical sense of the word). But he says practically nothing of music. Others may very well see in this a "symptom." What is important however, is that in each case the operation or "generic procedure" that allows one to identify the type of truth a given form of art can bear is similar to producing a mime or the kinetic diagram of a movement intended to signal, negatively, that thought itself is an event exceeding the expressive capacities of this given form of art.[8] The generic procedures basically repeat the same gesture through various media and techniques. The arts, in this regard, are on an equal footing. Yet the absence of a traditional hierarchy of the arts does not mean that there is no paradigm for the generic procedures. As a matter of fact, the primacy of the poem reappears on the operational level. Be it spacing and effacing (dance), simplification (theater), or the pure transition of the evanescent (cinema), the movement of thought always seems to have to be described from the pure and general subtractive operation furnished by the model of the Mallarméan poem. This fundamental operation, as described by Badiou, is that of the Idea's oblique capture at the threshold of its solidification in a world of objects. In other words, the capture of a substance that is, by nature, without substance, the paradoxical inscription of what is only revealed by a pure subtraction: the passage of the Idea into the sensible.[9] And if it is true that inaesthetics refuses any hierarchy of the arts (hierarchy in the sense of their ability to express the principle of an aesthetics or a metaphysics), one must recognize that the arts, in their very diversity and means proper to them, only express in various degrees and at various levels of clarity the simple truth that "art—as the configuration 'in truth' of works—is in each and every one of its points the thinking of the thought that it itself is" (PM 28/14). Admittedly, philosophy should always reveal "a truth of *this art*, an art-truth," (26/13) but only as a means to establish a truth more general, and in the end, the only one that matters: art produces truths that belong to it alone, art is "a thought in which artworks are the Real (and not the effect)" (21/9), and this thought cannot be reduced to philosophy, despite the fact that philosophy "welcomes and shelters" it (99/63). Thus inaesthetics can clearly be defined as an alternative to the three above-mentioned traditional schemas of the art/philosophy knot, each depending on a particular idea of the aesthetic and the attending classification of the arts. In the didactic (Platonic) schema, art is incapable of truth, or (which is the same), the truth that it can bear (the truth of semblance named appearance) is always external to it. Philosophy will thus tend to control it, to hem it to its didactic or apagogic vocation. In the hermeneutic (romantic) schema, art alone can bear truth; it is the real body of truth, the sensible manifestation of the Idea. In the classical (Aristotelian) schema such as it is expressed in the doctrine of *catharsis*, art again is incapable of bearing truth, because it accomplishes itself in its operation, that is to say in its therapeutic *effects*. Art does not come under theory, but under ethics. Ethics, therefore, must state the rules of "pleasing" and "touching." In the inaesthetic schema, however, one must recognize that art can bear truth. But this truth, which finds in philosophy its most general formulation and its axiomatic continuation, is, in the end, always the same, even though it is admittedly always singular—that is to say given "nowhere else but in art."[10] This truth of art that wants art to be indeed capable of bearing truth (in a relation both immanent and unique to truth), this truth should be able to formulate itself independently of any thought or particular theory about art. On a more general level, this truth connects to a pedagogical concern, itself very general: "Art is pedagogical for the simple reason that it produces truths and because 'education' (save in its oppressive or perverted expressions) has never meant anything but this: to arrange the forms of knowledge in such a way that some truth may come to pierce a hole in them" (21/9).

Inaesthetics as Anti-Aesthetics: Badiou in Rancière's Prism

"Some truth." Inaesthetics does not ask for anything more in order to maintain philosophy's function of edification: the privilege to say, if not the truth of art, at least that there is truth in art. But by the same token, the divide between art and philosophy finds itself to be founded on an accepted divide between art in general and what is not art—non-art. This would not be a problem if it weren't for the fact that the blurring of the border between art and non-art is one of the more important stakes in contemporary aesthetics, just as it is in artistic practices. Before raising the problem of truth in art, Rancière wishes to question the very unity of art as a category. He does not do this like Goodman or Danto: the point is not to define or "de-define," but rather to consider for its own sake a fluid relationship between art and non-art. This without refraining from recapturing artistic practices and discourses within the larger context of activities that participate in a common definition of the sensible. Here we touch a sensitive aspect of the Badiouian edifice, one that is perhaps the occasion for a fertile confrontation in our contemporary philosophical "moment."

It is pointless, indeed, to criticize Badiou for not having taken into sufficient consideration the dimension of sensation, of *aisthesis*, of perceptions and affects; for having lost sight, in the axiom's subtractive and impersonal asceticism, of the concrete and intensive implication of the poetic subject in the poem's flesh.[11] One might as well immediately criticize him for not being Deleuzian. No. Badiou's interest lies precisely in the distance he takes from any "logic of sense," in the name of an ontological project whose inaesthetics is most likely just a propaedeutic aspect.[12] The real problems lie elsewhere: in the particular montage that governs the very definition of inaesthetics and in the differential relationship he establishes with the field of aesthetics at large (philosophical and non-philosophical).

Two types of remarks seem necessary at this juncture. First, it would be prudent to ask what still connects inaesthetics to a familiar form of aesthetic thought, where a refusal of *mimesis* has become its favored theme. In aesthetics just as in ontology, Badiou's Platonism is an anti-Aristotelianism: for him, Mallarmé's greatness is to have reflected upon and activated the rupture of the poetic act from the seductions of presence, either actual or represented. We saw this: poetry neither describes nor expresses anything; it does not reflect the world but instead buttresses itself against language in order to ensnare it. Inaesthetics, as it has been defined through the Mallarméan paradigm, thus inherits a "latent"[13] aesthetic, which is none other than that of anti-*mimesis* (and its easily discernible trace in the history of aesthetics, from Plato to the Kantian analysis of the sublime to German romanticism). The inaesthetic's anti-aesthetic is nothing but the focal point of all resistances against a diffuse schema, which is correctly associated with Aristotle's *Poetics* and with the representational regime of tragedy. As Jacques Rancière explains, however, this form of "anti-aesthetic consensus" characteristic of our period also "pre-emptively ensures that there is well and truly a univocal concept of art."[14] It seems as though the idea of an art "proper" is confirmed each time the abuses of "classical" aesthetics are denounced.

This brings us to our second series of remarks. As we will show, they may reveal, in turn, questions regarding the divide between art and non-art, this divide being itself only one of the manifestations of the supposed identification in the field of artistic productions. That inaesthetics should deny on principle that philosophy ought to make art its object does not mean we are done with Art. If what is needed is a genuine *critique* of art as a concept, it is not enough to untie the classical knot of philosophy and art, and then to substitute in its place a montage immanent to art, since the desired critique is intraphilosophical in its effects. Badiou holds that art is a sure thing, once it is admitted that it will not be considered as the object of philosophical reflection, but instead as a field of operations. Better yet, he still needs to believe in art, in its autonomy, in order to say that it can bear truth, without going so far as to place philosophy in art's shadow. For Badiou, the excess of romantic philosophy was to have identified the productions of art with a mode of being of the sensible where the Idea was to be absorbed. But whether he wants to or not, his radical anti-aestheticism, his virulent rejection of the classical doctrine of *mimesis*, brings him closer than he would like to the romantic regime and some of its favorite commonplaces: the idea of "absolute art," the primacy of the open, potentially infinite artistic process over the finite form of the artwork, etc.[15]

Art and Non-Art

In fact, things are much more complicated. As Rancière has shown in several books in the past few years, the specificity of the romantic or "aesthetic" regime (which has so strongly directed our different "modernisms" in their wish to devote each particular art to the demonstration of art's unique power) is the abolition, along with the "mimetic" activities of representation's classical regime, of all distinctive criteria in artistic modes of production.[16] There is thus nothing "proper" to art aside from what social conventions assign to it. Its productions belong to the same unconscious expressive power that exists throughout the sensible, from the writing of stones to the *Comédie humaine*, from the hum of the cosmopolitan city to works by Varèse, Cage, or Scanner. Aesthetic claims about art's autonomy variously state, therefore, the same paradox: "Art is to be recognized by its characteristic indistinction."[17] The essence [*propre*] of art, in its ability to harness the process of the sensible as a transition to the Idea, is to entertain a relationship of indiscernibility with non-art. Nothing is really truly proper to art. Or again: "The aesthetic identification of art is the principle of a generalized disidentification."[18] Thus, modernist avant-gardes have sought in various ways the self-suppression of art as a separate practice and its replacement by a new understanding of aesthetic experience (i.e., the identification of art with the elaboration of new forms of life). This is evident even with the purest adepts of the doctrine of art for art's sake. It is well known that Mallarmé himself was the poet of fans, postcards, prose, and occasional verse, as well as the "throw of the dice" … Badiou has naturally little to say about this aspect of Mallarmé: he refuses to reflect on the consequences that would naturally arise from his radical anti-aesthetics (which is, in the end, an anti-*mimesis*). The Idea passes (nothing more) into something so unlike it: this is the core of Badiou's Platonism, which is enough to endow him with a unique place at the heart of a constellation that Rancière describes as the "aesthetic" regime of our post-romantic landscape. He is the partisan of an "incontestable modernism," but a "twisted modernism,"[19] because for him, what is specific to the arts is no longer identified by their materials or their specific language, but by their ideas or ideational processes.

Is the Idea's force (or stamp) enough to preserve us from the aesthetic indiscenibility of both art- and life-forms? Yes, provided the Idea's passage is an event forever renewed. This is why, according to Rancière, Badiou "wants to make eternity pass into the ever-renewed separation that lets the Idea shine in the vanishing of the sensible, to affirm the absolutely singular yet always similar character of the advent of the Idea by preventing its inscribed cipher from becoming lost in the muteness of stone, the hieroglyph of the text, the décor of life or the rhythm of the collective."[20] Rancière deploys in full detail all the consequences that derive from this fundamental tension proper to the "aesthetic" regime of art that Badiou expresses in his will to reconcile two contradictory requirements: on the one hand the requirement of a "pedagogical poem," or a theater that would foster the courage required by truth; on the other hand "the modernist requirement of the autonomy of art."[21] From this perspective, the curious stature of cinema, most "impure" of all arts, takes on a special importance: everything occurs as if its role were to contain, "in the margins of art, the constitutive impurity of the aesthetic regime of the arts through which art's singularity emerges."[22] Cinema is the place of all shady exchanges, of all "false movements," which constantly push the threshold of art and non-art. Badiou knows something of this, having proposed a (properly Platonic) reading of *The Matrix*.[23] Even masterpieces are interspersed with clichés, with dull, banal, and vulgar materials imported from daily life. But this impurity of cinema is essential to its being a mass art:

> For you can always penetrate into the art of cinema through what it offers that *is not art*, although it is present in abundance. Whereas with other arts it is the other way around. It is always in the medium of the arts' grandeur that you experience their non-artistic part, their shortcomings. One may say that in the movies you can always *step in*. You can start from the most common representations, from your most nauseous sentimentality, from your vulgarity, your cowardice even. You can be the absolute average viewer. Your bad taste is not a problem, it can be given access too, as part of your basic disposition. It will not prevent you from being elevated by the film. You may even reach powerful and sophisticated levels in the end. You won't have to take the return trip. Whereas in the aristocratic arts, you may always slide backwards. This is the great advantage of the democratic art of cinema: you can go to the movies on Saturday evening in order to relax, and still get caught and elevated by surprise.[24]

Can Contemporary Art Educate Us for Truth?

The preceding quote already suggests that the ambivalent montage known as "inaesthetics" translates less a theoretical contradiction or tangle (as Rancière suggests) than a concern for the ethical and political efficacy of art. What is at stake is the educational potential of art. Badiou makes the wager, not only that art is capable of producing immanent truths, but that art *teaches* truth. As we saw, this very education must occur under the condition of philosophy, so to speak. It is philosophy's responsibility to claim that art can provide an education to truth. And it is indeed a wager, which brings us back (this time most directly) to our first question: how much truth can art still bear? Because the whole problem comes from the fact that truth, like the event, is rare. In the opening citation, the definition of inaesthetics stems from "the existence of several independent works of art." What to do, in this case, with most artistic productions? Must these be relegated to the ranks of non-art, placed alongside standard products of the culture industry that feed the usual aesthetic consumption? And what to do if, as Badiou writes, "art is dubious," if "the present of art is only its own uncertainty, its fusion (or confusion) in the vague productions of bodies (or of capital-bodies)?" What to do if "art repudiates all truth, or creates truth from the consumable absence of all truth?"[25] "Inaesthetics is clear if art is obvious. As the horizon of art, does not non-art impose, strangely, an aesthetic? An aesthetic of chaos, for example?" In this case, inaesthetics must defend the axiomatic strength of art, "and reclaim, if need be, a return." The work is twofold. First, philosophy must pull itself together and not abandon its own productions to a commentary that, "under the guise of its devotion to the experimentation of the body of art," increasingly "incorporates production, fills a gap, compensates as best it can in the chalky concept, the sinister deficiency of the sensible."[26] Second, it is necessary to dream, to invoke (short of creating it) "a new *regulated* art": "as rigorous as a mathematical demonstration, as surprising as an ambush in the night, and as elevated as a star."[27] This formula of Badiou's occurs in the twelfth of his fifteen theses on contemporary art (collected under the title "Draft for a Manifesto of Affirmationism"). How to say it more clearly? Despite all its "latent aesthetics," inaesthetics is not just another aesthetics: it's a slogan. ▪

Translated from the French by Laura Balladur.

....

1   [*Partage du sensible*. The French *sensible* means, like the English "sensible," "perceptible by the senses," but does not carry the English overtones of "well-reasoned" or "making good sense." It might also be rendered as "sensorial," "sensate," "phenomenal," or, neologistically, "sense-able."—Trans.]
2   PM 7/xiv. [For a list of Badiou's principal texts and their corresponding abbreviations, see the introduction to this issue. In the present essay, citations containing two page numbers separated by a forward slash refer first to the French edition and second to the published English translation.—Ed.]
3   Alain Badiou, "Le devoir inesthétique," in "Philosophie et art: La fin de l'esthétique?" special issue, *Magazine Littéraire* 414 (November 2002): 29.
4   See TS 92–128; C 108–29 ("La méthode de Mallarmé"); and PM, chapters 2, 3, 5, and 10.
5   Qtd. in Pierre Macherey, "Le Mallarmé d'Alain Badiou," in *Alain Badiou: Penser le multiple*, ed. Charles Ramond, (Paris: l'Harmattan, 2002), 401.
6   Ibid., 400–401.
7   On the topic of a "conditional" philosophy [*une philosophie "sous condition"*], see MP.
8   On this topic, Jacques Rancière discusses a "metaphorization of the advent of the Idea": "We might say that in [Badiou's] work the general status of artistic manifestation consists in signifying and symbolizing the passage of an idea, in showing that a body is capable of it, that a site is capable of harboring it, a group of being seized by it." "Esthétique, inesthétique, anti-esthétique," in Ramond, op. cit., 489; reprinted in Jacques Rancière, *Le malaise esthétique* (Paris: Galilée, 2004). Translated by Ray Brassier as "Aesthetics, Inaesthetics,

Anti-Aesthetics," in *Think Again: Alain Badiou and the Future of Philosophy*, ed. Peter Hallward (London: Continuum, 2004), 226–27.
9   That the Idea should only pass is of course essential if one wants to avoid the romantic idea of incarnation (the descent or installation of the infinite in the finite).
10 On this topic, it should be pointed out that the double characterization of truth as both immanent and singular (a double characterization that is the distinctive trait of inaesthetics) is somewhat redundant. If, indeed, immanence means that "art is rigorously coextensive with the truths it lavishly produces," singularity only brings forth a supplemental restriction ("these truths occur nowhere else but in art").
11 See Martin Rueff, "Critique de l'esthétique négative: À propos de l'inesthétique d'A. Badiou," *Poé&sie* 96 (2001): 117–43.
12 On the nature of the "propaedeutic" project, its difference from the Deleuzian ontology of the multiple, and some reflections in the realm of aesthetics, see Badiou's *Deleuze*.
13 See Macherey, op. cit., 45.
14 Rancière, "Esthétique," 478/218.
15 Badiou clarifies his anti-romanticist stand in "Le XXIe siècle n'a pas commencé: Interview avec Élie During," *Artpress* (March 2005), forthcoming.
16 See especially *Le partage du sensible* (Paris: La Fabrique, 2000) and *L'inconscient esthétique* (Paris: Galilée, 2001).
17 Rancière, "Esthétique," 480/220.
18 Ibid., 481/221 (translation slightly modified).
19 Ibid., 483/222.
20 Ibid., 485/224.
21 Ibid., 491/228.
22 Ibid.
23 See Alain Badiou, Thomas Bénatouïl, Élie During, Patrice Maniglier, and David Rabouin, *Matrix: Machine philosophique* (Paris: Ellipses, 2003).
24 Alain Badiou, "Le cinéma comme emblème démocratique," in "Cinéphilosophie," special issue, *Critique* 692/693 (January/February 2005), forthcoming.
25 Badiou, "Le devoir inesthétique," 29.
26 Ibid.
27 Alain Badiou, "Fifteen Theses on Contemporary Art," http://www.civiccentre.org/SPEAKERS/Keynotes/Badiou.Abstract.html. See the commented version of the same text in "Troisième esquisse d'un manifeste de l'associationnisme," in *Circonstances 2* (Paris: Léo Scheer, 2004).

THE LEOPARD.

Something Else Is Possible: Thinking Badiou on Philosophy and Art

Nico Baumbach

I Introductions

"Something else is possible." For Alain Badiou, this is what art today must say.[1] What is at stake in asserting that an indefinite thing that is not has the possibility of being? Why is this the domain of art?

The reader of Badiou will need to entertain, if provisionally, the forgotten game of philosophy, that is, in Badiou's definition, "thought thinking itself," and take seriously the question of "what is possible" in relation to "what is." For Badiou, this is the question of how to think an event in relation to being. Badiou rehearses two alternative responses that he views as symptomatic of the refusal to really confront this question. The first alternative is: *everything is possible*. This position sees no limit to what can be expressed or imagined today. Not content with a mere "something else," this position embraces the open, unequivocal affirmation of unlimited possibility. The second alternative is an inversion of the first: *everything is impossible*. This position responds to our distance from this sort of abstract speculation by suggesting that we turn our backs on the seductive but illusory gesture of trying to think that which is not, and declare once and for all that there's nothing beyond our finite experience. Badiou in his reflections on art suggests that both these latter claims, although contradictory, are simultaneously behind most artistic production today and, what's more, to his mind, they are the same claim.[2] Together they announce a world of progress and a world without events: the desire for infinite innovation within an essentially closed world. To say that everything is possible—there is no end to novelty, variation, the realization of latent consumer fantasies—means only that everything is impossible—there is no new thing that is not made up of a series of effects that cannot be calculated or assimilated to a certain conception of the world that remains fundamentally unaltered.

Something else is possible. Minimal and abstract, the proposition is neither empty nor equivocal—as a succinct summation of one of the central wagers that is Badiou's philosophical project, its implications are decisive.

Mallarmé, in a letter explaining his refusal to write an introduction for a friend's book, explains that art cannot tolerate introductions. Art, he claims, is "like a woman with her lover and has no need for the third party—the husband." What Mallarmé calls art, Badiou calls "the event," but it is fitting that the event take the form of art through the metaphor of love, as art and love are two of the four loci of events for Badiou, which include the additional realms of science and politics. No husbands needed, but are we left then with something that has no ramifications outside the finite experience of a single individual—the woman, the reader of the poem? If we must lean it can only be, as Paul Celan would have it, "on inconsistencies." Badiou's philosophy proceeds from two disjunctive fidelities. He insists on the adherence to the conception of the event as that which is subtracted from the third party, any and all places of support. In other words, the event and its truth is that "something else" which cannot be subsumed under any of the figures of what we could call husbandry: namely, according to Badiou, any form of historicism, contextualization, or categorization. At the same time, however, Badiou insists upon the importance of maintaining the third party. So what is this third party, free of all foundation, but keeping vital watch over its own uselessness? The third party is what Badiou calls "philosophy."

If there are signs in the English-speaking world of an encounter with Alain Badiou's "return to philosophy," we would have to say that the encounter remains in a period of latency. There is no shortage of introductions, but they tend to focus on the question of what, for Badiou, it means to do philosophy, whereas the actual practice of what Badiou calls philosophy is still relatively unexplored. Yes, the question of what it means to do philosophy is part of the process of actually doing it; that is, it is philosophy's business to define its own terrain. But to approach Badiou's work with the will to fidelity, no matter how skeptical or critical, we must confront the realization that merely to mark and categorize Badiou's contributions to or attempted interventions in the history of philosophy would be—by Badiou's own insistence—strictly anti-philosophical. Moreover, the terrain of philosophy itself, as Badiou has presented it, is one of essential dependence on its four conditions. If the project of fidelity to Badiou is to take place, it should proceed not simply from commentary on his own work, but in two ways: through the production of more actual philosophy in the mode that he claims for it, and outside philosophy through the independent procedures called art, math, politics, and love.

While philosophy's existence, for Badiou, is dependant on the existence of truths, philosophy itself does not produce truths. Philosophy is thinking the mutual but disjunctive construction of truths, which fall under four "procedures" of which philosophy itself is not one. By Badiou's standards the test of philosophy's own legitimacy should come under these four headings. That is, the test is not within the four procedures themselves, nor in philosophy itself as a truth procedure, but in philosophy's relation, or in Lacan's sense "non-relation," to the four procedures of truth.

Of Badiou's "generic procedures," I would suggest that his philosophy of art has received the least attention from critics. Commentators on Badiou have, for obvious reasons, focused on the more provocative of his fidelities: his identification of ontology with mathematics, his Maoism and political militancy, and his striking inclusion of love as one of the specific conditions of philosophy. If Badiou's understanding of art has received less engagement, the obvious reason is that what Peter Hallward calls "his broadly modernist conception of art"[3] may appear comparatively familiar in relation to the other three procedures. In addition, though Badiou's use of certain poets remains a consistent motif throughout his writing, the sense that art as a procedure of truth is ancillary to the other procedures, if not philosophy itself, may derive from the fact that when Badiou "summons" the events constituted by the generic procedure of art the truths are most often utilized for thinking philosophy itself, and more specifically the philosophical problem known as "the event," rather than art.

Badiou warns against collapsing art and philosophy, though he does insist on knots, imitation, and sharing, and even necessary, localized sutures that exist between the two. To look then at the encounter between philosophy and art in Badiou's thinking, as I intend to do here, we cannot simply bracket the other procedures, nor can we work by analogy, but rather we must think the two together. "Thinking the two" is the project of the truth procedure of love, but here the two in question are not like two lovers who cannot be thought from the position of a third party; philosophy itself is the third party. Thinking philosophy and art is like thinking both a star and its constellation.

I will proceed from two directions within the conjunction philosophy and art; first by way of philosophy in its distance from and conditioning by artistic truth and then by way of art as not so much an object but a locus for philosophical prescription.

II The Intraphilosophical Effects of Art

What can we say about this relation that is not one in which the four independent procedures converge without finding a point of contact? Badiou's insistence on the necessity of philosophy to retain what we could call a hard notion of truth, provocative as it may be, is a more immediately comprehensible intervention than understanding what precisely philosophy's relationship to truth ultimately is. Badiou's attacks on the various proclamations of the end of philosophy or the reduction of philosophy to a matter of relativism or pragmatism (for him amounting to the same thing) are centered around a Platonic conception of truth as radically heterogeneous to fact, knowledge, common sense, understanding, and opinion. So while philosophy does not produce truth, its role is also significantly not production of knowledge. So what does philosophy do? "Philosophy is the locus of thinking wherein the 'there are' truths is stated, along with their compossibility" (MPe 141).[4] The "il y a" highlighted by Badiou is to insist that philosophy involves an affirmative practice. It is not a place for equivocation, but for axiomatic exposition. The word compossibility, derived from Leibniz, suggests that the philosopher is something like a non-dialectical mediator. In other words, the four types of truth are placed in what Deleuze might call an "inclusive disjunctive synthesis;" the task is to think them together in their mutual coexistence, while at the same time preserving their autonomy. Given this claim, it may come as some surprise that Badiou also insists that philosophy is fictional and its relation to the other truth procedures is one of imitation. "As a fiction of knowledge, philosophy imitates the matheme. As a fiction of art, it imitates the poem … it is like love without an object … political strategy without any stakes in power" (142). This is evocative of Lacan's "analytic discourse" in which the analyst assumes the locus of the object cause of desire, which is a matter of the excess or the place of the void where truth emerges in the form of a fiction, but not from the analyst himself. Truth must emerge from the analysand, or in the case of philosophy, from lovers, artists, scientists, or political activists. Philosophy is, then, like psychoanalysis for Lacan, a matter of ethics: staving off the sophist who refuses to recognize any affirmative truth, yet simultaneously "staving off disaster," which means not doing away with the sophist by assuming truth is substantial and can be produced by the philosopher herself.

To do art one does not need philosophy. If philosophy's role is seizing the truth of these procedures, it is decidedly not doing the procedures. This is not to say that a philosopher cannot, as Badiou himself has done, write plays and novels, but only that when writing a play, he is no longer a philosopher or, for that matter, a political activist, mathematician, or lover. Hence, Badiou's philosophical reflections on politics he calls metapolitics and his reflections on art, "inaesthetics." Inaesthetics "describes the strictly intraphilosophical effects produced by the independent existence of some works of art" (PM 7). We should understand by this not the description of the effects of the works of art themselves, but a description of the "intraphilosophical effects," which insofar as art is concerned is a matter of "localized prescription, not description."[5] In his *Ethics* he claims there is no "ethics in general," and indeed it would seem that for him there is no aesthetics in general. This is primarily a matter of making any aesthetic reflection a matter of what Badiou calls the situation. "Every philosophical enterprise turns back toward its temporal conditions in order to treat their compossibility at a conceptual level" (IT 91). Philosophy is then a matter of the historicity of the relationship to the generic procedures themselves.

Given Badiou's classicism and anti-historicism, it is important to note his insistence on the situatedness of every philosophical project. This goes for art as for the rest. In Badiou's recent "Fifteen Theses on Contemporary Art," which we will look at in detail below, the word "contemporary" is essential. If Badiou's theses prescribe art that is both universal and eternal, for him this is inseparable from a confrontation with the historical moment.

Desuturing Philosophy and the Poem: Historicity versus Act

The sophistic position of anti-philosophy exists either as the refusal of the possibility of truth *tout court* or as a blockage caused by the handover of truth to some other generic procedure. This is what Badiou calls, using Jacques-Alain Miller's term derived from Lacan, suturing. The question of compossibility is then a matter of desuturing. We must separate Badiou's position from the more familiar insistence that despite the claims of the various postmodernisms or poststructuralisms, one must maintain the status of the Kantian diremption model or the semi-autonomy of art's claim to truth production in relation to politics or philosophy.

For this reason we must look at why Badiou rejects this model as his own. Unlike Habermas, for example, Badiou does not see the question about the relative autonomy of artistic truth in relation to other forms of truth as one about the inheritance of the enlightenment, but rather he views it as a classical question. We can identify Badiou's separation from Kantian aesthetics in his rejection of Aristotle's conception of art. Badiou provides three models for understanding philosophy's relation to art. The models emerged with the inception of philosophy, but he sees them as carrying over into the twentieth century. "Three possible relations of philosophy (as thought) to the poem are *identifying rivalry* [Parmenides], *argumentative distance* [Plato], and *aesthetic regionality* [Aristotle]. In the first case philosophy wants the poem; in the second, it excludes it; and in the third, it categorizes it" (IT 95–96). It should come as no surprise to anyone familiar with Badiou's insistent fidelity to Plato (in part a tactical gesture stemming from a rivalry with Nietzsche, Heidegger, and Deleuze over the stakes of philosophy) that while not sanctioning it, Badiou finds more philosophical purchase in Plato's ban on poetry than Aristotle's categorizing of it. "For Aristotle—as little a poet as is possible in his technique of exposition (Plato, on the other hand, and he recognizes it, is at every moment sensible to the charm he excludes)—the poem is no longer anything but a particular object proposed to the dispositions of knowledge …. With Aristotle, the foundational debate is finished, and philosophy, stabilized in connection to its parts, no longer turns back dramatically upon what conditions it" (94). Hence, Badiou's philosophy of/on art is significantly not an aesthetic philosophy. According to Badiou, an aesthetic model leads to what Lacan calls "the discourse of the university," which is strictly opposed to Badiou's own conception of philosophical thinking. Philosophy's role is not interpretive—it is not about making "sense" of the four generic procedures. On the contrary, philosophy's role is "founding a unique place in which under the contemporary conditions of these procedures, it may be stated how and why a truth is not a sense, being rather a *hole in sense*" (MPe 102). Philosophy, like the four procedures, subtracts itself from both sense-making and sensual experience; the "how" and "why" must be stated through reason. "Philosophy is an insensate act, and by this very fact rational" (MPe 142). Badiou is therefore defending the philosophy of art as not aesthetic or poetic, nor, on the other hand, a matter of making sense of art by understanding it, categorizing it, or defining its parameters. Philosophy is restricted to the "rational act" of seizing the truths of art.

Badiou indicates several suturings that have historically blocked the practice of philosophy. Positivism sutured philosophy to science. Marxism in certain formations sutured philosophy to the political in fidelity to Marx's claim that philosophy's role is no longer to "interpret" but rather to "change" the world. If there is a particular sophist that is situated as the enemy when it comes to the relation of philosophy and artistic truths, it is Heidegger. Heidegger, according to Badiou, sutured philosophy to the poem. Nonetheless, Heidegger remains a great sophist and in regards to philosophy's relationship to the poem, he cannot be ignored. Badiou sees Heidegger's act of suturing as on the one hand a failure in regard to philosophy, but on the other hand, as possessing a saving grace that endows it with a "ground of historicity" (MPe 74), since Heidegger rightly identified the "Age of Poets." Badiou grants that an "Age of Poets," spanning from Hölderlin to Paul Celan, marked not so much the death of philosophy, but a historical sequence in which philosophy lost its "free play" and poetry became the "locus" of enacting the truth of "being and time" (69). This epoch, characterized by "inconsistency and disorientation," was articulated in a kind of subtractive metaphysical poetry. "The scintillating dryness of these poems cut open a space … of historical pathos" (71). Heidegger's work, despite its failure, grasped the event. "The reformulation of that which both joins together and separates the poem and philosophical discursivity is an imperative which, thanks to Heidegger, we must submit ourselves to" (92).

Heidegger is, then, the end of aesthetics, though not the end of the co-existence of art and philosophy. "Until today, Heidegger's thinking has owed its persuasive power to having been the only one to pick up what was at stake in the poem, namely the destitution of object fetishism, the opposition of truth and knowledge, and lastly the essential disorientation of our epoch" (74). Still, because Heidegger failed to grasp the matheme, he turned artistic truth into something sacred. In regards to Heidegger's claim of an "original indistinction" between the poem and the logos, Badiou claims that Parmenides is "not yet philosophy." Badiou continues, "for every truth that accepts its dependence in regard to narrative and revelation is still detained in mystery; philosophy exists only through its desire to tear the latter's veil" (IT 92). If philosophy exists as a certain desacralization and denarrativization, these turn out to be precisely true of artistic truth as well. That is, art, while having access to narrative and the iconography of the image, finds its truth in an immanent interruption with "the sacred authority of the image or the story" (IT 93).

The placement of both narrative and the image as heterogeneous to the rational evokes Lacan's distrust of the imaginary. In order to desuture philosophy or the poem from narrativization, both must borrow from another truth procedure: mathematics. As we've seen, compossibility means we can't think of these procedures in isolation. It is a matter of nondialectical relationality. Badiou is adamant about not confusing different procedures and claims that any given truth procedure itself involves a process of purification. Still, the purification is never complete; every procedure will remain permeated by the other procedures. Badiou freely acknowledges that each procedure will find reason to borrow from the others and they will get tied in knots. Indeed, philosophy's role as thinking compossibility would lose its force if the autonomy of each procedure could be delineated in advance of any event within one of the procedures. This is central to Badiou's philosophical project in its relation to the different procedures—a denial of rivalry, an assertion of independence and yet an ever renewed tension or conflict that demands a subtle and cutting precision to renew the integrity and vitality of each procedure and of the philosophical project more generally.

So, for example, fidelity to mathematical truth is not restricted to the domain of mathematics. Not only philosophical but also poetic, political, and indeed amorous practice (thanks to Lacan) must be presented from an "imperative of consistency

... which turns out to be incompatible with any legitimation by narrative, or by the initiated status of the subject of enunciation" (IT 93). This is of course adamantly not a version of positivism. Badiou finds in figures like Gödel, Cantor, and Cohen a way to think inconsistency as that which underlies consistency, but the mathematical paradigm that permeates philosophy and the other procedures is used to undermine all manner of doxa and what we could loosely call aestheticization. We find ourselves confronted with a mathematics of beauty and a poetry of near-pure abstraction and logic.

Wounds, Knots, and the Law

As we've seen, Badiou's attack on the poetic suture concedes quite a bit to Heidegger, which is to say not the end of philosophy, but the end of aesthetics. Aesthetic reflection as a productive discipline, he seems to be saying—despite the indication that he would never have endorsed the Aristotelian model—comes to an end with Heidegger. It is striking that, despite all the persuasive attacks Badiou makes on what he calls the sophistic position holding that the traumas of the twentieth century have put an end to philosophy, he clearly supports the notion that modernity has seen an end to both moral and aesthetic philosophy, and even to ontology insofar as it is to be thought as within the domain of philosophy. It makes one wonder whether the return to philosophy isn't to a rather impoverished form. And indeed Badiou makes such a claim: "philosophy is under the conditions of art, science, politics, and love, but it is always damaged, wounded, serrated by the evental and singular character of these conditions. Nothing of this contingent occurrence pleases it" (IT 101). All the procedures of truth not only condition philosophy, but also put it into question. Plato, he suggests, recognized that philosophy suffers from the "wound" of art to the concept. Badiou insists that all the conditions of philosophy are also its wounds. "Poem, matheme, politics, and love at once condition and insult philosophy. Condition and insult: that's the way it is" (101).

When philosophy's role cannot be interpretive, journalistic, or literary and cannot be reduced to the status of algebra, it may seem unclear what language philosophy is written in. Badiou's answer is that while philosophy maintains its distance from the generic procedures, since they condition it, it must have recourse to the effects of their truths. While philosophy desutures, it preserves and even engenders tangles. So philosophy does not place a ban on art even within philosophy itself. What saves philosophy from becoming art is a matter of jurisdiction. This is the position that might lend credence to Deleuze's alleged accusation that Badiou is a secret Kantian.[6] Maintaining the category of truth seems to necessitate the adherence to an impersonal law, one determined by reason or rationality as distinct from sense or understanding. Badiou says this about "occurrences of the literary" in philosophy: they "are placed under the jurisdiction of a thought that they do not constitute. They are localized in points at which—in order to complete the establishment of the place in which why and how a truth hollows sense and escapes interpretation is stated—one must precisely, through a paradox of exposition, propose a fable, an image or a fiction to interpretation itself" (IT 104–5). This claim is striking as a weak point in Badiou's philosophy not because philosophy should not have recourse to the literary, but rather in the broader sense of what is meant by compossibility. It reads as a rather strained attempt to smuggle literary devices back into philosophy without conceding anything to so-called anti-philosophy.

Beyond this "paradox of exposition," poetry plays another more specific and more necessary role in philosophy. The nomination of an event "is *always* poetic" (100). When philosophy attempts to present what in the poem constitutes its truth, what he calls "truth's proving of itself" within the poem, it "falls under the imperative of having to propose to sense and interpretation the latent void …. This presentation requires within language the deployment of literary resources; but under the condition that it occur at this very point; thus under the general jurisdiction of an entirely different style" (104). The act of naming the void so central to Badiou's conception of the philosophy is itself literary but in such a way as to be marked as a gesture that refers back to another authority.

Philosophy is therefore knotted up with art, but it must rigorously subtract itself from art's aim. Philosophy's duty to art is to "envisage … the poem as truth of sensible presence deposited in rhythm and image, but without the corporeal captation by this rhythm and this image" (102). It reduces the material of representation to nothing, leaving only presentation. The impoverishment of philosophy is that it must seize the truth of art (and each of the other procedures) but without the jouissance attached to them. Philosophy is characterized by simultaneous impoverishment and excess—deprived of the power to create truth while granted jurisdiction over all truth.

As for philosophy relinquishing the jouissance of art, it is not clear to what extent art itself has access to this jouissance. "Imaginary captation" is hardly prescribed to art by Badiou.[7] On the contrary, it is precisely what needs to be subtracted. Rhythm and image seem ultimately to have a similar role in art to the one they have in philosophy—extrinsic to truth, they subsist as only residue or the site of deposition. And if, as we saw earlier, while philosophy may "imitate" art, in a peculiar reversal, artistic truth must subtract itself from all fictional or mimetic aspects. Like philosophy, both anemic and revitalized, Badiou characterizes poetic truth alternately by lack and excess, as figured correspondingly by Mallarmé and Pessoa.[8] "Excess," of course, is not the discourse of the university, universality as encyclopedic, but rather an inverse method of breaking from particularity toward the impersonal through a kind of infinite dispersion. We could think of Beckett's distinction between himself and Joyce: "He was always adding …. I realized that my own way was in impoverishment, in lack of knowledge and in taking away, in subtracting rather than adding."

III Theses on Contemporary Art: An Annotation

In Badiou's recent "Fifteen Theses on Contemporary Art"[9] we see philosophy conditioned by the truth of art at work. Uncontaminated by reflections about the relation between art and philosophy, it is simply a matter of philosophy: succinct, demanding propositions about what it means to do art. There is no enumeration of the specific evental sites to which the contemporary artist must be faithful, but we could perhaps locate these names or sequences as underlying the individual propositions. What is on display is what Hallward calls his "broadly modernist conception of art," insofar as the emphasis is on impersonality and abstraction.

Badiou's canon, if we can call it that, seems largely still within the framework of the so-called Age of Poets, but to subsume Badiou's theses under the rubric of modernism would not only lazily collapse the impersonality of Mallarmé with that of Eliot, but more importantly would ignore the strictly anti-modernist tendency of the theses—that is, the powerful polemical attack on the will to formal innovation. Instead, I suggest we take seriously what Badiou would call the theses' punctuality. What follows then is only a modest gesture at understanding Badiou's most recent intervention into the relation of philosophy and art—a kind of loose annotation to supplement and open up what we have been pursuing thus far.

1. Art is not the sublime descent of the infinite into the finite abjection of the body and sexuality. It is the production of an infinite subjective series through the finite means of a material subtraction.

All of Badiou's philosophical prescriptions emerge out of a diagnosis. If artistic or aesthetic production is to be a truth procedure, it must say something other than what counts as art within the art world, the accepted discourses surrounding contemporary aesthetic production, and the culture at large. The diagnosis identifies what is counted as art—call it art's sickness. He provides two dominant tendencies and calls them "romanticism" and "formalism."[10]

What Badiou identifies as romanticism, a tendency that he claims still dominates artistic production, is itself a kind of subtractive aesthetic in which sublimation is viewed as oriented toward abjection—exposing the finitude of the body and sexuality. It's not hard to think of much recent work that in the guise of provocation offers up the body as the limit of experience. According to Badiou, this is "only the reversal of the ideology of happiness"[11] and is but another figure for resignation. In other words, the ever-present reminder from consumer culture that happiness and fulfillment are within our grasp, as figured in the still-powerful, if dated, tradition of the "Hollywood ending," finds only corroboration in the romantic gesture that seeks to expose mortality as the final word on human experience.

In Badiou's view, dominant practice, obsessed with finitude as the marker of substantial truth, places infinity on the side of formal innovation. Badiou makes it clear that he believes art will inevitably create new forms, but as a motivation for art, this drive is only a kind of complicity. In this sense he is decidedly not modernist as the term is usually construed. Infinity for him is to be located at the level of what we can crudely call content, whereas formal experimentation should be limited.

2. Art cannot merely be the expression of a particularity (be it ethnic or personal). Art is the impersonal production of a truth that is addressed to everyone.

This claim is true of all truths for Badiou. The insistence is on universalism, which must be established through impersonality. The singular abstracted from any particularity is the only meaning of universal address for Badiou. Badiou is, of course, well aware that what gets called globalization or empire comes with its own form of universalism. His proposal is that whereas the representation of the particular—be it an ethnic group or community or some form of so called "personal expression"—might be conceived as one form of opposition to this "abstract universality of money and power,"[12] what we need is a different form of universality that is concrete.

> *3. Art is the process of a truth, and this truth is always the truth of the sensible or sensual, the sensible as sensible. This means: the transformation of the sensible into a happening of the Idea.*

We see here both the locating of the specificity of artistic truth in the sensible and the insistence on its "transformation" into the idea. Like Deleuze, Badiou sees the impersonal effect of the work as ultimately conceptual or ideational. There is no aesthetic truth, only truths of the aesthetic. Still, it is important to remember that Badiou places the artwork at the edge of the void of sensible experience, which is to say that the process of subtraction or purification is never complete. In this way, the word "happening" is important here; the truth process is an idea-effect, but cannot be reduced to the concept, which is what philosophy works to bring out and articulate. It is important to note that Badiou says that the role of philosophy in regard to science and politics is to identify a "thinking," whereas for art it is matter of "saying." Thinking is "the non-dialectical or inseparable unity of theory and practice" (IT 79). As presence, art stands short of being able to make any distinction between theory and practice, the conceptual and experimental. The experiment of art is immanent, and as the positing of the mere existence of itself, it needs philosophy to delineate its truths. It is, like all truth procedures, a way of thinking, but as an act, it refuses its conceptualization.

Badiou locates the political importance of art explicitly in this thesis. Art's main political value is to resist the new sensible relations to the world proposed by globalization and provide a "proposition about a new definition of what is our sensible relation to the world."[13] Art's value today is about political emancipation, because "without art, without artistic creation, the triumph of the forced universality of money and power is a real possibility."[14] The "something else" posited by an artwork must be other than what is allowed or understood by capitalist experience.

> *4. There is necessarily a plurality of arts, and however we may imagine the ways in which the arts might intersect, there is no imaginable way of totalizing this plurality.*

In addition to an argument against the Wagnerian "total work of art" as a necessarily anti-subtractive conception that would ignore the necessity of the void intrinsic to any truth (a false "excess") or indeed its contemporary variant in the will toward an all-encompassing virtual reality or multimedia experience, we can see Badiou here making an argument against the suturing of the truth of art to any particular form of art. This is significant in part because he could be accused of the tendency to do just that. When Badiou writes about art, he is usually writing about the poem or about literary works more generally, with work on theater and the inclusion of figures like Beckett and Proust among his pantheon of events. One of the four truth procedures listed in *Manifesto for Philosophy* is "the poem," not art (61). His work does contain passing references to music and painting—the events marked by Haydn or Malevich, for example—and in a fascinating essay on cinema, we may be pleased to discover his sensitivity to the progressively subtractive work of the great contemporary Iranian filmmaker Abbas Kiarostami. Nevertheless, given both the propositional nature of artistic truth and poetic nature of the naming of philosophical truths, one should at least open up the question whether, in Badiou's thinking, the compossibility of the different arts within the plurality of arts doesn't tend to find its suture in poetic truth. And given that art is one of the conditions of philosophy, we may wonder whether a rigorous philosophical engagement with the truth of visual art would not alter the practice of philosophy and the other corresponding conditions.

5. Every art develops from an impure form, and the progressive purification of this impurity shapes the history both of a particular artistic truth and of its exhaustion.

We find here both the assertion of the historicity of artistic truth that we have noted before and also an insistence on progress. Works consist in a series, and though the truth and the series may be singular, it seems an individual work is not, since it pursues a process of a fidelity also pursued by other works that it tries to push further to the point of exhaustion. In part, we are seeing here another thesis against the practice of formal innovation. New forms for Badiou are not ex nihilo, but emerge from a passage that happens within the process of purification.

Badiou refers to certain procedures as "saturated," which means that the procedure has become consistent with the regime of sense. It is from the point of view of an event, emerging out of the process of purification, that this saturation comes to light, inaugurating a break or rupture within the history of artistic practice—e.g., after Schönberg, classical music is no longer a viable truth procedure. The question of exhaustion should probably be pushed further however, since it seems that all art for Badiou is itself a kind of art of exhaustion, pushing the sensible to its limits. And since this art of impersonality is to a certain extent modernist or more specifically Mallarméan, when will the art of exhaustion exhaust itself?

6. The subject of an artistic truth is the set of the works which compose it.

The artistic configuration as process of formalization must in a certain sense be repeatable, which is only to say that the void opened up by a single work initiates a process, not that it could ever be a matter of adopting a formula. The single work subject to a truth remains for Badiou a "finite fragment."[15] In addition, we should note that artistic truths are not understood as the work of an artist. The artist may lend his name to the event constituted by his own work, but the subject to the truth is the works themselves and not the individual who was an instrument in their creation. Indeed, the artist is, "finally, what disappears in art."[16] Badiou is of course proposing an ethic radically antagonistic to the cult of the artist in which the artist is identified with the work and subsequently rewarded. There is a kind of martyrdom to artistic creation. He claims the ethic of art is "desperation." We must separate this ethic from its simulacrum, the fake martyrdom of the romantic artist. Of course, the "desperation" should not be marketable, like David Blaine suspended over the Thames, but nor should we be seduced by more subtle variations in which the apparent disappearance of the artist as creator only draws more attention to the elusive figure behind the work, rather than to the work itself.

> *7. This composition is an infinite configuration, which, in our own contemporary artistic context, is a generic totality.*

The generic totality is by definition unconstructable, an infinite set. It contains its own void or point of rupture, which is why there is no totality for Badiou except the generic totality. This is to say that in principle there is no limit to the number of works that can compose the subject of an artistic truth.

> *8. The real of art is ideal impurity conceived through the immanent process of its purification. In other words, the raw material of art is determined by the contingent inception of a form. Art is the secondary formalization of the advent of a hitherto formless form.*

The idea of "secondary formalization" suggests Freud's concept of secondary revision. The analogy here would be between the relation of secondary revision and the dream work to art and its raw material. For Freud, "secondary revision" gives coherence and legibility to the fragmented manifest content of the dream work. Art lends consistency to its raw material, the real or void of what conditions it; it is not itself that real. Nonetheless, the real only emerges through the artwork itself.

> *9. The only maxim of contemporary art is not to be imperial. This also means: it does not have to be democratic, if democracy implies conformity with the imperial idea of political liberty.*

Non-imperial art is evocative of what Deleuze and Guattari call the minor. Art should relinquish its claim to authority while at the same time stubbornly refusing appropriation. It is significant that the maxim of contemporary art should be in a negative form, a proscription rather than a prescription. Art, which is meant to make exist what is not allowed to exist, must justify its existence through the artistic act. Artistic experimentation in its loosest sense is not endorsed by Badiou. Art must begin from a refusal.

> *10. Non-imperial art is necessarily abstract art, in this sense: it abstracts itself from all particularity, and formalizes this gesture of abstraction.*

> *11. The abstraction of non-imperial art is not concerned with any particular public or audience. Non-imperial art is related to a kind of aristocratic-prole-*

tarian ethic: alone, it does what it says, without distinguishing between kinds of people.

Abstract art is not the evacuation of content, but of particularity. We see again that Badiou opposes the notion of art as ever being a matter of asserting the truth of any particular subject position. Art as presentation but not representation should intervene at the edge of the void of the situation, which means, for Badiou, not being able to be included in the meta-structure or state of the situation. All art is like Mallarmé's book: "it is the one that comes into being by itself; it is made, and exists, by itself." For Badiou, Mallarmé's seemingly extreme assertion of art's autonomy means that the event constituted by an artwork is that part of the artwork that cannot be counted or claimed. What has been called Mallarmé's hermeticism is for Badiou precisely the statement of universalism and a figure for democracy, though one contrary to any notion of consensus or the common denominator.[17] That which is addressed to everyone equally will, like a star, necessarily seem elevated, distant, and strange, qualities that should not be mistaken for hermeticism or elitism.

12. Non-imperial art must be as rigorous as a mathematical demonstration, as surprising as an ambush in the night, and as elevated as a star.

Here we see the analogy to the other procedures—their sharing or imitation. We can also see Badiou's localized use of the literary for philosophical purposes. Art is informed by the other procedures with which it must be made compossible. From mathematics it borrows rigor and consistency as well as a certain irreducibility. The ambush evokes surprise and political risk and the star suggests both distance and authority. All three may indicate the "new," and Badiou would like to maintain the importance of the new in what could be considered a modernist vein. But again we must recognize that he is not talking about new forms. He says art must "create a new possibility," but he insists this is not to "realize" a new possibility.[18] Again, this latter is the philosophy of the market—there are infinite possibilities within our finite world. Art should say "something else" is possible. Dominant art insists that all is possible because all is impossible. That is, within our closed, globalized, liberal, capitalist world, innovation is infinite. For Badiou, art should on the contrary refuse innovation, but say that another world is possible.

13. Today art can only be made from the starting point of that which, as far as Empire is concerned, doesn't exist. Through its abstraction, art renders this inexistence visible. This is what governs the formal principle of every art: the effort to render visible to everyone that which for Empire (and so by extension for everyone, though from a different point of view), doesn't exist.

This is a corollary to the maxim of art as non-imperial. Empire is the state of the situation, but not the situation itself. The gesture of art is to present that which Empire cannot count. From this vantage point we can understand Badiou's insistence on abstracting from particularity. The assertion of the particularity of a specific group, however oppressed, is a matter of making it countable within the state. The oppression itself is what the state ignores and what must be made visible by abstracting the particularity on which the state relies.

> *14. Since it is sure of its ability to control the entire domain of the visible and the audible via the laws governing commercial circulation and democratic communication, Empire no longer censures anything. All art, and all thought, is ruined when we accept this permission to consume, to communicate, and to enjoy. We should become the pitiless censors of ourselves.*

Art is always giving form to the void of the current configuration of artistic production or indeed of the imitation of artistic production. The self-censorship Badiou advocates, then, is not the crude form of proscription of content, but rather a matter of rejecting the lure of sublimation as Freud conceived of it in its most basic form—the conversion of libido to something socially desirable in a thoroughly conventional sense and therefore in Badiou's sense "imperial." But, as Badiou suggests elsewhere, art must necessarily engage in a rigorous subtractive mode with the vulgar productions of the culture industry. That is, art is not indifferent to the culture of consumption. In the case of cinema for example, Badiou proposes that one direction of the purification process of cinematic truth should be directed toward what Adorno and Horkheimer called the prudish pornography of Hollywood film. It could be argued that Hollywood has since become less prudish, but as Badiou points out, it was the proscriptions of the Hays Code that lead to the use of metonymic desire in classical Hollywood, its saving grace, but a process that has become saturated through Empire's progressive ban on censorship. Since the classical period, the culture industry has taken the direction of explicit use of "extreme violence, cruelty" and "the motif of erogenous nudity" (IT 116–17) while remaining as prudish as ever in regard to desire. These forms constitute raw material that needs to be submitted to artistic purification. This process should be directed "not through an aggressive posture with respect to inherited forms, but through mechanisms that arrange these forms at the edge of the void, in a network of cuts and disappearances."[19]

> *15. It is better to do nothing than to contribute to the invention of formal ways of rendering visible that which Empire already recognizes as existent.*

Art must abstract itself from the production of the new in commodity culture. Unlike the other procedures, as a matter of the sensible, art is especially susceptible to being folded back into what Empire recognizes. We might be able to perceive in this statement a reversal of what Badiou sees as Wittgenstein's anti-philosophical claim that "everything that can be expressed can be expressed clearly. Everything else must be passed over in silence." Badiou's claim for art is that which Empire allows expression must be censored, not of course by the state, but by the artist herself. Only what is passed over in silence must be given expression.

....

IV Artistic Specificity: Conclusions, Questions

Find an artist who is not trying to make a name for himself and not just one who says he is not trying to make a name for himself. Find an artist not invested in pathos or the false materialism that unveils the animal nature of man as the limit of experience. Find an artist who does not seek formal novelty. I told an artist friend what Badiou's theses proscribed and his immediate response was: "But what else is there?" Badiou's wager is, of course, something else.

We see in Badiou's theses the way in which diagnosis is followed by prescription, but in original and striking ways. The diagnosis merely marks the empty space for what is missing that an artistic truth would offer. If Badiou is proposing a kind of aesthetics of resistance, it cannot be a simple matter of reversal or inversion of dominant forms or mere avoidance of the symptoms. The prescription must involve some element of forcing. We can view here the philosophical importance of the void in Badiou's work. It marks a place for resistance both immanent to dominant and oppressive practice, but also necessarily unacceptable to it and unanticipated by it. Subtraction is the elimination of the terrain of the opposition, but it must be a rigorous and rational procedure and not the sort of confident indifference that more often than not repeats what it sought to ignore. This is a point which sharply separates Badiou from the strain of post-Deleuzian aesthetics that seeks justification for artworks based on the notion that they exhibit unconstrained raw affect.

What makes art its own generic procedure, what gives it its "eventual and singular character," is that it is the truth of sense or, as Badiou says, "of the sensible." Since as we saw, all truth is a matter of making a hole in sense, rupturing the regime of sense-making, art has the peculiar position of presenting the truth of that which truth itself interrupts. Sensual material is reduced to its "minimal image." Art is then the self-negation of its own material, a breaking of its own mirror. As Badiou says, "to make something appear (swan, star, rose) to appear only insofar as it is canceled out is constitutive of the poetic act" (PM 161). Inaesthetics is then not simply meta-aesthetics but the reduction of the aesthetic to its own absence or void. It is this that allows Badiou to claim that art is pure presence. Art is the assertion of the existence of a "formless form." But what we could call inaesthetics seems to be characteristic of both the philosophical expounding on art and artistic truth itself. Both privilege logos over pathos. The distinction is a matter of philosophy's claim to historicity. According to Badiou, "one could maintain that poetry is the thought of the presence of the present. And it is precisely because of this that it is not in rival with philosophy, which has as its stake the compossibility of time, and not pure presence" (IT 99). Art is a kind of interrupted philosophy, philosophy an interrupted art. Art stops short before the proposition, philosophy stops short before jouissance.

We are confronted with a seeming paradox. Art is distinguished from philosophy in two significant ways. First, it is a truth procedure, whereas philosophy is not. Secondly, its means or material is imaginary and sensual experience. But its material, its relation to the object world, is precisely what needs to be evacuated for artistic truth to reveal itself. Hence art's purifying itself of non-art starts to seem a lot like non-art's purifying itself of art. In other words, art starts to seem a lot like philosophy. If the act of art reduces art to the minimal difference between art and non-art so as to give way to the idea, then the articulation of the idea supplied by a philosophy that equally refuses to provide any context or elucidation of the process may become superfluous.

A series of questions follows. What justifies Badiou's end to aesthetics, which for him means the end of narrative and image? If this is truly an historical claim, why do we remain in a generally classical framework? Though Badiou insists that there is no ban on narrative or image even within philosophy, they are clearly devalued for him within art. We must question this Lacanian undermining of the imaginary, particularly as it pertains to art, a subject which in Badiou's own opinion was not Lacan's strong suit. Finally, we must ask whether the locus of truth in any given generic procedure really derives from within that procedure. To what extent are the truths seized by philosophy concretely dependent on the integrity, or to use Badiou's word, "consistency," of each generic procedure? The insistence on progress and sequence within a set of works that constitute the subject of a truth makes any dialectical play between works or across procedures seem limited. One has to wonder whether the different generic procedures can not only share with, but actually condition one another without the mediation of philosophy. Is it too crude to ask whether within Badiou's philosophy itself, fidelity to the matheme might be conditioned by an aesthetic of austere impersonality or vice versa? That is, how can we be sure that the jurisdiction actually lies in philosophy and reason and not elsewhere? Is philosophy possible for one who, through lack of exposure, has not recognized the event of ontology as mathematics? Is art? For Badiou, does one necessarily fail ethically as a philosopher if he limits his purview to political and aesthetic truths and their compossibility without necessarily refusing science or love the possibility of truth? Does philosophy demand fluency with all the generic procedures of truth? If so, must one, within art, have fluency with the plurality of arts?

If we take seriously, as I believe we should, Badiou's insistence that art is one of the four specific conditions of philosophy as well a locus to which philosophy must direct its thought, then we cannot subsume what Badiou has to say about art under either his taste or his aesthetic. Perhaps we cannot ignore the question of whether Badiou's admiration for certain poets as well as his own philosophical style may not overdetermine his philosophical pronouncements on art, but we can always subtract precisely those elements. We must do justice to the attempt, rare today, to reassert philosophy as holding place for both poetic and mathematical truth, not to mention political and amorous truth, while refusing at once any transcendent point from which to evaluate these truths and any value to the encyclopedic categorizing of them. To claim simply that there is a transcendent function that overdetermines a certain conjoining of the conditions would cut short one of the richest and most ambitious attempts to revitalize philosophical thinking. Nonetheless, the questions remain necessary, constitutive even of a certain phase of affirmative practice. There must be a place in philosophy for a distance that doesn't condemn us to a forced choice between fidelity and silence. In the best of Badiou's work, we encounter a rare voice of rigorous commitment cutting through the rhetoric of accommodation, equivocation, and ideological affirmation toward a point that hits upon what is essential in the historical moment. The theses on art provide an example of Badiou's philosophy in action. Hardly a stale modernism, they gesture toward something like a new Platonic realism. The practice of thinking the void in any situation is one that must always be renewed, and Badiou's focused interventions offer a set of claims that are meant to be polemical and contentious. We are left with a worthy challenge: To think a non-imperial art, an art of beauty without pleasure, demonstrative, surprising, illuminating, other-worldly, and unconsumable.

"Something else is possible" is what Badiou says art must say. After our litany of critical questions, let's end with a final question of a different nature. Let's pose the wager not as an axiom, but an open question: Is something else possible, something outside available forms and systems of knowledge, something that can't be reduced to finite permutations of language and bodies? And if so, if we accept this proposition, what are the consequences? ■

....

1   Alain Badiou, "Fifteen Theses On Contemporary Art," *Lacanian Ink* 23 (2004): 110.
2   Ibid., 111.
3   Peter Hallward, *Badiou: A Subject to Truth* (Minneapolis: University of Minnesota Press, 2003), 193.
4   [For a list of Badiou's principal texts and their corresponding abbreviations, see the introduction to this issue.—Ed.]
5   Quoted in Hallward, op. cit., 195.
6   In his book on Deleuze, Badiou claims that Deleuze often tried to "pin on" him the label "Kantian," but he does not go into detail about Deleuze's justification for the criticism. See, for example, De 77.
7   Of course, for Lacan, jouissance is not identical to "imaginary captation," but when Badiou speaks of the jouissance of art that must be subtracted from philosophy, he aligns it with the pleasures of narrative, image and rhythm.
8   See Hallward, op. cit., 198.
9   The numbered italicized sections below are Badiou's theses as presented in December 2003 and can be found in English translation by Peter Hallward at http://www.lacan.com/frameXXIII7.htm. My commentary follows. Oddly, the publication of Badiou's own commentary on the theses in *Lacanian Ink* 23 under the title "Fifteen Theses on Contemporary Art" does not include the theses themselves, but leaves the reader to infer them from the commentary.
10 Badiou, "Fifteen Theses," 103.
11 Ibid., 105.
12 Ibid.
13 Ibid., 107.
14 Ibid.
15 Hallward, op. cit., 196.
16 Badiou, "Fifteen Theses," 109.
17 Cf. thesis 9.
18 Badiou, "Fifteen Theses," 111.
19 Quoted in Hallward, op. cit., 196.

THE LION.

Badiou and Beckett:
Actual Infinity, Event, Remainder

Andrew Gibson

Actual Infinity

This essay is part of a sustained and ongoing project whose object is to think the work of Alain Badiou and Samuel Beckett together.[1] I am not aiming to produce yet another "philosopher-based" account of Beckett. Nor am I concerned to tell the story of Badiou's own considerable interest in Beckett or to elucidate his work on him. My purpose is rather to think through a certain set of (to me, ungainsayable) conceptual relations between two oeuvres. This is not an idle matter. My interest is in thinking the two together as a complex nexus and focal point for some important contemporary aesthetic, ethical, and political questions. In a still larger context and in the longer term, what I am hoping to do is to characterize and explore the full implications of what I call a "thought of intermittency" as it has been emerging over the past twenty years, chiefly in France, and which, at the present time, I associate chiefly with the work of Badiou, Jacques Rancière, and Françoise Proust. Beguiled, firstly by grand theory and then by cultural studies and the smorgasbord of postmodern liberalisms, the Anglo-American academy has granted it scant attention, failed to notice it for what it is or get the measure of what it might mean for us. Beckett is crucial. This is not just because, as I indicate here and will show in much more detail elsewhere, he is a great modern thinker of an intermittent world, but because the philosophers I have just mentioned partly develop their "thought of intermittency" out of modern literature, with Mallarmé, above all, as guiding light. Indeed, here philosophy looks belated; though I suspect that Badiou would also urge us to add that, in the same context, modern literature itself looks belated in comparison to modern mathematics.

The concept most crucial to my attempt to think Badiou

and Beckett together is what I call "the pathos of intermittency."[2] Since the phrase appears in neither oeuvre and, for Badiou, "pathos" is always a negative term, I clearly have some explaining to do. In "Philosophie et mathématique," Badiou asserts that, from Plato up to and including Kant, philosophy and mathematics are inter-involved. For Descartes, Leibniz, Spinoza, and many other philosophers, only mathematics can properly instigate the crucial, founding break with ignorance, myth, and superstition. Mathematics and intellect are inseparable. Mathematics is the primary form "of an integrally laicized thought" (C 159).[3] But romantic philosophy more or less completely separates philosophy from mathematics, with Hegel playing the decisive role. The anti-philosophical stance of positivism does no more than mirror the anti-mathematical stance of romanticism. For romantics and positivists alike, mathematics is neither a founding condition of philosophy nor a kind of thought.

Hegel and the romantics reject mathematics because they "temporalize the concept" (161).[4] The romantics believe that infinity can only be conceived of in terms of time, as a kind of "temporal ecstasy" (161). In comparison with the heady excitement of this conviction, the crystalline, idealized, mathematical conception of infinity seems barrenly abstract. For mathematical infinity is indifferent and impermeable to the passing of time. So Hegel gets what he wanted: mathematics loses its status as a means of thinking infinity.[5] In the process, however, he and the romantics set up a structure whose essence is pathos and from which we have yet to recover. Mathematics thinks infinity strictly in relation to the "closed power" of an order of signs (162). By contrast, the romantics can conceive of infinity only as a boundless exteriority, an openness without end. The trouble is that, against this horizon, the tragic historicity of finite beings becomes all the more sharply perceptible. We are separated from infinity by an uncrossable limit. By the same token, infinity becomes an object of insatiable yearning. It is placed within a structure that opposes it to transience, historical mortality, the birth and death of ideas.

In this respect, we are still very much in the shadow of romanticism, however irreducibly modern we say we are. But the romantic legacy is profoundly disabling. Certainly, it flatters our narcissism, our need for tragic grandeur, for an auratic conception of the infinite. But it prevents us from setting out on the adventure (not least, the political adventure) that has potentially been ours since the modern proclamation of the death of God. The contemporary world precisely demonstrates this. More or less secretly, we believe ourselves to be prisoners of our historicity and materiality. We are immersed in *"the pathos of finitude"* (176, italics mine). This insistently drives us back in the direction of religion. Here modernity confronts its most forbidding impasse, of which "postmodernism" in any interesting sense now appears to have been a short-term, short-lived, insufficient formulation. The question is all around us, at the current time: how can modernity move decisively beyond its romantic determinations? For Badiou, the only way of doing so—"l'unique voie royale que je connaisse" (163)—is putting mathematics back at the heart of philosophy. This is crucial, above all, insofar as mathematics presents us with a flat, solid, laicized concept of eternity, and therefore offers us the chance of getting away from the pathos of finitude.

Set theory in particular spells a "radical desacralization" of eternity (164).[6] On 25 March, 1974, *Der Spiegel* ran the headline, "Macht Mengenlehre krank?" ("Does set theory damage your health?").[7] Badiou might answer that, if so, then so much the better.[8] Badiou takes set theory to be massively significant for modernity.[9] This is because it gives an account of an actually existing, accessible infinity, which he equates with Being. For Aristotle in the *Physics*, infinity is a notion that is inescapably associated with time. Infinity can be conceived of only in relation to a temporal sequence, to time as a process of becoming that we cannot grasp in its totality. This means that, as a whole, infinity has only a potential existence. Infinity in this description—potential infinity—is an indeterminate, variable quantity which increases beyond all finite limits. This is the standard conception of infinity according to what is known as classical finitism. But set theory provides an abstract account, not of a potential but of an actual infinity. Infinity or, better, infinities are actually there, all at once. The assertion of actual infinity is the cornerstone of Badiou's thought.[10] For he takes Being itself to be actually infinite.

The account of actual infinity that set theory provides is awesomely sophisticated. It produces "a total dissemination, a disunification, of the concept of the infinite" (EE 305). In other words, as its founder Georg Cantor put matters, there is absolutely no "'Genus Supremum' of the actual infinite."[11] Set theory presents us with an infinity of infinities. These infinities are of different sizes. An infinity of one kind of object can differ in number from an infinity of another kind. However, infinities are also determinate. This is true in two ways. Firstly, set theory regards infinite pluralities, not, vaguely, as limitless, but as objects or sets; that is, a given infinity has a determinate membership. Cantor asserts, for example, that, if the totality of all finite, positive integers is infinite, that is, if it surpasses in magnitude every finite quantity, it is also, for all that, "a definite quantum, fixed in all its parts."[12] Given any unending sequence of increasing numbers, there is a smallest actually infinite domain containing them all. This is intrinsic to Cantor's very definition of a set as "any collection of definite elements *which can be united by a law* into a whole."[13] For the most significant of later mathematicians—certainly those most important to Badiou, like Gödel and Cohen—set theory produces completed infinities that possess identifiable and determinate number-theoretic properties.

Secondly, an infinity is also determinate in that it can be conceived of as existing all at once. Cantor understood the definition of number as requiring, not "the addition of ones" (in a temporal sequence), but "a single act of abstraction."[14] The sheer, peremptory radicality of this "act" is very appealing to Badiou. In Cantor's wake, the mathematician most responsible for the axiomatization of set theory was Ernst Zermelo. Zermelo, too, sought to avoid selecting units in succession, to make possible a simultaneous or "timeless" conception of a set. Not all modern mathematical procedures work like this. The procedures Badiou most distrusts—constructivist procedures—are strictly successive. But for Badiou, sets are not just constructible objects, but objects that already exist. His conception of mathematical entities is in this respect Platonic, and quite distinct from the Euclidean emphasis on counting.[15]

Cantor himself took Locke, Descartes, Spinoza, Leibniz, Hobbes, and Berkeley all to task for dismissing the concept of actual infinity.[16] But that the philosophers have been wary is perhaps not surprising: the implications of the concept are far-reaching. Cantor asserted that "there is no distinction between the finite and the vast realm of infinity that comes within the orbit of mathematics."[17] He treated mathematical infinities like finite objects: the "unified treatment" of the mathematical domain is precisely what is involved in Cantor's discovery of what he called the "transfinite" realm. In dissolving the frontier between finite and infinite, Cantor allows man to share what had been solely God's preserve.

This is not true, however, in any grandiose (romantic or humanist) sense. It lays no salve to either our anthropocentrism or our *hubris*. Both Aristotle and Christian theologians rejected the use of completed infinities: in Aristotle's phrase, "the infinite cannot be a quantum."[18] The advocate of what is known as classical finitism recoils from Cantor's universe. He or she obstinately insists on the pragmatic imperative: neither experience nor application suggests any basis or need for the idea of actual infinity. "Actual infinity" does not have any empirical sense, and can be set aside as a fascinating but idle by-product of mathematical ingenuity. But if classical finitism is pragmatic, it also salvages the religious domain, the conjunction (pragmatism and theology) being very significant, not least today. For the classical finitist argues that, if infinity can be grasped at all, it is in other than worldly terms. The theological leap is the only possible resort. Badiou argues that the finite ontology of classical finitism has long been closely intertwined with an infinite theology.[19] If, from a worldly perspective, infinity is always potential infinity, that is, if it must always remain tantalizingly incomplete, the only possible way of conceiving of potential infinity as a whole is thinking it as God. The theological or mystical and the pragmatic dispositions can thus go placidly hand in hand. So much is clear from the example of Wittgenstein. Not surprisingly, Wittgenstein was fiercely hostile towards set theory.[20]

If Badiou and Beckett share anything, it is an antipathy to theological leaps and pragmatic imperatives alike.[21] This is a matter of intellectual rigor perhaps even more than ethical principle. But there are problems in any case with classical finitism. Mary Tiles makes the objections to potential infinity very clear:[22] the classical finitist asserts that infinity is only potential, not actual; that is, any attempt to think it can do so on the basis of complete, finite segments. Potential infinity is never complete and can never be completed. The concept of potential infinity is thus intrinsically linked to a concept of becoming. The potentially infinite is "an inescapably temporal notion."[23] For if infinity is determined spatially, it must be actual (or space is either finite, or inseparable from time). However, any general concept of becoming is illogical since, if becoming becomes, it must transform itself in becoming, putting itself beyond conceptual reach. Cantor understood this: the concept of potential infinity must imply, not just limitlessness, but limitless variability. Thus to think variability on the basis of any given, finite segment is to think variability on the basis of a variable, and to lose "any fixed support for the study."[24] The only way of thinking variability at all is to decree its "domain" beforehand, through a definition.[25]

This is what mathematics superlatively does. There can be no prior, existing, general categories for thinking potential infinity—Aristotelian universals, for example—because they will themselves be transformed in becoming. (Cantorian set theory spells the death of such categories insofar as they restrict the thought of infinity.) The only precise way of establishing a "domain" is to think it as a "set of values" that is at once "definite" and actually infinite. This is one of Cantor's "core principles": any potential infinity in fact presupposes a corresponding actual infinity.[26] Variability can only be thought intelligibly and free from contradiction within a completed domain. But this means that the concept of potential infinity collapses into a concept of actual infinity the presentation of which is accomplished by mathematics. It is through the discipline of mathematics and it alone that such a general concept as infinity can be established. Classical finitism itself requires an account of generalization which, in this context, set theory can best provide. In many ways, for as long as we remain bound up in a thought of infinity—and it is hard to imagine our not being so, at least in some sense, whilst the culture remains in thrall to religious and post-religious formations—set theory holds out the most complex and subtle system for addressing it.

That rather understates the case: the universe of set theory is prodigious, extraordinarily fertile in inventive discoveries. On the one hand, almost as soon as Cantor had achieved his most important breakthroughs, set theory was thrown into brief disarray by what Bernays later called "the shock of the antinomies."[27] It was assailed by contradictions and paradoxes, like Russell's paradox and the Burali-Forti paradox, which threatened it with the charge of inconsistency, peculiarly damning for mathematicians.[28] Set theory clearly required a more solid foundation than Cantor had been able to give it: the consequence was its rapid axiomatization. This was achieved in the so-called ZF (Zermelo-Fraenkel) axioms. On the other hand, in Badiou's phrase, set theory as a whole "has constantly been enriched with new monsters," above all, through theory of the "large cardinals" (EE 344).[29] Looked at in detail or for any length of time, the book of set theory in fact turns out to be an endlessly fascinating bestiary.

To begin very simply: mathematicians distinguish between ordinal and cardinal numbers. Ordinals are the counting numbers. They denote a process of ordering and are sometimes explained in terms of the places in a queue. (Think of the numbered tickets at the delicatessen counters in supermarkets). Cardinals denote magnitude, answer the question, "How many?" and are arrived at by "pairing" not "queuing."[30] The correspondence of the set {knife, fork, spoon} to the set {1, 2, 3} means that its cardinality is 3.[31] The obvious objection, here, is that this is merely to number a cardinality by an ordinal. Are cardinals not just ordinals by another name? This is in fact the case so long as we remain within the realm of finite number. But in the realm of infinite number, as I've said, there exists an infinity of infinities. Once it has been established that infinities may be different in size, this gives rise to the separation of the notion of cardinality from that of ordinality, because cardinality is linked to the existence of one-to-one correspondences, whilst ordinality is linked to a generalization of the counting process. There can be no one-to-one correspondence, for example, between the infinity of the real numbers and that of the natural numbers, because there are not as many numbers in the second infinity as there are in the first.[32]

Equally, there are numbers like inaccessible cardinals that cannot be "reached from below," that is, by a process of addition.

Thus cardinality takes on a life of its own. With the power set axiom, this life takes on staggering proportions. The power set axiom—for every set, there is always its power set[33]—generates new orders of cardinality, an infinitely increasing sequence of infinite cardinals. The consequence of this has been "the pursuit of the large cardinals program" that "has formed the core of modern research into pure set theory."[34] This program has spawned the vast, chimerical creatures that lurk beyond the bounds of the ZF axioms: Mahlo, weakly compact, hyper-Mahlo, ineffable, measurable, Ramsey, supercompact, huge, and n-huge cardinals.[35] There is a point at which infinite numbers become too large for set theory to deal with, where infinity escapes numerical treatment. There can also be no set of sets, because its power set will always exist and be larger than it.

But size isn't everything. Infinite cardinals are not only very big indeed. In mathematical terms, they "are extraordinarily ill behaved."[36] Indeed, bad behavior, or at least illogical behavior, seems sadly common in the universe of set theory. Most fundamentally of all, an infinite set can be put into a one-to-one correspondence with a part of itself—the sets of the natural and even numbers, for example, $\{0, 1, 2, 3, \ldots, n\}$ and $\{4, 6, 8, 10, \ldots, n\}$—even though there are self-evidently many more numbers in the first set than the second. Dedekind was the first to point this out. He took it to define an infinite set. Or take Cantor's diagonal argument: according to this, no matter how rationally and completely the mathematical description of a line is constructed, the description of itself clearly generates holes in itself, irrational numbers which it could not itself have taken into account.[37] Thus the work of exhaustive denumeration proves the truth of non-denumerability. Or take Cohen's concept of "forcing," one that is extremely important for Badiou: there is a restriction on the sets that we can find in the universe of set theory according to the ZF axioms. There are some sets and subsets about which it does not allow mathematicians to talk. But Cohen showed that it was possible to add such sets to the universe of set theory by a method of "forcing." As a consequence of "forcing," in the words of one mathematical study, "marvelous things happen."[38]

Marvelous, but disconcerting: it becomes possible to prove, as Cantor so devoutly wished to, that the power set of the first, smallest infinite cardinal is equal to the second infinite cardinal. This is represented as $2^{\aleph_0} = \aleph_1$, the formula for Cantor's famous Continuum Hypothesis. The trouble is that it also becomes possible to prove that $2^{\aleph_0} = \aleph_2$, $2^{\aleph_0} = \aleph_3$, and so on. The position of $2^{\aleph_0}$ in the sequence of infinite cardinals is in fact not only undetermined but "*extravagantly* undetermined."[39] Furthermore, to the concepts of monstrosity and extravagance, we must also add that of trauma or catastrophe, in the sense in which Hallett writes of the "traumatic" or "catastrophic" stages in the development of numbers.[40] He is thinking for example of ω, the first limit ordinal or transfinite number. Cantor produced it according to a *Hemmungsprinzip*, a principle of limitation which breaks up the sequence of ordinals. The first transfinite number expresses the natural, regular order of the entire set of finite ordinals as a limit which the natural numbers approach but never reach. Badiou puts the point like this: where Hegel sees only a supposedly unending sequence, Cantor's actual infinity requires "another place," the limit ordinal, another initial point of being (EE 184). In that respect, ω institutes a "traumatic" breach.

The universe of set theory bristles with strange features: infinite cardinals can be doubled and remain the same size.[41] As Cantor was the first to prove, $\mathbb{N} \times \mathbb{N}$ may have the "same number of elements as $\mathbb{N}$." If a is an infinite cardinal then by definition we have $a = a + 1$. But therefore $a + 0 = a + 1$, and we apparently have the contradiction $0 = 1$.[42] The "non-commutativity" of transfinite ordinals means that the sum of two elements in a given order is not the same as the sum of the same two elements when the order is reversed: $a + b \neq b + a$. It would not be hard to continue this list. As Pierre Verstraeten points out, the virtue of set theory, and the advantage it has over "other modes of thought," is that it presents the multiple in terms of strict consistencies, but without canceling out the inconsistency from which they spring.[43] Thus the most demanding and rigorously logical procedures unceasingly produce, require, or run up against lacunae, discontinuities, and incongruities. It may seem as though I have resorted to an overly dramatic language to convey the point, that I have converted the universe of set theory into a kind of Disneyland of number. My intention is something like the reverse. I have simply scooped up the daubs of color in my account from mathematicians' own non-mathematical accounts of their work. (They are well worth the scooping). But much more importantly, I have tried to highlight the strange richness of actual infinity, not just because Badiou does, but because he also repeatedly emphasizes what he calls its "neutral banality" (C 164).

The paradox is crucial, and we must try to think it through as rigorously as we can with reference to both Badiou and Beckett: number exists as both "une foisonnante diversité et une sourde monotonie," an abundant diversity and a dull monotony (NN 227). What in one respect are "myriad multiplicities" are, in another, virtually indistinguishable (227). The prolific richness of actual infinity is also a "flatness endless," to quote a Miltonic, Milton-inverting inversion from Beckett's *Lessness*.[44] In set theory as in Beckett, the invention or discovery of a host of precise and exquisite differences is inseparable from the confirmation of a principle of sameness. Badiou associates this "ingrate identité formelle," this intractable formal identity (EE 271) with actual infinity. I quote his phrase because it echoes a sentence from Beckett's *Assez* that Badiou himself repeatedly quotes: "Terre ingrate, mais pas totalement."[45] The sentence closes not only "L'écriture du générique," Badiou's essay on Beckett in *Conditions*, but the book itself. Beckett himself translates the phrase as "Stony ground, but not entirely."[46] For Badiou, however, "Terre ingrate" principally means "thankless Earth." The features of actual infinity may in one respect seem curious, intriguing, even scintillating. But there is another respect in which actual infinity is thankless because it lacks feature. If it is "not entirely" intractable, that is because, in principle, it can always be supplemented.

To understand the point, we should recognize that, for Badiou, mathematics says what can be said about Being. Mathematics is ontology. Mathematicians tend to think that the consequences of set theory are finally anarchic, and that it can therefore have no ontological authority. Badiou would argue that that is to think the meaning of ontology only within certain restrictive limits. His own logic is startlingly conveyed by a kind of shrug at the end of *Le nombre et les nombres*, §15.1 (pages 174–75). In 15.1, Badiou confronts the *fourmillement* (welter) of numbers. Numbers are themselves innumerable. They exceed the ordinals beyond all reason: "this 'more than' vacillates beyond the thresholds of sense" [*ce "plus" vacille au-delà des lisières du sens*]. For each ordinal, there will be as many more different numbers as there are parts of the ordinal. The ordinals themselves are "an inconsistent multiplicity." By how incalculably much more so, then, is the number of numbers. Indeed, given any particular ordinal, the exact quantity of the set of its parts is in any case unknowable, "undecidably" in excess of it.

The set of the parts is therefore, quite plausibly, "'immensely' bigger" (though also possibly only "'minimally' bigger") than the ordinal. Furthermore, any ordinal will provide the material for more possible numbers than there are elements in the ordinal itself. Once again, the excess in question is undecidable. The number of numbers is thus an inconsistency of inconsistencies. It is precisely at this point in his argument that Badiou shrugs: "in reality, the easiest thing to say is simply this: *Number is co-extensive with Being.*" Badiou rightly assumes that what we can say about Being is that, contrary to all habitual assumptions that, somewhere along the line, it will turn out to be a unity, in fact, it is always irreducibly multiple. Not only that: its infinite multiplicity infinitely exceeds our ability to express it. In a sense, there is nothing more to be said about Being than that. Insofar as any expression of its infinite multiplicity is possible at all, that expression is mathematical. However limited and even defective,[47] mathematics seems incontrovertibly to be the sole discourse that begins to approach the pure multiplicity of Being, in terms adequate to it, as an actual infinity.

There are two features of the mathematical account of actual infinity—two aspects of the relative adequacy of mathematics to Being—which need briefly underlining, not least because they are relevant to Beckett. The first is that, as Badiou puts matters, mathematics thinks the presentation of the multiple independently of questions of time and space.[48] Cantor argued that "spatial as well as temporal intuition and likewise all psychological elements must be kept out of the concepts and basic propositions of arithmetic."[49] As subjective, *a priori* forms of intuition, space and time "can contribute nothing to the thoughtful and rigorous analysis of continuity."[50] For Cantor, to conceive of infinity as a temporal or spatial question is to ignore the fact that neither time nor space "comes first." For both presuppose an independent concept of continuity. Time and space are constructed with the help of a continuum conceptually fashioned and already available. We should rather use a mathematical theory of the continuum to clarify our concepts of time and space.

Set theory, then, crucially separates the idea of continuity or discontinuity from ideas of temporal succession and spatial distribution. I have already noted the importance of simultaneity in Cantor's theory of sets. According to Dauben, "time, for Cantor, was nothing more than an auxiliary, related concept binding together movements in the natural world."[51] But equally, set theory rejects the principle of spatial definition. Set theory emerged from nineteenth-century theory of functions and real numbers. From Euler onwards, the theory of functions itself emerged as a rival to theories of space, in that the concept of a function was understood, no longer as a relation between geometric objects, as it was for Leibniz, but as a mathematical relation. Numbers specified structures that were otherwise unspecifiable. Above all, the concept of set alone finally appeared to be adequate to the infinitely complex structure of the points on a line. As Badiou says, insofar as it is conceived as a feature of "cosmological space," infinity always seems reducible to One (one God, one Nature, one Universe, etc.). But this is not the true modern infinity, which is "the pure multiple, that is, presentation" (EE 163). Mathematical attention to the structure of the line makes an appropriate concept of infinity possible. Alas for the romantically and the theologically inclined, gazing up at the night sky does not. Beckett knows this, too: "*the stars are undoubtedly superb*," he notes, "as Freud remarked on reading Kant's cosmological proof of the existence of God."[52]

Not surprisingly, in separating itself from questions of time and space, mathematical theory of the continuum also declared an "end to picturability." It is too seldom pointed out that modern mathematics turned to radical abstraction almost a century before modern art did. For mathematicians increasingly realized that geometrical "intuitions" were not far-reaching or precise enough to afford a clear account of the continuum. As Tiles points out, set theory did not actually start the collapse of the edifice of classical finitism. This happened much earlier, with the algebraization of geometry, which shifted the focus of mathematical concern away from geometric figures towards relational structures and defined representations or figures in terms of algebraic equations. These algebraic calculations subsequently took on a life of their own, going quite beyond what was picturable.

The crucial step came with the legitimization of the discontinuous, ill-behaved, and so-called "pathological" functions, like "the famous everywhere-discontinuous (and utterly unpicturable) Dirichlet function" of 1829.[53] Geometrical representation was not an adequate basis for questions about the behavior of such functions. To solve the problem, mathematicians resorted to algebra. Functions with infinitely many discontinuities in any arbitrarily small interval introduced an actual infinity of points of division. Algebraic representation described these more fully and precisely than geometric pictures. They made it impossible to draw a graph of the function in question, and left the arithmetical point continuum as the most effective means of modeling the geometric line. The question of how many points there are in a line was thus translated into the question of how many real numbers there are. Here precisely the turn to set theory eventually became inevitable, because the real numbers form an infinite collection. If, in Badiou's phrase, infinity "proliferates beyond everything tolerated by representation" (EE 168), set theory appeared to provide "an ever-increasing refinement in thinking beyond any picture of 'the real, physical world.'"[54]

Event

The concept of actual infinity is one pole of Badiou's philosophical universe. The other is a specific theory of the event. In essence, Badiou seeks to replace the Hegelian and romantic dyad of potential infinity and human finitude with the dyad of actual infinity and event. If the mathematical presentation of Being makes it seem monotonous, the event is what redeems it. The event is "the other side or the reverse of mathematics."[55] It is a "hazardous supplement" to "the indifferent multiplicity of Being."[56] It is an aleatory fragment, the chance occurrence of something that had no existence beforehand, could not be predicted or foreseen and had no prior name. The event is the means by which the truth of newness enters the world. If the logic of the event puts it at the opposite pole to actual infinity, the two are also intimately bound up with one another. The sixth meditation in *L'être et l'événement* (on Aristotle) is particularly clear about this. As Aristotle asserted and as we'll see further later, there is an intrinsic connection between the void and actual infinity: the void is its "point of being" [*le point d'être de l'infini*] (EE 88–89).[57] The void is the ultimate truth of Being. Badiou puts the point by way of oxymoron: the void is what "supports" all plural presentation (46). The void is, in a manner, all that is. If, as an infinity of infinities, the universe is inconsistent, that is because the void is at its heart. But the void is also always "in excess of Being" and of any given situation (89). In a sense—to introduce another oxymoron—it is greater than that situation. There is therefore always the possibility of an "explosive" movement, an "irruption of inconsistency" into a given situation, and its propagation (89–90). This movement destroys any illusion that the limits of the situation are the limits of the world. But such movements do not happen often. This is cardinal: in Badiou's philosophical system, the event has only "a *rare* existence" (Ee 60, italics mine).

What rescues Being from stifling monotony, then, is the "surgissement novateur" that is the event (EE 271). The possibility of the event is intrinsic to actual infinity itself. The concept of a universe structured in terms of actual infinity and event has an undeniable descriptive power. Badiou's post-Cantorianism offers a plausible model, for example, for thinking the universe constructed by scientific advance and the progressively ramifying systems of contemporary technology.[58] Badiou himself becomes progressively more convinced of the persuasiveness of his model. In "Philosophie et mathématique" (1989), he restricted himself to calling for the spread of modern mathematical concepts beyond mathematics itself. By the time he writes *Le Siècle* (2004), however, he is effectively claiming that certain aspects of twentieth-century culture, particularly its art, are best described in terms of actual infinity and the event.[59] He suggests that, in much modern art and music—Schönberg, Malevich, and Duchamp, for example—"the infinite is nothing other than the finite itself" (S 125).[60] It would not be hard to find literary equivalents of this; indeed, it would not be hard to construct a tradition of literary versions of actual infinity running from Mallarmé, Kafka, and *Finnegans Wake* through Roussel, Borges, and the *nouveau roman* to Perec and Ashbery. Modern art has also turned towards the event, or the possibility of the event. Modern art knows that it has no objective status. It knows that it does not incarnate any prior idea in its supposed wholeness and unity. In its resistance to objectification and its practice of "disincarnation," modern art becomes increasingly concerned with "précarités événementielles." The most radical examples of this are installations, happenings, and jazz (S 125). Here, again, it would not be hard to describe a many-sided modern literature of the event, including Mallarmé,

Kafka, Joyce and Woolf, Pound and Imagism, William Carlos Williams, and various traditions in postwar American poetry.

There is however a major problem here: the question of the historical residue. I shall call this residue "the remainder." This is my translation of *le reste*, a word that appears specifically in Badiou's essay "Six propriétés de la vérité." Putting Badiou and Beckett together makes me attach far more significance to the term than Badiou himself would wish to. To begin very simply: In Badiou's scheme of things, the event is the sole source and guarantee of what he calls truth. But if it is so, and is also rare, what of the commonplace world that is ungraced by it? In Badiou's philosophy, the world of events is the sole source of value. From its point of view, the situations to which events are counterposed and into which they break constitute their remainder. As we've seen, ontological discourse must separate itself from temporal and spatial reference. The remainder can therefore not strictly be characterized as a "dead time" or space. But we can nonetheless give it an empirical identity. Indeed, we can do so with reference precisely to the events that are significant for Badiou (artistic, political, scientific, the event of love). Here the remainder is the psychic deprivation of lovelessness; political oppression or reaction; the triumph of conservatism in the arts and of obscurantism over the sciences. By implication, since events are rare, the remainder comprises and must comprise the larger part of historical experience.

Badiou does not really theorize the remainder as such. It has practically no explicit place in his developed philosophical system. My argument is that, however liberated from "the pathos of finitude," a universe structured in terms of actual infinity and event cannot be immune to a pathos of its own. This is what I call the "pathos of intermittency." The point needs to be put starkly and in quite concrete terms. According to Badiou's *Ethics*, the ordinary situation "of the human animal" (in which we live, and cannot do otherwise) is determined by self-interest on the one hand and opinion or *doxa* on the other (Ee 46). The behavior of the human animal is a matter of what Spinoza calls "perseverance in being." This is nothing other than the pursuit of interest, or the conservation of self. It is the law that "governs some-one insofar as he knows himself" (46). In the ordinary situation, opinion—"presentations without truth," "the anarchic debris of circulating knowledge" (50)—will prevail. The event is "an immanent break" in a situation. As a consequence of it, "the human animal finds its principle of survival," its interest and its attachment to opinion "disorganized" (50). But the inertia of any given situation is properly formidable.

This is perhaps most obvious in the case of politics. Badiou explicitly accepts Rousseau's argument that "politics is rare" (EE 379). Politics is born of an allegiance to an event. But such an allegiance is not common. Furthermore, it is precarious. As Rousseau puts matters, "there is an inherent and inevitable vice which, from the birth of the body politic, tends unrelentingly to destroy it" (EE 379).[61] Politics is also inherently "fragile" (380). It is not necessary, does not have to be at all and does not usually happen. Simon Critchley amongst others has argued that Badiou's philosophy, and in particular his ethics, can seem too close to a virile heroics.[62] But alongside such tendencies, it is important to stress the delicacy and complexity of the event in Badiou's account of it. The event is characteristically "vulnerable" (EE 241). It may expire in the very instant of its appearance. Its origins are enigmatic, and it may pass unnoticed or fail to have consequences. Events can be smothered, obliterated, misconstrued, abandoned, and betrayed.

Badiou's conception of events is therefore characteristically austere. He summarily (and rightly) kills off the contemporary prestige of both a post-Heideggerian romance of *Ereignis* and a post-Deleuzian romance of becoming.[63] That events are rare and frail, however, does not mean that Being is not inherently unstable. The crucial issue, here, is what Badiou calls the State. Here, I deal with the term only in a political sense, though that is not the only sense it has for Badiou. Within the structure of the State, a part functions or appears, reductively, as the whole of Being. Thus, for example, as Badiou so brilliantly and scathingly argues in *Le nombre et les nombres*, contemporary economism functions according to a pitifully narrow reduction of the infinity of number.[64] This prevents any manifestation of the principle of the whole, which is inconsistency. It makes for "closure and assurance" (EE 114), and protects the supposed "normality" of a specific, given situation from the destabilizing force of the event. The State masks or represses or holds at bay the instability of Being. Badiou's grim realism on this point is refreshing and persuasive: in any ordinary situation, the weight of the State is likely to be overpowering. The event is unlikely and, if it takes place, is unlikely to have effects.

It seems to me that, in this respect, the key moment in the development of Badiou's thought comes with "Six propriétés de la vérité," a long and difficult essay that he published in two parts in 1985.[65] The essay provides an early, elaborated theory of Badiou's concept of truth before he has fully developed his mathematical ontology. In "Six propriétés," the specific truth in question is above all that of the analytic cure. It is clear that Badiou understands the cure in terms of events or *coupures* which break into a given analytic situation and fracture its language.[66] These *coupures* produce a subject who in turn breaks with established knowledge. Badiou not only tells us, as he will repeatedly later, that a truth divides a situation into two, but also that the division in question separates the truth from its remainder or *déchet*. (*Déchet* means waste matter, though also "down and out" or "outcast," which makes it eminently appropriate to Beckett. Part of my argument is that, where Badiou the philosopher briskly dispenses with the *déchet*, Beckett the artist stays with it.) Truths expose "negativity," rather than reactively transmuting it. They reveal what appears to be "a prodigious inertia … in the bowels of reality."[67] The subject of a truth must endure this inertia—and the *ennui* that it involves, the experience of "the thickness of duration" [*l'épaisseur de la durée*]—with "suppleness" and tenacity.[68]

We should remember, here, that inertia is a Beckettian word.[69] But Badiou is probably thinking chiefly of its significance in Sartre's *Critique of Dialectical Reason*. Badiou had once taken issue with what he had called the "broken dialectic" of Sartre's *Critique*.[70] In the Sartrean version of it, dialectics (the dialectic of the *en-soi* and the *pour-soi*) is neither pervasive nor caught up in a progressive, forward movement. Sartre asserts that, as existential subjects, we sporadically flare into authenticity, calling ourselves and the world into question. But we are also always bound to lapse back into the "massive indifference" of Being.[71] By the end of the eighties, Badiou himself is saying something similar.⁷² "What I call politics," he asserts, "can only be discerned in brief sequences, often quickly closed, dissolved in a return to business as usual."⁷³ As Peter Hallward aptly suggests, "whilst struggling to maintain his strictly political principles," Badiou increasingly adopts "a perspective similar to Sartre's historical-ephemeral pessimism."⁷⁴ Badiou himself evokes this pessimism near the end of *Jean-Paul Sartre* (1981): "Man exists only in flashes, in a savage discontinuity that is always finally reabsorbed into inertia."⁷⁵ This judgment on the *Critique* seems to anticipate much of his own subsequent progress. Indeed, the very phrasing of the judgment echoes on at least as far as *Le Siècle*, where "fraternity" in particular is announced as a "discontinuous passion" which "exists only as 'moments,'" whether within political movements, avant-gardes, or mathematical circles (S 88).⁷⁶ In fact, Badiou clearly owes much of his emphasis on the rarity of the event to Sartre.

After 1985, Badiou mainly formulates the remainder mathematically, in terms of actual infinity, situations, and the State. This neutral formulation reflects his strictly philosophical perspective. However, it is not intrinsic to the four domains—love, art, politics, and science—in which truths emerge as a consequence of events. Badiou repeatedly asserts the imperative of philosophical modesty in the face of truths.⁷⁷ But his philosophical perspective on the remainder is usually superior and detached. From the perspective both of the large world and the events that traverse it, however, the remainder is not neutral. The transforming power of the event casts a bleak light into the shadows that it does not transform. What I call the pathos of intermittency is generated in the gap between events and their remainder. Badiou expressly repudiates any "pathétique transcendantale."⁷⁸ It implies a passivity that is antithetical to his own insistence on "active force."⁷⁹ Yet the pathos of intermittency repeatedly shows itself at the edges or just under the surface of his work. He registers it in a political context; adopting a phrase with which Mallarmé summed up the years after 1880, for example, he writes of counter-revolutionary epochs, like the one that followed the defeat of the Commune, as times in which "a present is lacking." Such epochs are "captive to the idea that nothing begins or is going to begin" (S 113).⁸⁰

Intermittency also affects cultural history, as Badiou notes with regard to the vanished (socialist and anarchist) French "théâtre de combat" 1880–1914.⁸¹ Commenting on Breton's *Arcane 17*, he writes very strikingly of a negativity in modern love whereby "the weight of suffering endured seems bound to engulf everything."⁸² In the case of Sartre, as we've seen, he recognizes the pathos of intermittency in a philosopher to whom he has been close, but whom he is also concerned to hold at a certain distance. In the case of Lyotard, by contrast—in Badiou's more recent account of him, at least—it is precisely a thought of intermittency that he conjures up to leaven what he sees as Lyotard's later pessimism. Badiou profoundly agrees with Lyotard on the crucial importance of thinking multiplicity, events, and singularities. But Lyotard increasingly despairs of politics. He ends up believing that Capital is "the nocturnal name of Being" itself, that we cannot escape "the night" in which we find ourselves [*la nuit où nous sommes*] and which is the consequence of "the obsolescence and deletion [*rature*] of politics." Badiou agrees that it is no longer possible to believe in politically transformative action. But politics is not of this order: "It is of the order of thought. It aims, not at transformation, but at the creation of possibilities that could not previously be formulated."[83] However, like the occasional flarings of authenticity in Sartre, these will be "disparate" and disjoined.[84] They occur as interruptions of "the melancholy drift [*dérive*] of capital itself."[85]

In fact, Badiou cannot wholly escape a sense of the pathos of intermittency. Science is the only domain that concerns him in which no such pathos seems perceptible, specifically in the case of mathematics. Art stands at the opposite pole. The pathos of intermittency is chiefly evident in art, and notably in literature. Above all, it flickers insistently in Badiou's accounts of the modern poets who most grip him. Indeed, it is reflected in his very choice of poets: however sedulous the effort to pick a way round their melancholy, it would hardly have been possible to write about Mandelstam, Pessoa, and Celan without also evoking it. But it is not only modern poets in whom, almost in spite of himself, Badiou detects a particular form of pathos. The great comparison of Corneille with Racine in *Rhapsodie pour le théâtre* provides a more out-of-the-way example (RT 58–61). The contrast Badiou establishes is between Jansenist fatalism on the one hand and the pathos of intermittency on the other. For Racine, politics does not exist (remembering, here, that what Badiou calls politics always begins with an event). The State is all-powerful in its vigilance and cruelty. Victims are hapless, weak. Love is evanescent and finally inane. Furthermore, and crucially in the context of my argument, Racine does not mourn the loss of politics ("il n'en porte nul deuil"). A Racine play is an infernal machine, "un montage de diamantaire." By contrast, Corneille "knows the torment of the Idea." He was schooled by the events of Richelieu and the Fronde.[86] His struggle is to keep politics alive, to believe in its persistence in inauspicious times. When he recognizes, presumably after the defeat of the Frondeurs' challenge to the supremacy of the monarchy, that, for the foreseeable future, politics is finished—"that nothing is happening any longer" ("que plus rien se passe," writes Badiou, Beckettianly)—Corneille chooses to sustain an "anguished memory" of it in the creation of great "melancholics" and "suicidal figures." These are his "sentimentaux de la politique." Corneille transcends Racine's inexorable reality precisely in the desolate magnificence of his later protagonists.

Remainder

Beckett's preference was the exact reverse of Badiou's. According to Knowlson, he shared both Thomas Rudmose-Brown's "deep love for Racine's plays" and "his antipathy to Corneille's."[87] Badiou rightly asserts that Beckett's world is not constructed on rigorously deterministic principles.[88] In this respect, it is unlike Racine's and a little more like Badiou's own. But the narrow yet profound difference between the two tastes is nonetheless indicative. The preference for Corneille on the one hand and for Racine on the other points us quite exactly to two very different shadings of a mutual vision. In fact, *Badiou and Beckett both structure their universe in terms of actual infinity, the event, and its remainder. Both shrink the scope of one of the three terms. But the two terms that they respectively diminish are different ones, and are diminished in different ways*. On the one hand, whilst Badiou largely banishes the remainder to the margins of philosophy, as beneath thought, though without entirely annulling it, Beckett locates his work squarely within it, as the stuff of art. On the other hand, whilst a concept of the reality and truth of events is everywhere central to Badiou's thought, one can hardly claim this of Beckett. Beckett's world is one in which, by an ungainsayable logic, the event is always theoretically possible, to the extent that his characters invoke it and even appear to recall it, that his works conjure it, mimic it, assess the conditions that might make it possible. But it is also nonetheless a world in which the event can scarcely be said to take place at all (though it has many more or less ironic simulacra). We might recall Winnie in *Happy Days*: "Ah earth you old extinguisher."[89]

Beckett's is not only a world of "broken dialectic." It is, emphatically, Lyotard's nocturnal world, Mallarmé's world without a present. As Vladimir and Estragon in *Waiting for Godot* repeatedly state, nothing wholly dooms it to be so. There is no stark and absolute law in Beckett of the kind that so swiftly dooms Phèdre to ineluctable disaster. This is a crucial point: there is no Beckettian trap that automatically snaps shut, as there is a Racinian one.[90] But Beckett's world is nonetheless not obviously open to transformation or renewal. For this reason, where Badiou vigorously celebrates the intermittency of truth, for Beckett, it is a source above all of pathos and laughter. To the idea, crucial to Badiou's conception of philosophy, that the world should not be as it is, Beckett responds with pathos: it is seldom that the world even briefly promises that it might be otherwise. He also responds with laughter: our plausible and seemingly irrepressible reasons for revolt against the world are also absurd-seeming. In this respect, Badiou and Beckett might today seem to serve as custodians of the embers of the Enlightenment project for a new century, the one pugnaciously, the other ironically and melancholically. To a far greater extent than he would acknowledge, like Beckett, Badiou is a writer of vestiges. In suggesting as much, however, I don't mean to diminish the importance of either. Quite the reverse: the problematic at the heart of Badiou and Beckett's work is of major significance for contemporary thought, particularly once that work is put together as a whole.

But a large difficulty appears at this point. It is not hard to think of Beckett as writing the remainder and the missing event. But it may not be obvious that his work evokes an actually infinite universe. For Badiou, set theory provides us with an expression of actual infinity. Beckett's interest in mathematics has long been recognized. Ackerly in particular has shown how pervasive mathematical references are in his work. It is by no means immediately clear, however, that we can jump from scattered if widespread tokens of interest in mathematics in general to the idea that Beckett provides us with a literary equivalent of the set-theoretic universe. The problem is made the more difficult by the fact that, for many mathematicians and philosophers interested in mathematics, there can be no such "equivalent," save as a product of loose thinking. As we've seen, for Aristotle and the classical finitists, actual infinity has no empirical meaning. Wittgenstein is even harsher: mathematical statements can simply not be construed as statements about the non-mathematical world, and therefore have no cognitive content. Set theory is a "cancerous growth," and rather than clarifying notions (like infinity) that are common in everyday life, it merely adds to the confusion.[91] Whilst Russell was initially much more enthusiastic for set theory, he defended it, above all, as opening up "the Platonic world of unchanging, eternal 'forms,'" not as having any empirical bearing.[92]

Furthermore, when it comes to the relation between the mathematical and non-mathematical worlds, modern mathematicians themselves sometimes coincide with classical finitists. If, for Aristotle, we have no need for a concept of infinity in our ordinary dealings with the real, physical world, the same is true for David Hilbert.[93] In general, many mathematicians would agree with Hermann Weyl that there is a "deep chasm" between everyday experience and mathematical representation.[94] For others, however, notably Dedekind and Cantor, the separation of abstraction from concrete particulars is a false one. Rigorously considered, descriptions of the physical world are always rooted in abstract theories. Ordinary language is in fact capable of expressing mathematical concepts. But it resists the presentation of multiples of multiples, and therefore expresses them unclearly. Set theory provides determinate and coherent concepts for what are vague and possibly incoherent notions in ordinary discourse. Cantor subscribed to the same Platonic theory of mathematics as did the young Russell. But he also believed that number has a "trans-subjective" or transient reality in the physical world.[95] He insisted that the transfinite numbers of set theory existed *in concreto*.[96] They are required for any explanation of natural phenomena that aspires to be complete.

The problem with the position I have summarized by quoting Weyl is not its assumptions about mathematics but its assumptions about everyday experience. Here the most wildly adventurous mathematicians can sound oddly staid: unlike set theory, it would seem, the nature of everyday experience is a matter of common sense. Pollard wittily demonstrates, for example, what happens to *Romeo and Juliet* in a set-theoretic universe: commonsense questions start to get weird answers.[97] But this does not prove that the universe of set theory is incompatible with the real-life world, only that there is a poor fit between set theory and one kind of construction of real life, one specific form of aesthetic practice. Not surprisingly, perhaps, Pollard seems not to have read Robbe-Grillet or O'Hara. As Tiles says, the universe is, surely, actually infinite, and, if we cannot experience it as an actually existing infinite totality, we can nonetheless conceptualize our experience of the physical world in relation to an actual infinity.[98]

In practice, at least, Badiou agrees with Cantor and Dedekind. Mathematics presents the infinity of being "*in its most abstract form*" (EE 164, italics mine). Once he chooses to consider nature and the State—let alone love, subjectivity, and immigrant workers without papers—in mathematical terms, he has effectively decided in Cantor and Dedekind's favor: actual infinity is concrete. But he is not keen to say so; rather the reverse. For him as for mathematicians themselves, set theory offers formally exact descriptions of actual infinity where ordinary language is chronically inexact. "There is *no* infra-mathematical concept of infinity," he asserts, austerely, "merely vague images of the 'very large'" (EE 164). He is therefore deeply distrustful of any smooth move from mathematical thought to empirical world, not least by way of examples. This is partly responsible for the extreme abstraction of his ontology, which Hallward has repeatedly and I think successfully problematized.[99] But, since

Badiou is wary, in this respect, of a logic to which he must himself remain attached, the abstraction of his thought also has a curious and specific character, flirting here and there with the very empirical substantiations from which it otherwise maintains a principled aloofness.

Interestingly, at least one such "flirtation" runs directly counter to the spirit of Cantor. Cantor dismissed the concept of infinitesimals—infinitely small quantities, smaller than any assignable ones—in the most peremptory fashion. He saw them as one of the "ghosts and chimeras" of mathematics.[100] Badiou, however, has no such qualms. Infinitesimals have an important place in his discussion of number in *Le nombre et les nombres*.[101] Furthermore, his favorite passage from Leibniz evokes a world in which "'each portion of matter may be conceived of as a garden full of plants, or as a pond full of fish,' and where, moreover, 'each branch of the plant, each limb of the animal, each drop of its humors is in its turn such a garden or pond'" (EE 349).[102] What Badiou responds to, here, is the metaphor for the infinite recessions of an infinitesimal universe. But metaphorical discourse is "infra-mathematical." More pointedly still, so is quite a lot of Badiou's own discourse in the *Ethics*, for example. It repeatedly adduces an infra-mathematical concept of actual infinity. Badiou writes for example of representations of the self, whether held together by interest or determined by an event, as "the fictional imposition of a unity upon infinite component multiples" (Ee 54–55). An event such as "a loving encounter" offers a new "way of being" in place of "infinite differences" or "the ordinary state of relation to the other" (41).

Such concrete instances of an actually infinite universe are by no means confined to the *Ethics*. They can be found, for example, in the chillier world of *L'être et l'événement*. *L'être et l'événement* argues that "almost all situations are infinite," but are represented by the State as finite (EE 261). A citizen—say, Antoine Dombasle—does not coincide with any of the State's particular representations of him. As a voter, for instance, he is represented by a part of himself. In set-theoretical terms, "he is considered *as a subset* … or the singleton of himself"; "not Antoine Dombasle," says Badiou, "the proper name of an infinite multiplicity," but {Antoine Dombasle}, an indifferent and unitary figure (122). The State, writes Badiou, has "no concern" with "the *life* of people" as such (122). Its concern is with finite forms, as opposed to the actual infinity that is the condition of life in general and lives in particular. As Badiou asserts in "Philosophie et mathématique," "we ourselves" are (banally) infinite (C 165). Not surprisingly, therefore, Badiou's commentators repeatedly search for their own concrete versions of actual infinity: Jean-Claude Milner, for example, suggests that Cantor intersects with Freud. The unconscious is an actual infinity for the modern, speaking subject.[103]

It is worth noting here that, however skeptical of concrete versions of the set-theoretic universe, Pollard admits that there may be "near cousins of mathematical set talk … at the dim periphery of ordinary English."[104] I'd suggest that some of the "near cousins" to which Pollard refers can be found above all in modern literature. Indeed, Badiou is much concerned with Beckett's work as a "near cousin" of set theory. Critics who have discussed Beckett's work in a mathematical context have brought this out. There is evidence that Beckett's interest in mathematics stretched to at least some awareness of developments in contemporary set theory.[105] So, too, critics have provided mathematical accounts of certain works by Beckett that have come very close to describing them in set-theoretical terms, particularly as those terms are recast by Badiou. For Badiou, in an actually infinite universe, there is no One. There are only multiples of multiples. James Hansford's essay on *The Lost Ones* effectively suggests that its world is actually infinite. There is no unitary "perfect mental image of the entire system"[106] in *The Lost Ones*, writes Hansford. There is no recoverable plenitude in which "'one' and 'all' are combined."[107] The One that will unite the many is precisely "the 'lost one.'"[108] So, too, various commentators have drawn attention to the relation between limit and inexhaustibility in Beckett. This runs parallel to a similar concern in set theory. Hansford notes, for example, the serial endings in *The Lost Ones*. These "conclusions" are in fact provisional limits established in a world that is actually "without culmination."[109] Ellis suggests that Beckett's description of the "dark zone" of Murphy's mind specifically as a "*matrix* of surds"[110] fuses Heisenberg's concept of the algebraic matrix—a grouping of numbers arranged in a fixed rectangular field to identify and display the mechanics of atomic quanta—and the Pythagorean bugbear of the surd—a number inexpressible as terminating decimals, repeating decimals, or fractions. Ellis thinks that this combination suggests a gridded but "numerically irrational, infinitely repeating" structure.[111]

The critics have tended to suppose, however, that Beckett subjects mathematical thought to ironical mockery or demonstrates its limitations, particularly when it is cast in non-mathematical terms.[112] The assumption tends to be that Beckett opposes literature to mathematics, or that he promotes literature, affect, and corporeality over mathematics.[113] This seems an odd idea to me: Beckett tends repeatedly to "mathematize" the body. More importantly, his work is much closer to mathematics than it is to most literature. Like mathematics, it is characterized by its powerful will to abstraction; its radical withdrawal from a world of which it nonetheless retains a residual trace; its frequent concern with extraordinary paradoxes and what seem to be irreducible problems and impossibilities; and its formalization of material that is threatened with drastic inconsistency. Commentators are often reluctant to think of Beckett as abandoning the world of human, flesh-and-blood fullness. But on all the points I've just mentioned, he is surely far closer to the bleached world of mathematics. Beckett's attitudes to different kinds of mathematics, however, were surely themselves different. As Brian Macaskill suggests, insofar as Beckett is attached to a "language of number," it is close to that of a mathematician like Gödel, at the expense of a classical or Kantian conception of number.[114] Culik rightly argues that Beckett's irony actually strikes chiefly at Pythagorean mathematics and Euclidean geometry, or intellectual practices that Beckett associates with them. Not only that: it emerges from a grasp of issues like the limits of formal mathematical systems and the nature of continuity and the line that resembles that of set theory.[115]

Brater has shown how this irony works in *The Lost Ones*. The narrator's mathematics is "approximate at best, misleading or even erroneous at worst."[116] His passion for precision is chiefly rhetorical. But this narrator is neo-Pythagorean, and so are his calculations. As these calculations give way to a "chronic instability," so what

Beckett called the "irrationality of *pi*" assumes "its full Pythagorean terror."[117] In *The Lost Ones*, this serves as "an instrument of indeterminacy" and progressively traces "the futility of culmination."[118] In other words, what breaks down is the world of exact calculation that Badiou satirizes in *Le nombre et les nombres*. The seemingly exact calculations in *The Lost Ones* are opened up to the corrosive effects of an actually infinite world. Beckett does not evoke that world in its own terms, those of set theory, but rather in what Brater calls an "iconography of imprecision."[119] In doing so, however consciously, like Badiou, he "concretizes" certain features of the set-theoretical universe. Beckett's work can occasionally be specifically analyzed in set-theoretical terms. Edith Fournier shows for example that the relation between the two parts of *Sans* can be quite exactly described as a bijection.[120] But he tends rather to proceed through literary approximations to or analogies with mathematical thought, if in a medium, language, that, for mathematicians, is too inexact, ambiguous, and lacking in well-defined rules to be acceptable. Howard has argued that the mathematical comedy in *Watt* has a clear point: mathematics is no more adequate than language to a complete description of the self and world.[121] But the comedy of the use of "infinite series" in *Watt*—Knott's servants, the dogs that eat his leftovers, the exchange of looks amongst the Committee members—does not poke fun at mathematics as such.[122] It is an expression of the irony of supposedly finite forms, sufficient descriptions and exhaustive enumerations in an actually infinite universe.

Elsewhere, I shall be demonstrating what actual infinity concretely means in Beckett with some detailed analysis of the *Trilogy*. However, there is no compelling need for me to do so, at least insofar as Badiou's own work on Beckett provides some examples. As we saw earlier, there is an ineliminable link in Badiou's thought between actual infinity and the void. Badiou sees Beckett as concerned with "the fictive place of being" (B 28). He conceives of this "place" as precisely the point at which language arrests what is otherwise the infinite "flight" [*fuite*] of being towards the void (28). It is a fictive place because, as an artist, Beckett thinks figuratively, in fictions, rather than in the pure abstractions of set theory. Hence, I'd add, the importance of Brater's observation that Beckett replaces what he takes to be bogus precisions, not with a new precision, but with an iconography of imprecision.

The figurative and purely abstract worlds, however, are nonetheless analogous. The fictions in question are numerous: the strange, vague landscapes of *Molloy*, the labyrinthine streets of *The Expelled*, the muddy netherworld ("le souterrain," C 334) of *How It Is*, which Badiou thinks we grasp as properly infinite (SB 28). But these fictions take two basic forms, closed (as in *Endgame* or *The Lost Ones*) and open (as in *Molloy*). Behind both these forms, however, there is a single figure into which they blend, the *noir-gris* (black-gray) or "penumbra" of Being. This figure presents Being as on the edge of or indistinguishable from the void. Thus for example in *Worstward Ho*: "Dim light [*pénombre*] source unknown. Know minimum. Know nothing no. Too much to hope. At most mere minimum. Meremost minimum."[123] This figure of the penumbra spells the ruin of both dialectics and the Cartesian equation of truth with clarity and distinctness. Here closed and open locations, motion and stasis, stability and instability all become "reversible metaphors" for actual infinity (B 31).[124]

For Badiou, it is *Lessness* above all that represents the "outcome of Beckett's poetic effort" to assign a place to Being. I'll repeat his reading, but also extend it a little. *Lessness* pointedly and succinctly suppresses "all descriptive particularity" in "a uniform image of earth and sky" (B 29): "Never was but gray air timeless no sound figment the passing light. No sound no stir ash gray sky mirrored earth mirrored sky. Never but this changelessness dream the passing hour."[125] Movement and immobility are equivalent to one another: hence the contradiction of an apparently petrified body—"legs a single block arms fast to sides"—that the narrator can nonetheless assure us will make "one step more."[126] Here time is a figment: "Never but in vanished dream the passing hour long short."[127] As Fournier says, the fundamental situation in *Lessness* is that of Being thought atemporally.[128] Space, too, is indeterminate: more precisely, the features of closed and open spaces are indistinguishable. The "four walls" of the "issueless" refuge merge with what is also "all sides endlessness earth sky as one."[129] "Endlessness"—the endlessness of actual infinity—is the most crucial concept in *Lessness*. The breach in finitude is irreparable. Banal infinity actually and endlessly intrudes upon the finite: hence the importance, here, of the Beckettian figure of the ruin. To adapt the imagery of *Lessness* itself: the ruin is half-block, half-sand, a structure defined against the sand into which it is turning and by which it is invaded. Like the penumbra or purgatory, it is a crucial liminal figure in Beckett's work.[130] It serves as an image of the leakiness or porosity of finite forms, of their friability. *Lessness* presents this friability as immediate, graspable at once, not related to the passage of time. The figure of the ruin is precisely appropriate to a world in which—to return to an earlier quotation from *Le Siècle*—"the infinite is nothing other than the finite itself" (S 125).

At the same time, actual infinity in *Lessness* is constituted specifically as the remainder. When Fournier argues that the world of *Lessness* is open to interruption, to the idea of a "temps à faire" in which historical time begins again, she might almost be echoing Badiou's concept of the relationship between Being and the event. The trouble is that she doesn't seem to me to be right about *Lessness,* which emphatically writes off the possibility of the event: "Never but imagined the blue in a wild imagining the blue celeste of poesy."[131] Badiou tends to skirt round such Beckettian moments in favor of those he finds more affirmative. As I suggested earlier, in "Six propriétés de la vérité," Badiou says that truths expose a negativity or "prodigious inertia" as the very principle of the real. This inertia, which he otherwise largely writes off, is everywhere in Beckett. Badiou himself comes close to suggesting this in his early pamphlet *Samuel Beckett: L'écriture du générique et l'amour*.[132]

But what this also implies is the prevalence of the remainder: without the event, writes Badiou, the penumbra is indifferent, thankless (an "indifférente ingratitude" [SB 17]). There is always a "breach" [*ébrèchement*] in Being (17). But that does not mean that events are not intermittent and occasional. That the classic Beckettian text has long been *Waiting for Godot* is therefore not surprising. I don't mean to argue that *Godot* is an expression of the essential Beckett. But it is nonetheless a particularly clear and simple statement of some of the principal features of Beckett's universe. "Nothing happens," says Estragon, "nobody comes, nobody goes, it's awful!"[133] In the terms of "Six propriétés," this is precisely the world of the *déchet* (or, as Estragon puts it, "the meantime".[134]). Its subjects can only stubbornly endure its tedium. It is a world of actual infinity without events. True, its actually infinite character is initially less evident in *Godot* than in *Molloy* or *The Unnamable*. But *Godot* clarifies what Badiou means when he says—as he does repeatedly—that, strictly speaking, actual infinity begins with two. Indeed, the play demonstrates Badiou's point repeatedly and very plainly and starkly. Once the other intervenes, there is no longer one world. The world proliferates *ad infinitum*:

> ESTRAGON: We came here yesterday.
> VLADIMIR: Ah no, there you're mistaken.
> ESTRAGON: What did we do yesterday?
> VLADIMIR: What did we do yesterday?
> ESTRAGON: Yes.
> VLADIMIR: Why ... [*Angrily*]. Nothing is certain when you're about.[135]

The uncertainty in question is not hermeneutic. It is a produced by a lack of unity, irreconcilable difference, the irreversible dissolution of one into the multiple, the appearance of the principle of infinity within finitude. There is no limit or endpoint to the process.

Moreover, *Godot* (including the stage directions) might be thought of as a series of discursive sets: clipped, precisely constrained, tightly structured and repetitive variations that often take place on the basis of a specific and more or less explicit axiom or decision ("let's make a little conversation," "let's ask each other questions," "let's abuse each other").[136] These localized patterns are both exhilarating and banal. They are characterized, precisely, by a curious amalgamation of "foisonnante diversité" and "sourde monotonie." Any given sequence quickly runs its course and reaches its limit. Hence the frequency with which Vladimir and Estragon declare that they are "tired," "weary," or "exhausted";[137] but hence, equally, the swiftness with which they spring back from exhaustion. There is no determinate or given end to the construction of sequences, and Vladimir can also assert that he and Estragon are "inexhaustible."[138] This is not surprising: as Estragon puts matters, "There's no lack of void."[139] Like sets, the exchanges that constitute the play are founded on the void. There is always scope for another "little canter." Equally, each such canter will always be haunted by the knowledge that it is nothing more than "blather."[140] *Godot* even has its equivalent of the empty set, a reiterated stage direction: [*Silence*].

Of course, the obvious objection to this reading is that things do happen in *Godot*: Pozzo and Lucky arrive, for example. But that merely confirms how close Beckett's thought of the event is to Badiou's, as opposed to Heidegger's or Deleuze's: events are sporadic and extremely infrequent. They are not to be confused with diurnal appearances and disappearances, however odd and unpredictable these may be. That, between acts one and two, the tree unexpectedly puts forth leaves is not an ironic rejoinder to Estragon. The point is precisely that the tree sprouts leaves *and yet* nothing happens. The world has its processes, shivers and tremors—that is, there is a kind of play in Being—but such disturbances should not be confused with events. Mere surprises or unexpected changes do not constitute events. They might rather be thought of as a phantom or delusive events, pseudo-events. Estragon may momentarily wonder whether Pozzo is Godot, but his confusion is short-lived.

To put the point very simply: Godot has become a classic because its world is that of the big non-event. We have come to understand this world very well. In the inert world of the non-event, history has not begun. Time is therefore indistinct. The obscure flicker of surprise or unexpected change does not of itself produce time. *Godot* has gripped so many people so intensely because it is an extraordinarily limpid and powerful expression of a problematic, vestigial, melancholic late modernity. I take Badiou, too, to be a proponent of this modernity, though the melancholy dimension to his philosophy is only thinkable from outside it, since Badiou himself axiomatically proscribes melancholy. In the era of the end of metaphysics and the collapse of the grand narratives, both of which are far more significant for Badiou than he likes to admit, truth and value logically emerge as intermittent or rare. Badiou and Beckett are what I call vestigial or melancholic modernists in that each commits himself to truth and value, in spite of their occasional and unpredictable character. For Badiou, however, what matters is the force of intermittency. For Beckett, what matters is its pathos, though in a sense that implies neither sentimentality nor defeatism. It may even be that we have to some extent to choose between Badiou and Beckett, though always with the possibility of choosing differently tomorrow, as Badiou says of the choice between Mallarmé and Rimbaud. Certainly, to think Badiou and Beckett together, I'd suggest, is, in this respect and at this particular historical moment, precisely to think ourselves. ∎

This essay was funded by a Leverhulme Trust Research Fellowship for 2003–2005.

....

1   *The Pathos of Intermittency: Alain Badiou and Samuel Beckett* (forthcoming).
2   I borrow the second word from Daniel Bensaïd. Bensaïd characterizes Badiou's (and Rancière's) concept of truth, politics and the subject as "intermittent." See "Alain Badiou et le miracle de l'événement," in *Résistances: Essai de taupologie générale* (Paris: Fayard, 2001), 154–55.
3   [For a list of Badiou's principal texts and their corresponding abbreviations, see the introduction to this issue.—Ed.]
4   For a critique of Badiou on Hegel and mathematics, see Juliette Simont, "Le pur et l'impur (sur deux questions de l'histoire de la philosophie dans *L'être et l'événement*)," *Les temps modernes* 526 (May 1990): 27–60, especially 54–55.
5   See C 171–75.
6   My unannounced shift from "mathematics" to "set theory" at this point is deliberate: the work of the great nineteenth-century mathematicians—Hamilton, Bolzano, Weierstrass, Dedekind, Cantor—suggested that all the concepts of mathematical analysis could be reduced to those of natural number, set, and membership. See Moshé Machover, *Set Theory, Logic and Their Limitations* (Cambridge: Cambridge University Press, 1996), 64. According to Cohen, "the notion of 'set' is the most fundamental concept of mathematics." See Paul J. Cohen, *Set Theory and the Continuum Hypothesis* (Reading, MA: Benjamin-Cummings, 1966), 50. Of all the branches of mathematics, set theory is the one that supplies compel-

ling formal reasons for viewing mathematics as a whole as a coherent enterprise. Its only serious rival is category theory (which has also recently increasingly attracted Badiou's attention). For arguments to this effect, see Stephen Pollard, *Philosophical Introduction to Set Theory* (Notre Dame: University of Notre Dame Press, 1990), 5–6. In Badiou's work, "mathematics" usually means set theory in the first instance.

7   Quoted in Pollard, *Philosophical Introduction*, 40.
8   Better, at least, this sickening than Heideggerian convalescence as involved in the concept of *Verwindung*; on which see Jon R. Snyder, "Translator's Introduction," Gianni Vattimo, *The End of Modernity: Nihilism and Hermeneutics in Post-Modern Culture*, trans. and intro. Jon R. Snyder (Cambridge: Polity, 1988), xxvi.
9   In *Le Siècle*, Badiou argues that the twentieth century did in fact seek to break with romanticism, but by means that themselves were largely romantic. It failed to learn Cantor's lesson with regard to actual infinity, and was thus unable to escape its own latent religiosity (124–25).
10 Badiou is quite sparing in his use of the term itself, preferring others, like "infinite multiplicity." But he is perfectly aware of its appropriateness to his thought. See for instance "Platon et/ou Aristote-Leibniz: théorie des ensembles et théorie du topos sous l'œil de la philosophie," in *L'objectivité mathématique: Platonisme et structure formelles*, ed. Marco Panza and Jean-Michel Palanskis (Paris: Masson, 1995), 66.
11 Quoted in Michael Hallett, *Cantorian Set Theory and Limitation of Size* (Oxford: Clarendon, 1986), 13.
12 Quoted ibid., 35.
13 Quoted in Joseph Warren Dauben, *Georg Cantor: His Mathematics and Philosophy of the Infinite* (Princeton: Princeton University Press, 1990), 170, italics mine.
14 Quoted in Hallett, *Cantorian Set Theory*, 128. However, Hallett himself argues throughout that Cantor remained persistently caught up in an ordinal definition of number (that is, one involving counting in succession).
15 If Badiou assumes that sets are already existing objects, that is because, like Cantor, Gödel, and Cohen, he platonically affirms the independence of mathematical truths. Mathematical realities are not derivable from nature, but their formation is nonetheless a process of discovery of a steadily evolving, shared, impersonal world of ideas, where what matters is consistency in concepts and an orderly relation to prior concepts that are already present and have already been tested. The creation of a consistent and coherent concept, here, is actually the discovery of a permanently and independently existing, real, abstract idea. To deny this is to ignore the way mathematics works and has worked. There is a sense in which mathematical truths remain immune to history in a way that is not the case, say, with judgments in aesthetics. Euclid's status in mathematical inquiry, for example, is very different to Aristotle's in literary criticism.
16 See Dauben, *Georg Cantor*, 122.
17 Hallett, *Cantorian Set Theory*, 15.
18 Aristotle, *Physics*, trans. Thomas Taylor (Frome: Prometheus Trust, 2000), 60.
19 See in particular the thirteenth meditation in EE, pages 161–68, for an argument to this effect.
20 This is precisely demonstrated in Ray Monk, *Wittgenstein: The Duty of Genius* (London: Vintage, 1991), 415–19. Of course, thinking actual infinity can also provoke the theological leap. Cantor himself sought refuge from the implications of his own work in a distinction between the "ordinary infinity" revealed by set theory and the "absolute infinity" beyond reason or number, which was God's.

21 *Pace* Mary Bryden and others, I see no evidence at all of "the idea of God" in any significant sense in Beckett's work. But see Mary Bryden, *Samuel Beckett and the Idea of God* (Basingstoke: Macmillan, 1998). Beckett does of course pervasively make use of the Christian machinery; and, at times, of the Hebraic and Islamic. For some traces of Islam in the *Three Dialogues*, see my "*Three Dialogues* and Beckett's Tragic Ethics," in *Three Dialogues Revisited*, ed. Marius Buning, Matthijs Engelberts, Sjef Houppermans, and Danièle de Ruyter-Tognotti, *Samuel Beckett Today/Aujourd'hui*, no. 13 (2003): 43–54. Those who want to argue for (a more or less residual but serious) Christianity in Beckett should take the full force of Knowlson's account of his sacrilegious and riotous behavior with members of the San Quentin company in the Matthäuskirche in Berlin. See *Damned to Fame: The Life of Samuel Beckett* (London: Bloomsbury, 1997), 648–49.
22 See Mary Tiles, *The Philosophy of Set Theory: An Introduction to Cantor's Paradise* (Oxford: Blackwell, 1999), 9–31 for the full case. My account of it is substantially indebted to hers.
23 Tiles, *Philosophy*, 25.
24 Cantor, quoted in Hallett, *Cantorian Set Theory*, 25.
25 A domain is the set on which a given function is defined, e.g., the completed, homogeneous number domains, natural, real, and rational numbers.
26 See Hallett, *Cantorian Set Theory*, vii.
27 Abraham A. Fraenkel, "Historical Introduction," in *Axiomatic Set Theory* by Paul Bernays (New York: Dover, 1968), 3.
28 Russell's paradox asserts that it is impossible to decide whether all sets that are not members of themselves constitute a set, since if they do they don't, and vice versa. The Burali-Forti paradox asserts that, paradoxically, the ordinal of the set of all ordinals must necessarily be larger than any of the members of the set, and so would be an ordinal which is not contained in the set of all ordinals. Thus the set of all ordinals is not an allowable set.
29 For Badiou on constructivism as contrasted with Ramsey, Mahlo, and Rowbottom and their work on the "large cardinals," see EE 342–48.
30 Cantor distinguished between *Zahl* and *Anzahl*, number in its cardinal sense and number as an ordering of elements. See Joseph W. Dauben, "The Development of Cantorian Set Theory," in *From the Calculus to Set Theory, 1630–1910: An Introductory History*, ed. I. Grattan-Guinness (London: Duckworth, 1980), 195.
31 I take my example from E. J. Borowski and J. M. Borwein, *Collins Dictionary of Mathematics* (Glasgow: HarperCollins, 2002), 65.
32 A rational number is any number that can be expressed as a ratio. An irrational number is one that cannot (e.g., π, $\sqrt{2}$). A real number is any rational or irrational number. A natural number is one of the counting numbers (usually identified with the positive integers, 1, 2, 3, 4, … , etc.).
33 That is, for every set, there is the set of all its possible groupings: from $\{a, b, c\}$, for example, we derive a, b, c, ab, bc, abc, and $\emptyset$ (the empty set).
34 Hallett, *Cantorian Set Theory*, 101.
35 I take my list from Ian Stewart, *From Here to Infinity: A Guide to Modern Mathematics* (Oxford: Oxford University Press, 1996), 69.
36 Pollard, *Philosophical Introduction*, 68.
37 As described by Stewart, the principle behind the diagonal argument is the assumption that the real numbers are countable (that is, they can be numbered off by the natural numbers). One proceeds to argue for a contradiction by listing the reals out as decimal expansions. One then forms a new decimal whose first digit after the decimal point is dif-

ferent from that of the first on the list; whose second digit differs from that of the second on the list, and in general whose *n*th digit differs from that of the *n*th on the list. This new number cannot then appear anywhere on the list, "which is absurd since the list was assumed to be complete." See *From Here to Infinity*, 66.

38 John N. Crossley, C. N. Ash, A. C. Brickhill, J. C. Stillwell, and N. H. Williams, *What Is Mathematical Logic?* (Oxford: Oxford University Press, 1972), 77. For helpful accounts of forcing, see pages 70–77; Tiles, *The Philosophy of Set Theory*, 185–91; and Peter Hallward's *Badiou: A Subject to Truth* (Minneapolis: University of Minnesota Press, 2003), 344–45.
39 Pollard, *Philosophical Introduction*, 69.
40 Hallett, *Cantorian Set Theory*, 114.
41 See Ian Stewart, *Concepts of Modern Mathematics* (New York: Dover, 1995), 135.
42 The examples are from T. S. Blyth, *Set Theory and Algebra* (London and New York: Longman, 1975), 80 and 88. Blyth demonstrates the second point in helpful, pictorial form.
43 Pierre Verstraeten, "Philosophies de l'événement: Badiou et quelques autres," *Les temps modernes* 529/530 (August/September 1990), 242.
44 Samuel Beckett, *The Complete Short Prose, 1929–1989*, ed. S. E. Gontarski (New York: Grove Press, 1995), 199.
45 Samuel Beckett, *Assez* (Paris: Éditions de Minuit, 1966), 11; cf. C 366.
46 Beckett, *Complete Short Prose*, 187.
47 I mean this, of course, only in the sense in which Gödel showed set theory to be inherently defective. Gödel proved that, if axiomatic set theory is consistent, there exist theorems which can neither be proved nor disproved within the system of axioms, and that there is no constructive procedure which will prove axiomatic set theory to be consistent. Gödel's discoveries were "dramatic" for mathematics and led to a new understanding of its inherent limits, in that he demonstrated that there were certain forms of mathematical knowledge to which mathematicians would never attain. See Ian Stewart, *The Magical Maze: Seeing through Mathematical Eyes* (London: Weidenfeld and Nicolson, 1997), 162 and 185–87; and *Concepts*, 292.
48 See EE 293. Badiou insists on the point with regard to time, rebuking the eminent mathematician Gilles Châtelet for stressing mathematics as means to liberation from spatial but not from temporal "slavery." See his review of Châtelet's *Les enjeux du mobile: Mathématique, physique, philosophie* (Paris: Seuil, 1993) in "Les gestes de la pensée," *Les temps modernes* 586 (January/February 1996), 203. Châtelet's book is translated as *Figuring Space: Philosophy, Mathematics and Physics*, trans. Robert Shore and Muriel Zagha (Dordrecht: Kluwer, 1993).
49 Hallett, *Cantorian Set Theory*, 121.
50 Dauben, *Georg Cantor*, 108.
51 Ibid.
52 Samuel Beckett, *Disjecta: Miscellaneous Writings and a Dramatic Fragment*, ed. Ruby Cohn (London: Calder, 1983), 141.
53 Pollard, *Philosophical Introduction*, 27. For a more detailed account, see pages 25–27; and Tiles, 79–82.
54 See Tiles, *Philosophy*, 69–73.
55 Alain Badiou, "L'ontologie implicite de Spinoza," in *Spinoza: Puissance et Ontologie*, ed. Myriam Revault d'Allonnes and Hadi Rizk (Paris: Kimé, 1994), 69. What Badiou takes to be Spinoza's implicit (as opposed to his professed) ontology involves an apprehension of the event.
56 MP 89; C 177.

57 Aristotle, *Physics*, book IV, §8, 75–76.
58 Badiou shares none of Heidegger's antipathy to technology, pointing out that the contemporary problem is not technology in itself, but the drastically limited conception of technological possibilities that prevails under advanced capital. See MP 34.
59 More precisely, this is true of art before what *Le Siècle* refers to as the Restoration, that is, the period of reaction that begins around 1980.
60 As *Le Siècle* has not yet appeared in print, all references are to the French typescript.
61 See book III, chapter X of the *Social Contract*. Jean-Jacques Rousseau, *Discourse on Political Economy* and *The Social Contract*, trans. Christopher Betts (Oxford: Oxford University Press, 1994), 118–20, especially at 118. Cf. Žižek's critique of Badiou and Rancière as caught "in the snare of 'marginalist' politics" in which "momentary explosions of an 'impossible' radical politicization" contain the seeds of their own failure and abruptly retreat "before the existing Order." Slavoj Žižek, "La malaise dans la subjectivation politique," *Actuel Marx* 28 (2000): 145.
62 See Simon Critchley, "Comment ne pas céder sur son désir," in *Alain Badiou: Penser le multiple*, ed. Charles Ramond (Paris, L'Harmattan, 2002), 232 and passim.
63 Badiou takes Deleuze to task precisely for putting the event everywhere. See for instance his review of Deleuze's *Le Pli: Leibniz et le baroque* in *Annuaire philosophique 1988–1989* (Paris: Éditions du Seuil, 1990), 171. Cf. Eric Alliez, who rightly argues that, for Badiou as opposed to Deleuze, the event is not one of the world's ways of being, but a "truth of separation." See "Que la vérité soit," in *De l'impossibilité de la phénoménologie: Sur la philosophie française contemporaine* (Paris: Vrin, 1997), 83.
64 See also EE 112–13.
65 Alain Badiou, "Six propriétés de la vérité," *Ornicar? Revue du camp freudien*, 32 (January–March 1985): 39–67; and 33 (April–June, 1985): 120–49.
66 Ibid., 32:42.
67 Ibid., 33:121.
68 Ibid., 33:121, 33:134.
69 See for instance Beckett to Lawrence Shainberg, 7 January 1983. Quoted in Knowlson, *Damned to Fame*, 685.
70 See "Le (re)commencement du matérialisme dialectique," *Critique* 23, no. 240 (1967): 445.
71 See Badiou's "L'entretien de Bruxelles," *Les temps modernes* 526 (May 1990): 1–26; and "Saisissement, dessaisie, fidélité," *Les temps modernes* 531–33, vol. 1, *Témoins de Sartre* (October–December 1990): 14–22.
72 For Badiou's own view of his later faithfulness to Sartre, see "L'entretien de Bruxelles," especially 19–26.
73 Quoted in Bensaïd, "Alain Badiou," 163.
74 Hallward, *Badiou*, 70. Cf. Eustache Kouvélakis, "La politique dans ses limites, ou les paradoxes d'Alain Badiou," *Actuel Marx*, 28 (2000): 47.
75 Alain Badiou, *Jean-Paul Sartre* (Paris: Potemkine, 1981), 14. This work is part obituary, part critical pamphlet, and part meditation on an early influence to whom, however unconsciously, Badiou himself will increasingly be drawn back. For another use of the same metaphor, see "Saisissement, dessaisie, fidélité," 22.
76 The same point is evident, in a different fashion, in the gulf that yawns between Badiou's early optimism and his later pessimism regarding the political will of the masses. The young Badiou asserts that "les masses pensent … et les masses pensent juste" (I 100). More recently, however, he has asked "Where is this 'creative' capacity of the multitudes?"

The question is followed by a critique of "the repertoire of movements belonging to the petit-bourgeois masses." See "Beyond Formalization: An Interview with Alain Badiou" (unpublished typescript), conducted by Peter Hallward and Bruno Bosteels (Paris, July 2002), trans. Bruno Bosteels and Alberto Toscano.

77 See for instance "Art et philosophie," PM 21–29.
78 Alain Badiou, "Sur le livre de Françoise Proust: *Sur le ton de l'histoire*," *Les temps modernes* 565/566 (August/September 1993), 246.
79 Alain Badiou, "Depuis si longtemps, depuis si peu de temps," *Rue Descartes* 33:103.
80 Cf. Badiou's presentation of Joan of Arc as an exception to a "miserable epoch," "L'insoumission de Jeanne," *Esprit* 238 (December 1997): 28.
81 See "Préface: Destin politique du théâtre, hier, maintenant," in *Au temps de l'anarchie: Un théâtre de combat 1880–1914*, ed. Johny Ebstein, Philippe Ivernel, Monique Surel-Tupin, and Sylvie Thomas, 1:7–14 (Paris: Séguier, 2001).
82 André Breton, *Arcane 17* (Paris: Jean-Jacques Pauvert, 1971), 115, translation mine. Cf. S 113–17. True, Badiou mitigates this effect by concentrating on Breton's interest in the transformation of negativity into affirmation. The catalytic function of the event, however, means that transformation is both willed and unwilled, not only voluntary but "miraculous" (S 115). There is no inexorable or compelling logic to Breton's escape from melancholy. It is a matter of chance, not necessity.
83 That politics is "intellectuality" in the first and determining instance is for Badiou an Althusserian principle. See "Qu'est-ce que Louis Althusser entend par 'philosophie'?" 29. This is his best and most sympathetic essay on Althusser.
84 Alain Badiou, "Le gardiennage du matin," in *Jean-François Lyotard: L'exercice du différend*, ed. Dolorès Lyotard, Jean-Claude Milner, and Gérald Sfez (Paris: Presses Universitaires de France, 2001), 104–5.
85 Ibid., 101. Interestingly, this emphasis is already apparent in Badiou's 1984 essay on Lyotard. Here, as in the essay of 2001, he argues for example that "the proletariat" is not an empirical category but the name for "a series of singular events." See "Custos, quid noctis?" *Critique* 40, no. 450 (November 1984), 862. However, the point is missing in his contribution to the debate on *The Differend* at the Collège Internationale de Philosophie in 1989, where he was mainly concerned to accuse Lyotard of reducing the multiple to the unitary principle. See "Débat général," in *Témoigner le différend: Quand phraser ne peut: Autour de Jean-François Lyotard*, ed. Francis Gibal and Jacob Rogozinski (Paris: Osiris, 1989), 87–126. For Badiou's contribution, see 109–13.
86 I take it that Badiou is thinking of Richelieu's inclusion of Corneille among the group of *les cinq auteurs*, for which Richelieu provided the inspiration himself.
87 Knowlson, *Damned to Fame*, 49. Cf. also pages 122, 154, 208, 212, 246, and especially 426, where Knowlson helpfully discusses the influence of "Racinian claustrophobia" on Beckett's drama.
88 To be exact, in Badiou's version of him, Beckett before 1960 is at least Racinian insofar as he is inclined to "a somber belief in predestination" (B 40). By contrast, the later Beckett is un-Racinian insofar as he is concerned to examine the minimal conditions of freedom.
89 Beckett, *The Complete Dramatic Works* (London: Faber and Faber, 1990), 153.
90 In lecturing on Racine at Trinity College Dublin, Beckett himself apparently referred to the typical Racinian "situation circle." See Chris Ackerly, "Samuel Beckett and Mathematics," *Cuadernos de Literatura Inglesa y Norteamericana* 3, no. 1 (May 1998): 80.
91 Quoted in Monk, *Wittgenstein*, 439. See also 328–29 and 468.
92 Ray Monk, *Bertrand Russell: The Spirit of Solitude* (London: Vintage, 1997), 159. In any

case, Monk's book makes it clear that Russell increasingly felt defeated by Wittgenstein's arguments.
93 See Tiles, *Philosophy*, 17.
94 Hermann Weyl, *The Continuum* (Kirksville, MO: Thomas Jefferson University Press, 1987), 93.
95 Dauben, *Georg Cantor*, 132.
96 Ibid., 145.
97 See Pollard, *Philosophical Introduction*, 46–51.
98 See Tiles, *Philosophy*, 22.
99 See in particular their arresting exchange on the subject in "Beyond Formalization," where Badiou's bluff rejoinder to Hallward's question—"Abstraction lies at the basis of all thought"—seems to me to sidestep Hallward's point.
100 Dauben, *Georg Cantor*, 234.
101 See in particular NN 221–24. However, Badiou has reason to feel that it is historically possible to take infinitesimals seriously now in a way that Cantor could not. See 221.
102 Translation mine. See Nicholas Rescher, *G. W. Leibniz's "Monadology": An Edition for Students* (London: Routledge, 1991), 26. Beckett's notes on Henri Poincaré's *La valeur de la science* in the Whoroscope Notebook appear to show an interest in a similarly atomistic account of infinitesimals. Ackerly relates it to the opening pages of *The Unnamable*. See Ackerly, "Samuel Beckett and Mathematics," 92.
103 See Alain Badiou, Christian Jambet, Jean-Claude Milner, François Regnault, Antoine Vitez, and François Wahl, *Une soirée philosophique* (Paris: Potemkine/Seuil, 1988), 28.
104 Pollard, *Philosophical Introduction*, 51.
105 See for instance Hugh Culik, "Mathematics as Metaphor: Samuel Beckett and the Esthetics of Incompleteness," *Papers on Language and Literature* 29, no. 2 (Spring 1993): 131–51; Brian Macaskill, "The Logic of Coprophilia: Mathematics in *Molloy*," *Sub-Stance* 57 (1988): 13–21; J. Alane Howard, "The Root of Beckett's Aesthetic: Mathematical Allusions in *Watt*," *Papers on Language and Literature* 30, no. 4 (Fall 1994): 346–51; Edith Fournier, "Samuel Beckett, mathématicien et poète," *Critique* 46 (1990): 660–69; and Ackerly, "Samuel Beckett and Mathematics," especially 77. Culik argues that Beckett probably knew of Gödel's work, and suggests that Gödel may very well be "the mad (?) mathematician" in Beckett's German letter "who used a different principle of measurement at each step of his calculation" (*Disjecta*, 173). Cf. Macaskill on Beckett and Gödel, page 19.
106 Beckett, *Complete Short Prose*, 204.
107 James Hansford, "*The Lost Ones*: The One and the Many," *Studies in Short Fiction* 26, no. 2 (Spring 1989): 126.
108 Ibid., 127. For a similar emphasis on a Beckettian subtraction of the One from the infinite, see Jeremy Parrott, "Infinity Minus One: Mathematics and the Search for Self in Samuel Beckett," *British and American Studies* 4 (1999): 23–33.
109 Hansford, "*The Lost Ones*," 125.
110 Beckett, *Murphy* (London: Calder and Boyars, 1969), 66, my italics.
111 Reuben J. Ellis, "'Matrix of Surds': Heisenberg's Algebra in Beckett's *Murphy*," *Papers on Language and Literature* 25, no. 1 (Winter 1989): 120–23.
112 See for instance Ackerly, "Samuel Beckett and Mathematics," passim, especially 99–100; and Howard, "The Root of Beckett's Aesthetics," passim, especially 346.
113 See for instance Vivian Mercier, "Poet and Mathematician," *Hermathena* 141 (Winter 1986): 66–71.
114 See Macaskill, "The Logic of Coprophilia," passim. In this respect, one might think of

Beckett as inverting the structure of thought that allows Kline to claim that the historical progress of mathematics over the past two centuries has been disastrous. See Morris Kline, *Mathematics: The Loss of Certainty* (Oxford: Oxford University Press, 1980).
115 See Culik, "Mathematics as Metaphor," 134, 138–40, and 144–45. Culik suggests that Beckett's insistence (particularly in the German letter) on the nothingness behind all linguistic formulations is consistent with Gödel's account of the "holes" in the completeness of all mathematical systems. This idea is particularly illuminating in relation, not only to Badiou and Beckett's use the metaphor of the hole, but to Badiou's account of the relation between actual infinity and the void.
116 Enoch Brater, "Mis-Takes, Mathematical and Otherwise, in *The Lost Ones*," *Modern Fiction Studies* 29 (1983): 97.
117 Beckett, *Disjecta*, 145.
118 Brater, "Mis-Takes," 97, 95.
119 Ibid., 97.
120 As Fournier puts the point, every element (phrase) in the first part has an "image" and only one in the second part, and vice versa. See Fournier, "Samuel Beckett," 668–69.
121 Howard, "The Root of Beckett's Aesthetic," 346.
122 Ibid., 349.
123 Beckett, *Worstward Ho* (London: John Calder, 1983), 9. Cf. *Cap au pire*, trans. Edith Fournier (Paris: Éditions de Minuit, 1991), 10.
124 On the penumbra as anti-dialectical, see in particular SB 7 and C 334–35, where Badiou asserts that it is separated from all contradiction with light.
125 Beckett, *Complete Short Prose*, 197.
126 Ibid., 198.
127 Ibid.
128 See Fournier, "Beckett," 669. Unlike Badiou, however, Fournier also argues that the situation in itself is not limitless, though it can be infinitely explored.
129 Beckett, *Complete Short Prose*, 201.
130 Cf. *Le Siècle*, where Badiou asserts that twentieth-century poetics was above all "a poetics of the threshold" (19).
131 Beckett, *Complete Short Prose*, 199. It is precisely the equivalent of this sentence in the French text (*Sans*) that Fournier takes as a sign that history can begin again, that the event remains possible. See her *Têtes-Mortes* (Paris: Éditions de Minuit, 1972), 73. There is certainly a little more justification for this reading in *Sans* than in *Lessness*. Fournier's claim that *Sans* evokes a "paradisal refuge of supreme vacuity" (668) which historical time, the event, and responsibility would all disrupt suggests a very odd notion of paradise.
132 See in particular B 17–18.
133 Beckett, *Complete Dramatic Works*, 41.
134 Ibid., 38.
135 Ibid., 16.
136 Ibid., 47, 59, 70.
137 Ibid., 54, 61, 71, 78.
138 Ibid., 58.
139 Ibid., 61.
140 Ibid., 60, 61.

CINEMA JOURNAL
Journal of the
Society for Cinema and Media Studies

Cinema Journal prints recent scholarship by members on a wide variety of subjects from diverse methodological perspectives. A "Professional Notes" section informs **SCMS** members about upcoming events, research opportunities, and the latest published research.

The field of cinema and television studies is diverse, challenging, multi-cultural, and multi-disciplinary. **SCMS** brings together those who contribute to the study of film and television to facilitate scholarship and represent their professional interests, standards, and concerns.

2005 CONTENTS INCLUDE:

Rob King on the Triangle Film Corporation

LeiLani Nishime on the Mulatto Cyborg

Mary C. Betrán on the New Hollywood Racelessness

Jaime Bihlmeyer on the (Un) Speakable FEMININITY in *The Piano* (1993)

Sylvia Shin Huey Chong on *The Deer Hunter* and the Primal Scene of Violence

In Focus: Postfeminism and Contemporary Media Studies

SUBSCRIPTION RATES: Individual $42, Institution $83, Canada/Mexico, add $22; other foreign, add $28 (airmail).

SEND TO:
University of Texas Press, Journals Division, Box 7819, Austin, Texas 78713-7819
Phone # 512-232-7621, Fax # 512-232-7178
journals@uts.cc.utexas.edu

Badiou, Derrida, and *The Matrix*: Cultural Criticism between Objectless Subjects and Subjectless Objects

Stefan Herbrechter

> *Il arrive que quelque chose arrive. Que quelque chose nous arrive. Et ces points d'exception, dont toute vérité procède, l'art a pour mission de les garder, de les faire briller, de les détenir, stellaires, dans le tissu reconstitué de notre patience.*[1]

> *... dès lors que l'humain n'est plus le fin mot de l'histoire ...*[2]

Post-Theory and Posthumanism

This essay takes Alain Badiou's philosophical ideas to the movies. In doing so, it follows a lead provided by Badiou himself, who recently published his thoughts on *The Matrix*.[3] For Badiou, art, and by implication all creative cultural signifying practices, is one of the four possible "truth-procedures" (the other three being politics, science, and love) through which a subject (of truth) can "arrive."

This article pursues a combination of several interests: in the context of the latest wave of apocalyptism about theory, that is, the increasing intensity of the talk about "post-theory," what can be done to defend the acquisitions of theory against a simplistic anti-theoretical backlash on the one hand and a post-theoretical desire to outdo theory by some kind of simple linear succession and repression, on the other? The current candidate for this, a seemingly "straightforward" succession, is "posthumanism." In the face of these two current "post-theoretical" options it seems important to defend theory against both reaction and succession in the face of the "event" or advent of what is sometimes referred to in a rather too celebratory fashion as "posthumanity" or "posthuman condition."

Instead, adapting Bruno Latour's phrase from another but not unrelated context, it will be argued here that "we [may] have never been theoretical [enough]."

What seems extremely desirable in this context is a return to a political thinking about the subject, aided by, for example, Alain Badiou's philosophical model, and which would be based on a renewed critical practice extended to all cultural forms, to evaluate and create possibilities for intellectual interventions in the current ideological debate about the future of "humanity" and the new situation arising after the supposed event of the posthuman. It is true that posthumanism in this respect plays an ambiguous role in the present argument. On the one hand, it is a discourse that comprises the controversial discussion about the increasing "prosthesization" of the human, the gradual replacement of essentialist humanism by "man's" technological other, his successor (with its focus on techno-scientific and late capitalist or postmodern cultural practices, which often leaves theory uncalled for and therefore somehow needs to be recaptured and rejoined by thinking and theoretical/philosophical questions). On the other hand, posthumanism may also be seen as the current or most advanced form of a (post-)theory, namely as the latest wave and the most radical critique of the liberal humanist subject.[4]

The Subject of Science Fiction: Philosophy Goes to the Movies

Using Badiou for a reading of *The Matrix* will here serve to explore the possibility of a cultural criticism that is re-theorized and ready to engage with the posthuman subject. *The Matrix Trilogy*[5] has almost instantly become a cult movie series and has had enormous influence on the general "cultural imaginary." Taking Badiou to the movies means testing his thoughts on critical practice, on a reading of cultural forms, even if this may be against some of Badiou's own principles about "truth-procedures."[6] The fundamental conviction that informs this double reading is that change—be it political or cultural—can only occur through critical subjects performing critical and theoretically informed readings. Badiou's notion of the subject of truth is important for cultural criticism because it will add (following Heidegger, Lacan, Deleuze, and, to some extent, Derrida) a very particular focus on truth as an event for a subject in a singular but concrete situation, which nevertheless is not fixed but remains to be fulfilled. This notion of the event is, in psychoanalytic terms, very close to being "traumatic," on the one hand, while on the other it is certainly not unrelated—despite Badiou's refreshing but also in many ways troubling polemic against all forms of "ethics" that involve notions of heterological otherness—to an ethico-political thinking that sees the event as a dis-propriation of the subject. This subject is separated from its (imaginary) identity, and identity therefore forms an untenable ground for any (political) decision without the acknowledgement of the irreducible precedence of a radical other.

The kind of reading of *The Matrix*, through Badiou and others, suggested here, attempts to show, however, that a reconciliation between a political philosophy of the truthfulness of the event and an ethics of alterity can be productive for cultural criticism. It thus proceeds by introducing a Derridean fictional "as if" [*comme si*] into the argument and the reading. This reading of *The Matrix* is informed by a thinking of the event along Badiou's lines but at the same time produces critical insights into Badiou's work, philosophy and theory, and about "culture," as the sum of its signifying practices.

Science-Fiction-Theory

Science fiction (film) is of course a very specific form of fiction (a very specific form of the "as if")—a visualization of what remains to-come *and* what is already thinkable, envisageable. Like any fiction, SF narrates stories about the transformation of subjectivity. It transposes these stories into an "other" place (*u-topos*) and an "other" time (*u-chronos*), which means it is concerned with a presence that always differs from itself and is always deferred (very much like Derrida's *différance*). It thus repeats and activates the original trauma of identity formation (as understood in Lacan's explanation of the mirror stage); hence the persistence of its "nostalgic" closures, its self-protective "returns" to the "self-same" in the form of transformed/transfigured/purified "humanity." What is at stake in the particular "economy" of SF is the reappropriation and repression of the "essence" of "man." A posthumanist reading of SF, strictly speaking, must therefore be a deconstructive reading of these moments of negation—negation of the otherness and the monstrosity that "shows" in the inhuman, the non-human, the trans-human—and instead must affirm this dangerous monstrosity unconditionally.

The question that follows is whether the transformation of subjectivity—dissolution, displacement, and re-subjugation/coagulation of subject positions—involved in SF is the expression of the desire for a "finally objectless subject" (as anticipated by Badiou, but also in the Nietzschean arrival of the "more (human)-than-man," the overman), or rather the fantasy of a "finally subjectless object" (a world thoroughly cleansed of everything human, for example in the sometimes dystopian, sometimes euphoric *Terminator* scenario in which humanity has been replaced by its machinic other)?

SF constitutes "a mode of awareness" that hesitates between the "belief that certain ideas and images of scientific-technological transformations of the world can be *entertained*" and "the rational recognition that they may be *realized*," and, on the other hand, "the belief in the immanent possibility of those transformations" and the "reflection about their possible ethical, social, and spiritual interpretations."[7] SF seems caught in the middle of a politics of science—the possible, the inevitable, and an ethics of truth, following Badiou—the advent of a subject to a truth-process necessary for the writing of the situation that saves the event. It seems therefore that the event of posthuman technology at once promises to overcome, domesticate, or eliminate the nonhuman, and at the same time helps incorporating it into the very essence of human truth. Science is thus that "fictional" event (of an "as if") that constitutes the posthuman truth of what Baudrillard would call our hyperreal condition, or the "derealizing" of human space.

The Matrix is a "philosophical film," and in a sense the film of philosophy as the quest for truth and especially the truth about (social) reality (Plato's cave, Descartes' evil demon, and Baudrillard's evil demon of images constitute one filiation of *The*

Matrix, while Marxism, (Christian) messianism, and Greek mythology are its ideological inventory). More precisely, however, *The Matrix* is a film about the "event" (of truth and its transformative power). One could say that what Badiou, science fiction, theory, and posthumanism share is a certain irreducibly utopian thinking—a messianism with or without messiah,[8] and a certain preoccupation with the "*comme si*" and the trans- or performative. Fiction represents a reality of the "as if"; speculative theory about the event (either as traumatic or fatal) does the same. In this sense, both areas share a recognition that the virtual is always at the heart of human reality, or as Derrida would say, an "as if" is always possible. It is always possible to assume an "as if," whose performative force in fact creates the event by pre-empting it. Derrida claims that it is with the history of the "as if"—in its undecidable performative and constative aspects—that the "humanities-to-come" will have to engage.[9] But theory would have to deconstruct the performativity and constativity of the "as if" whose dominant discourse occurs through fiction (as "what *figures* but also what *makes*").[10] This is why fiction or literature, including science fiction, of course, must be one of the main sources and targets for theory that questions the event by evaluating the possibilities of its arrival. The question is: can anything arrive from (science) fiction's "as if" and from its underlying posthumanist notions of virtuality?[11] What *arrivant* lies beyond the virtual? This is the question that informs *The Matrix* and many other post-representational science fiction films—i.e., films whose posthumanism propels them towards imagining a future where cinematic representation even of the most virtual and technologically sophisticated form threatens to break down and render obsolete the filmic logic as such.[12] While keeping in mind the usually conservative turn given to these science fiction scenarios at their points of resolution, science fiction can undoubtedly inform the thinking of the event (the "as if") and the subject in terms of its inventing an imaginary other space through which cultural change may arrive, as long as the distinction between the performative and the constative remains meaningful. But what if, as Derrida asks, the belief that an event usually takes place by breaking through the order of the "as if," and that therefore the place of the real is sufficient to displace the logic of the "as if," what if "the place itself becomes virtual, freed from its territorial ... rootedness and when it becomes subject to the modality of an 'as if'?"[13] In that context, the only event possible must be the "as if" itself. Derrida therefore, logically, pushes the logic of the "as if" to its extremes—by positing that "only the impossible can (truly) arrive":

> No surprise thus, no event in the strong sense ... the pure singular eventness of *what* arrives or of *who* arrives (which is what I call the *arrivant*), it would suppose an *irruption* that punctures the horizon, *interrupting* any performative organization, any convention, or any context that can be dominated by conventionality. Which is to say that this event takes place only to the extent where it does not allow itself to be domesticated by any "as if," or at least by any "as if" that can already be read, decoded, or articulated *as such* .... It is too often said that the performative produces the event of which it speaks.

One must also realize that, inversely, where there is a performative, an event worthy of the name cannot arrive.[14]

A reading of science fiction and posthumanism is thus concerned with its own impossibility and its unthought, its "real" so to speak—where the logic of the "as if" must break down and something altogether other *will have* arrived. This future anterior regulates the question of the "event" as it is being thought in theory today. Badiou, Derrida, and Baudrillard all play with this apocalyptic logic, of how to speak so that the event can arrive; or, how to break out of the matrix—whether it be interpreted as capitalism, metaphysics, or hyperreality. The only hope of establishing a meaningful link with truth and reality lies in renouncing any link in exchange for a mere possibility of the truthful event ("as if" this were possible). The only subject thinkable under these circumstances is that "Thing," that entity, that void which establishes a link by cutting itself off (in a process of *déliaison*), by subtracting it(s)self.

Dire l'événement, est-ce possible?[15] Only as its impossible-possibility. In accepting the pertinence of this question one must be allowed to project Badiou's specific problematic of "being and event" and their relation onto fiction and in particular science fiction. Cultural criticism's task in this specific context would then become a reading of the event and its impossible-possibility as articulated through the "as if" of (science) fiction. Both Derrida and Badiou share to some extent at least the idea of the event as incomplete inscription process with, on the one hand, a traumatic truth-to-come, as a kind of Kantian regulative idea and, on the other, a singularity and situationist specificity of a truth-for-a-subject that provides a possibility for an *ad hoc* and unpremeditated "*lien social*"—Badiou's "(la) politique"[16]—in its very structure of general *déliaison*.[17]

The Matrix, Posthumanism, and the Event

What is the event in or of *The Matrix*? There are in fact two cases of "eventuality," occurring in the two central scenes, which together have the structure of an anastrophe and a catastrophe in this cosmic drama. The first event would probably not fulfill Badiou's criteria—it is Neo's moment of recognition, realizing the true extent of human oppression by the machines. The second, the properly apocalyptic or catastrophic moment and event of truth, is Neo's "becoming" posthuman, his definitive entry into and embodiment within the matrix cyberspace. It may be possible to read Neo's resurrection and second coming as an event in the context of current posthumanist thinking, i.e., as an event that creates the situation out of which the posthuman subject must derive its fidelity to the event as a truth-process. The question that theory may thus put to the text of science fiction is: in what sense is this advent of the posthuman an event? What happens to its subject? What happens to its body? What is its truth? And what is its real?

To start with the first event scene: it is a fairly standard occurrence of recognition. It is an induced event in which Morpheus, the gatekeeper of reality and figure of benign paternal authority, proposes a choice to Neo, whom he believes to be the "One,"[18] or the future savior of humanity: Neo's choice is between the blue pill of forgetting, of acceptance of continued enslavement in hyperreality, and the red pill of recognition, resistance, and truth. Greek mythology, Christian messianism, and Marxist notions of ideology are all at play in this moment of recognition; Plato's cave, the question of faith and knowledge, and the ambiguity of subjectivation coincide in this "choice" that Neo is offered. The red pill initiates a tracing process necessary to find out the exact location of Neo's real (his unimaginable true self), his body. The scene of Neo's death in virtuality and rebirth into reality is a kind of inverted mirror stage. He is literally liquefied and turned inside out, and melts into his own mirror reflection in a form of psychotic self-annihilation and identification with the other. The next thing one realizes is the apocalyptic scenario of mankind's true condition. The world that the *Terminator* films had merely anticipated has already been and gone, the apocalypse has already taken place without, as usual, arriving completely. Humanity has lost its battle against its successor, the machines, and is now, in turn, being exploited as a provider of natural and environmentally friendly human battery cells. In a later scene Morpheus holds up a battery to Neo that looks, somewhat reassuringly, like a Duracell—some things evidently last longer than others (a clear similarity with the endurance of other brands in SF like Coca-Cola in *Blade Runner*, for example). As a result of Neo's awakening, his now conscious body has become useless to the machines and is flushed out of its cocoon and recuperated by Morpheus's group of cyberrebels, who greet him with the ominous words: "welcome to the real world" (thus anticipating the later reference to Baudrillard's "desert of the real").

The event structure of this scene of course has nothing to do with the significance given to the term in either Badiou's or Derrida's (or Lyotard's) thought. A simple Althusserian reading of the subject's interpellation, misrecognition, and ideology's necessary overdetermination would be sufficient to analyze this scene. Nevertheless it is an event that is based on a decision, not by a free subject, but rather a decision of the ideological other (under the conditions of the subject-supposed-to-know). It is a decision which clearly changes the subject's place in the imaginary and symbolic order and also displaces his real, even though it merely exchanges one master signifier for another. For Neo, it is an *Er-eignis*, a Heideggerian *enowning*, through which a change if not in true subjectivity, then at least in identity, takes place. It is a moment when the self rebuilds itself through an appropriation of its own other, a moment of "secretion" in which the otherness of this other is ejected and made "obscene." Neo's former virtual existence in the matrix now becomes the new real (unimaginable, unspeakable) of his real life among the rebels. The electronic sound sequence heard during the liquid mirror scene, just as the mercury-like liquid is about to engulf Neo's interior (a scene which seems almost like the inversion of the final moments of the T2000 model in *Terminator 2*), indicates the expiring of the (digital) ghost in the machine, Neo's virtual existence. Virtuality from now on is what structures Neo's desire, the void of his truth. In this sense Neo (re)becomes similar to the proto-post-human living at once in and out of cyberspace, and which is celebrated by so many posthumanist texts. Ironically, it is now that Neo's situation resembles more closely our own, in facing an uncertain future of posthumanity, the impossible-possibility of a real encounter with death in virtuality. Only the previous recognition of his virtual condition as loss, however, can allow him to experience the reality of his desire. Although there is nothing that may be objectively called truth here—all this happens in a SF that anticipates a dystopian future; for the viewer the moment before Neo's recognition is just as real or unreal as the moment after—the basic logic of identity formation holds, whether fictional or not. This is the peculiarity of the fictional "as if." The question however is, can and should this logic be resisted? Is it "false" and should it thus be ignored or overcome?

The second scene could be read "as if" it fulfilled the criteria of Badiou's notion for an event. It is an event without decision, something absolutely unforeseen happens: an apotheosis. Neo's physical death is reversed, he becomes the One, the Subject to truth who determines the situation by changing the matrix. In the process one could say that he becomes "posthuman." Badiou's event is closely related to the idea of a political subject: what seems appropriate here to claim the advent of subjectivity for Neo is his very function as messiah, as the One. Badiou himself uses the resurrection of Christ as narrated by Paul as an example of an event and of the advent of a subject to truth. Neo's subjectivity, his specific and singular future anterior, lies in determining the universal truth out of the multiplicity that may constitute his being in the posthuman situation. Neo's subjectivity is that which he will become as the result of the event and his fidelity to it; and the event is that which acts as a supplement to Neo's being and forces him towards a truth process that remains truthful to the event-supplement. In that sense, Neo's subjectivity (re)creates the event, which is ultimately depending on faith. Outside of this subjectivity, the event strictly speaking does not exist. Neo's subjectivity depends on his own belief, as the Oracle (and also the little boy whose mind bends the spoon) explains. The event is also that which makes the world, i.e., the matrix, meaningful for the subject and thus open to change and militant action. The structured but multiple character of the new situation we might call posthuman is the result of the (unnamable) event, which calls for truth and the universal. One could argue that the knowledge of the matrix's existence for Neo unfolds a situation which is interrupted by his becoming posthuman, by that which exceeds his being, his not or no-longer being (which is not death). This event seems to develop *ex nihilo*. The event is therefore the truth of the situation, its previous void or real which leads to a complete restructuring of the matrix—the matrix or the system turned against itself, just like Neo was turned inside-out before. What has been defining Neo as subject is his fidelity to the event. Although, strictly speaking, the "Neo-subject" comes after the event, and is a result of it, the truth process demands a trauma-like re-inscription of its traces within the situation, very similar to what Slavoj Žižek refers to in *The Sublime Object of Ideology* as the traumatic logic of the symptom, which again shows the affinity between science fiction, posthumanism, theory, and philosophies of the event.[19]

The subject, however, cannot completely appropriate truth because it exceeds him or her in its irreducible multiplicity and eventfulness. The truth-event's repositioning makes it possible for the subject to perceive the hitherto blind spot of the real; in

Neo's case this is his being neither virtual nor physical but in-between. This "existence without existence," or spectrality, may however be the inevitable *différance* (deferred difference) of any ontology based on the idea of presence and origin.[20] The posthuman event thus cannot be a revelation, but rather constitutes an act of interpreting (re)in(ter)vention. As Žižek claims: "Event is the traumatic encounter with the Real ... while its denomination is its inscription into language .... In Lacanese, Event is object *a*, while denomination is the new signifier that establishes ... for Badiou the new readability of the situation on the basis of Decision."[21] Badiou's subject, like Althusser's and Lacan's, is therefore never outside ideology but is always ideological and hence political rather than ethical. Neo's transubstantiation and apotheosis could thus serve as a sign of the immortality and universality to which the subject has access through his fidelity to the event.

Badiou's subject is the wager of a subject without an object, pure subjectivity that does not constitute itself "on the back of" an object. Badiou's starting point here is the claim that "the form of the object cannot in any way sustain the enterprise of truth,"[22] only a subject can. Badiou therefore wants to "de-objectify the space of the subject" and his version of the post- or trans-humanist subject is "the very same subject dissociated or subtracted from reflexive jurisdiction, un-constituting, untied from all supports unrelated to the process of truth."[23] Does not cyberspace promise to be precisely the ideal location for a finally objectless subject?

On the other hand, of course, cyberspace is part of the ongoing deterritorialization, delocalization, or dislocation of the subject, which contradicts Badiou's notion of truth for a subject; he calls a subject "the local or finite status of a truth. A subject is what is *locally born out.*"[24] Truth always precedes this local subject in the sense that "the subject is woven out of a truth, it is what exists of truth in limited fragments." Truth arrives through the subject, it passes through it. Truth, for Badiou, following Lacan, is "making a hole in knowledge."[25] The subject therefore is a (pre-ontological) "void"[26] that constitutes the "very gap filled in by the gesture of subjectivization."[27] Badiou's axioms for a truth-event-subject complex are the following: a truth is "post-eventual" (a process that works its way backward from a naming of the event as a void; in our case, that would be the moment "we" became "posthuman"). The process of a truth is fidelity to this event (Neo's posthuman subjectivity lies in his fidelity towards the name and the event of his "becoming the matrix"); the name of the event is connected to the "terms of the situation" which nevertheless ultimately remains "infinite" and can never be fully present (Neo's spectrality therefore seems structurally necessary as symbolic of a new "posthuman" cyber-subjectivity). As long as the knowledge of a situation does not exceed its "infinity," that is, as long as the situation is "open" and accepted in its irreducible multiplicity, there will have been truth (as long as the posthuman remains untotalizable as event, fidelity to its truth remains possible and "universal"). Neo remains a (posthuman) subject as long as his substance remains multiple or undecidable, as long as he resists the transcendental position of totalized experience as presence, as long as he remains the generic subject of a truth process, as long as he is not seen as either the result or origin but rather as in excess of the posthuman situation, or, indeed, as long as he remains a "faithful connection operator" between truth and the event as name. Neo's transubstantiation, his becoming (part of) the matrix could thus be described, following Badiou, as his "subjectivization," "the emergence of an operator that is consecutive to the interventional naming that decides the event."[28]

It does not seem irrelevant that Neo's advent and subjectivization are in fact first triggered by the treason of a false operator, Cypher, who plays the Judas part in the story. Symbolically, one could say that it is the treachery of the void or the number, the digit that nearly spoils the posthuman event, or at least wrongly names it. Badiou, however, would resist the looming metaphysical closure involving truth, knowledge, and subject here by positing that truth must ultimately remain unknowable to its subject: "If a truth is something new, what is the essential philosophical problem concerning truth? It is the problem of its appearance and its 'becoming.' A truth must be submitted to thought, not as a judgment, but as a process in the real" (IT 61). The event remains undecidable in the very decision of the subject of which it is an effect: "The undecidability of the event induces the appearance of a *subject* of the event. Such a subject is constituted by an utterance in the form of a wager. This utterance is as follows: 'This event has taken place, it is something which I can neither evaluate, nor demonstrate, but to which I shall be faithful.' To begin with, a subject is what fixes an undecidable event, because he or she takes the chance of deciding upon it" (62). Neo, as posthuman subject, is a "local moment of the truth" which necessarily transcends his finality in being infinite: "every truth transcends the subject precisely because its whole being consists in supporting the effectuation of that truth."[29] However, this subject is confident through belief (which takes the form of "event-knowledge") and the generation of "namings" that only have referents in the future anterior.

This naming process forms the possible nexus between Badiou's thought, Christianity, science fiction, and posthumanist utopia: such names, Badiou asserts, will have been assigned referents or meanings when that situation will have come into being in which the indiscernible, which is only represented (included), is finally presented, as a truth of the former situation. Would it thus be possible to argue that Neo's posthuman adventure presents the truth of his former recognition, of his void and the annihilation of his virtuality? Does the posthuman name a truth that will have been, that the apocalypse has already taken place, that the human never existed? This would return me to my starting point in terms of (post-)theory. Could it now be said that the truth of the posthuman will have been in naming the radically human and will thus allow one to ask: have we ever been human (enough)? Again Badiou would probably resist closure here by claiming: "It is entirely impossible to anticipate or to represent a truth, as it comes to be only in the course of evaluations or connections that are incalculable, their succession being solely ruled by encounters with the terms of the situation."[30] But can one really have it both ways, so to speak: a situation determining a truth which unfolds out of random encounters, or the "objectless" subject as either the "real" of a situation or a mere hypothesis: "a subject is … at once the *real* of the procedure … and that which uses names to make hypotheses about truth?"[31]

This is where I would like to return once more to the scene of the posthuman event in *The Matrix* and ask the question of its political and ethical implications: is not Neo's (fictional, "as if") posthumanity also an invention and intervention of the other? It is, after all, through the encounter with Agent Smith, the sentient program that polices the matrix—that is, with ideological "agency" as such—that Neo's posthumanity comes into being, as excess of the matrix, and therefore as its truth. It is not so much an encounter with Agent Smith as imaginary other, as other-than-*me* (i.e., not his bodily similarity, his virtual humanity) but rather as other-than-other (Agent Smith's unknown ontological status: who or what is "he"; his post-subjectivity and "void"; the undecidability between human-body and machine, but pure anti-representation, similar to the protean T2000 model that can "inhabit" any human form) which needs to be appropriated by Neo in order to make truth in the form of political resistance arrive. It is clear from the start that it is not their difference that separates Neo and Agent Smith, it is their uncanny resemblance, their uncanny and ironic sameness which accounts for much of the viewer's fascination with Smith.

The real of the posthuman out of which Neo's emancipatory politics could evolve, the impossible of the situation, is thus in fact humanity's lack of being (in-the-world). But what if the posthuman were just a perpetuation of this original lack? A renewed obliteration of the trace or the truth that long before the distinction between the human and the inhuman (the non-human, trans-human, and post-human) already existed in a kind of (Derridean) arch-virtuality, the hauntology of a spectral origin, more virtual and more real than any cyberspace, any space at all, virtual or real? What if the matrix (as a kind of Baudrillardian object-world of seduction) always precedes the human or posthuman, and every event, every twist and turn of the subject (human or posthuman) has already been marked, written, codified following an absolutely irretrievable origin which would be the birth of humanity, representation, and space?[32] Would Badiou's (ethics of) truth be able to recognize this? Can one say, in the face of Badiou's imperative, "Keep going!" [*Continuez!*], which he derives from Beckett's (absurdist) existentialism, as that which ethics calls out to the subject, that: as long as we stay away from the three forms of evil, as long as we don't betray the event of the posthuman, as long as we don't confuse it with its simulacrum, as long as we don't succumb to the terror of its absolutization (by, like Morpheus, obsessively giving names to everything that arrives—cf. his insistent "He's the One"—which Badiou identifies as the proper sense of religion)? Is there such a thing as localized posthumanity if it is true that there cannot be any humanity unless through "rooted particular truths?"[33]

In a sense, Badiou's objectless subject, as Peter Hallward points out,[34] seems diametrically opposed to Baudrillard's thought, for whom, it would seem, posthuman hyperreality is characterized by a disappearance of the subject and the threat of an object without subject. It is clear that both—Badiou's and Baudrillard's—are options that are being taken up within current posthumanist thinking, and indeed are at work within the logic of *The Matrix*. For Baudrillard, the evil lies in the fact that in hyperreality the apocalypse can no longer happen. One could argue that in *The Matrix* Neo is just the kind of paroxyst that Baudrillard would have in mind. *The Matrix*, famously, cites Baudrillard in a scene towards the beginning when the hacker Neo illegally sells virtual experiences (the future of drug dealing) to a client. He stores these disks in a hollowed out copy of Baudrillard's *Simulacra and Simulation*,[35] which opens at the starting page of the last chapter, "On Nihilism." So the film is at once inspired by and also comments on (i.e., fictionalizes or virtualizes) Baudrillard—the hollowing out of the book might be seen as symbolic in this context. *The Matrix* describes *le crime parfait*: the elimination of the real world, of the original (fatal) illusion. In this sense the machines who (re)invented the world as illusion of an illusion, as a perfect copy, deprive humanity of its "evil." Neo could thus be seen, in Baudrillardian terms, as a paroxyst-terrorist, who situates himself within this apparent impossibility of exchange of one world for another and thinks through this "undecidability between subject and object."[36] Neo, in his exploding of the matrix from inside, illustrates Baudrillard's impossible nostalgia for (theoretical) terrorism that tries to overcome the terrorism of the system and regain the possibility of finality, of death, and hence for the possibility of a subject. In a sense Neo's final challenge to the matrix at the very end, when he promises certain changes to the reality program of the matrix, could also be interpreted as resonating with the final sentence in Baudrillard's "On Nihilism." Neo's future realm may be that of the object, of immortal appearances independent from meaning, which is "where seduction begins."[37]

For both Badiou and Baudrillard, in a sense, the event has happened and it is now just a matter of imagining it, if we can or dare. Hence the inevitable doubling of the event as described in *The Matrix*: the moment of recognition—that the event has taken place, and the moment of action—what to do with the event, or bringing about/driving home (the truth of) the event. *The Matrix*, however, is part of the symptom (not in the sense of pathology, but of the underlying structure of the unthinkable real). Neo, by incorporating the other (Agent Smith), becomes the Other, he becomes the matrix, and, paradoxically, he embodies the matrix and thus truly becomes the digital self he always was. The question is whether this is still human, already posthuman, or merely inhuman?

In terms of *The Matrix*'s dénouement it may be worth recalling Slavoj Žižek's account of a virtual catastrophe, and linking it to Neo's Baudrillardian gesture of overreaching:

> The prospect of the accomplished digitalization of all information [cf. Neo's instant access to the matrix, he is no longer relying on being materially jacked in] … promises the almost perfect materialization of the big Other: out there in the machine, "everything will be written," a complete symbolic redoubling of reality will take place. This prospect of a perfect symbolic accountancy also augurs a new type of catastrophe in which a sudden disturbance in the digital network (an extra-effective virus, say) [cf. Neo's virus-like threat to infect and thus to change, maybe even destroy, the whole matrix] erases the computerized "big Other," leaving the external "real reality" intact [cf. the prospect of humanity's liberation and rebirth into reality].[38]

Žižek's skepticism, however, should warn us against Neo's idealism, namely that the denegation of this virtual catastrophe may not lead to the desired result: "although, in 'real life,' nothing whatsoever happens, and things seem to follow their course, the catastrophe is total and complete, since 'reality' is all of a sudden deprived of its symbolic support ...."[39]

Conclusion: Bad-you

What is most curious about Badiou's thought, maybe ironically: there is literally no space for a significant other (no "you") in Badiou's subjectivity. Badiou's political thought is a thought of I's and We's, not you's. It seems however that something like the truth as attainable for a subject should require a combination of elements which nevertheless do not necessarily form a dialectic. It is not a question of fusing or collapsing the two moments referred to here in *The Matrix* but which may rather be true for any narrative involving subjectivization, i.e., in fact for any narrative. The moment of recognition analyzed in terms of an ethics of truth, as formulated by Badiou, whose ethics nevertheless asks political questions about a subject and its access to the truth in a specific situation, produces a post-evental subject that involves agency and a universal notion of truth. It is not strictly speaking dialogic and turned toward the other. It may constitute a *déliaison* rather than a *lien social*. It cannot escape a certain violence, and Badiou's ethical imperative of the "keep going," of the demand of the subject to be true to himself and to honor the fidelity to the event (like Lacan's injunction to never give up on your desire), is interestingly close to Camus' Sisyphean existentialism. As Simon Critchley rightly objects, it is the heroism which makes this ethical attitude vulnerable to the most reactionary forms of humanism.[40]

On the other hand, everything Badiou says about the potential conservatism of an ethics of alterity translated into multiculturalism, communitarianism, or "silly left culturalism" and identity politics is absolutely pertinent and true (and a lot of cultural criticism has to acknowledge responsibility here).[41] As mentioned above, Badiou's subject has the structure of a trauma; its goal is to remain true to the traumatic event and to speak its truth. But as the reading of *The Matrix* tries to show, the actual moment of recognition and return is indeed necessarily a moment of radical alterity and leads to an inevitable forgetting of the real. This is where Baudrillard's "desert of the real," Lacan's void, and Badiou's event differ somewhat from Derrida's notion of otherness. "Tout autre est tout autre"[42] does of course mean that radical alterity is tautological and hence beyond any logic and philosophical enquiry, but it also means that this universalism is precisely not pure (e.g., mystical or anti-philosophical) because it is at the same time specific and singular, situated, one might say. The concrete other which is always other to a self and also other to any other only arrives through this structural opening. It is always a concrete other that is foreclosed by a subject. This makes the other specific while remaining other. It is thus the second moment, the moment of self-appropriation as action-transformation—the event-apotheosis-miracle proper—that needs to be supplemented by an ethics of alterity—which is strictly speaking not a simple ethics, as Derrida says in his reading of Levinas, but an "ethics of an ethics," a specific kind of meta-ethics that prevents (Levinasian) ethics from drifting off into theology (or non-philosophy, as Badiou would say). Derrida returns ethics towards philosophy and towards politics. The best illustration for this is a statement by Derrida in *Altérités*:

> Of course, in order to respect the entirely other of alterity, alteration itself—which always presupposes a contact, or an intervention, a socio-political, psycho-, etc. transformation—alteration itself would have to be impossible. If the other remains at an infinite distance, and this is the condition on which the other is other, not only can the other not touch me, or affect me, but the other cannot even alter anything. This relation to the entirely other would ultimately leave everything unchanged, unaltered. And it is of an irrefutable logic that pure alterity should be incompatible with the logic of alteration. There is a moment, I feel, when one must re-start negotiating—this is of a political, or historical concern. This means that if one restricts oneself to the pure respect for this alterity without alteration, one always runs the risk of lending oneself to immobilism, to conservatism, etc., that is, to the obliteration of alterity itself …. There is no reasonable, rational response to this question. There is no logic.[43]

To return therefore to my initial question: why is it that at this historical moment, just when technologically we are about to invent a global public sphere for all humanity, this humanity disappears and is reflected back to us as the inhuman, or the posthuman? Does this announce a disappearance, a return, or a re-invention of the human?[44] The anxiety and desire of "becoming posthuman" may signal a certain need to reconceptualize the human as long as theory keeps remembering the location of thought and agency. As long as the subject is being thought as at once "emergent" (i.e., we have always been posthuman *and* (therefore) never human enough), and as long as theory does not forget a certain historical materialism (e.g., of the body and its processes of embodiment).[45] Subjectivity as both the process and result of an event, to return to Badiou, is the unsurpassable of theory, of thinking, which nevertheless continually has to be thought through every time. The subject of theory refers to both events that were seen in *The Matrix*: the event of recognition which starts a process of self-reflection and hybridization that always originates in the other and in the name of an absolutely Other; and the event of apotheosis understood as the interminable project of purification, becoming universal, immortal, etc. Between these two poles, theory and reading, thinking and culture, carry out their ongoing work of re-writing the event. Any posthumanism, following Badiou, must be interrogated in terms of its betrayal of the event (disavowal, imitation, ontologization).[46] As long as this fidelity to the event allows for a critical interrogation by the same subject that is also the effect of the event, whose task it is to be truthful to "its" event, theory has a place—a place between politics and ethics, between a truth-event, and the question of the other.

Finally: What does this mean therefore for my attempted return to cultural criticism and the current practice of theory? When speaking of post-theory and post-humanism in relation to the question of technology and the future of "man," we must avoid certain pitfalls staked out in this reading of Badiou, Derrida, and others through the "symptomatic" productions (or texts) reflecting the current cultural imaginary (e.g., *The Matrix*, the posthuman, etc.). With Badiou we must ask how truthful posthumanism in theory and practice is to the event it represents in anticipation (i.e., our "posthuman condition"). Against Badiou, we must also recognize that any ethical moment of truth is always already split by an other, by an "as if." The posthuman must be interrogated both as to its truth and its other. This interrogation can only occur through reading, i.e., through the co-incidence of the subject and the event which *is* reading. Whether this is thus an ethical or a political imperative, both or neither, remains undecidable. ∎

....

1   Alain Badiou, *Beckett: L'increvable désir* (Paris: Hachette, 1995), 79. [Hereafter cited parenthetically in the text as B. For a list of Badiou's principal texts and their corresponding abbreviations, see the introduction to this issue.—Ed.] "It so happens that something arrives. That something happens and arrives to us. It is the mission of art to protect, to let shine forth, starlike, these exceptional situations, out of which every truth emerges, and keep them in the reconstructed tissue of our patience." (Unless indicated otherwise, all translations are mine.)
2   Jean Baudrillard, *Le paroxyste indifférent: Entretiens avec Philippe Petit* (Paris: Grasset, 1997), 15: "… as soon as the human is no longer the last and finest word of history …"
3   See Alain Badiou, Thomas Bénatouïl, Élie During, Patrice Maniglier, and David Rabouin, *Matrix: Machine philosophique* (Paris: Ellipses, 2003), 120–29. Badiou here produces a sketch of a philosophical analysis of David Cronenberg's *eXistenZ* (1999), Vincenzo Natali's *Cube* (1999), and *The Matrix*. Badiou ends by stating that for him *The Matrix* is, from a philosophical point of view, the strongest of the three because it remains closest to Plato. Its main question is: "what is a subject who fights its enslavement by an appearance which is itself a subjectivated form of enslavement to biology?" (125).
4   Cf. Stefan Herbrechter and Ivan Callus, "What's Wrong with Posthumanism?" in "Theory's Others," special issue, *Rhizomes* 7 (Fall 2003), http://www.rhizomes.net/issue7/callus.htm.
5   *The Matrix*, dir. Andy and Larry Wachowski (Hollywood: Warner Brothers, 1999); *The Matrix Reloaded* (2003), *The Matrix Revolutions* (2003).
6   See for example Badiou's hesitation when asked (by Peter Hallward) about the "autonomy of truth" in relation to the specificity of "a culture": "Does the identification of procedures of truth always pass through philosophy, necessarily or unnecessarily, or is it a question of situation, of culture? It's an open question and a fairly complicated one" (Ee 139). Later on he nevertheless seems convinced that "[i]n the end, a culture, to the extent that it can be thought or identified by philosophy [or theory?], is a singular interconnected configuration of truth-procedures" (140).
7   Istvan Csicsery-Ronay, Jr., "The SF of Theory: Baudrillard and Haraway," *Science Fiction Studies* 18 (1991): 387.
8   On messianism without messiah, see Jacques Derrida, *Specters of Marx: The State of the Debt, the Work of Mourning, and the New International*, trans. Peggy Kamuf (London:

Routledge, 1995); and "The Deconstruction of Actuality: An Interview with Jacques Derrida," *Radical Philosophy* 68 (Autumn 1994): 28–41.

9   See Jacques Derrida, "The Future of the Profession, or the University without Condition (Thanks to the 'Humanities,' What *Could Take Place* Tomorrow)," in *Jacques Derrida and the Humanities: A Critical Reader*, ed. Tom Cohen (Cambridge: Cambridge University Press, 2001), 52–53.
10 Ibid., 48.
11 Cf. Derrida's notion of the "invention of the other," first in *Psychē: Inventions de l'autre* (Paris: Galilée, 1987), 11–61, and reiterated in "The Future of the Profession," where he refers to "this thinking of the possible impossible, of the possible *as* impossible, of an impossible-possible that can no longer be determined by the metaphysical interpretation of possibility or virtuality" (54).
12 See for example Tom Cohen's reading of *Terminator 2* as a fight against "the invasion, from a fantasized 'future,' of an anti-representational and post-humanist logic," in *Anti-Mimesis from Plato to Hitchcock* (Cambridge: Cambridge University Press, 1994), 260. What is at stake in posthumanism is the survival of representational logic in general. The question is whether the zero/one digital logic is still (too) "metaphysical" (death being the "absence of information"). How to symbolize the absence of information on a screen?
13 Derrida, "The Future of the Profession," 34. *The Matrix* partakes in the whole logic of the virtualization of (the end of) work that Derrida discusses in this context, by providing a particularly bleak prospect of "telework," within virtual communities and communication for a humanity "blissfully ignorant" of its own enslavement—a "disembodiment" of work which is hailed by some utopians, but which in fact merely constitutes a new phase in capitalist exploitation and alienation (43ff.). See also Baudrillard, *Le paroxyste indifférent*: "[I]n our new logistics of interaction, man-machine, there is no longer any question of work. Man and machine form an interface. There is thus no more subject of work" (41–42).
14 Derrida, "The Future of the Profession," 53–54.
15 A question addressed by Derrida in 1997, in Montreal; cf. "Une certaine possibilité impossible de dire l'événement," in *Dire l'événement, est-ce possible?* ed. Gad Soussana and Alexis Nouss (Paris: L'Harmattan, 2001).
16 Cf. PP 12–13, 18.
17 For this notion of the "lien social," see Jacques Derrida, "Fidélité à plus d'un," *Cahiers Intersignes* 13 (1998): 221–65; for Derrida's notions of "democracy-to-come" and "literature," see for example "This Strange Institution Called Literature: An Interview with Jacques Derrida," in *Acts of Literature*, ed. Derek Attridge (London: Routledge, 1992), 33–75.
18 Note, of course, the anagrammatic logic at work in neo, one, and eon.
19 See Slavoj Žižek, *The Sublime Object of Ideology* (London: Verso, 1989), 55–84.
20 Cf. Derrida on "hauntology" and "spectrality" in *Specters of Marx*, passim.
21 Slavoj Žižek, "Psychoanalysis in Post-Marxism: The Case of Alain Badiou," *The South Atlantic Quarterly* 97, no. 2 (1998): 242.
22 Cf. Alain Badiou, "On a Finally Objectless Subject," in *Who Comes After the Subject?* ed. Eduardo Cadava, Peter Connor, and Jean-Luc Nancy (London, Routledge, 1991), 24–25.
23 Ibid., 25.
24 Ibid.
25 Ibid.
26 As Žižek remarks in his critique of Badiou's combination of psychoanalysis and "post-marxism" in relation to (Oedipal) "inhuman excess" in the human: "Don't these lines expose the elementary matrix of subjectivity: you become 'something' (you are accounted

a subject) only after going through the zero-point, after being deprived of all those 'pathological' (in the Kantian sense of empirical, contingent) features that support your identity, thus being reduced to 'nothing'—'a Nothingness counted as Something,' which is the most concise formula for *subject*." Žižek, "Psychoanalysis in Post-Marxism," 256.
27 Ibid., 257.
28 Badiou, "On a Finally Objectless Subject," 28.
29 Ibid., 30.
30 Ibid., 31.
31 Ibid., 32.
32 It would doubtless be possible to trace the idea of a "matrix" reality back to ancient forms of mysticism in cultures of "writing" like, for example, the Arabic notion of *mektoub* or similar Jewish notions that seem to constitute a proximity with many "Jewish" thinkers including Walter Benjamin and Jacques Derrida.
33 Peter Hallward, "Translator's Introduction," Ee xiv.
34 Peter Hallward, "The Singular and the Specific: Recent French Philosophy," *Radical Philosophy* 99 (2000): 15a.
35 Jean Baudrillard, *Simulacra and Simulation*, trans. Sheila Glaser (Ann Arbor: University of Michigan Press, 1994).
36 Baudrillard, *Le paroxyste indifférent*, 62–63.
37 Baudrillard, *Simulacra and Simulation*, 164.
38 Slavoj Žižek, *The Plague of Fantasies* (London: Verso, 1997), 164.
39 Ibid.
40 Cf. Simon Critchley, "Demanding Approval: On the Ethics of Alain Badiou," *Radical Philosophy* 100 (2000): 16–27.
41 Alain Badiou, "Euroamerican Left and the Myth of 'New' Capitalism," *The Red Critique* 3 (March/April 2002), http://www.geocities.com/redtheory/redcritique.
42 Cf. Jacques Derrida, *Donner la mort* (Paris: Galilée, 1999), 114–157.
43 Jacques Derrida, in *Altérités* by Derrida, Pierre-Jean Labarrière, Francis Guibal, and Stanislas Breton (Paris: Osiris, 1986), 31; see my forthcoming translation and preface in *Parallax* 10, no. 4 (2004).
44 Cf. Baudrillard's cry of frustration in *Le paroxyste indifférent*, 39: "It's always the same. The moment one starts intellectualizing a phenomenon it disappears into facts."
45 Cf. N. Katherine Hayles, *How We Became Posthuman: Virtual Bodies in Cybernetics, Literature, and Informatics* (Chicago: University of Chicago Press, 1999), 193, 283–84, and 291.
46 See Žižek, "Psychoanalysis in Post-Marxism," 239.

Badiou without Žižek

Bruno Bosteels

1

Ever since Jacques Lacan first published his "Kant with Sade," originally intended to serve as a preface to a modern edition of Marquis de Sade's *Philosophy in the Bedroom*, it has become somewhat of a commonplace among psychoanalysts, philosophers, and cultural critics alike—often in polemical dialogue with one another—to present readings of the type "*Y* with *X*," whereby *X* would signal the secret "truth," or the inherent dark underside, of *Y*. As Lacan writes: "*Philosophy in the Bedroom* comes eight years after the *Critique of Practical Reason*. If, after having seen how attuned it is to the latter, we demonstrate that it completes the latter, we will say that it gives the truth of the *Critique*."[1] Unlike Lacan, but in order to underscore the logic behind much of his argument, I will follow Slavoj Žižek's usual practice to put the term "truth" in this context between quotation marks. My reasons for doing so are furthermore pivotal to the very issues that are at stake. Indeed, it is first of all the status of truth in philosophy as well as its distinction from another "truth," or rather, from a peculiar type of knowledge of, or in, the real—seemingly available only to psychoanalysis—that are put into question in this interplay between Kant and Sade. In other words, if Sade gives us the "truth" of Kant, this also implies a radical destitution of the philosophical categories of truth, of the good, of the moral law, and so on, in the name of something far more radical—"enjoyment," the death drive, or what one commentator in a bold oxymoron has called "pure desire"—which those familiar philosophical categories cannot fail to disavow, and which instead shines through on another stage, or in another discourse, such as the analyst's: a dramatic stage or discourse which, in this sense, would have been greatly inspired and anticipated by Sade.

Not only can we imagine situations in which a person's stubborn sense of duty for its own sake would come to acquire exactly the kind of "pathological" dimension that Kant's definition of the moral law as pure practical reason in the strict sense would have to forsake. But Lacan is also able to show in what way the typical Sadeian scenarios of endless torture and perverse suffering can be said to obey a universal maxim of their own, the ground for a true "right to enjoyment" [*droit à la jouissance*] which, both in terms of the radical rejection of all "pathological" interest in well-being and in terms of the form of this maxim, which is also its only substance, must be recognized as strictly conforming to the requirements of Kant's universal moral law. Lacan phrases this Sadeian maxim as follows: "I have the right to enjoy your body, anyone can say to me, and I will exercise this right, without any limit stopping me in the capriciousness of the exactions that I might have the taste to satiate by doing so."[2] However, this imperative would still present us with little more than a formal homologue to Kant's categorical imperative, based on a Sadeian version that is actually not even found in so many words in *Philosophy in the Bedroom*, if it were not for at least three further motives, which I take to be the real key to the dynamic behind Lacan's difficult text, as well as behind those readings for which it has been this text's fate to serve as a model.

The three motives in question are in fact variations on a single theme, namely, that of the philosopher who is being unmasked, undermined, and subverted by the libertine. Lacan, first of all, insists on the fact that in Sade's imperative, the split between the subject of enunciation (the figure behind the grammatical "me" in "so anyone can say to me") and the subject of the enunciated (the figure who says, or is said to say, "I have the right") is openly acknowledged, whereas this split is actually obfuscated or concealed behind the idea of an autonomous subject—simultaneously legislator, agent, and subject of/to the law—in Kant. This means that, even if in both cases the law actually comes from the outside rather than from a little voice within, Sade is more open about this than Kant: "In which the Sadeian maxim, by pronouncing itself from the mouth of the Other, is more honest than appealing to the voice within, since it unmasks the splitting, usually conjured away, of the subject."[3] Second, by reducing itself to a mere instrument of the Other's will to enjoyment, the Sadeian subject in a sense gives body to the object-cause of desire that in strict Kantian terms would have to remain absent from the domain of the moral law. This was, after all, Kant's great revolution—to have shown that the moral law cannot be accomplished without robbing its subject of every representation of a possible object. With Sade, however, this meta-law, regarding the encounter between the law and a subject who ought to remain objectless, is completely overhauled. We thus already see a higher Law emerge, a Law for which Lacan in his text typically uses a capital L so as to distinguish it from the regular moral law, and the object of which, far from remaining unknowable as the Kantian Thing-in-itself, is actually made to appear, in a thorough reshuffling of the transcendental aesthetic, as the agent-instrument of Sadeian torment: "Do we not have this object here, descended from its inaccessibility, in the Sadeian experience, and unveiled as Being-there, *Dasein*, of the agent of torment?"[4] Third and finally, we can also formulate the general relationship between Kant and Sade as one in which the latter forces the confession of that which is lacking in the former: "Thus Kant, by being put to the question 'with Sade,' that is to say with Sade filling the office, for our thought as well as in his sadism, of an instrument, confesses to what is covered by the meaning of 'What does he want?' which henceforth is no longer missing for anyone."[5]

In these three formulations from "Kant with Sade," beyond a simple homology between the Kantian imperative and the reconstructed Sadeian maxim, we see a deeper and asymmetrical pattern develop, one which ever since the publication of Lacan's trendsetting text has frequently come to overdetermine the type of interaction envisaged between philosophy and psychoanalysis. Sade, for all his fantasies about nature's complicity in the omnipotence of perversion, proves to be both more honest and more radical than Kant. The libertine, like the psychoanalyst who finds inspiration in his bedroom, is one who gives us the painful "truth" that is otherwise hidden, disguised, or disavowed by the philosopher. The interpretive scheme behind Lacan's text reveals the secret double bind that ties even the most sublime moral law to the dark continent of morbid desires and obscene superego injunctions—a continent first conquered by Freud more than a century after parts of it had been discovered by Sade. To be exact, Sade's notion of a "right to enjoyment," actually elaborated only by Lacan, suggests to what extent "the law and repressed desire are one and the same thing," or, as we also read further on: "This demonstrates from another point of view that desire is the obverse of the law. In the Sadeian fantasy, we see how much they sustain each other."[6]

In sum, what we obtain from "Kant with Sade" is the matrix for an as yet unheard-of subversion of philosophy by, and through, psychoanalysis: "Here Sade is the inaugural step of a subversion, of which Kant, no matter how amusing it might seem in view of the man's coldness, is the turning point, one that has never been noted, as far as I know, as such."[7] If we use the horizontal bar as a symbol of repression, whereby that which lies beneath the bar is repressed by, and at the same time necessarily grounds and sustains, whatever is standing on top, we can concentrate the conclusion of Lacan's text in a simple formula:

$$\frac{\text{Kant}}{\text{Sade}} = \frac{\text{law}}{\text{desire}}$$

Whenever the inherent underside of this formula is shown in broad daylight, as could seem to be the task of a critique of morality inspired by Lacanian psychoanalysis, the result of this turnabout or anamorphic shift also inevitably reveals the inherent split that divides the moral law from within. Starting from desire, or from *objet petit a* as the object-cause of desire, the discourse of the analyst would thus allow us to interrogate and come to grips with the constitutive divide of the subject, in this case the moral subject. Without this view from below, in fact, the split in the subject would not even be visible in the first place. Finally, insofar as some version or other of the subject typically occupies the center stage in all modern philosophy, the analyst's discourse, following the model provided in "Kant with Sade," also allows us to put into question the very status of philosophy itself in the name of everything that the latter's beloved truth(s), whether practical or theoretical, cannot but disavow and push away beneath the bar of repression.

2

Today it seems almost unavoidable to give an updated version of this type of reading in the guise of a confrontation of "Badiou with Žižek," whereby Žižek would giddily come to play the role of a modern or postmodern Sade in the boudoir of Badiou's secret Kantianism:

$$\frac{\text{Kant}}{\text{Sade}} = \frac{\text{Badiou}}{\text{Žižek}}$$

This combination is nearly unavoidable not only because Žižek was one of the first thinkers to devote a long commentary to Badiou's philosophy, in the central part of *The Ticklish Subject: The Absent Centre of Political Ontology*, but also because, in the same "Wo Es War" series for Verso in which *The Ticklish Subject* appeared, Žižek was responsible two years later for publishing the translation by Peter Hallward of Badiou's *Ethics: An Essay on the Understanding of Evil*, which in many ways produced a breakthrough for Badiou, just as Hallward's exhaustive introductory guide to Badiou's philosophy came to us prefaced with much well-deserved praise by Žižek.

In English-speaking parts of the world, Badiou's work thus seems to have been thoroughly mediated by Žižek's idiosyncratic brand of Lacanianism, in some cases before any of this work was even beginning to be available in translation. This mediation, moreover, takes the shape of what almost seems to be a preemption, which in actual fact will turn out to have been a retroactive self-criticism as much as the anticipatory critique of another thinker who is only recently becoming better-known. I will have to come back to the strange temporal loop involved in the process of this forced reception, since it is not foreign to the rapport between philosophy and psychoanalysis in general—or, at least, it does not seem to me to be foreign to Žižek's work in terms of the peculiar rapport it establishes between Lacanian psychoanalysis and contemporary European philosophy. But first I want to attempt briefly to systematize Žižek's criticisms of Badiou. This will then lead me to propose a new set of demarcations so as to avoid the familiar subversive matrix of "Kant with Sade" by way of a rather more subtractive "Badiou without Žižek."

3

Aside from numerous isolated references, starting with his earliest books published in English, Žižek has devoted two extensive critical commentaries to Badiou's philosophy, both of which are available in multiple versions in journals and in books: the abovementioned chapter "The Politics of Truth, or Alain Badiou as a Reader of St. Paul" from *The Ticklish Subject*, an abridged version of which had been anticipated in *South Atlantic Quarterly* the year before; and a more recent article, partially written in answer to my views on Badiou and Lacan, published as part of the foreword to the second edition of *For They Know Not What They Do: Enjoyment as Political Factor* and again, in a slightly modified version, as a chapter both in Hallward's edited volume, *Think Again: Alain Badiou and the Future of Philosophy*, and in a special issue of *Communication & Cognition* edited by Dominiek Hoens.

In these texts, the lines of demarcation between praise and blame are not always easily drawn. Frequently, what is meant to be a critical rejoinder, such as the description of Badiou as "the last great author in the French tradition of Catholic dogmatists,"[8] could also be read as a vicious attack, with the subsequent result that Žižek in public and private conversations already has been somewhat at pains to clarify the exact nature of his responses to Badiou. This ambiguity is at least in part due to the fact that what presents itself as a straightforward summary of Badiou's philosophy is already heavily influenced and refracted by Žižek's own thought. This is a first example of the strange temporality of Žižek's line of reasoning: many insights from Badiou, before being allowed to stand on their own, are thus appropriated and transcoded in Žižekian and/or Lacanian language. No doubt this is a result of the overwhelming power of Žižek's thinking. Like most truly original minds, he too cannot not think in his own terms. However, we can also see the involuntary side-effect of this inability, which from another perspective of course looks like the gift of a rare ability: Badiou's thinking thus may appear to be more derivative than it actually is, since in his moments of greatest insight he would primarily be confirming the views of Lacan by way of Žižek while, conversely, many of his alleged blindnesses, or the risks of the so-called non-thought, seem to depend on inexplicably naïve and slightly caricatured principles, for which those recently expropriated insights can then serve as the perfect rebuttal in the hands of Žižek.

This is not just a matter of preemptive strikes as part of the usual art of philosophical warfare. Badiou truly does appear as an increasingly important accomplice in Žižek's work, but one whose own arguments, once they are expropriated and transcoded, almost magically come to serve as counter-arguments to the alleged misgivings of their originator. These misgivings, though, actually may be the product of a one-sided summary on the part of the commentator, instead of signaling an authentic blind spot in the texts that are being commented upon. On occasions, the allegedly neutral summary thus paints an almost unrecognizable portrait of Badiou's philosophy, while in other cases the perspective under attack seems to resemble, more than anything else, some of Žižek's own viewpoints, albeit from earlier works. Many of Žižek's counter-arguments by contrast seem to be faithful paraphrases, admittedly rewritten in Lacanese or Hegelese, of Badiou's thought properly understood. To disentangle this interpretive knot may well be a nightmarish labor worthy of Sisyphus. Perhaps this is even one of the reasons why to this date Badiou has remained uncharacteristically silent in response to the polemic provoked by his friend.[9]

On some topics, finally, Žižek seems to toy with a number of hypotheses that are loyal experiments which do not really break with Badiou's own thought, even though they push this thinking in rather unexpected and potentially extreme directions. Thus, when he discusses politics, art, science, and love as the four conditions of truth, or the four generic procedures that condition philosophy according to Badiou, Žižek insists on what we might call their uneven development, all the while suggesting that either religion or love would occupy a symptomatic position within (or outside) the series—either as the disavowed model for all four conditions or as something of an ultimately determining condition, which therefore would have to be counted twice, once as part of the series and a second time as the model for all four. "So, perhaps, if we take Badiou's thought itself as a 'situation' of Being, subdivided into four *génériques*, (Christian) religion itself is his 'symptomal torsion,' the element that belongs to the domain of Truth without being one of its acknowledged parts or subspecies," Žižek writes in *The Ticklish Subject*, whereas in his text for *Think Again*, perhaps under the influence of Alenka Zupančič's arguments along the same line, this function of symptomal torsion is attributed to love instead: "So is love not Badiou's 'Asiatic mode of production'—the category into which he throws all truth procedures which do not fit the other three modes? This fourth procedure also serves as a kind of underlying formal principle or matrix of all of them."[10] Žižek, as is only to be expected, then goes on to suggest the primordiality of psychoanalysis in this regard: "And insofar as Badiou recognizes that the science of love—this fourth, excessive, truth procedure—is psychoanalysis, one should not be surprised to find that Badiou's relationship with Lacan is the nodal point of his thought."[11] The hesitation itself between religion and love can serve as a further indication of the fact that Žižek, with regard to the status of the different truth conditions, is only experimenting with the limits and possibilities of Badiou's philosophy, without phrasing as yet any inherent and insurmountable shortcoming or deadlock.

No doubt we could make the same point about Žižek's discussion of the four subjective figures in Badiou's philosophy (the master, the hysteric, the pervert, and the mystic—even if these are old names that are not quite held up in Badiou's current theory of the subject that is part of *Logics of Worlds*, in which the figures of the subject are either faithful, obscure, or reactive—with a fourth figure, that of resurrection, squaring the circle with a renewed fidelity) in comparison with Lacan's famous theory of the four discourses (the master's, the hysteric's, the analyst's, and the university discourse). Here, too, Žižek's discussion confirms Badiou's fundamental insights, while complementing them with an even-handed exposé of the specific differences and overlaps that separate them from, or connect them with, Lacan. In fact, by underlining Badiou's obvious proximity to the figure of the master, including in Badiou's own definition, whereas it is rather the hysteric's discourse that serves as a model for Lacan, Žižek also candidly portrays how his own response to Badiou corresponds in large part to the hysteric's reiterated mockery and denunciation of the philosopher or master-thinker by answering all of the latter's proposals with an ironic rejection: *Ce n'est pas ça!*[12]

4

In Žižek's reading of Badiou, the actual criticisms can be divided into three registers, which in order of increased weight are respectively philosophical, political, and psychoanalytical in nature.

Criticism One

In philosophical terms, the argument takes two apparently incompatible forms. Žižek first of all accuses Badiou of being much more profoundly Kantian than Badiou himself has been able or willing to admit. Badiou's Kantianism, to which Žižek is dying to play the role of the Sadeian tormentor, would be particularly clear in terms of the rigid divide that, in Žižek's summary and spelling, separates the positive (phenomenal) order of Being from the radically other (noumenal) dimension of the Truth-Event: "What all this means is that there is a Kantian problem with Badiou which is grounded in his dualism of Being and Event, and which needs to be surpassed."[13] When Badiou proposes that one of the forms of "Evil" would consist in the disastrous sublation of this gap, that is, in the direct overlap or forced coincidence between the two radically incommensurate dimensions that are (or ought to be) Being and the Truth-Event, he would in a typical Kantian fashion be reminding us of the indispensable requirement to treat the accomplished Truth-Event only as a regulative idea, and not as a constitutive principle. This is how Žižek reads my line about the "as if" mode of the generic extension of a situation: "Can we imagine a more direct application of the Kantian distinction between constitutive principles (a priori categories which directly constitute reality) and regulative *ideas*, which should only be applied to reality in the *as if* mode (one should act as if reality is sustained by a teleological order, as if there is a God and immortal soul, etc.)?"[14] A Kantian modesty would be lurking in the notion of an ethic of restraint, explicitly assumed in Badiou's idea not to push the operation of forcing a truth all the way to include the unnameable point of the real of a situation in the process of its event-related transformation. Finally, even despite the so-called secularization of the infinite, realized in mathematical set theory, Badiou as read "with Žižek" would nonetheless remain caught in the notion of finitude that is central to Kant's critical-transcendental project: "Although Badiou subordinates the subject to the infinite truth procedure, the place of this procedure is silently constrained by the subject's finitude."[15] For Badiou, the subject is nothing but a finite instance of a truth process that in and of itself is strictly speaking infinite, and this gap between the finite and the infinite cannot be erased without getting involved in a "disaster" similar to the place and function of the "transcendental illusion" in Kant.

Žižek's answer to this first shortcoming, or this first disavowal, consists not only in unmasking Badiou's profound, albeit surreptitious, Kantianism, but also in countering it with a by-now familiar passage through Hegel. Instead of setting up an insurmountable gap between the positive order of Being and the radically heterogeneous order of the Truth-Event, Žižek thus proposes that a thoroughly Hegelianized Badiou would have had to transpose this split onto the order of Being itself. "The only way out of this predicament is to assert that the unnameable Real is not an external limitation but an *absolutely inherent* limitation," Žižek proposes in his text for *Think Again*. He continues: "*This* and only this is the proper passage from Kant to Hegel: not the passage from limited/incomplete to full/completed nomination ('absolute knowledge'), but the passage of the very limit of nomination from the exterior to the interior. The true materialist solution is thus that the Event is *nothing but* its own inscription into the order of Being, a cut/rupture in the order of Being on account of which Being cannot ever form a consistent All."[16] Badiou, in other words, would have been insufficiently clear about the immanent nature of the split within the multiple of Being. This can also be phrased in Badiou's own terms, as the split between presence, or presentation, and re-presentation. "The key to Badiou's opposition of Being and Event is the preceding split, within the order of Being itself, between the pure multitude of the presence of beings (accessible to mathematical ontology) and their re-presentation in some determinate State of Being," Žižek writes in *For They Know Not What They Do*; "The question, therefore, is that of the precise status of this gap between the pure multitude of presence and its representation in State(s)."[17]

An odd variant of this philosophical criticism—odd in the sense that it hardly seems compatible with the allegation of a profound Kantianism—holds that Badiou, by supposing that the order of presence somehow offers up a wildly profuse and anarchic multiplicity prior to its inevitable capture by the State or the metastructure of a situation—is also much more Deleuzean than he is able or willing to admit. Žižek questions this privilege of pure presence-without-representation by invoking an obvious counter-example from politics: "Today, however, extreme Rightist populists are also not represented; they resist State Power; so perhaps we should question this logic of multiple presence versus State representation. On this point, Badiou remains all too close to Deleuze."[18] Žižek also asks: "Is it not that there already has to be some tension/antagonism that is operative within the pure multitude of Being itself? In other words, is Badiou, in overlooking this topic, close to Deleuze, his great opponent?"[19] It is difficult to reconcile these two views of Badiou as a proto-Kantian and a crypto-Deleuzean, if for no other reason than that Deleuze frequently explained how his little book on Kant's critical philosophy, in clear contradiction with the Spinozian principle of joy as an affirmative passion, was his only reactive book written against and about an enemy. In another sense, though, the second philosophical reproach may confirm the first one: Badiou, we could then say, remains too close to Deleuze because of, and not in spite of, his undigested Kantianism. Pure presence and multiplicity can seem to be overprivileged precisely as a result of the presupposition of a purely external opposition, in contrast to an immanent split, between presence and re-presentation, or between Being and Event.

Criticism Two

Politically, much of Žižek's criticism focuses on the alternative, which is central to Badiou's recently published lecture series *Le Siècle*, between the two paths taken by the so-called "passion for the real" in the twentieth century, namely, the self-destructive path of purification, or purging, and the purely formal path of subtraction, or the play of minimal differences. Žižek connects this criticism with his more strictly philosophical arguments by imagining the consequences of a hypothetical alternative scenario, one in which Badiou would not have hesitated, as he still seems to have done in *Le Siècle*, between the plea for a strict fidelity to the violently self-destructive fury of the twentieth century and the need resolutely to move on from a politics of purification to a politics of subtraction. Žižek in this regard actually goes so far as to speak of a "blunder," to which he believes there is a certain necessity in

Badiou: "Why? Because *fully to follow the logic of subtraction would force him to abandon the very frame of the opposition between Being and Event*. Within the logic of subtraction, the Event is not external to the order of Being, but located in the 'minimal difference' inherent to the order of Being itself."[20] Complete loyalty to the logic of subtraction, in other words, would have forced Badiou to risk taking the next step in the obligatory passage from Kant to Hegel.

After calling him at the same time too Kantian and too Deleuzean, all the while quickly making his own much of the argument about the twentieth century's violent "passion for the real," Žižek thus almost seems to blame Badiou for not being quite Badiouian enough in making the move from purification to subtraction! In the new foreword to *For They Know Not What They Do*, in a concluding fragment not reprinted in the version for *Think Again*, he even adds an illustration of what the much sought-after politics of subtraction would look like. Thus, citing the fate of the four profiles of Marx, Engels, Lenin, and Stalin that used to appear at the top left-hand side of each issue of *Pravda*, Žižek recalls how, after de-Stalinization, it was not just that the profile of Stalin was removed so as to leave only Marx, Engels, and Lenin, but rather Lenin's profile was strangely redoubled, so that we end up with an uncanny repetition of Marx, Engels, Lenin, and … Lenin. This brings Žižek to ask rhetorically "what if the repetition of Lenin is the ultimate example of the logic of subtraction, of generating the minimal difference?"[21] Of course, if we leave the sphere of Soviet influence, another solution, one that is more likely to be favored by Badiou, could consist in adding the profile of Mao Zedong. When Žižek fails to consider this possibility, we could even say, mimicking his very own style, that there is a strict necessity to this failure in Žižek's approach. Why? Because *fully to follow the logic of Badiou's Maoism would have forced Žižek to abandon the allegation of a purely external opposition between Being and Event*. But, then again, by abandoning the notion of such a pre- or proto-Kantian dualism in Badiou, Žižek would also have lost the perfect opportunity to present himself as the Hegel or Sade of this closet Kantian.

Criticism Three

Žižek's most profound and harshest criticism of Badiou, which is also the real crux of the debate, is of course psychoanalytical in nature—even though the consequences of this criticism never leave untouched the spaces of philosophy and politics. We can summarize this criticism by saying that Žižek teaches Badiou a lesson or two in dying. To be more precise, if all philosophical wisdom, according to a common schoolbook definition, consists in learning how to prepare for death, then the fundamental lesson of psychoanalysis by contrast would teach us how to die twice—or, failing that, how to live in the uncanny or undead space in-between-the-two-deaths, that is, the physical and the symbolical.

This criticism will immediately strike a note of familiarity in the ears of anyone even mildly acquainted with Lacan's "Kant with Sade." Following the Lacanian model, Žižek himself in fact had performed a similar critique of Badiou's former teacher, Louis Althusser. In *The Sublime Object of Ideology*, Žižek shows how Althusser's theory of ideology as interpellation leaves out of the picture all the obscene scenarios of desire and drive that alone tie an individual to the mechanisms of interpellation by which this individual is turned into an accountable subject. "In short, the 'unthought' of Althusser is that there is already an uncanny subject that *precedes* the gesture of subjectivization," Žižek writes; "'Beyond interpellation' is the square of desire, fantasy, lack in the Other and drive pulsating around some unbearable surplus-enjoyment."[22] When Žižek opens his first major reading of Badiou by announcing how the latter's notion of fidelity to a truth is actually the exact equivalent of Althusser's notion of ideology, the trained reader already knows exactly what to expect next. Beneath and beyond Badiou's truth, Žižek will thus locate an ineradicable dimension of excessive enjoyment, for which Lacan, taking his clue from Marx, coined the term *plus-de-jouir*, or "surplus enjoyment":

$$\frac{\text{Badiou}}{\text{Žižek}} = \frac{\text{Truth-Event}}{\text{surplus-enjoyment}}$$

What Badiou's concept of truth cannot fail to disavow, in other words, is the dimension of perverse desires and the death drive that necessarily precedes, subverts, and outlasts any and all attempts to domesticate it. Badiou at this point would even run the risk of banality and the non-thought according to Žižek: "When Badiou adamantly opposes the 'morbid obsession with death,' when he opposes the Truth-Event to the death drive, and so on, he is at his weakest, succumbing to the *temptation of the non-thought*."[23] What is more, insofar as "his theoretical gesture involves a 'regression' to 'non-thought,' to a naïve traditional (pre-critical, pre-Kantian) opposition of two orders (the finitude of positive Being; the immortality of the Truth-Event) that remains blind to how the very space for the specific 'immortality' in which human beings can participate in the Truth-Event is opened up by man's unique relationship to his finitude and the possibility of death," Badiou's fundamental weakness can be overcome only by radically acknowledging the role of the death drive as a missing third term, or a "vanishing mediator," between Being and Event: "The Lacanian death drive (a category Badiou adamantly opposes) is thus again a kind of 'vanishing mediator' between Being and Event: there is a 'negative' gesture constitutive of the subject which is then obfuscated in 'Being' (the established ontological order) and in fidelity to the Event."[24] Using Lacan's discourse as an instrument of subversion, much in the same way that Lacan himself used Sade to give us the tormented "truth" of Kant, Žižek thus boldly lays bare that which cannot but remain obfuscated in Badiou's philosophy. In the end, it would seem that we have not gone very far beyond the matrix of Lacan's text. The radical point is still and always to unveil the dark and repressed underside of philosophy's grandest claims to truth: "The 'death drive' is thus the constitutive obverse of every emphatic assertion of Truth irreducible to the positive order of Being."[25]

5

Can we ever hope to extricate Badiou's thought from the complex picture drawn by Žižek? At first, it may seem a fairly straightforward, if not exactly small, task to respond to each of the three criticisms summarized above:

Response to Criticism One

Regarding Badiou's alleged Kantianism, to be overcome by a passage from Kant to Hegel, we should no doubt apply to Žižek some of his own observations, in *For They Know Not What They Do*, about the typical "deconstructivist" criticisms of Hegel's pan-logicism.[26] Žižek thus is one of the first to fall prey to the error that soon thereafter is to become common among perspicacious critics of Badiou, when he formulates as a reproach to Badiou what is actually a basic feature of Badiou's own thought, that is, the insight in the immanent deadlock, or impasse, of the ontological discourse of being—an impasse which for Badiou already signals the retroaction of an event, without which it would not be visible in the first place. Like the Derridean reading of Hegel, Žižek's claim about Badiou's hidden Kantianism breaks down an open door. In order to maintain the distance between Badiou and Lacan, similar to what Rodolphe Gasché had to do in order to keep the distance between Hegel and Derrida, Žižek is forced to impute to Badiou a nonsensically simplified version of "proto-Kantian dualism," summarizing the worn-out textbook platitudes about how the event "belongs to a wholly different dimension" and suchlike. Matters reach a peak when Žižek *refutes Badiou by means of Badiou* himself—presenting as a limit supposed to escape Badiou the elementary proposition of Badiou's entire philosophy, from his Maoist works all the way to *Being and Event*! Not only has Badiou repeatedly explained the reasons for his anti-Kantianism, often through a detailed reading of Hegel's *Logic*, but he has also always rejected the "leftist" or "rightist" deviations that would oppose freedom and necessity, forces and places, the masses and the State, or Event and Being as two externally opposed "orders" or "dimensions" (terms that, including the abundance of New Age-sounding large capitals, are strictly Žižek's only). This is precisely one of the major lessons that Badiou draws early on, so as never to abandon it, from the Maoist principle that "One divides into two"—a principle obviously more attuned, if only we were able to recognize as much, to Žižek's demand for a Hegelian dialectic than to any naïve proto-Kantian or even pre-Kantian duality.

As for Badiou's Deleuzeanism, Žižek is probably the first to perceive the perversity of this reproach, since much of his own book on Deleuze would not have existed, at least not in its present form, if it were not for Badiou's *Deleuze: The Clamor of Being*, in which the differend between the two is painstakingly documented. But even in terms of strict philosophical content, the argument that somehow Badiou would favor a wild, even vitalist notion of pure multiple presence, accessible outside of representation, completely fails to understand that for the author of *Being and Event*, being is only approachable in a kind of backward inference—drawn exclusively from the formal impasses, deadlocks, or absurd reasonings based on representation itself. Our only means to think being qua being are the immanent resources of thought struggling to come to grips with its own intrinsic excess. Nowhere is being given as such, not even as an unspeakable but still somehow showable experience. The excess of representation over presentation, in other words, is not some great insight supposedly missing from mathematical ontology, but rather the most fundamental feature of this ontology itself.

Response to Criticism Two

The political argument, regarding Badiou's failure fully to embrace his own suggestion of the need to pass from a politics of purification to a politics of subtraction, portrays as an admittedly incomplete linear progress what in actual fact consists of a distinction in terms of level of application that even today allows for a partial overlap, or a non-synchronous synchronicity, between the two. In his current work Badiou thus ends up arguing for a *destruction* of a regime of *appearing* or *existence* while at the same time on the level of *being* he restricts the change produced by an event to an effect of *supplementation* or *subtraction*. "Indeed, something that was not entirely present in *Being and Event*, and that I will now redeploy, finally going back to my oldest sources, is the real distinction between being and existence," Badiou says in an interview; "Finally, and to wrap up this discussion which is extremely important politically speaking, but also very abstract, I believe that I will assert that there is supplementation of being and destruction of existence whenever an event occurs."[27] As for the play of minimal difference, which in Žižek's hands gets to be compared, not to say reduced, to Lacan's logic of the signifier, itself equated with Hegel's logic of the re-mark as the play between a mark and the inscription of the empty place of this mark, and so on: this play has actually been criticized quite extensively by Badiou in relation to the Hegelian dialectic, both in the footnotes to *The Rational Kernel of the Hegelian Dialectic* and in a superb reading of the *Logic of Science* that appears in *Theory of the Subject* by way of anticipating the criticism of Lacan's overly structural dialectic. What is more, Žižek's two other canonical references for this logic of the void or empty place and its subsequent marks, namely, Jacques-Alain Miller's "Matrix" and "Suture," receive a heavy if not fatal blow from one of Badiou's fellow Maoists, Lucie Analbage, in a key chapter from *The Present Situation on the Philosophical Front*, before being tackled by Badiou himself in a special section from his book *Number and Numbers*. Ultimately, the problem with this logic is its complete inability to conceive of the transformative power of an event other than as the effect of a structural reiteration, even though the indefinite repetition of mark and place generates a semblance of dialectical movement that claims to be more radical than anything: "One could speak of a kind of 'ultra-dialectic,' a theory of movement such that it becomes impossible not only to grasp but more radically to *determine* the movement itself."[28] At best, the passage from one term to another, when they are identical, only leads to a "serial logic," that is to say, "one and then the other as minimal difference."[29] Any attempt to turn the play of minimal difference into the greatest insight of Badiou's philosophy at the very least would have to come to terms with this profound criticism of the Hegelian or Lacano-Millerian logic, which Žižek for obvious reasons is only too happy to privilege in Badiou's *Le Siècle*.

Response to Criticism Three

Finally, as for Badiou's failure to take into account the domain in-between-the-two-deaths, here too we could give empirical counter-evidence, such as the opening hypothesis in *Of an Obscure Disaster* according to which the "death" of communism, with the fall of the Soviet Union, is merely a second death, the first occurrence of which had long preceded its symbolical redoubling. More importantly, however, the complexity of the debate with psychoanalysis shows how superfluous is any pretense to restore the "proper" Badiou by pulling him out of Žižek's hands. Aside from opening up one can of worms after another, as though in a potentially endless series of Chinese boxes, such pretense also completely misses the point, since it is certainly not a schoolmasterly question of "correcting" Žižek's interpretation with empirical or theoretical counter-examples. We would then still fail completely to grasp the deep *necessity* behind Žižek's peculiar understanding, or misunderstanding, of Badiou.

6

The situation, in other words, is both more complicated and more interesting than would appear at first sight in view of our using "Kant with Sade" as a model. Žižek knows that at least two of Badiou's own texts seriously upset the scenario of a subversion of philosophy, of truth, or of the moral law, by its inherent other—an other that would be accessible in a primordial way to psychoanalysis. Thus, in *The Ticklish Subject*, Žižek is first of all obliged to consider how, in *Saint-Paul: The Foundation of Universalism*, the dualism of the law and its inherent transgression or sinful perversion is already described, including in explicitly Lacanian terms, only to be supplemented by the possibility of a truth beyond the law and its obscene other. In Paul's terminology, this domain beyond the morbid dialectic of law and sin is of course love, which for Badiou is only one possible condition of truth among others. Thus, we would have to complicate our initial formula somewhat so as to include this domain beyond the law and its underlying desire:

$$\frac{\text{Badiou}}{\frac{\text{Kant}}{\text{Sade}}} = \frac{\text{truth}}{\frac{\text{law}}{\text{desire}}}$$

Secondly, in *For They Know Not What They Do* and *Think Again*, Žižek responds extensively to my criticisms of his and Lacan's position, in which I took up arguments from Badiou's *Theory of the Subject* against the interplay of the twin figures of the superego and anxiety, best illustrated by Creon and Antigone in Sophoclean tragedy. As a supplement to this first tragic dyad, Badiou in his *Theory of the Subject* elaborates a second one, merely suggested but never quite taken up by Lacan himself, namely, the dyad of justice and courage as exemplified by the Aeschylean figures of Athena and Orestes. Aeschylus would thus assist Badiou in his attempt to move beyond, without ever ignoring, the morbid entanglement of the law and its violent origin in non-law, so as to break out of the deadlock that thus far seems to have kept the entire tradition of psychoanalysis as if spellbound by the tragic model of Sophocles.

Given these acute insights, in *Saint Paul* and *Theory of the Subject*, into the perverse interdependence between the law and its transgression, or between the ferocious superego injunction and the anxiety-producing confrontation with the real of enjoyment, Žižek in his polemic with Badiou obviously cannot merely reenact the matrix of "Kant with Sade."[30] How, then, does he proceed? Žižek's brilliantly perverse answer or, rather, his hysterical way out of the apparent deadlock of perversity, will consist in positing that there exists a Lacanian alternative, too, to the merely perverse interplay between law and sin, between law and desire, between the superego and anxiety.

At first, though, the fundamental psychoanalytical lesson may not seem to offer any way out of the perverse dialectic. Žižek admits this much in a long series of rhetorical questions:

> Is not Badiou's description of the intertwining of Law and desire full of implicit (sometimes even explicit) references to and paraphrases of Lacan? Is not the ultimate domain of psychoanalysis the connection between the symbolic Law and desire? Is not the multitude of perverse satisfactions the very form in which the connection between Law and desire is realized? Is not the Lacanian division of the subject the division that concerns precisely the subject's relationship to the symbolic Law? Furthermore, is not the ultimate confirmation of this Lacan's "Kant avec Sade," which directly posits the Sadeian universe of morbid perversion as the "truth" of the most radical assertion of the moral weight of the symbolic Law in human history (Kantian ethics)?[31]

Upon closer inspection, however, the entire effort of Lacan's psychoanalysis according to Žižek consists in avoiding the masochistic intermingling of the moral law and its obscene superego supplement. It is precisely Freud's limitation not to have gone far enough in exceeding this framework in which desire is the obverse of the law—not to have recognized that this is merely a view of the law as superego, which gives us no access to a higher Law beyond the law, a Law that stands in a new relation to the Thing. Žižek's habitual propensity to use large capitals left and right actually makes him loose sight of the difference between the law and the Law in Lacan's "Kant with Sade"—a difference which, as Bernard Baas has pointed out, may very well serve to mark the difference in this particular regard between Freud and Lacan.[32] However well that may be, forced by Badiou's rejection of the Pauline predicament to go beyond the morbid dialectic, Žižek clearly outlines the stakes of the Lacanian endeavor. "Freud's discovery—the ethics of psychoanalysis—does it leave us clinging to that dialectic?" Lacan himself had asked in *Seminar VII*, launching a question the answer to which is a resolute "No!" according to Žižek:

> ... for Lacan, there *is* "a way of discovering the relationship to *das Ding* somewhere beyond the Law"—the whole point of the ethics of psychoanalysis is to formulate the possibility of a relationship that avoids the pitfalls of the superego inculpation that accounts for the "morbid" enjoyment of sin, while simultaneously avoiding what Kant called *Schwärmerei*, the obscurantist

claim to give voice to (and thus to legitimize one's position by reference to) a spiritual illumination, a direct insight into the impossible Real Thing.[33]

Žižek's wager to avoid both and at the same time the perverse or morbid and the mystical or obscurantist position thus hinges on the ability to posit a domain beyond or, following the spatial logic of the bar of repression, perhaps it would be more accurate to say beneath, the relationship between the law and its violent and perverse other: "Lacan's 'Kant avec Sade' retains its full validity—that is, the status of the Kantian moral Law remains that of a superego-formation, so that its 'truth' is the Sadeian universe of morbid perversion. However, there is another way of conceptualizing the Kantian moral imperative which delivers it from superego constraints."[34] This other way of conceptualizing the law as Law reaches far beyond the constraints of the superego so as to delve into the uncanny depths of pure death drive: "For Lacan, the uncanny domain beyond the Order of Being is what he calls the domain 'between the two deaths,' the pre-ontological domain of monstrous spectral apparitions, the domain that is 'immortal,' yet not in the Badiouian sense of the immortality of participating in Truth, but in the sense of what Lacan calls *lamella*, of the monstrous 'undead' object-libido."[35] Badiou, even while being exceedingly aware of the perverse logic of law and desire, would nonetheless still fail to acknowledge this spectral domain where the drives are forever rampant.

Our complete formula thus would have to look somewhat as follows:

$$\frac{\text{Badiou}}{\frac{\text{Kant}}{\frac{\text{Sade}}{\text{Žižek}}}} = \frac{\text{truth}}{\frac{\text{law}}{\frac{\text{desire}}{\text{drive}}}}$$

Of course, there is an ultimate irony to the added detour by which Žižek seeks to avoid the perverse interplay between law and desire, all the while claiming to outsmart Badiou. Thus, if we exclude the middle sections of our formula, we still merely end up repeating a similar dialectic on a higher level, this time between truth and the death drive.

7

For Žižek, the key to the Lacanian way out of the deadlock of the law and its obscene underside is the notion of the act. As he writes in an important self-critical remark in the new foreword to *For They Know Not What They Do*: "The Lacanian name for this gesture of breaking the vicious circle of the superego is *act*, and the lack of a clear elaboration of the notion of act in its relation to fantasy is perhaps the key failing of *The Sublime Object*."[36] We might even say that Žižek's entire polemic with Badiou reaches its climax in this notion of the act, which in parenthetical additions is often equated, without further ado, with Badiou's notion of the event. Žižek certainly is not alone in doing this: Alenka Zupančič, too, seems to suggest in her

Ethics of the Real: Kant, Lacan that there is more than simply a family resemblance between both notions. So is the act ultimately synonymous with the event?

In the remaining pages I obviously cannot offer a systematic overview of Žižek's changing definitions of the act throughout his work. Nor am I qualified to embark upon a detailed comparison with the way the act is defined in Lacan's own seminar on *The Psychoanalytical Act*, a seminar which interestingly enough had to be cut short due to the "events" (or should we say "acts"?) of May '68 in France. All I wish to suggest is how there are two fundamental concepts of the act that circulate in Žižek's vast body of work, only one of which seems to be in strict keeping with Lacan's use of the concept. There is first of all the notion of the act as a traversing of the fundamental fantasy, eventually followed by the identification with the symptom as an unsymbolizable leftover of the process of symbolization, in which enjoyment and the signifier immediately coincide. A subject's defining act thus consists not just in interpreting his or her desire by integrating it into the existing symbolical network, but in assuming the ultimate nonexistence of the symbolic—its constitutive incompleteness. "The act involves the acceptance of this double impossibility/limit: although our empirical universe is incomplete, this does not mean that there is *another* 'true' reality that sustains it," as the example of Antigone perfectly illustrates: "Antigone's act locates her, as it were, in the *ex nihilo* of the interstices of reality, momentarily suspending the very rules that define what counts as (social) reality."[37] But then, especially in Žižek's more recent works, we also find a second, entirely different understanding of the act as that which not only heroically assumes and bears witness to the real as impossible but also profoundly transforms the entire symbolic order that sets the parameters for what is possible and impossible in the first place. Thus, opposing what he calls "the act proper" to other modalities such as the hysterical acting out, the psychotic *passage à l'acte*, and the symbolic act of formal self-assertion, Žižek writes: "In contrast to all these three modes, the act proper is the only one which restructures the very symbolic coordinates of the agent's situation: it is an intervention in the course of which the agent's identity itself is radically changed."[38] In a sense, this shift from one notion of the act to another, a shift which clearly involves a sharp self-criticism on the author's part, also coincides with a decisive reaffirmation of the fact that miracles do happen: "From 'impossible TO happen' we thus pass to 'the impossible HAPPENS'—this, and not the structural obstacle forever deferring the final resolution, is the most difficult thing to accept: 'We'd forgotten how to be in readiness even for miracles to happen.'"[39] Much less clear, however, is the question of who or what would exemplify this type of miracle, similar to the sublime illustration of the first act by Antigone.

My main hypothesis with regard to these two notions of the act then holds that while the first notion is openly indebted to Lacan, the second is to a large extent an attempt to appropriate, under the same Lacanian term of the act, whatever Badiou understands by a truly transformative process of change, which alone would deserve to be called an event. It seems to me, however, that the question is still very much open if and how we can get here from there: can we ever expect to get to the act as radical change by starting from the act as real, or from the act as confrontation with the vanishing cause of the real, after traversing the fundamental fantasy? As if to fill the void between these two notions, Žižek in more recent years also increasingly appears to favor a definition of the act in purely formal terms, as an intractable sticking to principles against all odds. The Pope's stubborn refusal to give way on the issue of abortion, for example, can then serve as an example of the authentic ethical act, against the pragmatic adaptability and feel-good spiritualism of the Dalai Lama: "The Pope, in contrast, reminds us that there *is* a price to pay for a proper ethical attitude—it is his very stubborn clinging to 'old values,' his ignoring the 'realistic' attitudes of our time even when the arguments seem 'obvious' (as in the case of the raped nun), that makes him an authentic ethical figure."[40]

If Žižek with his elaboration of the different notions of act merely wanted to note that Lacan has more to offer in this regard than Badiou wants to acknowledge, then we could end the discussion here and shake hands over yet another happy coincidence. But there is more: Žižek's understanding of the Lacanian act as real in fact not only presents itself as more radical than Badiou's event, but there also seems to come a point where respect for the act as a pure gesture of self-relating negativity and/or stubborn attachment to principle disables in advance any engaged fidelity to a cause of the kind to which Badiou feels obliged to pledge his fidelity following the example of one of his other mentors, aside from Lacan and Althusser, namely, Sartre.

Badiou once summed up the two options in the last truly engaging polemic in French politico-philosophical thought as follows: "Sartre against Althusser: that meant, at bottom, the Cause against the cause" (PP 10). With this wordplay, of course, Badiou is referring not just to any political Cause, but also more specifically to the Maoist *La Cause du Peuple* which could always count on Sartre's support, whereas Althusser's insights into Marx's discovery of a structural or absent cause did not seem to allow for a similar commitment: "One saw this very well in the choices and urgencies: Althusser on the side of Waldeck Rochet, when push came to shove; and Sartre, with the 'Maos,' despite everything."[41] Where in this debate, then, should we place Lacan? After all, did not Lacan by the end of his life abruptly dissolve his *École freudienne de Paris* only to give birth to the *École de la Cause freudienne*, often referred to simply as *École de la Cause*? This might seem to give us some anecdotal reason to put Lacan in the same camp with Sartre and Badiou.

Žižek, on the other hand, ends his final ruminations in *For They Know Not What They Do*, on the situation in the ex-Soviet Union, with a plea for a Lacanian leftist political project that would at least keep alive the memory of past causes, even if they have been thwarted by the turn to Western-style capitalism and neoracism: "Today more than ever, in the midst of the scoundrel time we live in, the duty of the Left is to keep alive the memory of all lost causes, of all shattered and perverted dreams and hopes attached to leftist projects."[42] However, the ultimate paradox of this hopeful project might well be its inherent incompatibility with some of the very same teachings from the Lacanian school that so deeply inspire Žižek. As the latter writes in *The Ticklish Subject*, in another good summary of his entire polemical reply to Badiou: "For Lacan, negativity, a negative gesture of withdrawal, precedes any positive gesture of enthusiastic identification with a Cause: negativity functions as the condition of (im)possibility of the enthusiastic identification—that is to say, it lays the ground, opens up space for it, but is simultaneously obfuscated by it and undermines it."[43] It would thus seem that any principled recognition of the real of enjoyment and drive as the absent cause, or absent center, of political ontology strictly speaking undermines in advance the possibility of identifying with a leftist Cause—other than a lost one! To put the question even more bluntly: what causes are there to be kept alive from a psychoanalytical perspective, if for the latter the most radical act consists in the subject's defining gesture of pure negativity that precedes and undermines every one of the possible candidates?[44]

8

This political paradox finally brings us back to the theoretical question which I announced at the start: What is the status of truth after psychoanalysis? From the preceding remarks we are now in a position to rephrase this question as follows: Is there or is there not a truth of the real? Is knowledge, recognition, or acknowledgement of the real not necessarily at loggerheads with the philosophical category of truth?

Lacan's own steps towards answering this question in his final works is reflected in a number of statements that have a typically aphoristic appeal. Badiou, in his 1994–1995 seminar on *Lacanian Antiphilosophy* concentrates in particular on one of these statements, originally made by Lacan in a 1970 speech to the *École freudienne de Paris*: "The truth may not convince, knowledge passes in the act" [*La vérité peut ne pas convaincre, le savoir passe en acte*].[45] Thus, whereas Lacan begins his international career, most notably in his 1953 discourse in Rome, by promising that psychoanalysis would bring not only truth but also wisdom, his later teaching starting in the 1970s increasingly moves towards a general antiphilosophical destitution of the category of truth, in favor of a peculiar kind of knowledge in the real. There is knowledge in the real, but there is also a real in knowledge. The act happens precisely when something of the real passes into a form of knowledge capable of transmission and as a result of which something drops out of the existing arrangements of knowledge, including their guarantee in the subject who is supposed to know. As Badiou comments: "For Lacan, there is no truth of the real, there is no knowledge of the real, but a function of the real in knowledge. There is also no knowledge of truth, but at best the truth of a knowledge in the real that works."[46] *Le réel passe en savoir*, meaning not only that the real passes into knowledge, but also that the real is not without knowing, as in the homonymous *le réel pas sans savoir*. While for Lacan, this form of knowledge in the real is best transmitted through the formal operations of mathematical logic, I would add that this role has been taken over by popular culture in the writings of a disciple such as Žižek. There is thus something arch-scientific about the act in Lacan, whereas in Žižek the act oscillates between an arch-aesthetic and an arch-political dimension. In both cases, however, the crucial point not to be missed is how the transmission of this knowledge in the real finds an impediment, rather than an aid, in the category of truth.

Ultimately, the philosopher's foolish illusion always consists in loving the force of truth, whereas in the analyst's discourse we could say that the real is always stronger than the true. "The analysis can only have as its goal the advent of a true speech and the realization by the subject of his or her history in its relation to a future," Lacan had written in one of his classical *Écrits*, but this promise of truth would later be dismissed as a lure better left to the care of other discourses, such as the university or master's discourse: "There are four discourses. Each one of them takes itself for the truth. Only the analytical discourse makes an exception."[47] For the later Lacan, therefore, the dividing line separates truth from a new type of knowledge that involves the relations between sense, nonsense, and the real, or between fantasy and enjoyment. Žižek could not be clearer in this regard:

> So, while the "classic," structuralist Lacan invites me to *dare the truth*, subjectively to assume the truth of my desire inscribed into the big Other, the later Lacan comes much closer to something like *truth or dare*: (the symbolic) truth is for those who *do not dare*—what? To confront the fantasmatic core of (the Real of) their *jouissance*. At the level of *jouissance*, truth is simply *inoperative*, something which ultimately doesn't matter.[48]

Lacan's answer, in other words, does not simply oppose truth and knowledge but rather adds another dimension, for which the real of enjoyment and drive constitutes the third mediating term. As Žižek also explains:

> In philosophical terms, Lacan introduces here a distinction, absent in Badiou, between symbolic truth and knowledge in the Real: Badiou clings to the difference between objective-neutral Knowledge which concerns the order of Being, and the subjectively engaged Truth (one of the standard topoi of modern thought from Kierkegaard onwards), while Lacan renders thematic another, unheard-of level; that of the unbearable fantasmatic kernel. Although—or, rather, precisely because—this kernel forms the very heart of subjective identity, it cannot ever be subjectivized, subjectively assumed: it can only be retroactively reconstructed in a desubjectivized knowledge.[49]

We thus begin to see how Žižek's claim through the act somehow to outstrip the radicalism of Badiou's notion of the event has a temporal no less than a spatial effect. Typically this plays itself out in terms of positing the act as a negative gesture that always necessarily *precedes* the masterly inscription of the event into a new set of parameters:

> That is the difference between Lacan and Badiou: Lacan insists on the primacy of the (negative) *act* over the (positive) establishment of a 'new harmony' via the intervention of some new Master-Signifier; while for Badiou, the different facets of negativity (ethical catastrophes) are reduced to so many versions of the 'betrayal' of (or infidelity to, or denial of) the positive Truth-Event.[50]

The same operation of seeking to occupy the place prior to that of symbolic meaning or truth also applies to Žižek's use of the notion of the subject as opposed to the subsequent process of subjectivization, which he sees as central both to Badiou and to fellow Althusserians such as Rancière, Balibar, and Laclau:

> Lacan introduces the distinction between the subject and the gesture of subjectivization: what Badiou and Laclau describe is the process of subjectivization—the emphatic engagement, the assumption of fidelity to the Event (or, in Laclau, the emphatic gesture of identifying empty universality with some particular content that hegemonizes it), while the subject is the negative gesture of breaking out of the constraints of Being that opens up the space of possible subjectivization.[51]

Of course, what is really pivotal in this distinction is the fact that the subject comes before subjectivization, with the latter in a sense already suturing the gap of which the subject is the strict correlative. It is precisely this logical priority that gives the analyst's discourse its leverage in the radical interrogation of any philosophical master discourse: "In Lacanese, the subject prior to subjectivization is the pure negativity of the death drive prior to its reversal into the identification with some new Master-Signifier."[52]

Finally, the attempt always more radically to recapture the prior act can also be phrased in terms of sublimation and the death drive. Žižek not only insists that "the whole of Lacan's effort is precisely focused on those limit-experiences in which the subject finds himself confronted with the death drive at its purest, prior to its reversal into sublimation," but he will also once again pit the death drive, which merely suspends the existing order in preparation for a new act of creation, against the event: "However, this 'merely' should be put in quotation marks, because it is Lacan's contention that, in this negative gesture of 'wiping the slate clean,' something (a void) is confronted which is already 'sutured' with the arrival of a new Truth-Event."[53] From the radical point of view of the preceding void, or the empty place, indeed, every consequent inscription of a new mark must seem utterly naïve in comparison—at best, it is the age-old lure of truth as a symbolic fiction and, at worst, the banality of pure non-thought. This literally makes it impossible to have faith in the category of truth in the wake of Lacan's return to Freud: "Lacan parts company with St. Paul and Badiou: God not only is but always-already was dead—that is to say, after Freud, one cannot directly have faith in a Truth-Event; every such Event ultimately remains a semblance obfuscating a preceding Void whose Freudian name is *death drive*."[54]

9

In the end, I would propose that we pay closer attention to the feverish pace and peculiar haste that seem to be more than purely incidental to the thought processes found in Žižek's work. I say this with the utmost respect: this is not just a repetition of the vulgar resentful notion, which is so common among intellectuals so as almost to become their defining feature, about how someone else always publishes too much or too fast. Quite the contrary, as Lacan could have shown in reference to his early text "Logical Time and the Assertion of Anticipated Certainty: A New Sophism," a text which is extensively commented upon by Badiou in *Theory of the Subject*, haste often has a strictly logical, almost speculative function. Badiou in fact had tried to show in his commentary that Lacan's notion of anticipated certainty, when one hastily jumps to a conclusion so as to outsmart the others in the famous prisoners' dilemma, fails to take into account the possibility that the other might be dumber than oneself and therefore slower in drawing the same inferences.[55] What Badiou could not foresee at the time, however, is the strange kind of speculative haste that is ultimately meant to imply, rather than to shy away from, the notion that the other is a fool. Žižek's haste to expropriate and often preemptively to vitiate the thought of some of the most provocative philosophers today—a project which is now culminating in a searching *rapprochement* among the trio Lacan-Deleuze-Badiou as *the* answer in French thought to the hegemonic role of Foucault-Derrida-Levinas—can and perhaps should be seen as part of a larger trend that for purely structural reasons pushes the hysteric-as-analyst always to undermine the master's discourse, now shown to be foolishly ignorant, with reference to a prior, more originary, or more radically disavowed act.

In Žižek's repeated interpretations of the type "*Y* with *X*," in other words, it is absolutely crucial that *X*, while ostensibly being a response to an already existing discourse, nonetheless appear to be logically, or even ontologically, prior to *Y*. Žižek does not even shy away from jumping back to the future with regard to his own works, as when he uses the new foreword to *For They Know Not What They Do* so as to present this book in retrospect as a critique of *The Sublime Object of Ideology*. Speaking of the praise of "pure" democracy and the Lefort-inspired critique of "totalitarianism" in this last book, Žižek confesses: "It took me years of hard work to identify and liquidate these dangerous residues of bourgeois ideology clearly at three interconnected levels: the clarification of my Lacanian reading of Hegel; the elaboration of the concept of act; and a palpable critical distance towards the very notion of democracy."[56] It seems unlikely, though, that those "years of hard work" correspond to the mere two years that lapsed between the publication of *The Sublime Object of Ideology* and *For They Know Not What They Do*. I would rather venture that the author, in keeping with an irresistible tendency to position himself in the absolutely prior place, has now done the same with his own work—almost as if to suggest that the self-criticism, in an impossible temporal loop, comes before the actual work. More importantly, this strange backtracking also erases the role of some of those same interlocutors such as Badiou whose notion of the event can then be said to have been anticipated by an act the radicality and pure negativity of which is supposedly ignored and obliterated by everything coming afterwards. No doubt this too is part of the reason why Žižek's criticisms of Badiou are so nearly impossible to refute.

In the purest Žižekian fashion, then, perhaps I can be allowed to conclude with a joke. This one puts two fools together in an insane asylum as they get caught up in a heated shouting match. The first yells: "You're a fool!" And the second: "No, *you*'re a fool!" "No, *you*!" "No, *you*!" and so on, back and forth, until the first person finally shouts out with a certain pride: "Tomorrow, I will wake up at five a.m. and I will write on your door that you're a fool!" to which the second person answers smilingly: "And I will wake up at four a.m. and wipe it off!" This is exactly what the death drive or the act can do for Žižek with regard to the pretense to truth of the event in Badiou. Before any inscription of a new truth even has a chance to take place, actually blocking this process in advance by virtue of a structural necessity, the death drive always already has had to come first to wipe the slate clean. In order to undermine the claims of philosophy, the analyst's discourse can always pit the subject against subjectivization, the void against semblance, the real against symbolic fictions, and in the most general terms, the death drive against fidelity to the cause of truth. Thus, in the debate between Badiou and Žižek, I cannot help but think that it is the analyst's irrefutable and endearing wager—his ever more radically abyssal act—always to wake up earlier than the philosopher! ∎

....

1   Jacques Lacan, "Kant avec Sade," in *Écrits 2* (Paris: Seuil, 1971), 120. This version is the last one corrected by Lacan. English translation by James B. Swenson, Jr. as "Kant with Sade," *October* 51 (1989): 55. Page numbers in subsequent citations refer to the French and English versions, respectively (with frequent modifications of the translation).
2   Ibid., 123/58.
3   Ibid., 125/59.
4   Ibid., 127/60.
5   Ibid., 131/63.
6   Ibid., 139/68 and 145/73.
7   Ibid., 120/55.
8   Slavoj Žižek, *The Ticklish Subject: The Absent Centre of Political Ontology* (London: Verso, 1999), 142.
9   The relation between master and hysteric seems to be one of codependence—both in Lacan's version and in the version that for some time was central to the renewed formulation of an axiomatic theory of the subject for Badiou. But this codependence is also asymmetrical in terms of one's need or desire explicitly to address the other. While obvious in Žižek, this need or this desire does not seem to be as pressing for Badiou—whence what to the public eye may appear to be a certain coldness on the part of the philosopher, a coldness which of course only further provokes and intensifies the desire for contestation on the part of the thinker whose model is the hysteric's discourse.
10 Žižek, *The Ticklish Subject*, 141; and "From Purification to Subtraction," in *Think Again*, ed. Peter Hallward (London: Continuum, 2004), 170. See also Alenka Zupančič, "The Fifth Condition," in *Think Again*, 190–201.
11 Žižek, *The Ticklish Subject*, 141; *Think Again*, 170–71.
12 See Žižek, *The Ticklish Subject*, 164.
13 Žižek, *Think Again*, 178.
14 Ibid., 173.
15 Ibid.
16 Ibid., 179.
17 Žižek, "Foreword to the Second Edition: Enjoyment within the Limits of Reason Alone," in *For They Know Not What They Do* (London: Verso, 2002), lxxiv–lxxxv.

18 Ibid., civ n104.
19 Ibid., lxxxv.
20 Žižek, *Think Again*, 178.
21 Žižek, *For They Know Not What They Do*, lxxxi.
22 Žižek, *The Metastases of Enjoyment: Six Essays on Woman and Causality* (London: Verso, 1994), 61; and *The Sublime Object of Ideology* (London: Verso, 1989), 124. See also Mladen Dolar, "Beyond Interpellation," *Qui Parle* 6, no. 2 (1993): 73–96; Judith Butler, *The Psychic Life of Power: Theories in Subjection* (Stanford: Stanford University Press, 1997), 106–31; and Alenka Zupančič, *Ethics of the Real: Kant, Lacan* (London: Verso, 2000), who concludes the debate most succinctly: "The (psychoanalytic) subject is nothing but the failure to become an (Althusserian) subject" (41–42n11).
23 Žižek, *The Ticklish Subject*, 145.
24 Ibid., 163 and 160. See also ibid., 169n25.
25 Ibid., 159.
26 For the original formulations, which I will paraphrase and apply to Žižek himself in the next sentences, see *For They Know Not What They Do*, 72–91.
27 Bruno Bosteels, "Can Change Be Thought? A Dialogue with Alain Badiou," in *Alain Badiou: Philosophy and Its Conditions*, ed. Gabriel Riera (Albany: SUNY Press, 2005). See also in another interview, with Peter Hallward and Bruno Bosteels, "Beyond Formalisation: An Interview," *Angelaki* 8, no. 2 (2003): "For the time being I don't want to accord a metaphysical privilege to subtraction. ... There is something like an ideological decision involved here, one that gives priority to subtraction (or minimal difference) rather than to destruction (or antagonistic contradiction)" (119); and later: "I am obliged here to reintroduce the theme of destruction, whereas in *Being and Event* I thought I could make do with supplementation alone" (131).
28 Lucie Analbage, "La dialectique en son semblant," *La situation actuelle sur le front philosophique* (Paris: François Maspero, 1977), 58–59. See also TS 21–68; and "Note complémentaire sur un usage contemporain de Frege," in NN 36–44. [For a list of Badiou's principal texts and their corresponding abbreviations, see the introduction to this issue—Ed.]
29 Alain Badiou, Joël Bellassen, and Louis Mossot, *Le noyau rationnel de la dialectique hégélienne* (Paris: François Maspero, 1978), 30.
30 In fact, only a few pages after having accused Badiou of falling prey to the temptation of banal non-thought with his view on the morbid dialectic of law and death, Žižek recognizes in this very same view one of Badiou's most complex psychoanalytical insights: "So when Badiou speaks of the 'morbid fascination of the death drive,' and so forth, he is not resorting to general platitudes, but referring to a very precise 'Pauline' reading of the psychoanalytic notions he uses: the entire complex entanglement of Law and desire." *The Ticklish Subject*, 150.
31 Ibid., 152.
32 Bernard Baas, *Le désir pur: Parcours philosophiques dans les parages de J. Lacan* (Louvain: Peeters, 1992), 53–55.
33 Žižek, *The Ticklish Subject*, 153.
34 Ibid., 168n17.
35 Ibid., 154.
36 Žižek, *For They Know Not What They Do*, xl.
37 Žižek, *Did Somebody Say Totalitarianism? Five Interventions in the (Mis)use of a Notion* (London: Verso, 2001), 175–76.
38 Žižek, *On Belief* (London: Routledge, 2001), 85

39 Ibid., 84.
40 Žižek, *Did Somebody Say Totalitarianism?* 182.
41 Badiou et al., *Le noyau rationnel de la dialectique hégélienne*, 15–16.
42 Žižek, *For They Know Not What They Do*, 271.
43 Žižek, *The Ticklish Subject*, 154.
44 In a last turn of the screw from after 9/11, Žižek places the line of demarcation between First and Third World: "It appears, in fact, as if the split between First World and the Third runs more and more along the lines of the opposition between leading a long satisfying life, full of material and cultural wealth, and dedicating one's life to some transcendent Cause." *For They Know Not What They Do*, lxxiv.
45 Jacques Lacan, "Allocution sur l'enseignement," in *Autres écrits* (Paris: Seuil, 2001), 305.
46 Alain Badiou, *L'antiphilosophie lacanienne* (1994–1995 seminar), session of March 15, 1995.
47 Jacques Lacan, "Fonction et champ de la parole et du langage en psychanalyse," in *Écrits* (Paris: Seuil, 1966), 302; and *Ornicar?* 17/18 (1979): 278.
48 Žižek, *For They Know Not What They Do*, lxvii.
49 Ibid., cv; also in *Think Again*, 256n18.
50 Žižek, *The Ticklish Subject*, 159.
51 Ibid., 159–60.
52 Ibid., 160.
53 Ibid., 160 and 153–54.
54 Ibid., 154.
55 Lacan, "Logical Time and the Assertion of Anticipated Certainty: A New Sophism," trans. Bruce Fink and Marc Silver, *Newsletter of the Freudian Field* 2, no. 2 (1988): 4–22. See also TS 264–74. For a short and suggestive commentary, see Dominiek Hoens and Ed Pluth, "What if the Other Is Stupid? Badiou and Lacan on 'Logical Time,'" in *Think Again*, 182–90.
56 Žižek, *For They Know Not What They Do*, xi.

One or Several Events? The Knot between Event and Subject in the Work of Alain Badiou and Gilles Deleuze

Bruno Besana

Introduction

> *There will therefore be different sets, and each of these will appear as one, but it will not be, given that the One is not*
> [*Plato,* Parmenides][1]

"There is some new in being" Badiou announces in the exact middle of his magnum opus, *L'être et l'événement.*[2] And this report does not refer either to any contemporary state of the research, nor to a particular situation of the unveiling of being. Something of the order of the new, of the unexpected, of the incalculable, in a word, of the eventual, comes to add itself to being. And it adds itself to being under the form of the "there is" [*il y a*], under the form of appearing. For his part, Deleuze takes into consideration the thousand accidents[3] that punctuate perceptible reality, the thousand events that inscribe themselves in the life of an individual, and which, moreover, constitute it as an absolutely singular life. It is thus, according to a plexus of reasons that must be analyzed, that Deleuze can propose a necessary knot between ontology and the theory of the event, declaring that "all the events communicate in a same and single Event, which no longer leaves space for accident," and again that "being is the unique event where all events communicate."[4]

A same and single concern, a same and single question of "philosophical taste" seems to traverse the two authors. To explain the infinite mobility of what appears, to explain its constitutive multiplicity and the differences that traverse it, wouldn't it be appropriate to pass on these same differences, these same multiplicities, from the side of the characteristics of being, by doing this in such a way that they become the proper object of ontology? The putting into question, even the dissolution, of the unity of being and the one of the *en kai on*[5]—whether declined in its Platonic or Aristotelian versions—would thus be the primary condition of this procedure. Badiou, Aristotelian insofar as he doesn't lend this justification, affirms without delay that "the point of departure of my speculative proposal could be formulated thus: can one unseal the one from being, break up the metaphysical hijacking of being by the one?" (CT 26).[6]

Before proceeding to an analysis of these two topical cases that can enable us to gauge the import [*sens*] of this philosophical intuition (a philosophical intuition that describes a field in which Badiou and Deleuze are in a certain sense the extremes), it seems to us interesting to anticipate a detail that will be taken more squarely into account in the second part of this work. In the case of the opening quotation from Alain Badiou, we have the presentiment that what is of the order of the event comes to add itself to being in the very movement of appearing; while, in approaching the quotation drawn from Gilles Deleuze, we have the impression that what is of the order of the event is on the contrary the fundamental trait of being *qua* being. But, if events are exactly what, in making the "event," determine the sensible and concrete appearing of phenomena, it follows that two different visions of the corporeality of being, of the "presence" of being, are here in play. Thus being, for Badiou, conceived in itself as non-eventual multiplicity, turns out to be disincarnated, absent, "void"; for Deleuze, on the contrary, being in its eminently multiple nature is what always makes event, in a physical and perceptible manner.[7] And it is in two parallel readings of the work of Plato that we can illuminate such a divergent assonance in the ways of conceiving being as multiplicity, which will constitute our point of departure for taking the concept of event into consideration.

First Part: Being and Multiplicity—Plato's Abysses

It is throughout the opening pages of *L'être et l'événement* that Alain Badiou exemplifies his major ontological hypothesis; and, to do this, in the guise of an introduction, he relies on the second part of the hypotheses on being of the Platonic *Parmenides*. It is a matter in this passage, Badiou tells us, of the "ontological decision whence my entire proposal originates, namely the non-being of the one" (EE 41). And in fact we find here the complete enumeration of the primary consequences of the assertion "the one is not."[8] In the first place, we encounter the positive determinations (in themselves and in relation to Others) of this one-that-is-not. In the second place are marked the determinations that one must think of Others (in themselves and in relation to the one) if the One is not, and principally the fact that, if the One is not, the others cannot be others-than-one but must be others of others. Thus "each term, considered as a set, is an infinite multiplicity: whenever we take the smallest possible, right away, because of the infinite division of parts [*parties*], what appears to be One reveals itself to be multiple."[9]

In the first place, it is the dialectic *unity-multiplicity* that is overturned: the multiple others are not multiple unities, but are multiples of multiples, whose unity is not what permits their distinction but their gathering, in counting them as "one" according to a given criterion. But the dialectic *identity-alterity* is also completely put into question. And it is by playing on the constant return between πολλὰ and ἄλλα that traverses the Platonic text, that Badiou advances his argument. In fact, if one saves the One, the multiple "Others" cannot be different from the One, which is not: it follows that they are different from other "Others," that they are different from each other. The difference between the others is thus originary, because the others do not differ from any "same." Thus, in commenting on the Platonic affirmation which states that "the others are different,"[10] Badiou concludes that "the other cannot here designate the gap between the one and the others-than-one, since the one is not. It turns out that it is in regard to themselves that the others are others" (EE 43).[11]

But there is more: if we look more closely, Plato, while saying that "what would appear to be One reveals itself to be multiple," tells us that the One is the proper *modality* of the *appearing* of multiplicity. Plato seems, for an instant, to furnish a new arrangement between the multiple and the one: the multiple would no longer be what participates in the one under different forms, but, on the contrary, the one would be the image, the appearing, of the multiple. And this because no multiple, as pure multiple, can appear. Plato in fact exhibits this hypothesis as a dream, because "inconsistent multiplicity is, as such, unthinkable. All thought supposes a *situation* of the thinkable, that is, a structure, a count as one, where the presented multiple is consistent, numerable" (EE 44). Badiou can thus see the work *chez* Plato not only as an ontology of the pure multiple, but also as a phenomenology founded on the possibility of recognizing the individuality of things: the one as appearing of the multiple. If it is therefore true that Badiou here inverts Plato by Plato himself in regard to the hierarchical order of the one and the multiple, it is at the same time true that he maintains the idea of a division between the transcendent plane of being and the immanent plane of phenomena (the problem will thus be that of the arrangement of the two planes, and it is there that we will come upon the theory of the event).

However, Plato concludes the *Parmenides* with the radical impossibility of such a hypothesis of the ontological consistency of the multiple. And this not because it would ruin the one (the ruin of the one being the opening hypothesis), but because it ruins the multiples themselves. For the *Parmenides* "the others are not the One .... But they are not any more several: to be several, they must before be one. Because if any of them is one, the total is nothing, and thus they are not even several."[12] From which he draws out: "if the one is not, nothing is"[13] and by this affirmation Plato seems to foreclose the possibility of the inconsistency of the one and the possibility of being as pure multiplicity. But Badiou inverts this inversion of the Platonic inversion, by suggesting that οὐδέν ἔστιν should be more properly translated by "nothing is" [*rien est*]. Which signifies that being *qua* being, the pure multiplicity of which the One is only the manifestation, is, but its being is inconsistent, void.[14] This statement appears clear if one grasps it from two sides. From one side, at the interior of a concrete situation, what is not countable is not, so "that prior to [the count as one] there is nothing, because all is counted" (EE 67–68).[15] From the point of view of being as appearing, the pure multiple is therefore strictly inconsistent, void. But from the other side, this void, this inconsistency of pure multiplicity, is being, subtracted from all presentation. Which mathematics seems to have grasped very well: "the primitive name of being, in set theory, is the void, the empty set [*l'ensemble vide*]. In a certain sense, it alone 'is.' And the logic of difference implies that the void is unique. It cannot in fact differ from another, since it does not contain any element that could verify this difference" (EE 108).[16]

For Badiou, then, in the wake of Plato, to account for phenomena it is first necessary to found an ontology where "being *qua* being" is taken into consideration, even if he articulates the theory to the problem of appearing, to the problem of the necessary unity under which phenomena appear.[17] Thus Badiou maintains a clear "Platonic" separation of the plane of speculation about being and the plane of speculation about appearing, even if its premises are inverted, or even if, in reading, most extreme, abyssal premises might be "repressed": being is pure multiplicity. It is in this sense that the idea becomes clear: "I try to found a Platonism of the multiple" (D 69).[18] A Platonism of the multiple, to which one must add a theoretical supplement, a supplement to ontology capable of explaining appearing to us, in its non-ontological, more-than-ontological, specificity. A theory of being *and* a theory of the event.

But it is in starting from the tangled reading of the Platonic corpus that we can perceive the different ways of conceiving the arrangement between being and phenomena in Deleuze and in Badiou. It is in starting from this perspective that we can perceive the different "carnal consistency" of being in the two authors: void, separated from phenomena, always *supplementable* by an event that unifies its presentation, for the one; evental, always *supplementing* its own actual state, for the other.

Deleuze effectively accomplishes in his turn an "inversion of Platonism in Platonism," but the reference for this operation will not be in a text on the "abstract" nature of being (the *Parmenides*),[19] but on the contrary in a text that poses the foundations of this problem in the immediate relation with the concrete order of things: *The Sophist*, one of the texts that weaves the structure of *Logique du sens*. Here Deleuze takes into consideration the speculations of an already mature Plato, who interrogates himself as to the dialectical structure of first ideas. And it is here that we see arise, not without a certain astonishment, the hypothesis of a perceptible that has lost every relation to a first model.[20] We certainly have here something of a negative hypothesis, exhibited to be denied. Nonetheless, it is a question of a hypothesis formulated in a detailed and powerful way.

The stage of *The Sophist* is well-known: the Stranger, the protagonist, tries to define the sophist, but the latter always slips away from definitions, because he presents himself capable of everything and thus impossible to classify under the definition of such or such discipline; his knowledge does not seem to be constituted in the image of any model, to the point that the Stranger, in the attempt to define the sophist, finds himself producing a veritable swarm of definitions. To get out of this impasse, the Stranger proposes to define him as an "imitator," and thus as a species of image-creators, but a creator of very particular images. The sophist in fact does not compose by the imitation of what exists, but produces illusions in a manner analogous to painters who must draw very large figures, changing their proportions to make them appear normal to the spectator situated at the foot of the work. If these "reproduced beauties in their true proportions, the superior parts would appear too small to us, and the inferior parts, too large, since we see one from close up, and the others from afar."[21] This amounts to saying that, by the practice of this art, one produces the sensation of seeing the image of something that exists, when on the contrary one sees only an absurd being, deprived of proportion, something that *is the copy of nothing*. The artist in question produces something that has no relation with "the true *proportions* of the *beautiful*," which, in Platonic language, signifies that it has no relation with a true model. These images reproduce nothing, and thus they "χαίρουσιν τὸ ἀληθές," they set the true to walk [*elles envoient le vrai se promener*].[22] And nevertheless artists produce images, appearances: what is, then, their status? How to name them? This is what the Stranger proposes: "What simulates the copy that is nothing, will this not be a simulacrum [φάντασμα]?"[23] The sophist thus lines up among these producers of simulacra, with the fine distinction that his simulacra are even more powerful, because products of speech and not of painting or sculpture.

Now *phantasma*, here translated by simulacrum, is in general terms an apparition: in general the word signifies "image of an object."[24] Thus, in the first place, phantasma is, in a manner a little anodyne, appearance. Deleuze takes into account the concept of simulacrum as image without model, and he defines it as "the effect of a resemblance, but which is constructed on a disparity, on a difference,"[25] on a sensation and not on a model. And from this he deduces a major consequence: if the simulacrum is no longer the imitation of a form, the copy of a primary and transcendent identity, and nonetheless an identity, then it can only be an effect, the unitary appearing of a pure multiplicity. It is the appearing of a crowd of differences; and because of this, in its very appearing as form, it *changes constantly*.

But for Plato the domain of difference, the domain where difference awkwardly accords with the identical, is the perceptible. Saying then that the simulacrum, appearance, is constructed on differences, is equivalent to saying that its genesis accomplishes itself in the perceptible. Deleuze, through such an attempt to read an "inverse of Platonism" at work at the heart of the Platonic reflection, seeks finally to operate a donation of sense with the perceptible. And it is in reading the most current sense of the word *phantasma* that we can understand the sense of such a donation of sense with the perceptible, with "appearances," that lies at the heart of what one usually calls the "inversion of Platonism." While in France one speaks of the simulacrum, elsewhere one speaks of appearance, which confirms that the limit and paradoxical case of the simulacrum treats at the same time of the normal regime of appearances.[26] Thus, more generally, we can say that, when Deleuze sees the problem of "simulacra" arise at the heart of the Platonic system, there he sees a new possible way of approaching the problem of appearances, a new possible way of approaching the problem of appearing, that is, of *all that appears*. It is thus on the basis of Plato's intuitions, of this "Plato who in the flash of an instant discovers that the simulacrum is not simply a false copy, but that which puts in question the very notion of copy," that Deleuze takes his departure to ask what a thought of the perceptible stripped of every model would be, a thought of the perceptible whose rules are immanent to the perceptible itself.[27]

The "paradoxical case" of *The Sophist* does nothing other than make evident the fact that phenomena are, strictly speaking, phenomena of nothing. The theory of phenomena, of things such as they appear, certainly founds itself on the idea that identity is appearance, but what, exactly, is such an "appearance of nothing?" What does it mean, exactly, that "there is no longer any admissible reason that the existents resemble what would be more essential than themselves?" (D 66). And how to arrange this with the other important given put forward by *The Sophist*, knowing that the simulacrum is what, in its appearing identity, changes constantly?

The example chosen by Deleuze shows us a phenomenon that is indissolubly the "simulation" of an identity and constant change, the "contraction" of always-surging differences. It is something that Badiou also notes when he says, in a rather concise manner, that where he himself "attempts to found a Platonism of the multiple," "Deleuze," on the contrary, "attaches himself to a Platonism of the virtual" (D 69). Stripped of its *vis polemica*, Badiou's remark is very interesting: according to Deleuze, Plato stages in *The Sophist* a hypothesis in which the actual presence of an existent is the concrete and perceptible presence, the actualization, of a non-actual multiplicity, of a virtual set of transformations that is nothing other than the being of the existent.[28] The being of the existent is thus a multiplicity, but a particular multiplicity, arranged in such a way that the reason for its appearing insists in it, appearing as identity and as change, an event that inscribes itself on the surface of the existent.[29] For this being is defined as what "incarnates or actualizes itself, differentiates itself" in the existent; and, inversely, the existent is "what differs, [and thus] has itself become a thing, a substance";[30] it is the difference become substance. And this is possible because being is certainly a multiplicity, but this multiplicity is "in itself a system of differential relations," an essence "fully differentiated in itself, which comes to differentiate itself in the actual."[31]

Every phenomenon is therefore the product of a process of differentiation; it is the actualization of such a multiplicity. If the existent is the unitary appearing of a multiple being, it is also that in which the process of differentiation of being appears. It is the place of inscription of "remarkable or singular points that result: events."[32] Forced to appear by the internal movement that constitutes its differentiation, virtual being actualizes itself *both* as *form* of the phenomenon *and* as appearing of an *event*; being actualizes itself in a changing and perceptible phenomenon, always making event. Being, pure multiplicity without foundation, is thus at the same time the principle of appearing identity, and the principle of the becoming of this identity. And identity is at the same time simulated, appearing of a pure multiplicity, and really one, the actual place of the inscription of the event, of the event of the virtual part of itself.[33]

It is thus that, even though the simulacra are not copies of anything,[34] Deleuze does not draw from this the hypothesis of an inconsistency of being. If being for Badiou, insofar as it is deprived of the One, is inconsistent, for Deleuze being as multiple is nothing other than this material consistency that appears here and now under the aspect of a unitary form, the place of inscription of perceptible events. For

Badiou, "the one is not, and nothing is"; for Deleuze "the simulacrum is not a copy of anything" [*n'est copie de rien*]. Thus in Deleuze's phrase one can in no way elide the "n," and it is in this sense that the entire weight of a being is in play, whose virtuality can only be understood in strict and indissociable relation with its own actual *presence*.[35] Whence one can say without delay, paraphrasing Badiou, that for Deleuze "being is event," because there is nothing other than being that can make event, and there is nothing other than the actual existent, identitarian incarnation of the process of differentiation of this same being, in which the event can take place.

The being that appears and the law of this appearing are therefore strictly immanent to the fact of appearing [*l'apparition*] itself. One of the great differences in relation to Badiou is at play here. No distinction is possible between ontology and phenomenology, because the event that comes to supplement being, in ensuring the count as one, is nothing other than being itself, seized in its dialectic of differentiation. Moreover, Badiou himself brings an element important for understanding their respective differences on this point. For Badiou, the one is the effect of an event that, in coming to supplement being-multiple, constitutes a law of the count by permitting the distinction of the individuality of phenomena. But because of this the one is that which, deprived of consistency, subtracts itself from ontology, and by which the principle, disappearing as event, subtracts itself also from phenomenology. For Deleuze, on the contrary, the one is. And it is doubly so: on one side it is the identity-one of the existent, which is at the same time real, produced and simulated; on the other, the One is being itself, "being in which all the events communicate," unique virtual difference that actualizes itself in an infinity of actual forms. Thus "for Deleuze … the One is the infinite reservoir of dissimilar productions. *A contrario*, I maintain that the forms of the multiple are, like the Ideas, always actual, that the virtual does not exist, but I sacrifice the One" (D 69).[36]

Second Part: From Event to Subject

In sacrificing a nodal point of Deleuze's thought, namely the strict correspondence between the univocity of being and the multiplicity of existents, in sacrificing a same and single being that says itself in an infinity of existents, Badiou ends by sacrificing the strict reciprocal immanence of being, the appearing in a multiplicity of phenomena and the law of this appearing. It is in this sense that we could perceive that Badiou's system—a "classic" system, as he himself likes to define it—unfolds a passage that goes from being *qua* abstract of its *hic et nunc* to the phenomenal presence of things, in passing by the law that separates and unites these two dimensions. From transcendence to the empirical, in passing by the transcendental as soldering and division. With Deleuze, on the contrary, his system seems to deploy itself all at the same place: the being of what appears is separable neither from its appearing nor from the law of this appearing.

Event and Absolute Immanence

The fundamental question that seems to turn at the heart of such immanentism can be formulated thus: given that what appears manifests itself as a changing, perceptible form, always traversed by events, what must be said of being in order to justify this? It is here, moreover, that the principal sense of the Deleuzian concept of "immanence" lies: what makes event is strictly immanent to what appears as form, to the point that there is always a coalescence between these two aspects. Every subsequent signification of the concept of immanence does nothing but return to this primary one: the strict immanence of the actual aspects of the existent (its formal presence) *and* its virtual aspects (what can always make event in it, coming to modify it in a manner simultaneously hazardous and internal). Thus when Deleuze speaks of immanence one should think of this neither as immanence to a transcendental subject,[37] nor as immanence to an arbitrary rule of composition of objectivities. On the contrary, immanence is defined as "A LIFE and nothing other,"[38] because it is in the singularity of a life that we can distinguish (in their necessary imbrication) an actual objectivity and a line that, according to a specific order, reunites it with the virtual set that makes event in it. And because of this we can distinguish the exterior form of the existent and its own interiority, the interiority acting in such a way that its multiple matter "holds," "makes one" of the thousand events that solicit it. Behold how immanence is, in the first place, nothing other than the strict coalescence between actually present matter and its "making event," its perceptible and changing being.[39]

How, then, on the basis of this movement, should being and the existent be described?

The duplicity actual-virtual is the proper movement of the determination of being, that is at all times unique and infinitely multiple, that can only exclude all ontological dualism, a being as virtual totality that "virtually pre-exists expressive individualities, but does not actually exist outside those individualities that express it,"[40] outside those singular lives that express it. Being is therefore *univocal*, a completely determined virtual totality that actualizes itself in existents that are as many individuating differences.[41] At the same time, the *immanence* of its actual identitarian manifestation and the virtual events that it actualizes is its fundamental ontological trait: immanence and univocity come back to the same. Being and event have a single sense (univocity), and it is for this reason that being appears *both* as consistent presence *and* as mutation, necessary disfiguration of this presence (immanence). Being is therefore event, and it is in this regard that Badiou is absolutely right to remark that, for Deleuze, "it is necessary to sustain that the plurality of events is purely formal, and that there is only one event, that is in a way the event of the One" (D 111). There is thus only a single event—the event of difference—that manifests itself in an infinity of modalities. At the same time all is event, there is nothing that is not of the order of the event: all phenomena are actualizations of events, have a form that follows from an event, and in which the event comes to inscribe itself.

The existent is therefore determined by what we could call a *double regime of the appearing of difference*: difference appears as event that inscribes itself in beings, and it appears as identity. Nevertheless, the two modalities of appearing form only one: *what appears is an identity that makes event*, and for this reason appears in a perceptible manner. Concrete form and event are the two indissoluble sides of the same manifestation of being, so that "there is no quality without an extension that subtends it and in which it diffuses itself …. And a quality is always an event."[42]

This signifies that an interiority always corresponds to the material exteriority of an existent. This is a "life that contains only virtuals, that is made of virtualities, events,"[43] which is the singular implication of events that compose it, that actualize themselves in it. Its interiority is that by which it is an existent, a life; its interiority is, one could say, its subjective coherence.[44] We can thus even affirm that every existent has a properly subjective interiority, which is like the interval between the *multiple* events that it contracts and the exterior *one*-form, which is only the perceptible trace of the latter. We will thus say that the actual form of an existent "is the complement or the product, the *object* of realization, but the latter has only the virtual for *subject*."[45] The subjective essence of the existent is the internal line which rebinds the thousand events that compose its concrete and perceptible life, the line, *produced by events themselves*, made in such a way that the existent remains *one* in the face of solicitations. Grasping the essence of the existent means grasping the eventual multiplicity that expresses itself in it.[46]

Such an essential knotting between identity and the event is made evident by the concept of haecceity, by which one designates "what makes the *individuality* of an *event*," as in the case of "a life, a season, a battle, a season, five hours."[47] In "haecceity" we rediscover the fact that every existent is a *haec* (the material presence of a something, in the plural) and an *ecce* (the cry of astonishment faced with an unexpected event); by haecceity one thus hears in the first place every thing, every material multiplicity unified by the fact of being able to be a unique place for the inscription of events. Furthermore, Deleuze employs the concept of haecceity for the description of the subject. Thus he wonders: "are we not such haeccities rather than an I?" How, in fact, to maintain unaltered the notion of subject (even an empirical subject), a *res cogitans*, when the very notion of object dissolves itself in that of haecceity? Every thing is such, every thing is one, by virtue of its unifying, "subjective" interiority. On what grounds could we therefore maintain a special status for the empirical human subject, on what grounds could we consider it originary?[48] Still further: on what grounds could we maintain its transcendental status, when for Deleuze every faculty can only be conceived as empirically formed? The interiority of a haecceity is thus that by which absolute impersonality gives onto the formed individuality of an existent. "The life of the individual has made way for an impersonal and nevertheless singular life, that is to say of the subjectivity and objectivity of what happens. … It is a haecceity, life of pure immanence."[49] The individual is not thereby eliminated, but is defined as the immanent line that rebinds the ensemble of events that compose it, and as the form in which they incarnate themselves. There is certainly a principle of organization of a series of events in an actual form, but this principle, whose effect is subjective (the law of the series as interiority of the existent) and objective (the form of the existent that holds together, that makes one, for a certain duration of time), is a produced and existent principle, according to the different modes and degrees of each existent. Lacking which an *existent* would not be *an* existent.

We can go a step further by taking into consideration Badiou's proposal in regard to this point of Deleuze's thought. The point of departure common to the two authors is explaining being *qua* pure multiplicity, which appears as semblance (count as one, simulacrum) of an identity. This identity is certainly real, but produced, secondary, derived, always submitted to an evental given (whether internal to the existent, as in the case of Deleuze, or external to the existent, as in the case of Badiou). But on the road taken by Deleuze, as Badiou underlines, since the principle of univocity implies that every existent is the expression of the same Difference, one risks losing the real difference between existents. Thus Deleuze, in order to maintain the strict immanence between existents that would be as much expressions of the same being, would end by carrying off every essentiality to its difference: the difference between the existents would be nothing other than a simulation.[50] Deleuze, in fact, as Badiou holds by underlining, "must mark in actual existents their co-belonging to the great virtual totality (CT 69).[51] In this way, the organicist Deleuzian paradigm that affirms "the primacy of process over equilibrium, of the movement of transformation over the affirmation of identity" finishes by "privileging weak difference over strong difference" (TS 71–72). For Badiou, in conclusion, "one sees the price one must pay for the inflexible maintenance of the thesis of univocity: that the multiple is finally only of the order of simulacra ..., that the world of existents is the stage of simulacra of being" (D 41). Against the Deleuzian continuism that would finish by ruining every real difference between existents and every reality of multiplicity, Badiou reknots Platonism to mathematics, as a means of thinking pure multiplicity wholly by assigning respective differences between the existents. And this because "in the Platonic style of sets, alterity resolves itself into punctualities, difference is assignable in a uniform and always elementary fashion .... This is a central trait, in particular because it limits the rights (Aristotelian as well as Deleuzian) of the qualitative, of natural and global difference" (CT 107–8). In marking sets as the count as one of pure multiplicities, set theory succeeds in describing individualities really different in their respective presentation by maintaining that they are ontologically pure multiples. But for this to be possible, the primary strong and fundamental difference must be that between being as pure multiplicity and the principle that comes to install there a count as one, the evental principle, because it makes the count come to presentation.

But Deleuze renounces precisely the strong distinction between being, the evental law of presentation, and the presented existent. And this is because form and event, in their coalescence, are the sign of the same being in the existent. It is here that we find the point of genesis of the difference between the two authors: for Deleuze such a transcendental division ruins the univocity of being and thereby immanence that alone can be affirmed without reintroducing an arbitrary transcendental schematism;[52] for Badiou, on the contrary, "to wish to write the ontological equation being = event" (CT 71), Deleuze will have, on the one hand, split the essence of existents in two (between virtual and actual), and, on the other, will have condemned existents to being only the simulacra of identities, to being only the multiple phantasms of the same One.

The hypothesis from which Badiou begins is that it is necessary to assume that "the pure multiple, generic form of being, never welcomes the event in itself as its virtual component; but, on the contrary, the event comes to it through a rare and incalculable supplementation" (CT 71–72), even though in this way, by affirming the existence of different situations, radically heterogeneous, submitted to rare and constitutive events, the idea of immanence comes to efface itself. Which Badiou willingly recognizes: "Deleuze always maintained that, in conceptualizing absolute beginnings (what I call the theory of the void) and singularities of thought incompatible in their constituting gestures, I fell back into transcendence. But if, finally, in order that a political revolution, an amorous encounter, a scientific invention, an artistic creation can be thought as distinct infinities, on condition of incommensurable separative events, it is necessary to sacrifice the immanence and univocity of being, I would do it. I do it. ... As Deleuze would have said: it's a question of taste" (D 136–37).[53]

Immanence and Its Constitutive Dimensions

For Badiou, therefore, being and event can only be thought in their disjunction, as being and extra-being, as a Two whose encounter gives way to the effect of the One by which phenomena present themselves. The event proposes itself as what permits the passage from pure, transcendent multiplicity, abstracted from its perceptible presentation, to the one, which is the mode of its immanent appearing. In fact, it is characterized by "having disappearing as essence," and that, in its inconsistent disappearing, it "gives consistency" (TS 82) to multiple being. Supplement of being and therefore subtracted from ontology,[54] disappearing in phenomena, the event would be a sort of "rarity of non-being"[55] whose proper function would be to justify the passage from being to existent, from ontology to empirical phenomenology. Unaffirmable by ontology, vanishing in phenomena, the event seems to situate itself on the plane of the transcendental, by simultaneously ensuring the cutting and soldering of being as being *and* appearing. The event is thus that which, in placing itself between ontology and phenomenology, permits the appearing of phenomena as structured *identities*: because "the same is not what is (being the infinite multiple of differences), but what happens" (E 27). The disjunction and relation between these planes is graspable thanks to the concepts of situation and site.

As we have seen, pure multiplicity "does not *exist*," not being representable as such; but, at the same time, "it is of the being of the existent to appear" [*il est de l'être de l'étant d'apparaître*]. There are thus always presentations that appear under the form of one, according to a knowable structure, a pure multiplicity inconsistent in itself. Such a "localization of the site, I call a situation" (CT 191); and the proper of the situation is that being, presented but unpresentable, appears there in an "untotalizable deployment." This latter is, moreover, the criterion that gives us the norm of a situation: a normal situation counts its elements for one, but does not include itself in the count. There is thus a part—in which lies the principle of representation of the situation—that is not representable by the situation itself.[56]

On the contrary, the proper of "extraordinary" situations is to make the law of the count of the situation appear. And extraordinary situations are notably the place of inscription of events (EE 212–13).[57] The event is described according to two fundamental traits. On the one side, it is what "ontology rejects in the this-that-is-not-being-qua-being" (CT 205) and, effectively, in belonging to itself, it breaks a fundamental law of ontology.[58] But on the other side it is inscribed as what installs a new count as one: "the event makes one-multiple, on the one hand, of all the multiples that belong to its site; on the other hand, of the event itself" (EE 200). Extraordinary, the event is thus transcendental in the sense that it places itself at the limit of empirical experience, a limit—normally not representable—on the basis of which the situation is renamed. It places itself in the situation like a structuring absence, something that does not properly appear, and that nonetheless is the condition of a new way of appearing. But how can an event come to inscribe itself in a situation, come to rename it, restructure it? A situation, in the first place, presents all its elements. These elements, ontologically, are in their turn multiplicities. But elements for the most part form subsets, thus responding to the law of the count as one. One says that most elements are presented and represented by the situation. But, by the axiom of foundation, there is one part of the elements that is not also a subset of the situation, a part that resists assimilation to this law. It is to this multiplicity not represented by the situation that the event first comes to give a name: in inscribing itself in it as in its proper site it paradoxically names it as unnamable, it names it as what subtracts itself from the totalizing rule of a situation, it names it as "void situated at the heart of the situation" (E 61). The event inscribes itself materially in its site, and thus "the eventual site is this given immanent to the situation that enters into the composition of the event itself" (SP 74). It is at the site that the event appears in the situation, and thus "the event is at once supplementary and situated—it is an event of this or that situation." The event is thus what presents the bare being that lies at the heart of a situation, and that which, on the basis of this impossible nomination, comes to rename all its elements.[59]

Suspended from the void, supernumerary in relation to the law of the situation in which it appears, the event is totally illegal, but at the same time it functions like a new principle of nomination. Its proper is that, in a historically structured situation, "it implicates a quantity of other significant statements, without one being able to deduce it from the axioms that organize the situation" (EE 273–74).[60] This signifies that its truth can only happen in the consequences that it produces. Still further, its truth defines itself as the complete deployment of the latter: and thus it can only be proved on condition of being able to address itself to every element of the situation, on condition of being universal.

By such a universalism, we understand that the proper function of the event is to permit each element to attach itself there "in its most extreme particularity," not in virtue of a common trait, but in virtue of its own difference.[61] Only thus can it attach itself potentially to every element (and thereby be proven), if it is true that "there are differences. One can even maintain that there are only these" (SP 105).[62] This universal procedure—which renders an event true by rebinding to it an infinity of differences—makes itself according to invariable modalities that Badiou calls "subjective."

Every event can only appear in a situation in a disappearing fashion, and it can therefore not anchor itself in the situation except by grasping an element, a concrete individual. Badiou calls the topical figure incarnated by such an individual a "figure of subjectivation." This is because, on the one hand, there is strictly nothing subjective prior to this figure, taking account of the fact that the event is "what happens, purely and simply, in the anonymity of a path"; and, on the other, because it is on the basis of this figure that all the elements of the situation can attach themselves to the having-taken-place of the event "in their most extreme particularity," which constitutes, as we will see, the proper of a "process of subjectivation." The typical example of such a figure, non-dialectizable by the laws of the situation and who introduces there an eventual break, is Christ. But the only point that makes Christ an eventual figure is the miracle of resurrection, by which each is saved to a new life, by which the law of death is vanquished. Given the event "resurrection," "what the particular person named Jesus said and did is only the contingent material that the event seizes for a wholly other destiny …. It is the name of what happens universally to us" (SP 64). The impersonality of the event can thus come to incarnate itself in an infinity of subjects by way of such a figure, and thereby inexorably become true. Such a subjective figure announces itself in the situation as uncountable: it announces itself as a sort of naked body, that as such speaks first to all the naked bodies, to all the elements uncounted by the present situation; these elements constitute in this way the preferred *site* of inscription of the event announced by this figure. But as every element, even though counted by the situation, is also a multiple element, a naked body, it follows that every element is potentially attachable to this figure. It is thus precisely in its nudity that it can trigger a universal consequence, that it can attach the totality of elements to itself.[63]

But how to discern that such a figure is really what conveys the event in its site, and that it is not, on the contrary, one uncounted element among others? This can only be decided afterwards, according to a specific procedure. And it is here that we come across the second subjective figure, the figure of fidelity. In fact, if "the event is only measurable according to the universal multiplicity of which it prescribes the possibility" (SP 48), then for an event to be such it is necessary that there be someone who declares its singularity, someone who declares that it slips away from the ordered course of facts and who simultaneously declares its universality: there must be someone who declares that the event has been a "universal singularity" (CT 224). This second figure of the process of subjectivation is one who, departing from an act of belief, puts in place a "faithful intervention"—namely, a "procedure by which a multiple is recognized as event" (224)—and thereby retroactively begins to build the truth of the event. This signifies that the faithful figure is a constant, incarnated in an individual, who functions to attach as many individuals as possible to an event, and by this transforms the illegality of the choice (of the having-taken-place of the event) into effectuated truth.[64]

And it is here that a subject comes to appear: "we call subject the support of a fidelity, thus the support of a truth-process" (E 39). The becoming-true of the event is that by which arbitrary individualities become properly "subjective," capable of declaring that such an event is what grasps them in their most extreme difference.[65] And fidelity thus defines itself as the operation of creation of an infinite number of faithful subjects. From the moment that an event takes place, two figures are necessary for its effectuation: a figure who incarnates the event, and a figure who declares the having-taken-place of this incarnation.[66] By these figures every subject is "suspended" by an event, and every event is "presentified" in a subject. Thus the relation between these different figures forms something like the set of invariable coordinates by which an event comes to deploy itself in the subjects that presentify it.[67]

Under the condition of an event, according to spatial (the set of figures) and temporal (the line that goes from an event to a proven situation) coordinates, a consistent present takes place. The event presently [*actuellement*] becomes true; it produces effects. But such a set of transcendental subjective preconditions only determines the possibility of the arising of a subject. So that a subject effectively takes place, a whole set of heterogeneous elements must be reunited: the subject is in fact not simple multiplicity, nor concrete substance counted for one, nor a transcendental structure, nor a result. It is rather the knotting of these points, the "local and situated configuration" by which occurs "the incorporation of the event to the situation" (EE 431). More precisely, as a present thing, furnished with matter,[68] the subject will be defined by the action of an event on an arbitrary matter (multiplicity), according to subjective figures. The subject is thus the present point of attachment of an event to the multiple matter of a situation, it is the most advanced fragment of an event that is no longer there, and of a deployed situation that is not yet there. The subject is the interval between uncountable being, the count, and the counted. It is the present moment of the operation of knotting of these planes, it is that by which an event now becomes true, it is the liminal point, the vanishing present, where an event comes to count the elements of the situation for one. And thus the present as duration is a sequence of subjects where each time it is decided that such an event is the count as one of the situation.[69]

Submitted to an enormous set of conditions (an event,[70] a process of subjectivation, the organization of this process according to invariable figures, the multiple matter of an individual), always suspended at the highest incertitude by the fact of itself being the most advanced state of the truth that it declares, the subject is rare and precious, the luminous point where the present finds its bearings in its incertitude, in its truth, by declaring the necessity of an action that could restore each element to its most extreme difference through its attachment to the event.

Presentification of an event in a situation, the "subject has no other being-in-situation than the multiple-terms that it encounters," but its "essence is much rather the trajectory that binds them" (EE 434); it turns out that it is defined as subject despite its multiple being. And it is by such a distinction between multiple matter and one essence (a funny distinction, if we consider that, for Badiou, being is multiplicity), that we will measure the difference from Deleuze. For Badiou perceptible, biological, carnal differences are taken into account as material for the construction of the subject, but can in no way influence the modalities and rules of its construction, which occur according to invariants that exceed it.[71]

In the two cases the subject will thus be defined as the interval between a multiplicity and an identity, as that which—in catalyzing some evental thing—makes happen the identity of a coherent world. But in one case this process works by starting from a disincarnated multiplicity, despite the very materiality that forms the flesh of the subject, and according to invariable modalities that catalyze the extra-ordinary chance of an incalculable and unique event, the original moment from which a thinkable world can occur. In the other case, the subject is nothing other than the catalyst of evental forces by which a material multiplicity expresses itself, happens to the perceptible, by determining by itself the rules of its own appearing. The subject thus appears knotted with double threads to the event, if it is true that the first actualizes the passage from the multiple to the identity of which the second is the power. The system of the world appears grasped according to a single principle, according to the intuition that leads to an explanation of appearing and its becoming by starting from difference and multiplicity. But in one case the system develops itself according to a defined structure that assigns each element its place: being and event, *by which* an organized world takes place, *according* to invariable modalities, *through* a subject. In the other case the system develops itself all at the same place: being is event, and by this it differentiates itself in an infinity of concrete existents whose interiority, that which guarantees its changing unicity of presentation, is a principle of convergence we call subject. Contradictory hypotheses traversing the same multiple terms, these systems thus form the most advanced limits of the space where our subjective identity takes form, in which we finally grasp ourselves as the evental product of a pure multiplicity. ∎

This text originally appeared in French in Ereignis auf Französisch*, ed. Marc Rölli (Munich: Wilhelm Fink Verlag, 2004). This version was translated by Justin Clemens.*

....

1   Plato, *Parmenides,* trans. Auguste Diès (Paris: Les Belles Lettres, 1991 [1923]), 164D.
2   EE 231. [For a list of Badiou's principal texts and their corresponding abbreviations, see the introduction to this issue.—Ed.] *Being and Event* quotations are taken from Oliver Feltham's forthcoming translation, which will be published in 2005 by Continuum Editions. Since the English version is not yet paginated, page numbers refer to the French edition. All our thanks to Oliver Feltham.
3   Apparently the history of philosophy is traversed by the question "What is? This noble question is supposed to discern essence, and opposes itself to vulgar questions that come back merely to the example or the accident." Gilles Deleuze, "La méthode de dramatisation," in *L'île déserte* (Paris: Éditions de Minuit, 2002 [1967]), 132. The accident, as that which opposes itself to essence, is "inessential," but, at the same time, since Aristotle it is even through the accident that it is possible to determine the difference between two individuals belonging to the same species: it follows that the characteristics that determine the singularity of the existent as such fall into the inessential, and that essence itself is therefore not determinable on a concrete plane. As we will see, the interest of Deleuze in the concept of event has a strict relation with the surpassing of such an opposition between an abstract essence and a concrete but inessential accident. It is in this sense that, in a passage of *Le pli,* he declares himself interested in Stoic thought, because it "overflows the Aristotelian alternative essence-accident"; see Deleuze, *Le pli* (Paris: Éditions de Minuit, 1988).
4   Gilles Deleuze, *Logique du sens* (Paris: Éditions de Minuit, 1969), 179 and 210.
5   We certainly recall the fact that "being is being united, is being one," but above all the following conclusion: "not being, is not being united, is being multiple." Aristotle, *Méta-*

physique, trans. Jean Tricot (Paris: Vrin, 1991 [1933]), theta 10, 1051B10. For Aristotle, in fact, every accidental determination expresses the existent grasped in the multiplicity of its characteristics, while every essential determination expresses the totality of the existent, its unity and its simplicity (one thinks here in particular of essential characteristics that express the genres).

6   For Aristotle, one must not research "the reason for which there is no reason: the principle of a demonstration cannot be demonstrated in its turn." *Métaphysique*, gamma 6, 1001A10. And Badiou shows that his proposal does not demonstrate itself, but illustrates itself in the efficacious action of consequences: thus ontology "must prove from its own interior the impotence of the one" (EE 29).

7   "There have never been but two schemas, or paradigms, of the Multiple: the mathematical and the organic …. Animal or number? Such is the cross of metaphysics, and the greatness of Deleuze … has been to opt without hesitation for the animal." Alain Badiou, "D'un sujet enfin sans objet," in *Cahiers confrontation xx* (Paris: Aubier, 1989), 166. Cited by Dan Smith in *Acts of the International Conference on Badiou*, Cardiff, May 2002 (unpublished).

8   Plato, *Parmenides*, 160B.

9   Ibid., 164D.

10 τά ἄλλα ἔτερα ἔστιν, commented on by Badiou (EE 43), is probably a citation drawn from *Parmenides*, 160D, where the exact expression is rather ἔτερον τῶν ἄλλων λέγεσθαι. One must remember that Badiou does not provide any notes to his texts, and generally never gives an exact reference for the passages that he cites.

11 Thus he finishes by translating τά ἄλλα ἔτερα ἔστιν by "the others are Others."

12 Plato, *Parmenides*, 165E.

13 Ibid., 166C.

14 Contemplating nothing does not authorize, by wanting to limit oneself to *Parmenides* alone, a decisive taking of a position *vis-à-vis* an ontology of the multiple or the one. It is thus that, in "the *Parmenides*, being a question of perfectly clear statements 'the one is' and 'the one is not' … one arrives at an inconsistency, at an absolute undecidability" (EE 98–99). Which comes to nuance slightly the proposal of *L'être et l'événement*: "No being separated from the one is conceivable, and this is at base what the *Parmenides* establishes. The one is only the principle of every idea, grasped from the side of its operation—of participation—and not from the side of its being" (EE 47). It is therefore in cutting into this undecidability that Badiou can define himself as a "modern Platonist, a Platonist of multiple being" (CT 103). Moreover, the anti-Platonist Deleuze never hesitated to define himself in the same manner: "if one thinks with the Plato of the final dialectic, where the Ideas are a little like multiplicities that must be gone through … [t]hen, yes, all that I say appears to me in fact Platonic." Deleuze, "La méthode de dramatisation," 162.

15 The consequence is triple: on one side, the one is not, because it appears but has no ontological consistency; secondly, the pure multiplicity is, but is as non-countable, unpresentable, "inconsistent," pure void-that-is (it *is* nothing); finally, there would be a counted multiplicity, presented, a multiplicity of unities, "consistent." Plato, in saying that "without the one nothing is" [*sans l'un rien (n')est*] would therefore say at the same time that the one is not, that the pure multiple is nothing, and that consistent multiplicity exists only on condition of the one. Platonic irony or Badiouian *coup de théâtre*?

16 From this, one could hold that being is unique, and every situation is therefore a presentation of the totality of being. It nonetheless remains that, from the point of view of internal structure, every concrete situation is ontologically different.

17 A problem that, according to his own "modern Platonism," Badiou announces thus: "Pla-

tonism *seems* to say that appearance is mobile, fleeting, unthinkable, and that it is ideality, understood here mathematically, that is stable, univocal, exposed to thought. But we can sustain, we moderns, the contrary. It is the world of appearances that always gives itself as solid, bound, constant …. And it is even rather being in itself, thought as the mathematicity of the pure multiple, that is neutral, inconsistent, unbound" (EE 193).

18 Only mathematics would be capable of accomplishing such a task, would be capable of thinking the multiple qua multiple: in this sense, "inasmuch as mathematics touches on being, it is intrinsically a thought" (CT 96). Badiou's entire work is in fact traversed by the equation mathematics = ontology.

19 Claude Imbert speaks very rightly, for Badiou as a reader of Plato, of a "place delivered from the calendar of experience." "Où finit le platonisme?" in *Alain Badiou: Penser le multiple*, ed. Charles Ramond (Paris: L'Harmattan, 2002), 357.

20 Plato, *The Sophist*, trans. Auguste Diès (Paris: Les Belles Lettres, 1985 [1925]), 221C–231C.

21 Ibid., 236A.

22 We follow here the "ironic" translation of *khairein* given by Jacques Derrida, "La pharmacie de Platon," in *La dissémination* (Paris: Éditions du Seuil, 1972), 85. [*Se promener* is to go or be out for a walk; *envoyer promener q.* literally translates as "send someone about his business."—Trans.]

23 Plato, *The Sophist*, 236B.

24 This is August Diès' translation of "*Budé*" that, in resting on the specific sense of the text, uses the word "simulacra," that is, appearance without model, appearance of appearance.

25 Deleuze, *Logique du sens*, 297.

26 Cf. the following translations of *The Sophist*, 236B: the English translation by H. N. Fowler for Loeb Classical Library, and the Italian translation of Giovanni Reale for Rizzoli.

27 Deleuze, *Logique du sens*, 295. And with that Deleuze starts his search in the history of ancient philosophy for a theory capable of justifying the existence of such simulacra, of such appearances stripped of every model. The first and most important reference in this sense is undoubtedly the thought of the first Stoa, and in particular the exclusive affirmation of the existence of bodies, the negation of the existence of the general and the negation of the equivocity of being affirmed by the categories. Whence a radical immanentism, at least according to the key of the Deleuzian reading: no space subsists any longer either for an abstract transcendent ideality or for an abstract model of the transcendent configuration of reality.

28 Deleuze will never abandon this idea, which will, on the contrary, become more and more profound in the course of his work: it is probably in *Cinéma* that it finds its most finished expression. Around the actual state of the existent, of its presence, we can draw, in a kind of circle, its immediate capacities for action; in a larger circle we can draw its point of view on the world, its habits in reacting to stimulations that befall it; on a still larger circle we can draw the ensemble of its life; and on a yet larger circle we can draw the totality of the world, the totality of being, grasped as actualizing itself in it. The actual existent has thus "a virtual image that corresponds to it as a double or a reflection; … there is a coalescence between the two. There is a formation of a bifacial image, actual and virtual." Gilles Deleuze, *L'image temps* (Paris: Éditions de Minuit, 1985), 92–93. Between the identity of the actual existent and being as virtual multiplicity, there is therefore continuity and circularity. And the relation between the two is such that on one side the existent expresses the totality of its virtual being, and on the other this same multiplicity makes event on the surface of the actual existent. In this, see also Deleuze, "L'actuel et le virtuel," in *Dialogues* (Paris: Flammarion, 1996), in particular 179 and 184.

29 "Philosophy [is henceforth] a theory of multiplicities that does not refer to any subject as

prerequisite unity." Gilles Deleuze, "Un concept philosophique," in *Cahiers confrontations* xx (Paris: Aubier, 1989), 90. See also the beginning of "The actual and the virtual": "Philosophy is the theory of multiplicities," in *Dialogues*.
30 Deleuze, "La méthode de dramatisation," 132, and "La conception de la différence chez Bergson," in *L'île déserte*, 132. (The latter originally published in 1956.)
31 Deleuze, "La méthode de dramatisation," 316. In fact it is necessary that being be completely differentiated: because of this there must be a superior, transcendent principle, which by a transcendental law renders possible its differentiation.
32 Ibid., 132.
33 The event is thus, properly speaking, foundation of the essence of the existent. We will remark that "accidents" and "events" are the two translations of the Greek συμβεβηκότα: the word is the past participle of συμβαίνω. The verb signifies "encounter," and the participle therefore indicates that "encountered things, things that happen." The concept of event is therefore what restitutes to their proper *essentiality* the least *existential* determinations of the existent. This is why, in the Deleuzian theory of the event, "there is no more space for accident."
34 [The French here reads "ne soient la copie de rien," which can be translated either as "the copy of nothing" or "not the copy of anything."—Trans.]
35 Pierre Verstraeten, in "L'apport de Badiou á la considération de la 8ème hypothèse du Parménide," in *Badiou: Penser le multiple*, 154, precisely underlines the analogy between the simulacrum of Deleuze and the idea of the count as one of Badiou. He further underlines the radically positive nature of the simulacrum, which has as its own proper power that of letting the multiple show through underneath its appearing. But it seems to us that, if the simulacrum certainly has this power, its "positive" nature is double: letting inscribe in itself a maximum of events, and giving a form, unitary, to these. The simulacrum is therefore like a "minimum of form" that holds together, that "makes one" so that a "maximum of event" can inscribe itself there. See Gilles Deleuze, *Logique de la sensation* (Paris: Éditions de la différence, 1981), 71 and 101.
36 For the moment, it is interesting to remark that, from the strict immanence of the event and the existent to being, of which they are the two expressive sides, it follows that all existents and all events are the expression of a single and same multiple matter differentiating itself infinitely. (We leave aside here the polemic that would consist in knowing if the difference between existents thus conceived is therefore real or formal, a hypothesis, this last, that is at the heart of the Badiouian reading of the virtual with Deleuze.) This has, moreover, a major moral implication: *if every existent is the actualization of the totality of being, it follows that nothing can befall it from the exterior*. All the events that it lives are nothing other than the expression of its own modality of actualization of being. On the modalities according to which the individuality of every existent, including the human, constitutes itself as contraction of events that constitute its essence, see Gilles Deleuze, *Foucault* (Paris: Éditions de Minuit, 1986), 125–26, and *L'image temps*, 111. On the Stoic matrix of this conception, see *Logique du sens*, 175.
37 In this regard, one notes in particular: Gilles Deleuze and Félix Guattari, *Qu'est ce que la philosophie* (Paris: Éditions de Minuit, 1991), 49; Deleuze, "L'immanence, une vie," in *Philosophie* 47 (Paris: Éditions de Minuit, 1994), 4; and Deleuze, *Logique du sens*, 120 and 128, where one notices that every supposition of a transcendental subject is in reality drawn from the habit of considering the empirical subject as a given constituting experience. It is for this reason that one must "seek to determine an impersonal and pre-individual transcendental field that does not resemble corresponding empirical fields." Deleuze, *Logique du sens*, 124.

38 Deleuze, "L'immanence, une vie," 4.
39 In this regard, Badiou underlines, in partial contradiction with the theses that he sustains in his *Deleuze*, that, with Deleuze, there is "an originally duplicitous theory of multiplicities…. Extensive and numerical multiplicities must be distinguished from intensive or qualitative multiplicities." To his mind, this originates in the fact that for Deleuze "the event requires a theory of the multiple heterogeneous to that which returns reason to being" (CT 57). In this way, "equivocity is reinstalled at the heart of being" (CT 68). But if the "organicist paradigm" is at work in Deleuze—which Badiou also willingly recognizes—is it not rather because it is the very being of things that makes event?
40 Deleuze, "La méthode de dramatisation," 142.
41 The concept of univocity is hence expressed in this way by Deleuze: "What is essential to univocity is that being … says itself in a same and single sense of all individuating differences," without one being able to divide the different manifestations of being according to categories (modalities of presentation) or genres (classification of real existents) a priori in relation to existents themselves. This signifies that existents have true individuating differences, concrete modalities of individuation of being. The being by which they are the individualizing actualizations is therefore not a supreme individuality, nor the supreme principle of individuation, but it is eminently *difference*: "being says itself in a single and same sense of all of which it says itself, but that of which it says itself differs: it says itself of difference itself." Gilles Deleuze, *Différence et répétition* (Paris: Presses Universitaires de France, 1968), 53. Being is therefore simultaneously difference that actualizes itself in a form, one that expresses itself, and the principle of the re-differentiation of the latter: being, arising simultaneously as form and as event, therefore disfigures the existent by which the figure expresses it. We remark that this idea accompanies the entirety of Deleuze's work, from *Différence et répétition* (1968) to "L'immanence, une vie" (1994).
42 Deleuze, *Différence et répétition*, 134–36. These two aspects form "the distinctive double trait of a thing in general: the quality or qualities that it possesses, the extension that it occupies, … the way by which the thing determines and differentiates an entire exterior space …." The influence of the thought of the first Stoa on this point is clear. See *Stoicorum Veterum fragmenta*, ed. Hans von Arnim, trans. in Italian by Roberto Radice as *Stoici, tutti i frammenti* (Milan: Rusconi, 1998), 300.
43 Deleuze, "L'immanence, une vie," 5.
44 Internal and non-originary coherence to which one could certainly give other names, in order not to reknot with the stratification of sense of the word "subject." One would speak in this regard of "haecceity."
45 Deleuze, "L'actuel et le virtuel," 180. Emphasis supplied.
46 That the form of the existent is strictly inseparable from events (the *sumbebekota*, formerly called *accidents*) that inscribe themselves in it, and that the internal relation between these two poles is nothing other than the *essence* of the existent, is at the foundation of what in "L'immanence, une vie" Deleuze calls *transcendental empiricism*.
47 Deleuze, "Un concept philosophique," 89–90; see also Deleuze and Guattari, *Mille Plateaux* (Paris: Éditions de Minuit, 1980), 318.
48 Each existent comes to form itself as the capacity of a part of matter to unify itself in responding to eventual solicitations that befall it from the outside, and that it can contract in itself or learn to repel: "what organism is not made of elements and cases of repetition, of water, nitrogen, carbon, chloride, sulphates contemplated and *contracted*, thus interlacing all the *habits* by which it composes itself?" And this is true for every individual form "even the rocks and the woods, animals and men." Deleuze, *Différence et répétition*, 102.
49 Deleuze, "L'immanence, une vie," 5.

50. Which would have as consequence the denial of strong differences between classes, and thus of returning politics to a continuity of fact, and thus to a position simultaneously anarchistic and petit-bourgeois.

51. In *Théorie du Sujet* Badiou starts from the constant that "Deleuze's ontology of the multiple is a veiled metaphysics," where the "integral infinite multiplicity … is the summit of the one," and where the individuality of existents is only of the order of simulacra (TS 40–41).

52. Thus Deleuze wonders if the thought of Badiou implies, "under the appearance of the multiple, a return to an old conception of higher philosophy," where "philosophy seems to float in an empty transcendence." Deleuze and Guattari, *Qu'est ce que la philosophie*, 144.

53. The citation, very long, has been abridged. It nevertheless seems appropriate to remark that in the same citation, a parenthesis tells us "I do not believe [that it is necessary to sacrifice immanence], but no matter here." A funny contradiction next to the peremptory tone of "I do it."

54. Thus, "if real ontology disposes itself by eluding the norm of the one, it is also necessary that there be a point where the ontological field remains in impasse. I have named this point the event" (CT 56–57).

55. We can wonder if there is a certain "tragedy" implicit in Badiou's ontological project, which places, on the one side, being as void, inconsistent and non-appearing, and, on the other, its presentation, which appears but is not. For Badiou every presentation of being in a situation is made in the clear consciousness of the void on which it rests, but simultaneously presentation is most often doubled by a "count of the count," by a representation whose end is to make the real appear the one of the count, and therefore to make the structure of presentation appear ontologically founded. Thus, for example, the strictly "representative" function of every static structure that, as Bernard Vainqueur has justly remarked, "has no other goal but to obviate the lethal perspective of a ruin of presentation." Vainqueur, "De quoi 'sujet' est il le nom pour Alain Badiou," in *Badiou: Penser le multiple*, 320.

56. This is confirmed in mathematics by the axiom of foundation, that simply says that for every non-empty set there always exists a subset such that the intersection between this subset and the given set is void (EE 208).

57. The event, in its auto-presentation, escapes the axiom of foundation. And if this last is a fundamental axiom of ontology, it follows that the event escapes ontology, which confirms the radical heterogeneity between being and event.

58. The event will be designated in the following manner: $e_x = \{x \in X, e_x\}$, which signifies that an event e—which is always indexed to the evental site X where it appears—is constituted by all the elements which belong to its site, plus itself.

59. The event is thus certainly that which, taking place, cannot be counted by the present situation. But what by definition is unpresentable is even a pure multiplicity. The event, extra-being that founds a count as one, is that by which it is possible that being as such irrupts into appearing. And it is at this paradoxical juncture that Badiou develops the concept of "evental site." The event is thus an extra-being that convokes being to appearing.

60. The passage cited here particularly concerns the statements that present mathematical events.

61. The universal address of every event, without which there would not be, properly speaking, either the becoming-true of an event, nor its having taken place, is the principal object of *Saint Paul et la fondation de l'universalisme*. There Badiou works out a strict relation

between the fact that the event is "one" and universalism. And, in fact, if it is considered from the point of view of the situation where it appears, the event is not even *rare*, it is *unique*. This is because in a situation all is counted according to the founding event, and nothing exists that is not countable by the law installed by this event. Nothing is outside the situation; nothing is uncounted. To exemplify this, Badiou pinpoints the strict imbrication between monotheism and universalism: "What does it signify that there is a single God? What does the 'mono' of 'monotheism' mean? Paul confronts, in renewing the terms, the formidable question of the One. His conviction, properly revolutionary, is that the sign of the One is 'for all'" (SP 80). It follows that "the only possible correlate of the One is universal" (80).

62   Furthermore, in relation to these differences by which it ensures the universal count as one, the event has a double aspect: on the one side, they are not taken into account by the event (otherwise it would not be universal), to the point that "the differences are indifferent and the universality of the true deposes them"; but, at the same time, "universality must expose itself to all the differences, and show … that they can welcome the truth that traverses them" (SP 113).

63   Thus Christianity, which announces itself to everyone in announcing itself in the first place to the excluded.

64   The most eloquent example would be that of Saint Paul, who effectuates the having-taken-place of the event "resurrection of Christ" in forming a universal church that deploys that event's consequences.

65   The subject must therefore not be confounded with the material support, the multiplicity, on which it comes to form itself, according to the modalities of the procedure of subjectivation: "for example, the subject induced by a fidelity to an amorous encounter, the subject of love, is not the 'loving' subject …. Lovers [any multiplicity] enter as such into the composition of a subject of love, which exceeds them both" (E 40). Or, again, the subject of an artistic revolution will be a work that exhibits a revolution to the highest degree. Such a work declares that such a revolution is what permits it to express itself to the highest degree outside all academicism, and thus in its proper difference. It thereby becomes subject at the same time that it proves the having-taken-place of the event.

66   The first figure is thus the condition of the second, but the second is the condition of the truth of the first.

67   But if fidelity has an infinite number of elements on which it acts, it is impossible that the totality of its consequences be completely deployed. Thus universalism can only prove to be a tendency, since at each present instant it can only produce a certain degree of exclusion. The uncounted arise and accumulate at the heart of the subjectivation-procedure: more and more elements come "to resist" the count. And the more difference accumulates, the more universalism has a tendency to defend itself, to "statify itself," by codifying its laws, and in counting fewer and fewer elements thus excluded: but in this way it is universalism itself (and thus the event) that is denied, because differences not currently subsumed by the count are henceforth inevitably denied or destroyed, and not left free to return from their difference in the count as one. Fidelity thus finds itself "obscured," it finds itself absorbed in "an *obscure figure* that limits its universalism" (SP 38–40). More and more multiplicities result uncounted by the situation, they come to constitute a true invariant figure (a *reactive figure*) whose double stake is, on the one side, to foreclose the situation itself by subtracting more and more elements from the count, and, on the other, by becoming a *possible* site for the inscription of an event. By the set of four figures (subjective, faithful, reactive, obscure), every subjective space deploys, from its birth to

its death, the entire process of subjectivation that has an event for beginning, its truth for finality, and subjects for its present.

68 "There is only a particular animal convoked by the circumstances to become subject. Or rather to enter into the composition of a subject. This means that all that it is, its body, its capacities, finds itself, at a given moment, required that a truth make its path" (E 37).

69 From the point of view of truth "subjectivation is that *by which* truth is possible," and the subject is a "finite fragment of a truth-process" (SP 13).

70 We will remark that if it is true that the event does nothing but render *possible* the advent of a subject, it is at the same time true that the event will have taken place only if at least one subject takes place. If there is event, it is therefore *necessary* that there be subject because, if there is no subject, there will not have been event. It is only with this nuance that we can thus accept the Badiouian formulation according to which the event only renders *possible* a subject.

71 It is interesting to note that from the ethical point of view this implies a major difference. In fact, ethics is described by Badiou as the set of criteria of fidelity to an event: it follows that bare life, the differences that constitute the subject are indifferent to ethics, which has only the Truth for object and has for its goal the construction of a subject (E 52). For Deleuze, on the contrary, ethics, which is in the same way the practice of construction of a subject to come, has for foundation the capacity to act as if the events that happen to us would depend on us, the capacity to become the space of inscription of events that, arriving entirely in us ceaselessly from the outside, come to compose our essence. Deleuze, *Logique du sens*, 174. We thus see in the two cases that ethics depends on the mode of inscription of the event, but that in Badiou's case, if this signifies indifference to concrete and contingent differences, it on the contrary signifies for Deleuze the quasi-exclusive attention to concrete and contingent differences, that for him are nothing other than the events themselves.

Badiou: The Grace of the Universal

Eric Alliez

The book by Alain Badiou dedicated to his "non-relationship" with Deleuze is followed by a *Saint Paul*, subtitled *The Foundation of Universalism*, and, forming a series with the latter work, a collection of interventions around the political, *Abrégé de Métapolitique*, which defines its collective efficacy as "principially universal" [*principiellement universelle*].[1] In an article submitted to the journal *Multitudes* following the harsh controversy elicited by his book on Deleuze, Badiou himself seems to indicate that there is more than a simple chronological succession here, that one must consider this political sequence *with his Deleuze as its starting point* and as constantly positioned *vis-à-vis Deleuze*.[2]

Above all, it is the following passage that one must read as a *warning*: "Our quarrel can be formulated in a number of ways. … For example: how is it that, for Deleuze, politics is not an autonomous form of thought, a singular section of the chaos, one that differs from art, science, and philosophy? This point alone bears witness to our divergence, and there is a sense in which everything can be said to follow from it."[3] This divergence—let us note immediately—is founded on a shared rejection of "political philosophy," as well as of an ethics subordinated to the consensual legislation of the universal human Subject, which would confer upon public opinion a kind of transcendental legitimacy (the democracy of "common sense"). Focusing on "this concession to the One that undoes the multiple's fundamental radicalness, whose guarantee one had tried to secure"[4] (the attack is Badiou's, but its parameters are equally Deleuzian), Badiou highlights the immediately political character of their shared conviction according to which "all true thought is a thought of singularities." As one might expect, however, this political character will also, just as immediately and contradictorily, define the "non-relationship" to Deleuze: it will do so at its point of greatest *generic* proximity, inasmuch as Deleuze was "the first" to "properly grasp that a contemporary metaphysics must consist in a theory of multiplicities and an embrace of singularities";[5] and also along its most *specific* dividing line, which registers the political question under the condition of an ontology that is indissociably abstract and concrete, when it is a matter of resolving, *for Badiou and against a Deleuze that is now entirely Other and not at all Intimate*, "the problem that defines contemporary philosophy: what exactly is a universal singularity?"[6] That is the last sentence of the article, preceded by this one, which remains mysterious in its militant consequences, for the one who will ignore the Pauline re-foundation of the universal proposed by Badiou: "the only power that can be attuned to the power of being is that of the letter."[7]

A letter whose line we had to reproduce in order to recall the montage of Badiou's *dispositif*: such as it is present itself and such as we seek to test it in the following all-too-brief notes.

First (Theorematic) Point
On the general political meaning of the Badiou/Deleuze coupling

Deleuze and Badiou conceive of ontology only qua *politics of being*, and they regard this stance as a fundamental requirement of contemporary thought. Thus, if it is not unfounded to posit their respective metaphysics as the two extreme, and absolutely hostile, poles which nevertheless constitute the contemporary philosophical field in its materialist necessity,[8] it won't be so much a question of political consequentiality and verification (what does "politically" mean, for the one and the other?), but rather of *a radical antecedence of politics tied to their respective metaphysics*.

So that this radical anteriority only *really* allows itself to be formulated in terms of a *precedent*, in terms of a constant, political antagonism, the apparent suspension of which is the condition of Deleuze's writing, and its reactivation the occasion for the *Saint Paul*.

Second (Recitative) Point
On the historico-political sublation of political precedent

Badiou's *Deleuze* opens with the primal scene of the Vincennes years, setting against one another the "Maoist" and the inspiration behind the "anarcho-desirers," an "enemy all the more formidable for being internal to the 'movement'" (De 2). Nothing (or almost nothing) is lacking in this description: an intervention brigade, an attempt to seize control over the direction of the department, a furious article with an eloquent title ("The Flux and the Party"),[9] etc., concluding with the double public condemnation: "'Bolshevik' versus 'fascist': what a fine pair we made [*nous voilà bien*]!" (De 2). And things in effect took a rather bad turn on the side of the Party, which deemed "fascist" the anti-dialectical theory of flux and Deleuze's apologia for the new "spaces of liberty"—thus throwing confusion into "his philosophy of life and of the natural One-All." But then—unlike Lardreau, who pushes the attack all the way to the ultimate and *politically primary* reasons for Deleuze's Bergsonism (if I have understood correctly: *a Mitterandism avant la lettre*)[10]—Badiou suddenly shifts register, in order to leave the quarrel behind.

Because with the "winter years" there comes the time for the sublation of conflict in History, when the counter-revolution announced by the *nouveaux philosophes* and realized by the new-Kantians displaces and overturns the alliances of thought. With the former being philosophically worthless and the latter having placed themselves outside of non-academic philosophy with their constant shuttling between Republicans and Liberals, it is truly, according to all available evidence, the change in political parameters that authorizes, at Badiou's initiative, "a period of truly sustained theoretical discussion" (De 5) with Deleuze.

Except that this cannot be pursued, from the standpoint of the Decision, without the prospect of an entirely different sublation, which is philosophically determinant in a wholly other way: sublation of the convergent perspective of the work with Félix Guattari into a divergent or contrasting collaboration. This philosophical *forcing*, which would be able to extract Deleuze from the anarchic confusion of the world—from the "democracy of desire" that is coextensive with this confusion in the master as well as the "vitalist terrorism" of his disciples … in order to reestablish the truth of Deleuzism, if necessary, *against* Deleuze himself.[11]

"Contrary to the commonly accepted image (Deleuze as liberating the anarchic multiple of desires and errant drifts), contrary even to the apparent indications of his work that play on the opposition multiple/multiplicities …" (De 11). Whence the very peculiar image of Deleuze as Metaphysician of the One, *Platonist in spite of himself, whose contradictory truth* (a Platonism of the virtual) *is only intelligible through and in the philosophy of Badiou*. Dialectics would force us, then, into the Decision of a Platonism of the multiple, or *set theory* [*ensemblisme*], posited as the authentic Platonism and the sole materialism consistent with the truth of the separation from the world.[12]

The only thing that matters here is that this question of multiplicities is always carried in Deleuze by an *infra-* or *micropolitical* principle (to articulate the opposite of metapolitics) that is systematically evacuated by the Commentator, together with the works cosigned "Deleuze-Guattari" which nevertheless confront, on this very basis, the question of *"becoming-revolutionary."* Because—as they affirmed ever since *Anti-Oedipus*—multiplicities must not only be declared, or described, they must also be *made, to the extent that the differentiating opening of life must, each and every time, be actualized in an immanent construction of fluxes* (or an assemblage: always collective, always determined) *which, qua desiring production, is the social power of difference*. It is in light of this *molecular revolution*, which is combined [*conjugue*] with the cosmic by positing the intensification of life as the only criterion, that there is not, *de jure*, a separate political sphere, that "Everything is politics" [*Tout est politique*]—even when the production of singularity is made to fall back on unity with the Signifier taking control of a concrete assemblage … Everything is politics because there is no unassembled desire, because desire is the effective operator of assemblage, and because there are only politics of assemblages on a plane of immanence or of composition that must itself be constructed.

Deleuzian politics thereby mobilizes the *process of rhizomatic subjectivation* of his entire philosophy. It is thus that Deleuze re-commences his philosophy with Guattari (see the *Dialogues* with Claire Parnet and *Pourparlers*)[13] according to the principle of a double-articulation:

- The expression (of the world) without construction (of assemblages) is blind: this is *exactly* the "natural mysticism" denounced by Badiou under the name of Deleuze (*the unthought of Deleuze*, or a bland and cobbled-together Deleuzism—at any rate a metaphorizing Romanticism in the guise of the Last Phenomenology).

- Construction without expression is empty [*vide*]: this is *exactly* the mathematical ontology of Alain Badiou, naming the void as multiple (as the basis of an axiomatic), declaring the *indifference* of truth to the world (the construction of eternal truths) in the "offering of the event" as the *grace of nomination* (the Great Logic of the Signifier).

Borne by the Deleuzian question par excellence, that of *becoming*, one must think that the forces of becomings operate a "double capture" between the two terms as that which passes (happens) between them [*ce qui (se) passent entre eux*], realizing their mutual heterogenesis in a *mode of life*. Because a mode of life is "expression" only to the extent that it is "construction." Life-experiment, as Deleuze says.

This would allows us to grasp:

- The initiation of the epistolary protocol with Alain Badiou—because contemporary philosophy is the constructivism of multiplicities at their point of greatest singularity: after *A Thousand Plateaus* dedicated to "multiplicities themselves," comes the time of the question *What is Philosophy?* the last address, cosigned with Guattari, and, with it, the time of the ontopolitical confrontation regarding *the problem of construction*.

- The brutal cessation imposed by Deleuze if *Badiou's unthought* comes down to the equation CONSTRUCTION = EXPRESSION = BECOMINGS, condemning the Other to inconsistency in the guise of the void.

Third (Constative) Point
On the question of the universal under the condition of the most contemporary politics

"Universal singularity" articulates the metapolitical form of construction separated from all the world's differences of expression, *"absented" from the infinite multiple of differences that truth deposes in its singular emergence* [*surrection*]. A singular surge, truth as such, is, in perfect Platonic observance, *"indifferent to differences"*; therefore, it is immediately universalizable *in the historical mode of politics* as a rule for its intrinsically universal prescription: to produce some 1 by abolishing the infinity of differences in the "figure [*chiffre*] of the same and of equality" (E 27).[14]

Founding the truth of politics on a politics of truth, the (re)foundation of universalism by Badiou delivers the "purest" version of it *because it is the most classic version* (in the Jacobin sense), but *the most contemporary version as well*, in the radicalness of the distance to the void that this truth measures (a Jacobinism of the postmodern age). Refusing the logical plane of cases of the individual subordinated to the State through the law, this (re)foundation summons the singular infinity of the situation in order to reduce it to the collective-universalizable One which—unless one ties oneself to the identitarian-minoritarian expression of differences—can be authorized only *through the self-proclamation of the event by the subject-without-identity that names it*. It is, above and beyond the fable it constitutes, the Christ-event "whose only 'proof' lies precisely in its having been declared by a subject" (SPe 5): resuscitated *for all*. Evental One, universal One.

What is key here is not so much the outcome of the rigorous alternative to Deleuze and to "Deleuzism" (immediately brought together, as they should be, in the controversy), but rather the prescriptive character of this universalism of the Subject-of-Truth, stated by Badiou *for all those* who aspire to destroy *the leftism [gauchisme] of the party of desire* (as Lardreau, in perfect fidelity to the other party, says, and I quote: "[A party] of lack, of the One, of knowledge [*savoir*], of war."[15]) Prescriptive *because the universal is itself the truth of the subject who pronounces the void of being*—from which Badiou, *in immanence*, knows how to draw out the consequences. After *Deleuze*, it is no surprise that the militant objective of the *Saint Paul* is to unfold the logic of rupture with the movement of vitalist affirmation *by showing the inconsistency of becoming in regard to the excess of the Real over reality*. This cannot be grasped except through Lacan, who posits the real in the predication of the "no" as intervention-subject.

Founder of the figure of the militant, "*Paul's unprecedented gesture consists in subtracting truth from the communitarian grasp*" (SPe 5). How extraordinarily contemporary is Paul! Because, in introducing the *for all*, the rupture of universal singularity with regard to the *identitarian singularity* of a closed subset is devoid of alternatives, save for the present communitarization of public space, fragmented into closed identities that offer so many new territories to the market. This (strangely?) cannot be written without inviting Deleuze to the marriage between capitalist logic and identitarian logic, a marriage where what is at stake is precisely the denial of emancipatory reality to any becoming-minor—Deleuze says it "exactly": "capitalist deterritorialization requires a *constant* reterritorialization" (SPe 10). This is a completely nominal exactitude, a misprision [*contresens*], since the thwarted deterritorialization of capitalism no longer exerts its influence upon an *absolute* form of deterritorialization that mobilizes *otherwise* relative forms, and since *becoming* is no longer the business of fluxes of desire liberated by capital, but the occasion for the "mercantile investments" to which capital gives rise ... But isn't this point of view precisely the point of view of capital? For we know that *a becoming that has been reduced to the primitive accumulation of reterritorializations* is no longer Capitalism and Schizophrenia—it is Capitalism and Paranoia ... I quote Badiou, from the same page: "What *inexhaustible potential* for mercantile investments in this upsurge—taking the form of communities demanding recognition and *so-called cultural singulari-*

ties—of women, homosexuals, the disabled, Arabs" (SPe 10, emphasis mine). Let us recall that Deleuze-Guattari's question is that of *a revolutionary ontology of* ("nearly imperceptible") *becomings* that never cease to undo the history of identities ("primacy of the lines of flight") and to deliver "blows" unforeseeable both to the sociologist and the militant. There also exists "a becoming-revolutionary that is not the same thing as the future of the revolution and that does not necessarily come from militants."[16] *The constructions of the militant tend to be cut off from the "socio-cultural" expressions of the world and from the becoming-molecular of multiplicities—they tend to stop the forces in the process of becoming, to miss the multitudes.*

Badiou responds with *the theorem of the militant*, which states: "What grants power to a truth, and determines subjective fidelity, is the universal address of the relation to self instituted by the event, and not this relation itself" (SPe 90). This relationship being in "itself" the eventual rupture of the separation from the world and its "particularities," *one requires the return of the decision* (decidere = to cut) *on the event in order to guarantee the transcendence of the Signifier, all the while filling the empty Subject with its unique content: its subjective fidelity to the event of separation in the universal communication of this subtractive foundation* ... In Pauline language, this zero degree of immanence is called love, understood as that of which faith is capable *in order to extract itself from the living autonomy of desire.*

It is thus, in the end, a matter of desire, of access to desire as a situation of *life from the perspective of sin* because the life of desire has been put under the condition of the transgression of the law, of the automatism of repetition which assigns the subject to the place of death ... Badiou highlights this point in his comments on the famous text of Paul (Rom. 7:7–23: *I had not known sin but by the law* ...), "Clearly, what is at issue here is nothing less than the problem of the unconscious" (SPe 79). On this point, one must concede to the Lacanizing philosopher. One does not acquiesce, however, without countering that "the problem" is nothing other than the priestly discourse of psychoanalysis that chains desire constituted as a lack in the Law [*manque à la Loi*] in order to impose upon the Subject, in the guise of subjectivation, the universal grace of its letter. How could it be otherwise, if it is *in the name of the unconscious* that the constructivism of desire is barred, in order to substitute in its stead the void of a truth *defined, index sui,* as "the only power that can be in accord with that of being"?

Whence the following outcome: if the universal is the metapolitical fantasy [*phantasme*] of the philosopher, psychoanalysis is his symptom, when his self-imposed condition is *to create the event of nothing destined for all.*

According to the rules laid out by the *Saint Paul,* the universalism of grace and the materialism of life let us attain the political fundament that governs the conflict between two paradigms of the multiple: "the multiplicity that, exceeding itself, sustains the universality" of its letter; and the *exact opposite* [*là tout contre*], the creative function of an Outside that pushes through the middle, below and beside the signifying cuts, the living lines, the broken lines, the becomings of multiplicities—*or multitudes*—as "a line of flight or of variation that affects each system in preventing it from being homogeneous."[17] ■

Translated by Ashley King. Translation revised by Alberto Toscano. This essay originally appeared as "Badiou. La grâce de l'universel" in Multitudes *6 (2001): 26–34. The editor would like to thank Alix Mazuet for her assistance in preparing the translation.*

....

1   [For a list of Badiou's principal texts and their corresponding abbreviations, see the introduction to this issue.—Ed.]
2   The article in question is Badiou's "Un, multiple, multiplicité(s)," *Multitudes* 1 (2000): 195–211. [Translated as "One, Multiple, Multiplicities," in TW 67–80.] This article was part of a Badiou / Deleuze debate that I opened up, with additional interventions by José Gil and Arnaud Villani, in the last number of *Futur antérieur* (43 [1998]).
3   Ibid., 196 (French) / 68 (English).
4   Cf. Badiou, "Contre la 'philosophie politique,'" in AM 19–34.
5   Badiou, "Un, multiple, multiplicité(s)," 196/67.
6   Ibid., 211/80.
7   Ibid.
8   I have developed this proposition in *De l'impossibilité de la phenomenology: Sur la philosophie française contemporaine* (Paris: Vrin, 1995).
9   ["Le flux et le parti: Dans les marges de *L'Anti-Œdipe*," in *La Situation actuelle sur le front philosophique*, ed. Alain Badiou and Sylvain Lazarus, *Cahiers Yenan* no. 4 (Paris: Maspero, 1976): 24–41; translated into English by Laura Balladur and Simon Krysl, with commentary by Bruno Bosteels, in *Polygraph* 15/16 (2004).—Ed.]
10 Guy Lardreau, *L'exercice différé de la philosophie: A l'occasion de Deleuze* (Lagrasse: Verdier, 1999).
11 [In this sentence and throughout, ellipses are the author's.—Ed.]
12 See the dossier Badiou/Deleuze presented in *Futur antérieur* 43.
13 Gilles Deleuze and Claire Parnet, *Dialogues* (Paris: Flammarion, 1977), available in English translation by Hugh Tomlinson and Barbara Habberjam (New York: Columbia University Press, 1987); Gilles Deleuze, *Pourparlers, 1972–1990* (Paris: Éditions de Minuit, 1990), translated by Martin Joughin as *Negotiations, 1972–1990* (New York: Columbia University Press, 1995).
14 See also AM 166.
15 Lardreau, op. cit., 84. Commentary: the second-to-last term is, at the least, disputable; the last one, risible. The first two notions, on the other hand, are historically proven.
16 Deleuze, *Dialogues*.
17 Ibid.

WINGLESS INSECTS.

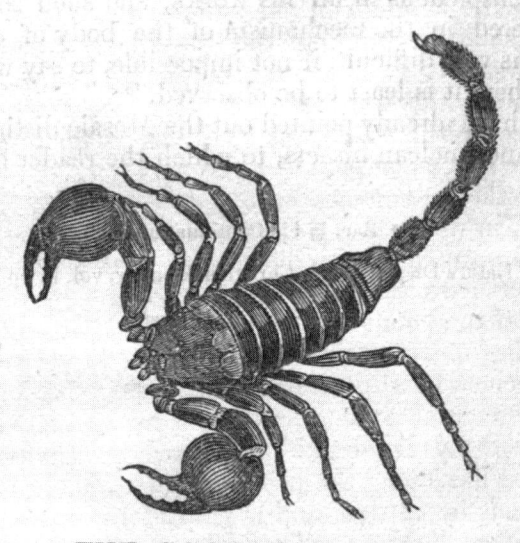

THE SCORPION.

The Badiou-Event

Carsten Strathausen

I

An event has taken place, we are told, in the realm of contemporary philosophy. It carries the name of Alain Badiou. Slavoj Žižek was among the first to proclaim it, others have remained faithful to it, and a truth-procedure appears to be gathering momentum in American academic circles.[1] On a superficial level, the proclamation of the "Badiou-event" attests to Badiou's deliberate break with the "sophist dogmas" of today's philosophical establishment, be they of a hermeneutic, analytical, or postmodern shading. Here is a philosopher who does not join the tenor of the "end of philosophy," but instead insists on the possibility of, even the need for, philosophical thought today. Critical of the linguistic turn that has dominated philosophy over the last decades, Badiou denounces historicism, relativism, and postmodernist pessimism in favor of a renewed commitment to universal truth and subjective faith.

Most importantly, Badiou rejects what he considers the neo-Kantian moralism of our times, evident not only in what he calls the Levinasian/Derridean fetishization of "otherness," but also in Western societies' obsession with human rights and international law. The latter, Badiou claims, are based on the erroneous assumption that humans are more prone to doing evil than doing good. But the Good, in Badiou's view, always precedes Evil, since the latter only results from the corruption of the former. The current ideological framework of ethics, by contrast, "equates man with a simple mortal animal" instead of recognizing him as the "Immortal" he really is (Ee 16).[2] Opposed to this "negative and victimary definition of man" that inevitably leads to nihilism, Badiou posits an affirmative "ethic of truths" that aims to restore our faith in the human potential to assume the responsibility of subjectification and to live up to truth:

> So Evil is possible only through an encounter with the Good. The ethic of truths—which simply serves to lend consistency to that "some-one" that we are, and which must manage to sustain, with its own animal perseverance, the intemporal perseverance of a subject of truth—is also that which tries to ward off Evil, through its effective and tenacious inclusion in the process of truth. (91)

By this point, it should be obvious that Žižek's attribution of a Badiou-event in contemporary philosophy carries a deeper meaning. It applies one of Badiou's central categories to his own work, and critics have aptly referred to "the triad event-subject-truth" as constitutive of his philosophy.[3] To speak of a Badiou-event is to imply not only that a profound rupture of the current status-quo has taken place, but also to make a series of far-reaching claims (about truth, about the subject(s) of truth, about the historical consequences of the event, etc.) that are implicit in Badiou's understanding of the term.

And this is where we encounter the first problems. According to Badiou, philosophy "does not itself produce truths" nor does it provide the space in which events are to occur. Events only take place in what Badiou calls the "four conditions of philosophy," that is, the matheme (science), the poem (art), political intervention, and love (MPe 35). The task of philosophy, by contrast, "is to propose a unified conceptual space in which naming takes place of events that serve as the point of departure for truth procedures" (37). So, while events cannot be conceived in advance, but simply occur haphazardly, truths, on the other hand, must be produced on the basis of the new modes of thinking enabled by an event. The task of philosophy, then, is to gather the various responses (i.e., the names given) to individual events and to provide the unifying concepts that assure their overall "compossibility." Although critical of Heidegger, Badiou often uses Heideggerian formulations to describe the "welcoming" and "sheltering" task of philosophy. Philosophy "gather[s] together all the additional-names" given to events and thus creates "a conceptual site in which the generic truth procedures are thought of as compossible" (37).

Hence, there cannot be a philosophical event as such, because philosophy is the midwife of truth and not its parent. In fact, truths are always borne out without prior conception by an already existing subject. For Badiou, subjects are the potential *effect* of events and not their *cause*, because they emerge simultaneously with the truth procedure that arises from the event. Subjects are "woven out of a truth"; they are "that which a truth passes through" and thus become the "local or finite status of a truth," but never its origin.[4] The latter, Badiou insists, "is of the order of the event" (MPe 36). The event, however, does not last; it "has always disappeared or been abolished; there will never be any knowledge of it" (IT 86). Truths, on the other hand, are the infinite development of the eventual implications carried forth by subjects faithful to the original event. It follows that truths always take shape within a given state of the situation. They are both local and universal at the same time: "Every truth is both singular and universal,"[5] Badiou insists; they are universal in their impact (otherwise they would not be "true") but singular in their origin (because they are carried forth by *particular* individuals operating within a *particular* situation in response to a *par-*

ticular event).⁶ Let me call this singular/universal nature of truth the *first constitutive paradox* of Badiou's thought; I shall return to it at a later point.

For now, I want to emphasize the importance of distinguishing between a truth and the event that causes this truth. Every fusion between the two, Badiou cautions, "leads back to a *christique* vision of truth, since a certain truth is but an eventuating self-revelation."⁷ In short, philosophy neither produces truths nor does it stage or represent the event(s) that called them forth. Why, then, do some of Badiou's leading critics entertain the non-sensical proposition that Badiou's work amounts to a (philosophical) event? Far from being a mere inaccuracy or minor terminological slip, the notion of the Badiou-event, I submit, is symptomatic for critics' desire to make Badiou's philosophy *matter* in the most radical sense of the term. It expresses the hope that his thought, like a true event, would shatter the reified status quo not only in the realm of philosophical discourse, but with regard to the existing social order as such. For every event violently ruptures the state of the situation from the outside. In political terms, it amounts to nothing less than a revolution. The various truth-procedures following the event, by contrast, confront the much more laborious task of slowly altering the situation from within. Based on discursive negotiations with and antagonistic struggle against its adversaries, a truth-procedure resembles not so much a *militant revolution* but the *deliberative process of reform* we already find institutionalized within Western democratic societies.

Critics' deliberate effort to treat Badiou's work like an event rather than a philosophical gathering of disparate truths signifies a deliberate effort to disassociate his ideas from the realm of existing liberal-democratic systems. Indeed, Badiou himself openly avows his utter disdain for what he calls our entrenched "democratic totalitarianism" along with its "moral terrorism" based on opinion polls and sustained by the utter lack of thought (i.e., what Heidegger called the *Gerede* of the "man") (Ee lv, liii). According to Badiou, the current liberal-parliamentary system and the "communicative sociality" promoted by Habermas, Rawls, and other liberal philosophers ultimately serves to keep the immortal subject-to-be hostage inside the shell of a mortal animal (51). Breaking out of this shell, however, requires both faith (to believe in the occurrence of an event) and action (in order to engage the real-life consequences of the event) on the part of the subject-to-be. The latter must act according to its belief and remain faithful to the event by confronting and ultimately modifying the existing state of the situation.

This intricate relationship between theory and practice is central to Badiou's philosophy. Inspired, no doubt, by Althusser's "theory of theoretical practice," Badiou refers to his own philosophy as a "thought-praxis" and insists on the pragmatic dimension of human subjectivity necessary to uphold the development of truth-procedures (Ee 106, 115).⁸ "I shall call thinking the non-dialectical or inseparable unity of a theory and a practice" (IT 79), Badiou declares categorically. Indeed, this practical nature of thought appears to be one of Badiou's major strengths. Like for the early Marx, practice is said to be more than a mere vehicle for the implementation of a preconceived notion of "Truth." For Badiou, "Truth"—in the singular and spelled with a capital "T"—is empty, a mere void. It serves as "an operational category" that allows philosophy to "seize" the disparate truths in order to think their "compossibility" (MPe 141). In other words, philosophy does not simply find the "conceptual site" for the gathering of disparate truths as if it were already there, waiting to be discovered. Rather, it actively creates this site. Philosophy "is the act of Truth with respect to truths" and thus "testifies to the unity of thought" by connecting the local truths of a given situation (142).

According to Badiou, then, both (philosophical) "Truth" and (artistic, scientific, political, or libidinal) "truths" are based upon *acts of creation* and thus pragmatic in nature. Nonetheless, they are distinct in two respects. First, whereas local truths can be fully expressed in specific terms, philosophical Truth cannot. Truth is a void category, Badiou claims, for it cannot be thought in the fullness of its being. Since philosophy "desubstantializes" Truth, the latter never appears except as the void "background on which truths are seized" (143). This leads us to the second difference between Truth and truths, since the latter cannot emerge or persevere apart from the human individuals (or subjects-to-be) remaining faithful to them and acting in their support.[9] Truth, by contrast, remains the exclusive domain of philosophy and thus inaccessible to all potential subjects except as void. There is Truth, claims Badiou, and it is there *for us*, but not sustained *by us*. Instead, it is the sole prerogative of thought to reflect upon its own unity in the process of thinking Truth.

In the following, I shall argue that Badiou's philosophy plays with this equivocation between Truth and truths. Whereas the former is primarily concerned with the auto-constitution and self-transformation of philosophical thought as such, the latter simply reflects the subjective decision of a human individual to regard something—or anything whatsoever—as true. But this decisionism at the heart of Badiou's theory of subjectivity contradicts the very notion of Truth it is said to enact. The ensuing paradox of an allegedly "universal truth" nonetheless born of an "subjective decision" testifies to Badiou's inability to bridge the gap between theory and practice, philosophy and politics. In my view, Badiou does not sufficiently work through this paradox but instead hopes to dissolve it in and through mathematical terms. This attempt fails, because Badiou merely replaces the reigning "linguistic turn" in contemporary philosophy with his own "mathematical turn." Hence, contrary to Badiou and his supporters, I do not believe that he has radically altered or "interrupted" today's philosophical status quo. However, it is precisely *because the Badiou-event did not take place* that I consider his ideas a vital contribution to both the philosophy and politics of our current situation.

To support these theses, I shall proceed in several steps. First, I flesh out the relationship between event and truth with regard to the question of time (§II). The third part outlines some central aspects of Badiou's ontology, focusing in particular on the irreducible gap between mathematics and philosophy, Being and (Truth-)Event. Thereafter, I examine his concept of the subject in the context of other contemporary theories of subjectivity and decisionism (§IV). In the last part (§V), I discuss Badiou's most recent ideas developed in response to some of the criticisms raised above.

II

Since we have already established that Badiou's work cannot possibly be called an event in Badiou's sense of the term, the question emerges as to the provenance of his philosophy. What are its proper origins? Which historical event(s) does Badiou himself remain faithful to? What truth(s) have seized and shaped him into the "subject" he is today? Badiou's answer is straight-forward: Paul Cohen, Jacques Lacan, May 68, and Paul Celan are the most important names of events that "today condition philosophy" (MPe 88).[10]

My primary concern, however, regards the temporal structure of these events. "The event comes and goes in a flash," Jean-Jacques Lecercle states in his commentary on Badiou, and Badiou himself insists that "the being of an event is a disappearing."[11] Yet such a Benjamin-inspired formulation appears to be at odds with Badiou's own examples, many of which stretch over the duration of months or even years. The only way to avoid a contradiction is to argue that events cannot possibly be measured in terms of the situation at all. Events "rupture" or "supplement" the given "state of the situation"; they are defined precisely as that which is "unknown" and "new" to the existing status quo. Since the latter determines the parameters of historical understanding, of given knowledge, and, ultimately, of reality and time as such, it follows that "every event constitutes its own time."[12] The various historical dates specifying the duration of each event can only be supplied *retroactively*, that is, *after* the event has been named and a truth procedure has begun—hence the significance of the *futur antérieur* in Badiou's philosophy: the event "will have been there" and "will have lasted" according to its own measure of time.

So "there is no time in general," Badiou declares; "there are times."[13] Events are ephemeral, and each one introduces (a new) time. By contrast, the particular truth inaugurated by an event is eternal, bringing about "the abolition of time" and "the end of memory": "*A* truth is always the undoing of *a* time," Badiou claims (note the singular!) (De 64, 65). Although Badiou emphasizes that every truth forgets not simply "this or that, but ... time itself" and acts as if *this time* were the only one that ever existed, we must remember that, according to Badiou, Time in general does not exist. Every truth abolishes time, to be sure, but *this time is always a particular time inaugurated by a particular event* (64). This dual notion of time leads us to the second constitutive paradox of Badiou's thought. Just as truth is both specific and universal (first paradox), time is both singular and manifold (second paradox). Truth itself and Time in general, however, are void.

In other words, there are as many truths (and thus "times") as there are subjects faithful to them. Although these truths (and times) co-exist simultaneously alongside each other, every single one of them *must be absolute* in the eyes of those who uphold it, because every subject-to-be "lives *exclusively* in an unfolding presence, the present of eternal consequences," as Hallward put it.[14] According to Badiou, then, history (or rather: "histories") begin(s) over and over again each time a truth-event is said to have occurred. Obviously, this leads us to imagine a profoundly anti-social universe of isolated subject-units, each of them living in their own eternal time-bubble that defines their own particular "state of the situation." If so, the central question concerns the relationship among these histories and the situations they describe. Are they structured hierarchically according to a surface-depth model in which some are more comprehensive than others? Or is it all just a matter of different, yet equal perspectives depending on which situation you happen to inhabit? And is there an eternal, common ground shared by all historical situations alike? Without clarifying these issues, Badiou's political theory cannot possibly hope to move beyond the postmodern relativism and identity politics it rejects as today's sophistry.

III

Badiou claims to address these questions through his ontological reflections, which are based on mathematical set-theory.[15] Badiou's ontology is entirely axiomatic. To arrive at the notion of being qua being, Badiou insists, one must subtract from it all predicates and particular characteristics. What remains is a pure multitude without any structure whatsoever, since being cannot be thought as a whole without distorting the nature of what is. In Badiou's terms, the true ontological foundation of any multiple being is not "its consistency …, but its inconsistency, that is, a multiple deployment that no unity can assemble" (EE 66). "The one is not," Badiou incessantly repeats. There is no consistent unity of being, there is only the inconsistency of the pure multiple. But there exists, of course, the logical operation that creates *a* particular multiple and presents "the one," which, therefore, is always the result of an operation. In other words, the pure multiplicity of being can only be found(ed) negatively by *subtracting* it from any given situation as that which cannot be presented therein. Being is multiple, but any effort to present this multiplicity necessarily "one-ifies" it. Thus, the multiplicity of being vanishes from any concrete historical situation, yet continues to haunt it from within, taking the form of a void: "every inconsistency is in the final analysis unpresentable, thus void" (71). This void is not simply non-existent, but literally re-presents or "names" the unpresentable. The void is "the proper name of being," Badiou concludes, because it is "universally included" in every situation (100). In short: "the One is not, there are only actual multiplicities, and the ground is void" (De 53).

This is precisely what mathematical set-theory is able to theorize. According to Badiou, it helps us understand what happens when we try to access or present the pure multiplicity of being. In this sense, mathematics presents (the mode of) presentation itself; it is the means by which we can recognize being qua being. Set-theory expresses the pure multiplicity of being in terms of the relationship between the numbers of elements of a given set and the number of potential sub-sets that can be construed by combining these elements in all possible ways. The ratio is always 2^n, where n is the number of elements of the original set. So, for example, a set with three elements {a, b, c} features eight sub-sets: {a}; {b}; {c}; {a, b}; {a, c}; {b, c}, {a, b, c}, and the empty sub-set {} or $\emptyset$—the latter representing the void that is always included in any situation.[16] If, however, the number of elements within a given set is infinite (as is the case with any real-life human situation), then the number of this situation's sub-sets if infinitely greater than that, namely 2^∞.

We owe this insight, Badiou argues, to the "event" of Georg Cantor's mathematical calculations. Cantor's achievement in set-theory was to allow for the precise—and hitherto considered absurd—mathematical comparison between two infinite sets. His theory measures the difference between, on the one hand, the infinite number of elements in a given set and, on the other, the infinitely larger number of sub-sets that can be formed among these elements. According to Badiou, the latter relates to the former exactly like the inconsistent multiplicity of pure being relates to any particular "state of the situation." Both contain an infinite number of elements, but a situation organizes and thus "one-ifies" its elements (i.e., it comprises them within a set), whereas the pure multiple of being cannot be "one-ified" because there is not one set that comprises all possible sets. Cantor's theory thus provides a mathematical explanation for the necessity of the empty set to be included in any family of subsets. In ontological terms, this means that the (impossible) presentation of being qua being is always structured around the void of a given situation. The existence of this void, however, only comes to light through an event that ruptures the situation and thereby exposes the constitutive void at its center.[17] Which is to say that every situation (or set) has its own specific void (or empty sub-set).

In short, Badiou's epistemology seems to be modeled after his ontology. The various truths of a situation are gathered around the active void of philosophical Truth much like the situation itself is structured around the constitutive void of being qua being. One may grant Badiou this analogy, yet continue to question its alleged relevance for Badiou's theory of subjectivity. The latter hinges upon the occurrence of an event. Yet Badiou stresses again and again that it remains uncertain whether or not such an event has actually taken place: "It will remain forever doubtful if there really was an event, except for those who, by intervening, decided that it belonged to the situation," Badiou maintains (EE 229). Since Truth is void (meaning that individuals cannot be guided by objective, philosophical principles within a given situation), the alleged occurrence of a truth-event depends entirely upon the autonomous decision of a (potential) subject to give it a name and call it into existence. Unbound by any external restrictions and solely responsible to the event to which it will have owed its own future existence, Badiou's "subject-to-be" implies a radically independent notion of (humanist) subjectivity.

A brief comparison with Lacan's theory of the subject will help clarify this point. Badiou himself has acknowledged his indebtedness to Lacan, particularly as regards their shared propensity for mathematical formula.[18] Yet Badiou has also insisted on a crucial difference between his and the Lacanian notion of the void. The latter relates to the subject, whereas Badiou relates it to being: "Let us say that philosophy localizes the void as condition of truth on the side of being qua being, while psychoanalysis localizes the void in the Subject" (IT 87). For Lacan, the subject figures as a structural void within the symbolic order. A retrospective effect of its failed representation in language, the Lacanian subject, Badiou argues, remains passive and severed from the emergence of an event that defies structural causality. Lacan's ahistorical structuralism, in other words, does not allow for the possibility of a radically new beginning (i.e., an eternal truth) taking place within a given Order or historical situation. To avoid this impasse, Badiou's "evental" philosophy must regard the subject not as void, but *as the infinitely extended response to an event that exposes the void*. This response initiates a truth-procedure that breaks through the reified "state" of the situation, leaving (Lacanian/Althusserian) structuralism behind.

But if local truths are literally enacted by the "subject-to-be," what "objective" truth criteria can it rely upon to make its decision? Although Badiou's epistemology stipulates the existence of objective, universal Truth, it does not grant individuals the ability to access this Truth such that it could inform and guide their action. For Truth pertains solely to "philosophy" itself. In fact, Badiou rarely, if ever, refers to himself or other thinkers as "philosophers." Instead, philosophy operates exclusively via its false proxies, the sophists, and Badiou insists that anybody who claims him/herself to be a philosopher will soon find him/herself exposed as a sophist.[19] While "subjects-to-be" are busy sustaining self-made local truths, only "philosophy" as such is able to conceptualize the site for Truth itself. One might say, then, that philosophy, for Badiou, is the house of thought, which shelters Truth. And the true subject that dwells in this house are not (human) philosophers, but is thought itself, as Hallward rightly points out: "Badiou's axiomatic orientation presumes the singular autoconstitution not only of the subject and truth but of the medium of this very autoconstitution itself, that is, of thought as such."[20]

This subject of thought, however, does not help curtail the rank growth of simultaneous truths-procedures initiated by the unfettered decisions of all those potential "subjects-to-be" allegedly seized by an event. Indeed, many critics have rightly challenged what they call Badiou's "decisionism."[21] A second, closely related problem is the specter of neo-Kantianism that haunts Badiou's strict separation between (mathematical) Being and the (philosophical) triad event-subject-truth.[22] Both problems are due to Badiou's elevation of thought as an auto-constitutive force or substance. Before discussing Badiou's recent responses to these charges in part v, I want to shed more light on his theory of the subject by comparing it briefly with those of Ernesto Laclau, Louis Althusser, Judith Butler, and Jacques Derrida.

IV

The notions of subjectivity developed by Laclau and Butler share with Badiou two essential characteristics: they are (explicitly or implicitly) based upon Lacan's paradoxical understanding of the subject as (some form of) structural void, while, at the same time, trying to augment Lacan's psychoanalytic concepts with a more viable social theory that accounts for political agency and historical change. For Laclau, as for Badiou, the "ethical" dimension of a subject's decision is precisely what transcends the "normative-descriptive" setting of any particular situation. But, contrary to Badiou, Laclau contends that even the subject's most radical decision directed against the rule of tradition nonetheless remains partly informed by it. Badiou's subject is seized by the inexplicable power of an event that breaks entirely with the given state (or structure) of a given situation and thus enables radical action. Laclau's subject can likewise decide for social change, but it cannot change, *at the same time*, the entire social ground that informed this very decision in the first place. Hence, the notion of a *radical decision* that breaks *entirely* with the existing normative-descriptive situation is self-contradictory and evokes an impossible scenario. Such a decision, Laclau argues, would be based upon self-annulment as a means of self-assertion: "This is the way in which I would establish distances with 'decisionism': the subject who takes the decision is only *partially* a subject; he is also the background of sedimented practices organizing a normative framework which operates as a limitation on the horizon of options."[23] Laclau's more measured understanding of ethics fully brings to light the radicality of Badiou's "decisionism." Since, for Badiou, subject and truth are inextricably intertwined and require each other's presence, there simply remains no normative background and thus no court of appeals able to verify that an event has actually occurred. How, then, are we to distinguish between true and false events? And what is the ontological status of the subject prior to its faith and before taking any decision at all? Who or what *wills* this subject into existence? As demonstrated above, Badiou's answer to these questions is "thought" itself.

Yet Badiou's recourse to "thought" as the active force of Being does not prevent his philosophy to be caught in the same paradoxical structure that characterized the Althusserian scenario of interpellation.[24] Althusser tried to solve the problem of subjectivity with reference to Lacan's notion of the split subject. As I have argued elsewhere, Althusser's reading of Lacan is highly idiosyncratic and not without flaws.[25] For example, his belief in the ideological nature of *all* subjectivity along with his strict distinction between ideology and science forced him to stipulate the latter as a "subject-less discourse." This, however, is irreconcilable with Lacan's insistence of the constitutive function of the subject for the linguistic field. For Lacan, the subject is not simply absent in discourse, but literally dis-appears therein and emerges as a void only after its failed effort of linguistic representation. Althusser's structuralist model was unable to account for this temporal movement at the heart of Lacan's fading subject and rendered it static instead. Thus, the "subject" becomes a mere ideological effect generated by the self-reflexive process of a structural field. In the eyes of Althusser, structure is substance: "it is this field itself which sees itself in the objects or problems it defines," while the function of Marxist "scientists" is to ventriloquize these operations: "The true subjects (in the sense of the constitutive subjects of the process) … are not … 'concrete individuals,' 'real men'—but the definition and distribution of these places and functions. The true 'subjects' are these definers and distributors: the relations of production (and political and ideological social relations)."[26] He continues by saying that "these are relations" and therefore "cannot be thought within the category subject"—a hardly convincing response.[27] In the end, Althusser's entire project failed because he was unable to account "for the relation between structure and subject," as Bruno Bosteels rightly argues.[28]

Judith Butler, too, contends that Althusser's theory remains "trapped within the grammatical time of the subject" because "it is almost impossible to ask after the genealogy of its construction without presupposing that construction in asking the question."[29] If subjects come into being and require their identity only in and through the process of subjection, then what should we call the original entity on which that operation is to be performed? What precedes the subject before its subjectification? These questions cannot be answered without presupposing the subject in question. However, instead of simply discarding Althusser's theory in light of his paradoxical account of interpellation, Butler reads it as a symptom for the inevitability of paradox in any effort to account for subjectivity in general: "As a form of power, subjection is paradoxical," Butler categorically states at the very beginning of her book.[30] Given its contradictory nature, "the subject," Butler maintains, "exceeds the logic of non-contradiction, is an excrescence of logic, as it were."[31]

Butler's embrace of paradox with regard to theories of subjection and subjectivity is thoroughly Lacanian. Lacan, too, describes the subject in paradoxical terms as the lack of its anticipated failure of self-representation in language: "I shall have been for what I am in the process of becoming," Lacan contends, and his use of the *futur antérieur*, like Badiou's, indicates the temporal contradiction at work in the dis-appearance of the subject in language.[32] It follows that, in some sense, the subject pre-exists its own genesis, which consists precisely in the constant undermining of self-identity: "Strictly speaking," Žižek admits, "individuals do not 'become' subjects" according to the Lacanian formulation, as Althusser had falsely assumed, but "they always-already *are* subjects."[33] Similarly arguing along these Lacanian lines, the subject, for Butler, can only be understood as "a linguistic category, a placeholder, a structure in formation," while "the story by which subjection is told is, inevitably, circular, presupposing the very subject for which it seeks to give an account."[34]

Badiou, on the other hand, cannot possibly accept this formulation, because Butler, like Lacan and Althusser before her, regards the subject as an intra-structural attribute or effect within a given field, whereas Badiou defines the subject precisely as that which escapes from this field by responding to the extraordinary occurrence of an event. Otherwise, Badiou claims, we cannot possibly account for the emergence of something "new" and remain forever trapped instead within an all-comprehensive, structural totality (be that Lacan's "symbolic order" or Althusser's "complex structured whole"). Although I believe Badiou's critique of structuralist models of subjectivity to be apt, his own notion of an active and self-generating subject ends up reintroducing the classical model of humanist subjectivity structuralism had sought to overcome. To avoid this impasse, Badiou's "decisionism" must account in greater detail for the process of naming the event: who, or what, decides that there will have been an event at all?

Derrida has tried to provide an answer to this question. For him, the decision of the subject is always a passive and unconscious decision, since "my" decision is "the decision of the other in me."[35] In his comparative analysis of Badiou and Derrida, Hallward concludes that Derrida's theory of the "subject" is inferior to that of Badiou for two reasons. First, because Derrida fails to account for the universal dimension inherent in any decision that gives rise to a truth-procedure. In Hallward's view, the subject's decision, as theorized by Derrida, becomes a private, isolated, and secret affair: "Derrida's responsibility keeps itself 'apart and secret,' it 'holds to what is apart and secret,'" Hallward contends, whereas "Badiou's commitment, inspired by Lacan's logic of the *matheme* … pursues clarity for all."[36] If Derrida's subject thus remains obtuse to the generic yet universally valid consequences of its decision, it is—second point—equally blind to the particular circumstances in which the event will have taken place:

> Badiou's event remains *situated vis-à-vis* the state of the situation (the elements of the "symptomal" or "evental" site … are perfectly accessible "in

their own right"; they are inaccessible only from within the situation), whereas Derrida's messianic event is *simply* "monstrous" in the strong sense, consigned to a general "formlessness."[37]

One may certainly take issue with Hallward's characterization of Derrida's project in these lines. But I would like to concentrate on Hallward's claim that elements can be "perfectly accessible 'in their own right'" yet remain "inaccessible only from within the situation." Obviously, this distinction is crucial for Badiou's thesis that every event brings to light the *particular* void that pertains to any *particular* situation. The void is only invisible for those who remain in the situation; from an outside perspective, however, the void is fully there for all to see. This issue of perspectivism is inextricably connected to what I have called the two constitutive paradoxes of Badiou's thought. It led us to conclude that there are as many truth-events and historical situations as there are subjects faithful to them. What remains puzzling, however, is the relevance of Hallward's distinction for a *particular* subject-to-be that *must be located, by definition, within its own particular situation* and therefore could not possibly be privy to the outside perspective Hallward mentions. Once again, the central epistemological question regards the possible *relationship that exist between individuals located either inside or outside a particular historical situation*. Niklas Luhmann, the late German master of systems-theory, referred to such outside observations as "second-order observations." They are performed by those who observe the first-order observations of others. By observing observation, these second-order observers are able to see the "blind spots" (i.e., "voids") that remain hidden to first order observers caught in the immediate operations of their own immediate surrounding (what Luhmann calls "system" and Badiou calls "situation"). Yet the second-order observer, too, remains part of a surrounding system and hence obtuse to his own blind spots, which, in turn, can only be observed by a third-level observer, etc.[38]

The same holds true for Badiou's theory. If the "subject-to-be" names the event and recognizes the void thereby exposed, it will immediately become part of a new situation based on its own void (for there is no situation without void, according to Badiou's logic). In other words, the subject has recognized one void only to become blind to another, which is to say that there is no total vision, no absolute knowledge—except for God, of course. But since, for Badiou, "the One is not," one wonders who could possibly observe the eventual elements of a situation "in their own right," as Hallward claims? The answer, once again, is thought. For Althusser, it was the situation "that sees itself," while for Badiou, thought is able to reflect upon the Truth of its own unity.

To return to Hallward's description above, we must conclude that the eventual elements of a given situation are fully visible "in their own right" simply because Badiou's axiomatic logic—as revealed by "thought" itself—dictates that they are. This explanation is hardly more satisfying than Althusser's. I, therefore, disagree with some critics' insistence on the "foundational role" of mathematics as a way to solve the problem of decisionism in Badiou's thought.[39] If we regard mathematics as a metonym for one of the four conditions of philosophy (i.e., science), it remains unclear why it should be any more foundational than any of the other three—art, for example.[40] If, on the other hand, we discuss the role of mathematics in ontological terms, then, of course, mathematics is indeed "foundational"—but foundational for what? For being qua be-ing, as Badiou puts it. Mathematics presents the mode of presentation of being itself. It *is* the "real model" for ontology, certainly, but it *is not* the foundation for what ruptures the pure presentation of being, namely the event, and the process of subjectification it inaugurates. And since that is what we are concerned with here, I fail to see the extraordinary relevance of mathematics in this context.

In other words, one can easily support Hallward's claim that the foundational role of mathematics in Badiou's philosophy makes *a* difference for thought itself, but nonetheless insist on the fact that *this* difference *does not matter* in any way for the subject-to-be. This difference that makes no difference constitutes a major problem for Badiou's "thought-praxis," as Hallward himself clearly recognizes: "Indeed, once we admit that all aspects of a particular situation that might resist mathematization are of no relevance to ontology, some readers may conclude that such an ontology is of little relevance to particular situations."[41] Indeed, I am such a reader. In my view, Badiou's ontology is utterly irrelevant in the context of current political problems such as moral relativism and human agency *unless Badiou is able to forge an intersubjective (i.e., "objective" and not merely "subjective") connection between being and event*. Such a connection, however, must be based on Truth, not on truths or mere faith.

Moreover, once we admit that mathematics can give no support for the "impossible" decision facing the subject, the differences between Badiou and Derrida on this issue become less pronounced than Hallward is willing to admit. I would even suggest that Derrida is more clear-sighted about the vexed paradoxical relationship between the event and the subject than Badiou. As Derrida states:

> There is no event, to be sure, that is not preceded and followed by its own *perhaps*, and that is not as unique, singular and irreplaceable as the decision with which it is frequently associated, notably in politics. But can one not suggest without a facile paradox, that the eventness of an event remains minimal, if not excluded, by a decision?[42]

In other words, the subject must decide upon a name for the event because only "the decision makes the event," as Derrida argues, implicitly declaring himself in complete agreement with Badiou on this point. But, unlike Badiou, he fully acknowledges the ensuing paradox, because the subject, by making a decision about the event, immediately "neutralizes this happening that must surprise both the freedom and the will of every subject" so as to even deserve the name "event" in the first place.[43] This circular logic is inescapable, Derrida insists, lest we fall back upon the classical theory of subjectivity that both Derrida and Badiou want to avoid at all costs:

> *A theory of the subject is incapable of accounting for the slightest decision.* But this must be said *a fortiori* of the event, and of the event with regard to the decision. For if nothing ever happens to a subject, nothing deserving the

name "event," the schema of decision tends regularly ... to imply the instance of the subject, a classic, free, and willful subject, therefore a subject to whom nothing can happen, not even the singular event for which he believes to have taken the initiative: for example, in an exceptional situation.[44]

Derrida's response to this paradox is "to show hospitality for the impossible itself" by making room for "*a passive decision*, an originarily affected decision" as "the decision of the other" in me.[45] Whatever one may think about Derrida's ethics, Badiou's attempt to solve this problem axiomatically inevitably falls prey to the very decisionism he had hoped to avoid.

V

In his recent responses to his critics, Badiou has tried to make certain adjustments regarding some of his major concepts, the results of which are to be published later in the second volume of *L'être et l'événement*. But Badiou has already outlined some of these ideas in various recent interviews, claiming, for example, that "there is no decisionism at all" in his philosophy because "the crucial question is the event and the event is not the result of a decision." This clearly amounts to a fundamental change with regard to his earlier position, as Badiou himself somewhat reluctantly admits:

> The difficulty is that in *L'être et l'événement*, I say that the name of the event is the matter of a pure decision and I have to change that point .... I now think that the event has consequences, objective consequences and logical consequences. These consequences are separated by the event. The effect of the event is a profound transformation of the logic of the situation—and this not an effect of decision. The decision is uniquely to be faithful to the transformation .... So, I am not a decisionist at all ... *now*. (IT 172–73, my emphasis)

Badiou's explicit distinction between the "objective" and the "logical" consequences of an event tries to separate the *ontological fact* that events occur from the *historical contingency* of their various consequences. The latter, he argues, fully depend upon the subject's decision, but the former does not. However, the central problems of Badiou's theory remain intact in spite of these reformulations. How could we possibly recognize the "objective" consequence of an event defined precisely as that which exceeds the limits of present knowledge? Is not the central characteristic of the event its "non-objectivity," i.e., the fact that it cannot be measured in terms of the specific historical situation in which it occurs?

Since Badiou's ontology is axiomatic and based on mathematical principles severed from the event, it cannot help us address these questions. Quite the opposite: the strength of Badiou's ontology resides precisely in the fact that it remains severed from historical contingencies of any kind, including events. But this strength is also a weakness, because Badiou's ontology excludes that which cannot either be decreed or deduced from decrees.[46] This is not to deny that, given the inconsistent multiplicity of being, events may in fact occur all the time, as Badiou insists. From my own, Deleuzian-inspired perspective, I would even go further and argue that the entire ontological field is nothing but a gigantic mega-event of constant ruptures in the form of Bergsonian vibrations passing along the lines of an eternal *élan vital*, a kind of incessant trembling of deterritorialization and reterritorialization moving between various states of being.

Be that as it may, the crucial point is that any event in Badiou's terms cannot possibly be determined or expressed mathematically. Mathematics is obtuse to the event, and the event defies mathematics, because it cannot be deduced logically from Badiou's ontological structure. The event must be defined—in fact: decreed!—axiomatically by a subject-to-be located within a specific historical situation. Nothing else will do. Otherwise, we are confronted with an endless series of allegedly "objective consequences" without any particular source to which they can be attributed, in which case we would suddenly find ourselves living out Badiou's worst nightmare: being caught in the decidedly Deleuzian universe of the univocity of being. Worse still, without recourse to defining an event as "the real and absent cause of a truth," there can be no "logical consequences" of the event either (IT 86). Truth, then, simply ceases to exist, or, more precisely, will have never existed to begin with.

Badiou's recent distinction between the "objective" as opposed to the "logical consequences" of an event drives an ever stronger wedge between ontology and epistemology. This divisive logic further exacerbates rather than solves the problems of decisionism and (Kantian) formalism that continue to haunt his philosophy. In order to avoid the impression that Badiou secretly relies upon a (however disavowed) transcendental notion of subjectivity, he must try to *reconnect rather than separate* being and event in order to outline the *possible relationships between* them.[47] Badiou himself acknowledges this problem and concedes that he must "rethink the most basic concept of my thinking, which is precisely the notion of situation" (Ee 136). Like in the earlier passage cited above, Badiou again distinguishes between the being of the situation (ontology) and what he now calls its "being-there" or the "appearance" of the situation. And he admits "that ontology doesn't settle this question" because "it is beneath this point of distinction. Hence, the effectivity of a situation, its appearing, can't be deduced from its configuration of multiplicity. There is no transitivity between the one and the other" (137). In other words, there is no direct path leading from "being qua being" to "being qua appearing"; there is no bridge connecting mathematics to the particular state of a given situation. Ontology (stipulating the *unrelated existence* of elements as *pure multiplicity*) is severed from logic (describing *the relations among elements in a given set*). But then Badiou continues as follows:

> At this point, we'll have to ask about the laws of appearance. I think we can maintain the idea that mathematics still explains some of what happens, that we aren't absolutely obliged to leave the realm of the mathematical. Simply, we'll need a slightly new form of mathematicity, one that requires a minimal theory of relation, a *logic*. (137, emphasis in original)

In the context of Badiou's previous oeuvre, this statement is simply baffling. He now extends the purview of mathematics from the ontological to the situational/evental realm, claiming that there exists an ontological theory of relation (in the form of a mathematical logic) that underlies being qua being—a (Deleuzian) argument that Badiou's "subtractive philosophy" had denied from its very beginnings. This new form of mathematicity, Badiou asserts, is "category theory," and Hallward outlines some of its major principles toward the end of his book.

I am not in a position to verify the usefulness of category theory to address the problematic (non-)relationship between being and being-there in strictly mathematical terms. But, in plain English, I would venture to formulate the following three conclusions: First, Badiou still faces the challenge of providing a more precise account of the relationship between ontological being (i.e., set theory) and its appearance (i.e., category theory). So far, Badiou's recent comments basically lead to a "double use of the word logic," as Hallward rightly observes:[48] on the one hand, Badiou refers to the global or universal logic that pertains to the ontological realm itself, but, on the other hand, he discusses the local logic that structures the particular state of a given situation. I guess we will have to wait for the publication of the second volume of *L'être et l'événement* to get a better sense of Badiou's new theory.

As it stands now, however, it is safe to assume that the axiomatic structure of ontology will remain unchanged, meaning that it still cannot inform the subject's decision about whether and how to name the event. In Badiou's view, it is still the decision that defines a logic, and not the reverse: "there is a logic of truth, but not a truth of logic," Badiou contends.[49] Ultimately, any such decision will have to remain self-sufficient and exclusively founded upon the faithful conviction of a subject-to-be: "Consequently, the irreducible gap between logic and mathematics stems from the blind spot of a thinking decision, which is that every decision of this type installs a logic that it practices as necessary [although ...] it is a consequence of that decision," Badiou concludes.[50] But the question remains: who or what makes the decision?

Nobody, it seems. Instead, true agency, for Badiou, resides in the situation itself once an event has occurred, because truth literally sets itself into motion: "Truth is an index sui. Truth is the proof of itself. There is no external guarantee. So, the genericity of the procedure of truth is effective in *the process itself*" (IT 173, my emphasis). Of course, "we are actors," Badiou concedes, "but in such a way that we are targeted by, carried away by, and struck by the event" (Ee 125). Although I am deeply sympathetic to Badiou's basic idea on an intuitive level, this and similar statements fail to clarify the matter in philosophical terms. Bluntly put, many of us are "seized" by a whole lot of "events" every day, from bowel movements and philosophical ideas to family problems and the war in Iraq. How could I possibly decide *ethically* among these "events"? Am I not rather forced to understand "ethics" in a brute (and brutal) pragmatic sense as that which calls upon me to arbitrarily bestow a name upon any occurrence whatsoever, thereby elevating it to the level of event and literally subjectifying myself to the truth-process I have thus defined? If, on the other hand, "truth is not said of the object, but *says itself only of itself*," then Badiou ends up precisely at the same deadlock as did his teacher Althusser who, likewise, had insisted on the radical self-sufficiency of the complex structured whole of society.[51] Badiou's "thought" becomes Althusser's "complex structured Whole."[52]

My second conclusion is that Badiou's reliance on the self-generative and auto-constitutive process of thought (Truth) puts him in the same boat as the various "anti-philosophers" he so vehemently opposes. Badiou's recent comments simply refer to mathematics and logic to formulate the relationship between being and appearing, whereas others favor linguistic paradigms instead. But both sides have to come to terms with the constitutive paradox of their "thought" (or "language"), which aims to present that which, by definition, cannot be (re-)presented without being lost. Such a (re-)presentation is *necessarily paradoxical* in nature, and Badiou, like all philosophers, remains its prisoner. But in that case we do not need yet another mathematical "logic" or more philosophical "thought," as Badiou argues. Instead, we need to change the current socio-political situation so as to increase the likelihood for people to be "seized" in Badiou's sense of the term. Instead of waiting for the event to happen, we need to welcome the event by keeping open the possibility of its occurrence.

In political terms, this means that we must work within rather than trying to transcend the parameters of the liberal-democratic tradition understood in its broadest sense possible. This is my final conclusion, and I, therefore, reject Badiou's exhortation to "remain outside the electoral system, outside any party representation," which precludes rather than enables change in our given situation (Ee 98, 99). I think this refusal to participate in the existing political process is indicative of the fact that his decisionist philosophy cannot provide access to the common ground shared by all truth-processes (and "subjects-to-be") except as void. In order to achieve particular political goals, however, our focus must be on building "chains of equivalences" (Laclau/Mouffe) among different individuals/groups. And this can only be done if we try to fill out the void and assign (a temporary) meaning to "Truth" so as to rally people around it. Rather than assigning thought the task of gathering and unifying "truths," Badiou's philosophy should seek to gather and unify politically active "subjects" instead. But Badiou still puts his faith in the power of an event to affect people more profoundly than his own deliberate actions ever could.

Since I, by contrast, have not been "seized" by the revolutionary activities of the sixties, Badiou's political theory strikes me as marginal at best and dangerous at worst. Calling on people to withdraw from rather than engage with the democratic system, Badiou might indeed contribute to a weakening of democracy such that the demagogical declaration of false events becomes an ever greater possibility. Given the choice, I believe it is far better not to have any event at all than to have a false one like 9/11 and its disastrous aftermath. And if such a cautious, not to say pessimistic, attitude were in fact to prevent the possibility of any event ever to occur at all, as some critics might charge, then I would be ready to accept this necessity.

But I do not believe this to be a necessary conclusion. For there is Badiou, and there are others like him. And the more successfully they promote their defiant stance vis-à-vis existing liberal democracy, the more they force its supporters to make a conscious decision in favor of its basic principles, thereby replacing the mindless acceptance of the given status quo with a committed dedication to its constructive improvement. Indeed, radical democracy is something to believe in and fight for; it cannot simply be taken for granted. Badiou helps us to realize this necessity, because democracy does not only need strong allies, but also needs strong adversaries. Badiou fancies himself among the latter, but finally ends up, *malgré lui*, among the former. It is precisely in this sense, and this sense only, that I, too, will remain faithful to the proclamation of the Badiou-event. ∎

....

1. In his preface to Peter Hallward's study on Badiou, Žižek maintains that "if Badiou's recent work is *the* event of contemporary philosophy, Hallward's book bears the greatest fidelity to this event." Slavoj Žižek, preface to *Badiou: A Subject to Truth* by Peter Hallward (Minneapolis: University of Minnesota Press, 2003), xii (emphasis in the original). Similarly, Sam Gillespie wonders: "Do his [Badiou's] works not, in and of themselves, establish events?" Sam Gillespie, "Neighborhood of Infinity: On Badiou's *Deleuze: The Clamor of Being*," *Umbr(a)* 1 (2001): 92.
2. [For a list of Badiou's principal texts and their corresponding abbreviations, see the introduction to this issue.—Ed.]
3. Alberto Toscano, "To Have Done with the End of Philosophy," *Pli* 9 (2000): 224.
4. Alain Badiou, "On a Finally Objectless Subject," in *Who Comes after the Subject?* ed. Eduardo Cadava, Peter Connor, and Jean-Luc Nancy (New York: Routledge, 1991), 25.
5. Quoted in Hallward, *Badiou*, 28.
6. Lecercle puts it most succinctly: Local truth is "always truth *in* a situation, but it is not *of* the situation," because it originates in an event that transcends the situation. Jean-Jacques Lecercle, "Cantor, Lacan, Mao, Beckett, *même combat*: The Philosophy of Alain Badiou," *Radical Philosophy* 93 (January 1999): 8 (emphasis in the original).
7. Alain Badiou, "Art and Philosophy," *Lacanian Ink* 17 (Autumn 2000): 63.
8. Bruno Bosteels is undoubtedly correct in claiming that the "importance of Althusser's legacy ... remains unsurpassed perhaps even by Heidegger and Lacan." Bruno Bosteels, "Alain Badiou's Theory of the Subject. Part I: The Recommencement of Dialectical Materialism?" *Pli* 12 (2001): 203.
9. I shall argue later that this seeming dependency of Truth/truths upon human agency is a misperception.
10. Of course there have also been many others in the course of history—Badiou even dedicated an entire book to St. Paul and his faithfulness to the (mythical) "event" of Christ's resurrection. If anything, this highly idiosyncratic list of "events" (most of which are decidedly "Eurocentric") testifies once again to the subjective nature of (Badiou's theory of) the event.
11. Lecercle, "Cantor," 8; IT 87.
12. Quoted in Hallward, *Badiou*, 157.
13. Ibid.
14. Hallward, *Badiou*, 157 (my emphasis).
15. For a more comprehensive account, see Hallward, *Badiou*, especially 81–106.
16. This is Hallward's example in *Badiou*, 88.
17. More precisely, since the void is "the without-place of every place" and thus scattered everywhere throughout the situation, the event takes place at the "site" of the localizable edge(s) of the void. For more, see Hallward, *Badiou*, 114–20.
18. See, for example, Ee 121.

19 See, for example, MPe 144.
20 Hallward, *Badiou*, 319.
21 Hence, Simon Critchley speaks of "a certain heroism of the decision in Badiou's work" behind which he suspects the Nietzschean specter of an "active, virile will" whose political significance has been fatally demonstrated by Carl Schmitt. Simon Critchley, "Demanding Approval: On the Ethics of Alain Badiou." *Radical Philosophy* 100:24. Similarly, Jean-François Lyotard maintains that at the core of Badiou's emphasis on decision and faithfulness lies "the Schmittian theme of authority through decision." Jean-Francois Lyotard, untitled discussion of *L'être et l'événement*, *Le Cahier* 8 (1989): 242. And Jean-Jacques Lecercle concludes that Badiou's "system is too abstract to provide a clear procedure of decision" ("Cantor" 12). Even Peter Hallward, Badiou's most eloquent advocate, acknowledges what he calls "the roughly absolutist dimension of Badiou's work" given his self-assertive and non-relational understanding of the subject as "the unquestionable" (*Badiou*, 285).
22 In *The Ticklish Subject: The Absent Center of Political Ontology* (London: Verso, 1999), Slavoj Žižek speaks of a "return to a proto-Kantian formalism" evident in Badiou's work (173). In the words of Peter Dews: "The fact is that Badiou wants Kantian intransigence, without paying the price of a formal universalism." See Peter Dews, "Categorical Imperatives: Adorno, Badiou, and the Ethical Turn," *Radical Philosophy* 111 (January/February 2002): 37. Likewise, Simon Critchley worries that "the dualism of being and event risks reproducing the Kantian ... distinction of pure and practical reason, between the ontological order of knowledge ... and the ethical order of truth ...." ("Demanding Approval," 21). The Kantian specter also resurfaces at various points throughout Hallward's book, most strikingly in his central objection against Badiou's radical subtraction of relations from being, which "introduces a new dualism at the heart of his radically univocal arrangement" (*Badiou*, 276). Finally, Badiou himself states that Gilles Deleuze, too, repeatedly accused him of being a "neo-Kantian." See De 100.
23 Ernesto Laclau, *Emancipation(s)* (London: Verso, 1996), 83 (emphasis in the original).
24 Cf. Žižek, who argues that "Badiou's notion of the Truth-Event is uncannily close to Althusser's notion of ideological interpellation" (*Ticklish Subject*, 141). Hallward explicitly rejects this reading for what he considers to be "three good reasons," which, however, in my view, basically boil down to merely one, namely that "Žižek pays virtually no attention to the foundational role of mathematics in Badiou's thought" and therefore encourages the confusing and "misleading suggestion" to attribute "to Badiou the inversion of Althusser's categories of science and ideology" (*Badiou*, 149). Since I will discuss the role of mathematics at a later point, suffice it to say in this context that Hallward fails to demonstrate how Žižek's neglect of mathematics contributes to this misleading analogy with Althusser. If anything, Hallward's discussion appears to support rather than contradict Žižek's claim: not only does he continually emphasize the degree to which "Badiou's subject is in several ways inspired by" Althusser's theoreticism, but he even quotes at length Badiou's own acknowledgment of this debt to his former teacher (149).
25 For a more comprehensive treatment of Althusser's notion of ideological interpellation, see Carsten Strathausen, "Althusser's Mirror," *Studies in Twentieth Century Literature* 18, no. 1 (Winter 1994): 58–71.
26 Louis Althusser and Étienne Balibar, *Reading Capital* (London: Verso, 1979), 180.
27 Ibid.
28 Bosteels, "Alain Badiou's Theory," 218.
29 Judith Butler, *The Psychic Life of Power: Theories in Subjection* (Stanford: Stanford University Press, 1997), 117.

30   Ibid., 1.
31   Ibid., 17.
32   Jacques Lacan, *Écrits: A Selection*, trans. Alan Sheridan (New York: Norton, 1977), 86.
33   Slavoj Žižek, *The Metastases of Enjoyment: Six Essays on Woman and Causality* (London: Verso, 1994), 60 (emphasis in the original).
34   Butler, *Psychic Life*, 10, 11.
35   Quoted in Hallward, preface to Ee xliii.
36   Ibid., xxvi–xxvii (emphasis in the original).
37   Ibid., xxvii (emphasis in the original).
38   See Niklas Luhmann, *Social Systems*, trans. John Bednarz, Jr. and Dirk Baecker (Stanford: Stanford University Press, 1995).
39   Hallward, for example, defines mathematics as "the *real* model for Badiou's four conditions," a statement echoed by Justin Clemens, who speaks of "the mathematical foundations of Badiou's thought." See Peter Hallward, "Ethics without Others: A Reply to Critchley on Badiou's Ethics," *Radical Philosophy* 102 (July 2002): 27 (emphasis in the original); Justin Clemens, "Platonic Meditations: The Work of Alain Badiou," *Pli* 11 (2001): 65n.
40   Indeed, Hallward and Clemens seem to have no problem with discussing Badiou without reference to his artistic work, i.e., the many novels and plays he has written. And yet, this work would seem as "foundational" or important to Badiou's philosophy as a whole as, say, science and mathematics.
41   Hallward, *Badiou*, 106.
42   Jacques Derrida, *Politics of Friendship*, trans. George Collins (London: Verso, 1997), 68 (emphasis in the original).
43   Ibid.
44   Ibid.
45   Ibid.
46   Similarly Hallward, *Badiou*, 156, 174.
47   Similarly ibid., 276.
48   Ibid., 303.
49   Quoted ibid., 313.
50   Quoted ibid. (ellipsis and square brackets in original).
51   Quoted ibid., 286 (my emphasis).
52   As Hallward concludes at the end of his book on Badiou: "Thought … is precisely that which decides itself into existence, all at once, in the element of pure subtraction. Thought is what lacks any upper limit, and for that reason, it is effectively cut off from its lower, worldly (or animal) contamination" (*Badiou*, 319).

THE UNICORN.

"Fault lines": Simon Critchley in Discussion on Alain Badiou

Edited by Jon Baldwin and Nick Haeffner

Introduction

This discussion took place following the presentation of Simon Critchley's paper "Ethics as Subjectivation" at a conference held on Alain Badiou's ethics, politics, and notion of subjectivity at the London Metropolitan University, December 2003.[1] The fault line in the title might be considered as the line dividing a whole series of oppositions in Badiou; between, for instance, the subjective/objective; truth/knowledge; an ethic of the same/an ethic of the other; subjectivity/individuality; immortal/man; the Real/the symbolic; and, crucially for Critchley, between the exceptional and the everyday. Critchley suggests there is a risk in Badiou of subtracting the realm of the everyday, whereas for Nina Power, for instance, this subtractive element is precisely the virtue of Badiou's philosophy. Finally, Badiou's critical stance in relation to Levinas comes under scrutiny. Since Critchley has often been associated with a Levinasian-Derridean approach, the debate with Badiou and his critical supporters is an important and necessary confrontation.

The dialogue takes us through key notions in Badiou's thought such as the event, subjectivation, the transformation of knowledge by truth, and universality. There is also debate concerning the status of the political event, the rarity of the event, the religious event, the difference between an affirmation of an event (Badiou) and the possible demand that the event makes on us (Critchley), the issue of norms, an ethics of the other, Pascal's wager, pathos, the exceptional and the everyday, and Levinas and Kant. During the discussion, frequently voiced objections to Badiou are refuted by interjections from Peter Hallward, Ray Brassier, Alberto Toscano, and Nina Power. The background to the debate may be found in Critchley's "Demanding Approval: On the Ethics of Alain

Badiou" and Peter Hallward's "Ethics without Others: A Reply to Simon Critchley."[2]

Discussion

ANDREW GIBSON: My question has to do precisely with how you, Simon, think about rarity—the rarity of the event. If politics is not rare, if politics is everywhere, then is the event everywhere? Likewise, are subjects everywhere? Is subjectivation everywhere? If indeed this is the case, then it sounds much less like Badiou, than, dare I say it, Deleuze. Indeed, this is precisely what Badiou says about Deleuze: that he puts the event everywhere and thus anaesthetizes it. If it is the case that, as you say, the event is everywhere, then why do we need to take a distance from the State at all? Exactly what does the State consist of if politics is everywhere? Who exactly is guarding the State?

SIMON CRITCHLEY: That's a good question. I take it that for Badiou, you have two ways of doing politics: politics that would be directed towards the State, and politics that would take its lead from the people as a plurality. Politics from the point of view of the State is effectively depoliticizing because it has to render invisible the plurality that is the people. This is a theme in Rancière, the distinction between policing and the political, and also similar to the distinction in Arendt between the political and the social. So politics conceived of at the level of the State makes politics invisible, it is essentially depoliticizing. So can the State be eradicated, can it be transformed, will it wither away? At this particular point in history I take it that's improbable.

For Badiou, there seems to be a complete autonomy of politics from the operations of the State (which are depoliticizing). I don't want to go that far; however there is a certain coherent logic to that position, which you find throughout history, if you think, for instance, of the great autonomist movements. Instead, I want to think about politics as erupting in … no, maybe erupting is too strong a word. In the way I am thinking about it, politics would be very minimal, it would just be about taking possession of the workplace, or at least finding representation in the workplace. Or if you were a doctor or nurse in a practice, then politics would be a case of making sure that the practice responds to the conditions you want it to meet. So in this sense I see politics as everywhere, as being a really quite banal, or rather mundane, call to forms of mobilization that begin from the place where you are, where your are working (or where you are not working), the place where you are active and where you are thinking.

GIBSON: Is this, then, the ubiquity of micro-politics? And the State therefore as some kind of empty machine that functions? Is there not a danger here of returning to a model which has the powerful few keeping the machine going, whilst the masses busily do their politics elsewhere? Alternatively, what Badiou gives me via the model of the rare political event on the one hand, and on the other what I call the remainder—that is, the world which is left untransformed—is a way of thinking about, for instance, the relationship between the developed world and the third world.

CRITCHLEY: Yes. If I say micro-politics then we end up thinking about it in too conveniently a Foucauldian or Deleuzian way, and I'm not too sure that's exactly what I mean. It would certainly be a question of politics being an activity. There is a phrase in Marx towards the end of *Capital*, volume one—incidentally there is very little in *Capital* on political organization—where he talks about the "association of free human beings." I think politics in that sense becomes a way of thinking about forms of association which could be really rather minimal or much larger. I take it this idea would have been the engine that was behind the unionisation movements from the late nineteenth century onwards.

What I worry about with the idea of the rarity of the political event is that it makes politics into this heroic act, which we await. It worries me because of its Heideggerian and national aesthetic connotations in the German tradition. So if we instead think about politics as a multiple mundane activity, which is about the ways in which people think about the place in which they act, then that is a way of loosening that heroism up.

JERRY REINELT: I want to also ask about the rarity of the event. In your paper you were contrasting Christianity and Judaism, but I think unfortunately you were also contrasting the dramatic conversion experience with someone who was born a Jew, and I consider this a problem. In Badiou's examples when discussing subjectivity he mentions Saint Paul, but Paul's event was something which happened just once in history. This makes me wonder about how common can events be? Do they have to be such dramatic things as a religious conversion experience would be?

CRITCHLEY: I take it that the example of Saint Paul reveals subjectivity in a particularly pure way, hence its exemplary status. In actuality it may well be impure. The example of Paul offers a response to the question, "What law can structure a subject in relation to an event in which the only proof is that a subject declares it?" With Paul, we have the vision of the resurrected Christ, which is that in relationship to which I become a subject. This reveals the relationship between subject and event in a rather pure way. Actually, I'd like to think of it as more complex and impure in every day life.

Another thing that worries me about Badiou, which I didn't mention in my paper, could take us into a discussion on psychoanalysis. Admittedly I'm placing a Kantian spin on Badiou, but I see the relationship between subject and event as having a structural autonomy. What is interesting in, for instance, Judaism and psychoanalysis, is that they are accounts of the subject in which the subject is defined in relationship to an event which is heteronomous. This could be the experience of the law or our relationship to the unconscious: that is the way in which the structure of trauma, in Levinas,[3] is a relationship to an event which makes me the subject that I am, but I have no way, as it were, of appropriating that: it always escapes me. So my position is like a structural-Judaism, and in Badiou's approach I see a more structural-Christianity. I want to argue for a more structural-Judaic approach, to use these caricature terms.

REINELT: In terms of getting away from the once in a lifetime experience of the event, what's the difference between someone who is born a Christian and someone who is born Jewish, in the structural sense of which you speak?

CRITCHLEY: I haven't really figured this out properly. The notion of the subject converting itself in relationship to an event interests me because it's a powerful way of describing one's motivation towards acting on the notion of the good. The fact that we are drawn ineluctably to using religious language to describe this interests me and deserves analysis. But I do pause. I want that conversion in relationship to a demand which I can never meet, which always already unseats and divides me. That's the picture I want to propose.

JERRY PALMER: I take your point about Paul and the road to Damascus being a particularly pure example or even a metaphor, of what Badiou means by subjectivity. I was struck by the idea that the subject and the event are mutually self-defining, that there is some kind of foundation of both which occurs simultaneously in a single moment or movement. I assume that this moment is a complete destabilization of everything that was previous, a kind of ecstasy in the etymological sense, a destabilization and re-foundation simultaneously.

CRITCHLEY: Yes, your name changes: you were Saul now you are Paul.

PALMER: If the individual only experiences events that are similarly rare, giving them a fleeting glimpse of, or experience of, subjectivity, then what is the individual the rest of the time? This seems to me to go back to the paradox that everyone always pointed out in Sartre's would-be ethics, which again, like Badiou, proposes that the ethical foundation is exactly that moment of destabilization and re-foundation. But as soon as you have re-stabilized, re-found yourself, then you are immediately, in Sartre's terms and by definition, back in bad faith. This was the problem that he always ran up against and which he tried to resolve when he wrote about Genet.[4]

It seems to me that this paradox is also in Badiou: you cannot have this constant destabilization and re-foundation of the individual because you'd be in a permanent state of trauma and would not have an ego. Something that Sartre also comments upon at length is that all the saints who tried to relive the road to Damascus as their basic commitment to religion all say the same thing: you can only do it once. Afterwards, you're condemned to trying to recreate that wonderful moment which just never quite reappears.

CRITCHLEY: Yes, I'd be interested to know how Badiou would be defended on that.

PETER HALLWARD: Badiou never talks about wanting to commemorate or repeat the event. In fact, the event isn't even something you really experience or are a subject to. The event is a suspension; it's the moment in which inconsistency is exposed for a second. Inconsistency is what we are, but in situations in which we live we are always counted, we are made to be consistent, made to fit some criteria—say white, male, student, teacher, whatever it is, all the criteria that apply—the point is that you count in the situation in which you are included. An event does something that suspends that count so that the inconsistent, shapeless, indeterminate entity that you are can appear in a consequential way. *Can* appear in a consequential way, it may or it may not. So it's sort of an invitation to act on that possibility, that's all it is. It can be extremely tiny. In political terms it can be about helping the organization and demonstration of a few people around workers' hostels in Paris, it's not just one of these big epic events. The question to ask, in terms of an event, if you could ask questions, is does it suspend the rules whereby you are counted as such and such person, and what do you do with this?

To go back to your paper, Simon, although I am sympathetic to some of the points you are making, it seems to me that there are some big distinctions to make; one is the difference between a demand and an affirmation, and the other is the difference between acting and thinking.

It seems to me that in Badiou an event does not make a demand on you, precisely because you cannot experience it or cannot be receptive to it. The exposure of inconsistency does not make a demand—it is inconsistent, it is unthinkable, it has no imperative, it cannot address you even, not strictly speaking. So that is why, as Andrew suggested in regard to Françoise Proust,[5] Badiou refuses an inaugural passivity or sensitivity or receptivity to some kind of appeal or demand or call from the other or the infinite or the beyond. All that falls under theism for him, for there is nothing fundamentally other than inconsistency, which is just that—inconsistent. So I don't see how it can make a demand. Instead, it happens that you can make an affirmation. It happens, and Badiou uses the metaphor of grace, it is possible to affirm ...

CRITCHLEY: An affirmation of what?

HALLWARD: Well, of inconsistency, and always in a subtractive sense and never to present it. To present it would be disastrous. It would be the Heideggerian theme of "here we all are in our resolution and our strength and in our rare militant mobilization." It would be the heroic move that you are quite rightly worried about. Insofar as Badiou shares this concern, I don't see how he can be criticized on this.

The other point is that thinking is not acting according to certain norms or criteria. If it were, then you would have a kind of ethical behaviorism, acting a certain way with norms you can invoke to legitimize or justify certain behaviors, which you can then test to see if they are universalizable or not. But again, that is not what Badiou is after.

CRITCHLEY: What is "*Continuer!*" if not a norm? It functions as a norm.[6]

HALLWARD: As a necessary condition of thinking, yes. Thinking doesn't happen in an instant, so to persist, to persevere, to continue, all those describe the process of thinking. In Badiou, thinking is always inventive, non-normative, always disruptive, always aligned to the inconsistent, it's a leaping around in the un-norms. The unknowableness of the norms is really crucial. I don't see how you can have a doctrine of justification based on unknowable norms.

CRITCHLEY: Mystics have, there are all sorts of examples.

HALLWARD: Yes, but where is truth? You don't talk about truth.

CRITCHLEY: Does the event remain? Does it remain as unknowable and inexperiencable once you, as it were, affirm it, and decide to bind your subjectivity to it?

HALLWARD: It has an implication or a consequence.

CRITCHLEY: There seems to be a moment of obscurity in Badiou, the moment when you submit to or affirm an event. But then it does not remain obscure. There is a sense in which you could rationally explicate that, make sense of that. It becomes a way of leading a life that can be explained to others. Whereas what you were saying sounds both a little too minimal and mystical.

HALLWARD: You can share with others; you can build an institution or organization. Organization is the effort to lend some kind of institutional weight to a truth, which is to say, to a non-normative, inventive, searching around for ways in which thinking can be sustained. Yes, maybe it doesn't last too long, and maybe it is always caught in certain kinds of compromise.

CRITCHLEY: There is a question as to what the notions of norm and normativity means. There is an allergy to the normative in French philosophy: Derrida always claims something like, "I have nothing to do with norms." But if you think about normativity in a much broader sense then thinking itself is normative. Forms of conscious activity are normative—normativity is the structure of experience as such, not some separate moral realm. We can have different notions of normativity.

PALMER: Going back to Badiou's ethics: what is an ethics that has no implication for my relationship with others? Robinson Crusoe had no ethics; he didn't need them, not at least until Man Friday arrived. If there are no others then there is no need for an ethics anyway.

CRITCHLEY: Crusoe had God.

PALMER: For me, the field of the other is the essential launching point for ethics. I can't see how an ethics which conforms to the analysis Peter gave of Badiou's ethics and conception of the event, actually produces something which can have any kind of basis for any kind of relationship with any other. I was very interested in love as one of Badiou's fields. It works very well with two people, as a couple, but as soon as there is a third person—a child—it suddenly doesn't work.

CRITCHLEY: But the subject in Badiou is not necessarily an individual subject, it can be a group or an organization, so to be a subject can be to be alongside others.

One of the questions I have for Badiou is the distinction between the subject and the pre-subjective state. Before you become a subject you are an individual, I'd be interested in what the status of this creature is, and what its rights would be.

AUDIENCE: Can I ask a question: is the subject only in existence insofar as it is conscious of itself? I'm thinking of the distinction in Marx between a class in-itself and a class for-itself. If the subject is only constituted through events, then I have a problem with that. There seems a kind of voluntarism about Badiou's politics, and also a way in which there is no kind of developmental process there. That somehow we only become subjects insofar as we become conscious through those rare events. In Marx a class can become conscious of itself and that moves it into political action, it also exists in-itself and for-itself. So there is a problem insofar as the subject is only constituted in these isolated events.

CRITCHLEY: Yes, I think I agree up to a point. I'm sure there are ways of getting around the voluntarism in Badiou, but it's a worry that I have. It's like the idea of the subject as autarkic, self-originating in relationship to something. I'm enough of a Freudian to worry about that—we are autarkic in relation to all kinds of stuff that we can barely understand.

But in Badiou's defense, when I was talking about the structure of the event in the reading of Paul, there was not just grace and faith but also love and hope, this perseverance with the process. That's a very concrete account of the subject. Maybe it happens once but that could be a way in which a whole lifetime could be described.

NICK HAEFFNER: I think there's a danger of conflating subject and individual ego in this discussion, of conceiving Badiou's notion of subjectivity in terms of Kantian autonomy, rather than radical heteronomy. I would suggest that the subject in Badiou happens at the point when you realize your radical heteronomy. The truth process exists after you, even after your death, and constitutes you in a field of social relations. In Badiou's account of the subject there is a great emphasis on self-denying, being self-less, and self-sacrifice. There is a giving up on what used to be called the bourgeois individual to something which exceeds you. Paradoxically, that is when you achieve your fullest development as a human being, and here I'm reminded of Hegel's argument in the *Phenomenology* that the highest stage of self-consciousness is the realization that you are socially constituted and that therefore self-hood is inextricably bound up with sociality. In contrast, the Sartre of *Saint Genet* and *Being and Nothingness* seems to posit an autonomous, Cartesian ego which at its most authentic is self-sufficient and essentially unitary. I take it that Badiou would reject the primordial existence of a unitary ego in favor of inconsistent multiplicity.

CRITCHLEY: The process of being faithful to a truth process, even if it began as being heteronomous to me, becomes my affair, my project. It becomes something that I take on board, assume, and affirm as part of the subjective process, which is my existence. So there is an autonomization of that.

RAY BRASSIER: I'd just like to follow on from some of the points Peter made. It seems to me that Badiou is a rationalist; his is an ethics of thoroughgoing rationalism. The point is that rationality has got nothing to do with justification. It's not about justifying cognitive norms. Rationality, for Badiou, is all about gambling precisely when you find yourself in a position when justification is impossible. So you wager that something unintelligible took place in the absence of any specifiable cognitive criteria capable of verifying or justifying that something took place. For example, Paul gambles that Christ rose from the dead. He didn't experience the event of the resurrection. Events don't really happen, you never experience an event—you gamble that something unintelligible took place. It's on the basis of that that the first subjectivation occurs. Subjectivation then initiates a subject procedure, which is not the same as the core originary reciprocity between event and subject. The subjective procedure is an inductive process. On the basis of an unintelligible wager, you simply draw the consequences from having gambled that this unjustifiable, unverifiable, occurrence took place. Drawing those inductive consequences initiates a subject. So it's first subjectivation, then a subject procedure, and the third moment is not about universality as subsuming the maximum breadth of subsumable instances, but it's about constructing an indiscernible universal. Because through the generic procedure you transform the situation in which you find yourself, a situation in which you wager that something unintelligible took place, in such a way as to reconfigure the criteria for verification so that it allows the possibility of thinking what was previously unthinkable, unverifiable, indiscernible. The constructing of an indiscernible, which completely overhauls and transforms the parameters of cognition, of justification, of verification, is a constructive or revolutionary process. This is why the model of evental rationality—which Badiou submits to—is based on no appeal to something other and is rigorously pathophobic. As soon as you start to appeal to intuitions or affects you are always going to end up justifying or legitimating what you feel or what you feel is possible …

CRITCHLEY: Ultra-Kantian then.

BRASSIER: It's the gamble on the basis that from something which is originally unintelligible, something as absurd as Christ rising from the dead, you can construct something which will reconfigure the parameters of knowledge and be ultimately intelligible for everyone in a way which cannot currently be imagined from within the existing parameters of the situation.

CRITCHLEY: That's very interesting, Ray. On this indiscernible universality: does the universal become discernible insofar as it becomes part of your subjectivation?

BRASSIER: The way in which the indiscernible changes or reconfigures the possibilities of knowledge is through what Badiou calls the forcing. That is where you construct the generic adjunct or supplement to an existing situation. That is the moment of transformation and that is where truth reconfigures the parameters of knowledge. It becomes possible to know things which were previously unknowable. That is why this is a revolutionary rationalism. It is all about discovering what was previously unknowable, not about justifying what everybody thought they knew.

CRITCHLEY: I just have a couple of thoughts on that. In the way you describe it—I'm not sure if this will irritate you—but it sounds very close to a version of Pascal.

AUDIENCE: Absolutely, very Pascal.

CRITCHLEY: Is that bad? In Pascalian logic, which is rationalistic—based on geometry—we have an absolute unknowability of the divine, and you then wager on that, gamble on that, knowing absolutely nothing. The logic of it is ultra-Protestantism, ultra-Lutheran, which is why the Jesuits gave him such a hard time. You gamble on that absolute unknowability and you become a subject at that point; a subject which has a rationalistic core. Pascal says, "two extremes: to exclude reason, to admit nothing but reason."[7] Once you've bound yourself to the event then it becomes a question of rationally articulating that. It strikes me as interesting that there is a commonality there between Pascal and Badiou. Your other points about Badiou I take on board, I just need to read more!

HALLWARD: The point about Pascal is that he is full of pathos.

CRITCHLEY: Why is pathos so bad? "The heart has its reasons of which reason knows nothing."[8] I mean, why this sort of …

HALLWARD: Well, that's a problem I think with Badiou, although he has a very sympathetic meditation on Pascal in *Being and Event*. He says that whatever else we do, we mustn't turn Pascal, who is a great thinker of the militant process of truth, into the thinker of a merely moral subject. Badiou would want to drive a very strong wedge between Pascal as a thinker of truth—in the very strict sense—and a thinker who is interested in how we justify ethical and respectable behavior.

CRITCHLEY: But that's a misunderstanding of my position, as if I'm claiming that talk about justification is arguing for some sort of bourgeois prudence. That's not it at all. There need to be procedures for justification of what you decide to act upon, unless it simply becomes that you act and accept the will of my action as such. I think that Badiou is trying to think ethics in relationship to situations. That is, he is considering the legitimacy of actions in situations in relation to the question of whether it is addressed to all—universality—and this, as it were, justifies or legitimates one's action in relationship to certain situations, and de-legitimates or does not justify actions in other situations, for instance, Nazi Germany.

AUDIENCE: But isn't that a problem? What seems to be missing in Badiou is the mediation between the universal and the individual.

CRITCHLEY: I think you're right. The fault line in our thinking about ethics is the fault line between the universal and the particular, and the different forms that this has taken in the history of thought.

I want to come back to the question of pathos. Is the objection to pathos that pathos is not universalizable? Which actually is the Kantian objection to pathos.

HALLWARD: Yes. But it's a bit more. Pathos and suffering and questions of comfort and being well and at ease in the world are all irrelevant for Badiou. They don't think, they are thoughtless and he subtracts them out.

CRITCHLEY: Well that's a risk. There's a risk in subtracting, or throwing out the pathetic baby with the bath water!

NINA POWER: But pathos simply happens all the time.

CRITCHLEY: No, it's not what happens all the time.

POWER: But it is.

CRITCHLEY: I think the opposite.

POWER: Pathos is everywhere, everyday. It's every tiny tragedy of every cake you didn't get to eat or every friend you miss or whatever. It happens all the time. Surely what is interesting about Badiou's project is its very subtractive dimension?

CRITCHLEY: Well, yes. It's an ultra-rationalistic anti-humanist attempt to construct an ethics in relationship to an ontology which some people find convincing—but I find less convincing. Sure it's impressive.

The classic argument against pathos is that if you base ethics on pathos—sentiment—then you cannot universalize ethics. This is, for instance, Kant's objection to Hume's ethics based on sympathy. It accounts for the objection to the role of pity in Rousseau's ethics. The argument is that we must eliminate pathos because it is not rationally vindicable.

ALBERTO TOSCANO: But surely it is a question of where the place of pathos lies? What if pathos lies in the series of consequences of subjectivation? Badiou talks a great deal about courage, enthusiasm, and has an entire typology of anxiety. So, it is a question of two domains of pathos. Is the domain of everyday pathos continuous with that which is a consequence of the process of subjectivation? For Badiou it is a matter of the dissymmetry between those two domains: there is your political enthusiasm of militancy at the barricades, and also the thinking about your lost pet. Because there is not a straight mapping of individual onto subject there is no reason why these two domains of pathos should be mapped onto one another. Everyday pathos does not have to be eliminated; it's simply not significant. Badiou does not say that we don't have ethical relations with our friends, just that they are not philosophically significant. It's not that they should be destroyed. They are just insignificant. Part of the attraction about Badiou is that he does not think that philosophy can think about everything, because it can't. It shouldn't be interested about everything and maybe it should not be interested in what we do on an everyday basis.

CRITCHLEY: Yes, precisely there is the fault line between a position like Badiou's and a position like mine. We have a distinction between exception pathos and everyday pathos.

TOSCANO: Organized pathos, I'd say, rather than exceptional pathos.

CRITCHLEY: I'm arguing for an everyday pathos, and that is regarded as a bad thing?

TOSCANO: No, I'm just saying that this is a distinction that Badiou would make.

CRITCHLEY: The philosophical problem is the following: if we base ethics entirely on reason then we encounter the problem that runs through Kant—how do you motivate subjects to act on pure rationality? How do you invite a will to assume the moral law if the only compulsion to do it is rationality? Kant argues that if we have individual emotion, individual pathos, sympathy, and compassion—all of those terrible things!—then we end up in moral relativism. So then the question is: can we link an exceptional pathos to moral rationality? The response that he gives is respect. In the second critique it is a little bit different, it is pain. Pain in Kant would be an exceptional pain. That interests me greatly. I want to exceptionalize the notion of affect in order to deal with this question of how we link together rationality at the level of our ethical thinking and motivation at the level of subjective compulsion to act on the conception of the good. But I think that I would, at the end of the day, want to get back to ordinary pathos at some level. But then I'm an old life-world phenomenologist!

MIKE KING: My question is in support of Simon, and against the suppression of pathos. This suppression is congruent with Badiou's rejection of Levinas and the discourse of the other. Badiou is rejecting the Judaic—and the Judaic is the discourse of pathos.

CRITCHLEY: No, the Judaic is the discourse of law. I thought Judaism was the absence of pathos? The classic critique of Judaism is that it is an abstract relation to law. It's the Christian that has pathos by the bucket load! They call it love. They don't experience the legal circumcision of the body.

Regarding Levinas, I take the first couple of chapters of *Ethics* with a pinch of salt. I think Badiou, for polemic reasons, tells a certain story about Kantianism and Levinasianism and these are necessary caricatures; philosophy works through the leverage of straw men and women. But if you really do think about Levinas or Kant carefully, then it is much more nuanced than the picture Badiou paints. Levinasian ethics is a theory of subjectivation in relationship to an experience of exceptional affect in relationship to an event which is unknowable and inassimilable in relationship to which you wager. There is no more Pascalian thinker than Levinas when it comes to these things. So if you think these things through in a less caricatured way, I think you'll find all sorts of interesting commonalities. This is what I am more interested in.

The risk with the reception of Badiou is the suggestion that here is a brush which will sweep away all sorts of other things, but that never happens in philosophy. It's an illusion to which human beings are prone every ten or fifteen years, and then they discover someone else. Badiou is a new and powerful voice in a concert with others. But to make the distinction, as he does, between an ethics of the same and an ethics of the other, between Badiou-Deleuze equal good, Levinas-Derrida equal bad—is not really thinking.

POWER: He does say that we should keep the sophists!

CRITCHLEY: Oh, which would refer to those reactionary metaphysicians! That's very kind of him!

Afterword

Although it might be frowned upon by some of Badiou's supporters, Critchley's exhortation to think together Badiou-Deleuze ("good") and Levinas-Derrida ("bad"), instead of seeing the positions as mutually exclusive, may well have some mileage.

The ethical question in Badiou's work that Critchley wants to keep coming back to is why "keep going," why "*continuer*," why wager, why affirm (what is, after all, a rational principle) in the first place? In the dialogue, Critchley raises the classic philosophical problem, how to motivate subjects to act on pure rationality? In terms of Badiou's project, he asks, what is the nature of the demand that I affirm inconsistency? As Hallward argues, the inconsistency does not and cannot compel a demand from you, only an affirmation, a wager upon it; but why affirm or wager in the first place? Badiou writes that a "truth's first step is to wager .... One decides to hold to the statement 'the event has taken place,' which comes down to deciding the undecidable. … It is then a question of an absolutely pure choice, free from any presupposition other than that of having to choose."[9] Critchley is asking questions of the nature of this "presupposition" of choice, and imperative to wager and affirm. Why should I choose to give up my individuality for subjectivity? Or rather, what criteria do I have at my disposal and how am I to decide when "I am confronted with a pure choice between the 'Keep going!' proposed by the ethic of this truth, and the logic of the 'perseverance in being' of the mere mortal that I am" (Ee, 78). In essence, this may prove to be an investigation of one way in which Badiou's ethical thought is founded in Plato's notion of the good. It also concerns the status of Badiou's idea of "grace" and (dis)interestedness and how well, or otherwise, these ideas sit within the rest of his philosophy.

As has been mentioned, Badiou's philosophy is subtractive. Hallward, however, reveals an analogous problem to the one above in a critical footnote to his study of Badiou:

> Badiou concludes [in *Conditions*] that "there is only one maxim in the ethics of a truth: do not subtract the last subtraction." Clearly, however, this maxim cannot itself be derived from the practice of subtraction as such. What is the source, if not the altogether classical philosophy of the subject as subject of moderation? Of mastery, and self-control? Or even, of "*calcul*"?[10]

Finally, in a recent book on Deleuze, Slavoj Žižek pays attention to one of Badiou's definitions of Evil:

> The total *forcing of the Unnamable*, the accomplished naming of it, the dream of total Nomination ("everything can be named within the field of the given generic truth procedure")—the fiction (the Kantian regulative Idea?) of the accomplished truth-procedure is taken for reality (it starts to function as constitutive). According to Badiou, what such forcing obliterates is the inherent limitation of the generic truth-procedure (its undecidability, indiscernibility …): the accomplished truth destroys itself; the accomplished political truth turns into totalitarianism. The ethics of Truth is thus the ethics of the respect for the unnamable Real that cannot be forced.[11]

Žižek's next move is to ask "does Badiou, *the* anti-Levinas, with this topic of the respect for the unnamable, not come dangerously close precisely to the Levinasian notion of the respect for Otherness?"[12] The question, as before, concerns the source of the imperative not to force the unnamable. Žižek's damning response is to argue that for Badiou's philosophy, "the only way out of this predicament is to assert that the unnamable Real is not an external limitation but an *absolutely inherent* limitation."[13]

Thus it would appear that Critchley's insistence that Levinas can and must be thought with, and not against Badiou, has some force. His warning that philosophy seduces us into the promise that it will "sweep away all sorts of other things" and that it often "works through the leverage of straw men and women" throws down a timely challenge to read Badiou along the fault lines of his thought. ∎

....

1 The conference was organized by the London Metropolitan University *Communications and Subjectivity Research Group*, comprising Jon Baldwin, Paul Cobley, Jean Collingsworth, Nick Haeffner, and Jenny Harding. The group edit the journal *Subject Matters—A Journal of Communications and the Self*. Badiou will be the focus of the next edition (December 2004), email subjectmatters@londonmet.ac.uk for further details.
    Thanks are offered to everyone who attended and contributed to the conference. Janelle Reinelt, University of California, Irvine, expertly chaired the discussion. Apart from a few instances, participants have been identified from the tape-recording. Certain grammatical emendations have been made as well as minor editing of the full transcript. What is, unfortunately, "lost in transcription" is the generosity and wit of many of the contributors. Any mistakes or misrepresentations are entirely the fault of the editors (Jon Baldwin and Nick Haeffner). Our thanks also to Jason Barker, who commented on an earlier draft.
2 Essays in *Radical Philosophy* 100 (2000): 16–27 and *Radical Philosophy* 102 (2000): 27–31.
3 See Simon Critchley, "The Original Traumatism: Levinas and Psychoanalysis," in *Ethics-Politics-Subjectivity: Essays on Derrida, Levinas and Contemporary French Thought* (London and New York: Verso, 1999).
4 Jean-Paul Sartre, *Saint Genet: Actor and Martyr* (New York: Braziller, 1963).

5   The reference is to Andrew Gibson's paper "Badiou and Françoise Proust: The Refusal of Passivity," presented earlier in the day.
6   The reference is to the imperative "Keep going!" In his *Ethics*, Badiou writes that "the ethic of a truth is the complete opposite of an 'ethics of communication.' It is an ethic of the Real, if it is true that—as Lacan suggests—all access to the Real is of the order of an encounter. And consistency, which is the content of the ethical maxim 'Keep going!' [*Continuer!*], keeps going only by following the thread of this Real" (Ee, 52). [For a list of Badiou's principal texts and their corresponding abbreviations, see the introduction to this issue.—Ed.]
7   Blaise Pascal, *Pensées*, (London: Penguin Books, 1966), #183.
8   Ibid., #277.
9   Badiou, Alain, "On Subtraction," in TW 112–13.
10 Peter Hallward, *Badiou: A Subject to Truth* (Minneapolis: University of Minnesota Press, 2003), 405n50.
11 Slavoj Žižek, *Organs Without Bodies: On Deleuze and Consequences* (London and New York: Routledge, 2004), 105 (italics and ellipses in original).
12 Ibid., 106.
13 Ibid., 107.

Contributors

Eric Alliez is professor of philosophy at the École des Beaux-Arts de Karlsruhe. His publications include *Les temps capitaux*, vol. 1, *Récits de la conquête du temps*; vol. 2, *La capitale du temps*, pt. 1: *L'état des choses* (Cerf, 1991/1999); *La signature du monde, ou Qu'est-ce que la philosophie de Deleuze et Guattari?* (Cerf, 1993); *De l'impossibilité de la phénoménologie: Sur la philosophie française contemporaine* (Vrin, 1995); *Gilles Deleuze: Une vie philosophique* (general editor, Synthélabo, 1998); *Chroma Drama* (edited in collaboration with E. Samsonow, Turia + Kant, 2002); *Biografie der Organlosen Körper* (Turia + Kant, 2003).

Jon Baldwin is Lecturer in Communications at London Metropolitan University, and PhD candidate. He is co-editor of the journal *Subject Matters: A Journal of Communications and the Self*.

Jason Barker is the author of *Alain Badiou: A Critical Introduction* (London: Pluto Press, 2002) and the translator of Badiou's *Metapolitics* (London and New York: Verso, forthcoming).

Nico Baumbach is a graduate student in the Program in Literature at Duke University.

Bruno Besana is currently a teaching fellow in the Philosophy department at the Université de Paris VIII. He wrote "Deleuze lecteur d'Aristote," in *Déplacements* (Éditions Paris VIII, 2002); "Condition, intercession, brouillage: le problème de la formulation philosophique de l'évènement dans l'art chez Badiou, Rancière et Deleuze," *Cahiers de l'ATP*, 2004; as well as the introduction to the Italian translation of *La Fable Cinématographique* by Jacques Rancière (Éditions Mimesis, forthcoming).

Bruno Bosteels is Assistant Professor of Spanish at Cornell. He has also held positions as an assistant professor at Harvard University and at Columbia University. He is currently preparing two book manuscripts, *After Borges: Literature and Antiphilosophy* and *Badiou and Politics* (under contract with Duke University Press). He is also translating and introducing two books by Badiou: *Can Politics Be Thought? followed by Of an Obscure Disaster: On the End of the Truth of State* and *What Is Antiphilosophy? Essays on Nietzsche, Wittgenstein, and Lacan* (both for Duke University Press). He is also the author of numerous articles on Latin American literatures and cultures.

Élie During studied at the École Normale Supérieure (Paris) and now teaches philosophy at the Université de Paris x-Nanterre. His current work touches on metaphysics and early twentieth century philosophy of science (Bergson, Poincaré, Wittgenstein). As a counterpart to this, he has been reflecting on contemporary aesthetic practices. He recently edited the work *Matrix, machine philosophique* (with A. Badiou, T. Bénatouïl, P. Maniglier, D. Rabouin, and J.-P. Zarader, Ellipses, 2003), and conducted interviews with Bernard Stiegler, *Philosopher par accident* (Galilée, 2004).

Oliver Feltham teaches in the Comparative Literature Department at the American University of Paris and is a researcher at the Jan van Eyck Academie, Maastricht. He co-edited *Infinite Thought* with Justin Clemens, and translated Badiou's *Being and Event* for Continuum, to be published in 2005. He is working on a book on praxis and change in contemporary philosophy.

Andrew Gibson is Professor of Modern Literature and Theory at Royal Holloway, University of London, UK. His publications include *Joyce's Revenge: History, Politics and Aesthetics in Ulysses* (Oxford University Press, 2002), and he is currently completing *The Pathos of Intermittency: Alain Badiou and Samuel Beckett* (Oxford University Press).

Nick Haeffner is Senior Lecturer in Communications at London Metropolitan University and a visiting professor of film and TV at Boston University British Programmes. He is co-editor of the journal *Subject Matters: A Journal of Communications and the Self* and author of *Alfred Hitchcock* (2004). He is currently part of a team devising a traveling Hitchcock installation and is working on a cultural study of Thatcherism and British media.

Lindsey Hair is a PhD candidate in the Department of Comparative Literature at SUNY Buffalo. She is currently writing her dissertation on Badiou, Deleuze, and film.

Peter Hallward teaches in the Centre for Research in Modern European Philosophy at the University of Middlesex. He is the author of *Absolutely Postcolonial* (2001) and *Badiou: A Subject to Truth* (2003), and the editor of *The One or the Other: French Philosophy Today* (*Angelaki* 8, no. 2, August 2003). His book *Out of This World: Deleuze and the Philosophy of Creation* is forthcoming from Verso in 2006.

Stefan Herbrechter is Senior Lecturer in Cultural Analysis at Trinity and All Saints, College of the University of Leeds, UK, where he teaches courses in Cultural Studies, Critical and Cultural Theory, and Literature. He is the author of *Lawrence Durrell, Postmodernism and the Ethics of Alterity* (Postmodern Studies: Rodopi, 1999) and the editor of *Cultural Studies: Interdisciplinarity and Practice* (Critical Studies: Rodopi, 2002), *Discipline and Practice: The (Ir)resistibility of Theory* (with Ivan Callus, Bucknell University Press, 2004) and *Post-Theory, Culture, Criticism* (with Ivan Callus, Critical Studies: Rodopi, 2004).

Oliver Marchart teaches cultural studies at the University of Basel and political theory at the University of Vienna. Recent books include: *Laclau: A Critical Reader*, edited with Simon Critchley (Routledge, 2004), *Techno-Colonialism: Theory and Imaginary Cartography of Culture and the Media* (Löcker, 2004, in German) and *Beginning Anew: Hannah Arendt, the World, and the Revolution* (Turia + Kant, forthcoming, in German).

B. Madison Mount is a PhD candidate in comparative literature at Princeton University writing a dissertation on necessity and contingency in the literature and philosophy of German Idealism. He also works on phenomenology, the history of metaphysics, and contemporary French philosophy.

Presently an Associate Professor in German at the University of Missouri, **Carsten Strathausen** is the author of *The Look of Things: Poetry and Vision around 1900*, published in 2003 by the University of North Carolina Press. He has also written more than a dozen articles on a broad variety of topics, including European intellectual history, Marxist and psychoanalytic theory, and German literature and film. His present book project—*Aesthetics Unbound: Art and Politics in the Digital Age*—tries to revitalize aesthetic theory and practice within leftist political discourse.

Matthew Wilkens is a PhD candidate in the Graduate Program in Literature at Duke University and a member of the *Polygraph* editorial collective. He is writing a dissertation on allegory and event in American fiction.

Art / Theory / Criticism / Politics

OCTOBER

Edited by
Rosalind Krauss
Annette Michelson
George Baker
Yve-Alain Bois
Benjamin H.D. Buchloh
Leah Dickerman
Hal Foster
Denis Hollier
Mignon Nixon
Malcolm Turvey

"October, a quarterly of social and cultural theory, has always seemed special. Its nonprofit status, its cross-disciplinary forays into film and psychoanalytic thinking, and its unyielding commitment to history set it apart from the glossy art magazines." *Village Voice*

" . . . founded by some of the brightest forces in art criticism. The ideas offered about modern art are often radical and influential."
Magazines for Libraries

At the forefront of contemporary arts criticism and theory, OCTOBER focuses critical attention on the contemporary arts and their various contexts of interpretation. Original, innovative, provocative, each issue presents the best, most current texts by and about today's artistic, intellectual, and critical vanguard.

Recent highlights include:

OCTOBER 111, special issue on Ed Ruscha *(winter 2004)*
- Liz Kotz, *Language Between Performance and Photography*
- Alexandra Schwartz, *Second City: Ed Ruscha and the Reception of Los Angeles Pop*
- Ed Ruscha, *"Blue Collar" drawings [artist project]*
- Yve-Alain Bois, *Thermometers Should Last Forever*

OCTOBER 110 *(fall 2004)*
- Hal Foster, *An Archival Impulse*
- Claire Bishop, *Antagonism and Relational Aesthetics*
- George Baker, *An Interview with Pierre Huyghe*
- Tom McDonough, *No Ghost*

Come join OCTOBER's exploration of the most important issues in contemporary culture. Subscribe today!

MIT Press Journals
Five Cambridge Center / Cambridge, MA 02142
tel: 617-253-2889 / fax: 617-577-1545
journals-orders@mit.edu

published quarterly by The MIT Press
ISSN 0162-2870 / E-ISSN 1536-013X

 http://mitpress.mit.edu/october

DIASPORA

A JOURNAL OF TRANSNATIONAL STUDIES

▶ multidisciplinary studies of varieties of dispersion – their history, literature, social structure, politics, and economics

▶ discourses of nationalism, transnationalism, ethnicity, exile, postcolonialism, and globalization

▶ contributions from scholars worldwide

Recent Articles
12:1 (Spring 2003)

Theorizing Africa in Black Diaspora Studies: Caryl Phillips' Crossing the River Yogita Goyal

The 1.5 Generation of Russian Immigrants in Israel: Between Integration and Sociocultural Retention Larissa Remennick

The Hungarian Status Law: A New European Form of Transnational Politics? Michael Stewart

World Literature: The Unbearable Lightness of Thinking Globally Gregory Jusdanis

Andean Transnational Merchants: An Indigenous Community in Globalization José Itzigsohn

Subscription Rates

Individuals $31   Institutions $65

For subscribers outside Canada, the rates are payable in US funds.
For Canadian orders, please add 7% GST.

UTP – Journals Division, 5201 Dufferin Street, Toronto, ON, M3H 5T8 Canada
Tel: (416) 667-7810   Fax: (416) 667-7881   email:journals@utpress.utoronto.ca

Journal for Cultural Research

EDITORS
Michael Dillon, *Lancaster University, UK*
Scott Wilson, *Lancaster University, UK*

Journal for Cultural Research, formerly Cultural Values, is an international journal, based in Lancaster University's Institute for Cultural Research. It is interested in essays concerned with the conjuncture between culture and the many domains and practices in relation to which it is usually defined, including, for example, media, politics, technology, economics, society, art and the sacred.

Culture is no longer, if it ever was, singular. It denotes a shifting multiplicity of signifying practices and value systems that provide a potentially infinite resource of academic critique, investigation and ethnographic or market research into cultural difference, cultural autonomy, cultural emancipation and the cultural aspects of power. As such, culture has itself become, in many areas, a primary instrument of government and thus the desire not to be governed is impelled to think culture differently from the accepted forms of cultural identity and recognition. In the academy, research has become a defining feature of the cultural just as the cultural has become indistinguishable from questions concerning the governable.

This journal is also available online.
Please connect to www.tandf.co.uk/online.html for further information.

To request an online sample copy please visit:
www.tandf.co.uk/journals/onlinesamples.asp

SUBSCRIPTION RATES
2005– Volume 9 (4 issues)
Print ISSN 1479-7585
Institutional rate: US$306; £185
(includes free online access)
Personal rate: US$61; £47 (print only)

ORDER FORM
rcuv

PLEASE COMPLETE IN BLOCK CAPITALS AND RETURN TO THE ADDRESS BELOW

Please invoice me at the ❏ **institutional rate** ❏ **personal rate**

Name _____

Address _____

_____

_____

Email _____

Please contact Customer Services at either:

Routledge Journals at Taylor and Francis Group, 4 Park Square, Milton Park, Abingdon, Oxon, OX14 4RN, UK
Email: enquiry@tandf.co.uk   **Website:** www.tandf.co.uk

Taylor & Francis Inc, 325 Chestnut Street, 8th Floor, Philadelphia, PA 19106, USA
Tel: +1 215 6258900 **Fax:** +1 215 6258914 **Email:** info@taylorandfrancis.com **Website:** www.taylorandfrancis.com

POLYGRAPH
AN INTERNATIONAL JOURNAL
OF CULTURE AND POLITICS

CALL FOR PAPERS

BIOPOLITICS, NARRATIVE, TEMPORALITY
Issue Editors: Rod Frey and Alexander Ruch

Contemporary accounts of politics often coincide with strategies, theories, and experiences of temporality, whether they be historical periodizations, the experience of everyday life, or attempts to give figural or concrete form to such experiences through narration. If we understand narrative as the principal and necessary means through which one is able to make sense of time and temporal experience (and therefore also social change), we must recognize the centrality of narrative to any attempt to think politically; if we reject this claim, we must account for one's ability to make sense of lived experience in some other way. Beyond this dilemma, however, we must acknowledge the prevalence of narrative as a means for understanding life (everyday or otherwise), causality, and political action, not only in the abstract, but in relation to specific forms of narrative and the different experiences of temporality they engender.

The next issue of Polygraph aims to explore the politics of life today—provisionally defined as biopolitics—by examining the constructions of temporality at these various levels. How might a notion of the biopolitical take its form and mode of expression from differing theories of narration, periodization, or everyday life in the present age? How do different forms of narrative provide differing schema for understanding the temporal experience of contemporary life, and to what extent is a notion of everyday life itself contingent on specific modes of temporal understanding? Moreover, what is the relation between biopolitics and everyday life as we try to think the political or epistemic effectivity of narrative today?

We hope to examine these questions by bringing together analyses of the political with those of narrative and temporal experience in contemporary cultural production: literature, theater or performance art, cinema, television, and other contemporary or emergent media. How do contemporary narratives and modes of narration coincide with, inform, or make possible the experience of politics or temporality today? How can we understand the relation(s) between historical questions of periodization and social transformation and more empirical or cognitive forms of temporality explored in the fields of science? Through these juxtapositions, we hope to come to a more fully developed understanding of the politics of social life in the contemporary age.

Deadline for submissions: August 1, 2005

E-mail complete manuscripts (not abstracts) to the issue editors at rodger.frey@duke.edu and alexander.ruch@duke.edu. More information and guidelines for authors available at http://www.duke.edu/web/polygraph.